Reassuring the Reluctant Warriors

A volume in the series

CORNELL STUDIES IN SECURITY AFFAIRS

edited by Robert J. Art, Robert Jervis, and Stephen M. Walt

A list of titles in this series is available at www.cornellpress.cornell.edu.

Reassuring the Reluctant Warriors

U.S. Civil-Military Relations and Multilateral Intervention

Stefano Recchia

Cornell University Press

Ithaca and London

First published 2015 by Cornell University Press

Printed in the United States of America

Library of Congress Cataloging-in-Publication Data

Recchia, Stefano, 1978– author.
   Reassuring the reluctant warriors : U.S. civil-military relations and multilateral intervention / Stefano Recchia.
      pages cm. — (Cornell studies in security affairs)
   Includes bibliographical references and index.
   ISBN 978-0-8014-5291-8 (cloth : alk. paper)
  1. Intervention (International law)—Case studies. 2. Multinational armed forces—Case studies. 3. United States—Military policy—Decision making—Case studies. 4. Civil-military relations—United States—Case studies. I. Title.
   JZ6368.R43 2015
   322′.50973—dc23   2015007847

Cornell University Press strives to use environmentally responsible suppliers and materials to the fullest extent possible in the publishing of its books. Such materials include vegetable-based, low-VOC inks and acid-free papers that are recycled, totally chlorine-free, or partly composed of nonwood fibers. For further information, visit our website at www.cornellpress.cornell.edu.

Cloth printing   10 9 8 7 6 5 4 3 2 1

Contents

Preface   vii

List of Abbreviations   xi

Introduction: Multilateralism and the Generals   1

1. The Value of Multilateral Legitimacy   16

2. Institutions, Burden Sharing, and the
   American Military   34

3. Haiti, 1993–94: Multilateral Approval to Ensure
   a UN Handoff   66

4. Bosnia, 1992–95: Keeping the U.S. Military
   from "Owning" It   107

5. Kosovo, 1998–99: Reassuring the Generals
   With NATO's Buy-In   147

6. Iraq, 2002–3: Silence from the Generals   188

   Conclusion   228

Appendix: List of Officials Interviewed   251

References   257

Index   269

[v]

Preface

In the summer of 2013, after a chemical weapons attack that killed hundreds of people near the Syrian capital of Damascus, senior U.S. policymakers, including Secretary of State John Kerry and National Security Adviser Susan Rice, advocated a military response to punish the Syrian regime for its massive human rights violation and tilt the local balance of power against it (DeYoung and Faiola, *WashPo*, Aug. 31, 2013; Epstein, *Politico*, Sept. 9, 2013). Kerry and Rice persistently called for military action, even after it became apparent that United Nations or NATO approval would not be forthcoming and that America's staunchest ally, Great Britain, was unwilling to participate (Erlanger and Castle, *NYT*, Aug. 29, 2013). However, America's top-level military leaders—notably the chairman and vice chairman of the Joint Chiefs of Staff (JCS)—were opposed to rash unilateral initiatives in pursuit of regime change (Londono, *WashPo*, Aug. 30, 2013). Admiral James Winnefeld, vice chairman of the JCS, cautioned that "merely launching a few Tomahawk Land Attack missiles into Syria hoping to turn the tide of this war will not accomplish that objective." Given the administration's persistent calls that Syrian president Bashar Al-Assad should leave power, he warned, "there would most certainly be an appetite for more action," with the result that "the United States would most likely be drawn into a protracted conflict, and would need to be prepared for the expense."[1] JCS chairman Martin Dempsey agreed that "once we take action, deeper involvement is hard to avoid." Therefore, he emphasized, if the United States decided

1. Adm. James Winnefeld, *Testimony Before the Senate ArmedServ Committee*, 113th Cong. (July 18, 2013), 936.

to intervene, "we should act . . . in concert with our allies and partners to share the burden."[2]

President Barack Obama, faced with an administration divided between civilian interventionists and a reluctant military, initially wavered but then quickly ruled out using force to undermine the Syrian regime "without a UN mandate," or at least without support from regional multilateral organizations and/or the U.S. Congress (Landler and Gordon, *NYT*, Aug. 24, 2013; Londono, *WashPo*, Sept. 1, 2013). In subsequent days, Secretary Kerry fell in line behind the president, and recognizing that UN approval for military action would not be forthcoming, he expressed his cautious support for a peaceful multilateral effort to disarm Syria of its chemical weapons (Gordon, *NYT*, Sept. 14, 2013). About one year later, General Dempsey and Admiral Winnefeld indicated that they would back limited air strikes against Islamist insurgents in Syria, and in September 2014 the United States launched a targeted bombing campaign (Gordon and Cooper, *NYT*, Aug. 21, 2014; Whitlock, *WashPo*, Sept. 23, 2014). But the foreseeable effect of those air strikes was to strengthen rather than undermine the regional status quo and with it the Syrian regime's hold on power—thus making a local power vacuum that might suck U.S. troops into a protracted quagmire less, rather than more, likely.[3] President Assad welcomed American air strikes against Islamist fighters, declaring his support for "any international anti-terrorism effort."[4]

The Obama administration's behavior toward Syria, I argue, reflects a broader pattern of U.S. military intervention decision making. America's uniformed leaders usually behave as reluctant warriors in debates about coercive humanitarian missions and other wars of choice aimed at internal political change, emphasizing the risk of protracted peacekeeping and stabilization commitments. As long as U.S. civilian policymakers are divided over how to proceed—which is likely absent clear threats to American security—the risk-averse military can tilt the bureaucratic balance of power toward nonintervention. In such circumstances, even heavyweight civilian interventionists (such as Kerry and Rice in 2013) can be expected to recognize the need for United Nations or NATO approval—if only as a means of reassuring the reluctant military about

2. Gen. Martin Dempsey, Letter to Carl Levin, Chairman of the Senate ArmedServ Committee, July 19, 2013.
3. Given the rapidly evolving situation in the Middle East, at the time of writing, a renewed deployment of U.S. ground combat troops to the region could not be ruled out.
4. Albert Aji and Ryan Lucas, "Assad Backs All Efforts to Fight Terrorism," Associated Press, Sept. 23, 2014.

the prospect of sustained burden and risk sharing with international partners, and to ultimately facilitate a presidential decision to intervene.

In the course of working on this book, I have incurred numerous debts to individuals and institutions. Michael Doyle, Tonya Putnam, Dick Betts, and Bob Jervis provided sharp criticism and constructive advice during my doctoral studies at Columbia University. I was very lucky to be advised by such an extraordinary group of scholars, who complemented each other extremely well in their candid feedback on different aspects of the project. Their guidance was invaluable in advancing my research and thinking on U.S. military intervention, multilateralism, and civil-military relations. Michael and Tonya, in particular, have been my leading advocates and professional role models since I entered graduate school in 2005, and I will always be grateful to them for their support.

My research benefited greatly from a fellowship in foreign policy at the Brookings Institution. While at Brookings, I was able to interact with and learn from a number of remarkable individuals, including Michael O'Hanlon, Martin Indyk, and Bruce Riedel. O'Hanlon in particular provided helpful, incisive feedback on early draft sections of the manuscript. Being at Brookings also allowed me to gain access to a large number of current and former policymakers whom I interviewed for my project—more on this below. Subsequently, I developed the project further during a Max Weber fellowship at the European University Institute (EUI) in Florence, Italy. Chris Reus-Smit, my mentor at the EUI, offered valuable guidance and advice.

I also want to thank the roughly one hundred current and former policymakers—senior U.S. officials from the Department of State, the Department of Defense, and the National Security Council (NSC) staff, as well as several European diplomats—who graciously agreed to be interviewed for this project. With the exception of a few individuals who requested to remain anonymous, they are listed by name in the book's appendix. Here I would like to thank in particular James Dobbins, Marc Grossman, Steve Hadley, Morton Halperin, John Negroponte, Walt Slocombe, Strobe Talbott, and Generals John Abizaid, Donald Kerrick, Walter Kross, and Gregory Newbold. They were particularly generous with their time and in some cases agreed to be interviewed twice, for more than an hour in each case. Their insights and candid recollections have been crucial to the development of the argument presented in this book.

Furthermore, I am grateful to Rob Seibert, archivist at the Clinton Presidential Library, for advising me on the formalities for submitting several requests for mandatory declassification review of U.S. national security documents. Hundreds of pages of previously classified memos and diplomatic cables have been released pursuant to those requests.[5] Being able to triangulate the evidence from interviews and published memoirs with evidence from declassified documents has been immensely helpful for my research.

The department of politics and international studies at the University of Cambridge provided a wonderfully stimulating and supportive environment for completing the book. Several of my colleagues commented on parts of the manuscript, including Mette Eilstrup-Sangiovanni, Amrita Narlikar, and Aaron Rapport. I also thank Chris Hill, department head during my first two years at Cambridge, for making sure I had the time and resources for research and writing. Two small grants from the Newton Trust and the Philomathia Foundation provided welcome financial support aimed at steering the manuscript toward publication. Viktor Stoll displayed remarkable talents as my editorial assistant.

Working with Cornell University Press has been a rewarding experience throughout. I am grateful to Roger Haydon and the series editors for seeing value in the manuscript and making publication of this book possible. I also thank series editor Steve Walt for his exceptionally detailed and incisive feedback on the draft manuscript, which helped me significantly improve the final version. Karen Laun has been both cheerful and very effective as my production editor, and Jamie Fuller did a superb job as copyeditor.

My most important debts are to friends and family, who have been a constant source of motivation and support. Among my friends, Mike Beckley stands out as the one who has contributed most significantly to this project, from the time since we shared an apartment during graduate school in New York City. Mike provided terrific feedback on my argument as it developed over the years, and our conversations about U.S. foreign policy have always been illuminating and plain fun! Finally, the person who deserves the most gratitude is without doubt my father, Giuseppe. He has offered unwavering love and support as a single parent over the years, teaching me to think critically about politics and the world and instilling in me a curiosity for different peoples and different cultures. For several consecutive summers while I was working on this book, he hosted me at our family home in Brunico in the Italian Alps, where I found a peaceful environment ideally suited to research and writing. This book is dedicated to him.

---

5. Those documents are now available at http://clinton.presidentiallibraries.us /collections/show/36/.

Abbreviations

ArmedServ	Armed Services
Assist	Assistant
AU	African Union
CARICOM	Caribbean Community
CENTCOM	U.S. Central Command
CRS	Congressional Research Service
DC	Deputies Committee (National Security Council)
DCI	Director of Central Intelligence
Dep	Deputy
Dir.	Director
DOD	Department of Defense
DOS	Department of State
EUCOM	U.S. European Command
FT	*Financial Times*
IFOR	NATO Implementation Force (Bosnia)
IO	international organization
JCS	Joint Chiefs of Staff
KFOR	Kosovo Force (NATO-led)
KLA	Kosovo Liberation Army
Legisl.	Legislative
LTG	Lieutenant General
MoD	Ministry of Defence (Great Britain)
NAC	North Atlantic Council (NATO)
NAM	Non-Aligned Movement
NATO	North Atlantic Treaty Organization
NatSec	National Security
NYT	*New York Times*

NSC	National Security Council
OAS	Organization of American States
OSD	Office of the Secretary of Defense
PC	Principals Committee (National Security Council)
PermRep	Permanent Representative
Pol-Mil	Political-Military
Pres.	President
SACEUR	Supreme Allied Commander Europe
SC	Security Council (United Nations)
SCR	Security Council Resolution
SecDef	Secretary of Defense
SecState	Secretary of State
SumConcl	Summary of Conclusions
UNMIH	United Nations Mission in Haiti
UNMOVIC	United Nations Monitoring, Verification and Inspection Commission (Iraq)
UNPROFOR	United Nations Protection Force (Bosnia)
UNSC	United Nations Security Council
UNSCOM	United Nations Special Commission (Iraq)
USA	United States Army
USACOM	United States Atlantic Command
USAF	United States Air Force
USMC	United States Marine Corps
USN	United States Navy
VP	Vice President
WashPo	*Washington Post*
WMD	weapons of mass destruction

Reassuring the Reluctant Warriors

Introduction

MULTILATERALISM AND THE GENERALS

Why does the United States, the most militarily powerful country on earth, typically seek multilateral approval from the United Nations or NATO for coercive humanitarian missions and more generally for major interventions aimed at changing the domestic authority structure of foreign countries? Alexis de Tocqueville (1835: 585) famously remarked that "Americans, in their relations with foreigners, appear impatient at the least censure and insatiable for praise." Yet U.S. policymakers, like Americans more generally, vary significantly in their desire for international approval and praise. Policymakers who support quick military intervention, as this book will demonstrate, are often willing to bypass multilateral bodies for the sake of maximizing U.S. freedom of action. Meanwhile, America's senior military officers—including the chairman and vice chairman of the Joint Chiefs of Staff (JCS), the commanders of the unified commands, and senior officers on the Joint Staff—are consistently risk-averse vis-à-vis interventions aimed at internal political change, emphasizing attendant risks and likely long-term costs. The senior officers are also surprisingly willing to coordinate U.S. activities with foreign allies and partners for the sake of international burden sharing. This insight has led me to investigate how civil-military relations can influence U.S. efforts to secure multilateral approval for the use of force.

THE COSTS AND BENEFITS OF IO APPROVAL

Since the end of the Cold War, the United States has consistently sought the approval of international organizations (IOs) with mandates in the field of international security—primarily the United Nations and

NATO—before launching coercive humanitarian missions and other wars of choice aimed at internal political change. Thus, U.S. leaders sought UN or NATO approval before intervening in northern Iraq (1991), Somalia (1992), Haiti (1994 and 2004), Bosnia (1993 and 1995), Yugoslavia/Kosovo (1999), Iraq (2003), Liberia (2003), and Libya (2011).

If U.S. attempts to secure UN or NATO approval bore no meaningful cost, then such efforts would not be surprising. Even decision makers who are not known for their multilateralist instincts may acknowledge that IO approval can have marginal public relations benefits by helping to "sell" U.S. policy to domestic and international audiences. However, securing approval from the United Nations Security Council (UNSC) or NATO's North Atlantic Council (NAC) is often very costly to the United States. First, it may involve protracted multilateral diplomacy with other member states, lasting weeks or even months. That makes quick military action difficult, in the meantime allowing the political and humanitarian situation on the ground to deteriorate. In addition, persuading hesitant IO member states to offer their affirmative vote may require significant side payments and logrolling. Multilateral deliberations also involve a loss of secrecy, reducing the element of surprise and thus increasing the risk to American forces if and when they intervene. Finally, the resulting multilateral mandate may limit targeting options and force employment more generally, thereby further constraining U.S. freedom of action and undermining military effectiveness. Former deputy secretary of state Strobe Talbott sums it up as follows: "Multilateralism is hell, and it can be a real pain in the neck. Getting a consensus takes a long time. It often drives you toward the lowest common denominator. There is a lot of logrolling, and one may end up with not very sensible outcomes that are necessary to keep everybody on board."[1]

For instance, the United States spent several months before the 1991 Gulf War building up multilateral support for the use of force at the UNSC, offering hundreds of millions of dollars in economic inducements to obtain the cooperation of recalcitrant states such as Russia and China (Baker 1995: 287–325; Pilger, *New Statesman*, Sept. 23, 2002). Similarly, before intervening in Haiti in 1994, the United States devoted months to an all-out diplomatic effort aimed at securing UN approval: the Clinton administration not only explicitly linked bilateral economic assistance to support for its policy on Haiti but also engaged in logrolling with Moscow, agreeing to support a UN mandate for Russian troops in Abkhazia (Georgia) in exchange for Russia's cooperation on Haiti.[2] Further

---

1. Author interview with Strobe Talbott, Deputy SecState, 1994–2001 (July 9, 2009).
2. See chapter 2 of this book.

examples are the Bosnia and Kosovo crises in the 1990s, where the United States delayed military action for many months, in order to secure NATO's approval for coercive air campaigns. That allowed the humanitarian situation to deteriorate dramatically, and even after NATO approved the use of force, allied concerns over strategy and tactics resulted in highly restricted target lists, thus undermining the effectiveness of U.S. airpower.[3]

Table I.1 Post–Cold War interventions for which U.S. sought advance IO approval

Intervention (Operation code name)	Authorizing resolution	Policy objective
Northern Iraq 1991 (Provide Comfort)	UNSCR 688 (Apr. 5, 1991)	Protect Kurdish population, facilitate humanitarian assistance
Somalia 1992 (Restore Hope) Bosnia 1993 (Deny Flight)	UNSCR 794 (Dec. 4, 1992) UNSCR 816 (Mar. 31, 1993); NATO/NAC vote (Apr. 8, 1993)	Create secure environment for delivery of humanitarian aid Enforce no-fly zone over Bosnia
Haiti 1994 (Uphold Democracy)	UNSCR 940 (July 31, 1994)	Restore exiled Haitian president
Bosnia 1995 (Deliberate Force)	UNSCR 836 (June 4, 1993); NATO/NAC vote (July 25, 1995)	Protect UN safe areas, facilitate end of Bosnian war
Kosovo 1999 (Allied Force)	NATO/NAC vote (Jan. 30, 1999)	Stop ethnic violence, obtain Serb consent to NATO peace force
Iraq 2003 (Iraqi Freedom)	none*	Disarm Iraq of suspected WMD, implement regime change
Liberia 2003 (Joint Task Force)	UNSCR 1497 (Aug. 1, 2003)	Create secure environment for delivery of humanitarian aid
Haiti 2004 (Secure Tomorrow)	UNSCR 1529 (Feb. 29, 2004)	Facilitate delivery of humanitarian aid, help restore stability
Libya 2011 (Odyssey Dawn/ Unified Protector)	UNSCR 1973 (Mar. 17, 2011); NATO/NAC vote (Mar. 24, 2011)	Enforce no-fly zone, protect civilians from government violence

Sources: Salazar Torreon 2015; *NYT* archive; online repository of UNSC resolutions (www.un.org/en/sc/documents/resolutions/); NATO website (www.nato.int).
* SCR 1441, adopted on Nov. 8, 2002, did not explicitly authorize the use of force.

3. See chapters 3 and 4 of this book.

I argue in chapter 1 that multilateral approval from the UNSC or NATO's NAC is particularly valuable to the United States as a means of facilitating sustained international burden sharing—especially on peacekeeping and stabilization after major combat. First, by legitimating the international use of force, IO approval helps foreign leaders overcome domestic political obstacles to sustained cooperation with the United States.[4] Second, IO approval publicly commits other member states who offer their affirmative vote to supporting U.S. policy, thus making it unlikely that they will subsequently oppose further UN or NATO involvement aimed at successfully completing the mission. When the IO's own reputation becomes linked to mission success, member states that independently value the multilateral institution and the security benefits it provides have additional incentives to offer sustained operational support.

It therefore might not seem surprising that the United States typically makes the greatest efforts to secure IO approval for humanitarian interventions and regime-change operations that are launched in the absence of clear threats to American security and entail a high probability of open-ended commitments. Domestic support for such missions is often lukewarm to begin with and risks evaporating as an operation becomes protracted. Sustained international burden sharing, as facilitated by IO approval, is likely to be especially valuable in those circumstances for the purpose of maintaining domestic support in Congress and among the American people. However, policymakers debating the merits of intervention often disagree vehemently among themselves as to whether a foreign crisis threatens American security, whether armed intervention is likely to yield an open-ended commitment, and more generally about how difficult it will be to maintain U.S. domestic support. Consequently, policymakers can be expected to often differ in their cost-benefit analysis vis-à-vis multilateralism—specifically, in their assessment of whether the long-term burden-sharing benefits of a multilateral course will outweigh its short-term freedom-of-action costs. Simply inferring policymakers' motivations from observed outcomes risks confusing the researcher's own *post hoc* rationalization with the *ex ante* perspectives of policymakers who were debating the merits of intervention under the pressure of rapidly evolving circumstances and with only limited information available.

---

4. For similar arguments see Thompson 2006; Chapman 2011: chap. 5

WHY CIVIL-MILITARY RELATIONS?

To address the problem of policymakers whose perceptions and cost-benefit analyses vis-à-vis multilateralism may systematically differ, I combine a bureaucratic politics approach with insights from scholarship on civil-military relations. The bureaucratic politics paradigm, as applied to the study of foreign-policy decision making by scholars such as Graham Allison and Morton Halperin, rests on three basic propositions. First, foreign policy is not made by a central, unitary actor. To the contrary, many agencies and individuals participate in decision making and compete for influence. Second, decision makers representing particular agencies and departments typically adopt policy perspectives that reflect their organization's parochial interests. Put differently, where government officials stand on any given issue and what they perceive as being at stake is significantly influenced by where they sit. Finally, decision making is not just a matter of rational problem solving. Instead, decisions are usually the outcome of bargaining and coalition building among the relevant powers that be, and consequently they reflect "the pulling and hauling that is politics" (Allison and Halperin 1972: 50–57; Allison and Zelikow 1999: 255 and 294–312).

Critics of the bureaucratic politics paradigm have repeatedly challenged the hypothesis that "where you stand depends on where you sit" (see, e.g., Krasner 1972; Welch 1992: 121–22). The policy outlook of top-level government officials, notably cabinet members and other political appointees, is indeed frequently affected less by their organizational membership than by their previous experiences outside government and their party political affiliation. However, this criticism is less applicable to permanent career officials, who rise through the ranks of their organization until they reach senior positions in government. In the United States, top-level military officers, notably the chairman and vice chairman of the Joint Chiefs of Staff, are frequently the only career officials among the president's principal national security advisers. Consequently, they are perhaps the only high-ranking government leaders for whom, as Richard Betts explains, their "latent political function is still secondary to their manifest professional identity" (Betts 1991: 40; see also Szayna et al. 2007: 67–68).

America's senior generals and admirals, as parochial actors, are concerned with the health, vitality, and social prestige of their organizations, and when confronted with the possibility of foreign intervention, they seek to limit the liability of the armed services and the troops they represent (Huntington 1957: 69–70; Petraeus 1989: 497–98). Furthermore, given their prior battlefield experience and natural focus on planning and

[5]

implementing military operations, the generals and admirals are less likely than civilian policymakers, especially those without combat experience, to fall prey to unwarranted optimism regarding the likely duration and operational costs of prospective interventions (Betts 1991: 153–60; Horowitz and Stam 2014). Finally, most senior military officers are conservative political realists in foreign affairs, and as such they are inherently skeptical of humanitarian and other human rights-driven interventions (Holsti 2001: 44–47; Feaver and Gelpi 2004: 37–38; Pew Research Center 2011: 22–26). For those reasons, senior officers, notably in the U.S. Army and the Marine Corps, tend to worry that interventions aimed at changing the internal politics of foreign countries in a more liberal and democratic direction might result in open-ended commitments without an exit strategy and with dwindling domestic support (Petraeus 1989: 492; Betts 1991: 119–20; Clark 2001: 137–38; Bacevich 2007: 239–41).

Contrasting with the traditional view of the military as staying above the fray of politics, modern American generals and admirals have, on average, been skilled and effective bureaucratic players who have often bargained hard to advance their own views on national security and defend their organizational interests (Halperin and Clapp 2006: 27–33; Bacevich 2007). The senior officers' acknowledged professional expertise and control of military planning, combined with their high standing in American society, enables them to exert significant influence over military intervention decision making—especially when they are united in their opposition to a particular course of action. Top-level military officers have several instruments at their disposal to put pressure on civilian administration officials, ranging from the ability to present certain options as unfeasible in the intramural debates to press leaks, public statements, coalition building with powerful organizations outside government, and threats of resignation as a last resort (Betts 1991: 43–45; Feaver 2003: 87–90; Bacevich 2007: 247–49; Brooks 2009: 232–35). There is evidence that when America's top-ranking generals and admirals express strong reservations about the risks and likely operational costs of intervention, and civilian authorities are divided over how to proceed, the military can veto the use of force (Avant 1996: 51–90; Desch 1999: 29–33; Kohn 2002).

As subsequent chapters will demonstrate, civilian policymakers who view armed intervention as a matter of urgency to defend American interests and values abroad often do not feel bound by international norms requiring IO approval. When confronted with hesitant international partners at the UN or NATO, such "interventionist hawks," as I call them, are initially likely to be inclined to bypass those multilateral bodies to ensure quick military action. More dovish policymakers typically put greater emphasis on IO approval as a source of legitimacy and a catalyst for domestic and international support. However, among civilian leaders the interventionists will often be at an advantage. First, especially when confronted with nonliberal foreign opponents responsible for serious human rights violations, the interventionists can appeal to America's liberal political culture and sense of exceptionalism to build up public support for the use of force.[5] Furthermore, the civilian doves, on their own, may lack the professional expertise and determination to effectively challenge the interventionists' optimistic assessments about the risks and likely costs of military action.

That is where America's senior uniformed leaders play a central role, through their ability to veto armed interventions about which civilian authorities disagree. In such circumstances, pro-intervention civilian policymakers have to be able to mollify the military leaders, in order to keep the use of force on the agenda and gradually pave the way to a presidential decision to intervene. Specifically, the civilian interventionists need to make a persuasive case that the use of force is a last resort, that major international partners support the policy and are willing to shoulder a significant portion of the operational burden, and that there is a viable exit strategy for American troops. As a consequence, even the administration's most heavyweight interventionist hawks can be expected to recognize the need for multilateral approval—if only as a means of mollifying the reluctant military leaders by reassuring them about the prospect of sustained international burden sharing.

My argument is not that top-level military officers are always decisive in steering U.S. policy on armed intervention toward IOs. Civilian policymakers clearly may have other, independent reasons for seeking IO approval—whether complying with international norms, reducing international opposition, or increasing U.S. domestic support. However, multilateral approval is usually difficult to obtain for coercive humanitarian missions and other interventions aimed at forcibly changing the internal authority structure of foreign countries, given that such missions are prima facie incompatible with established norms of noninterference as enshrined in the UN Charter. Consequently, hawkish U.S. policymakers contemplating such interventions, if left to their own devices, may be strongly tempted to bypass relevant IOs in order to maximize America's freedom of action. The uniformed leaders' reluctance to use force for internal political change, especially when the policy's motivation is humanitarian or otherwise human rights–related, is then likely to play a salient role in steering those particular types of intervention toward a multilateral path.

5. On how America's political culture facilitates military intervention, see Hartz 1955: 13–14, 284–87; Hoffmann 2005; Desch 2009b.

[7]

The argument that America's senior military officers play an important role in steering coercive humanitarian missions and other human rights–driven interventions aimed at internal political change toward the UN or NATO is counterintuitive. Scholarship on civil-military relations has long emphasized that, although U.S. generals and admirals are reluctant to intervene abroad in the absence of clear threats to national security, when the civilian leadership orders them to do so, their preference is for deploying "overwhelming force" with as much autonomy as possible (Huntington 1957: 66–79; Petraeus 1989: 490–93; Feaver and Gelpi 2004: 43–53). One might infer from this that the senior officers should be suspicious of multilateral procedures that inevitably constrain American power. Decades ago, General Douglas MacArthur complained that "United Nations restrictions" impeded the effective employment of U.S. force during the Korean War. "If one nation carries ninety percent of the effort," he argued, "it's quite inappropriate that nations that carry only a small fraction of the efforts and the responsibility should exercise undue authority upon the decisions that are made" (quoted in Manchester 2008: 667). More recently, the American military has viewed the growing "capabilities gap" between the United States and its allies as raising serious issues of interoperability (Helis 2012: 169–74). Senior military officers also have long been wary of deploying U.S. troops under foreign command and subjecting them to international jurisdiction (Sewall 2002). Nevertheless, America's senior officers ultimately appear to be pragmatists on the question of multilateralism, as there is evidence that on average, they value international cooperation through bodies such as the UN and NATO more than civilian leaders do (Holsti 2001: 36–38; Szayna et al. 2007: 101–3).

DEFINING MILITARY INTERVENTION

This book focuses in particular on coercive humanitarian missions and regime change operations, but the category of military intervention is more encompassing. Being aware of the broader category may help us understand variation in U.S. efforts to secure multilateral approval across different cases and different types of intervention. I define military intervention as the *cross-border deployment of military forces by a state or group of states without the consent of the local government, involving actual or anticipated combat, aimed at influencing the behavior and/or changing the internal politics of the target state.* This definition excludes forcible interference by nonstate actors, such as revolutionary groups or terrorist organizations, and political or economic interference that does not involve the cross-border deployment of military forces. It also excludes foreign military deployments on a state's territory following an express invitation from the recognized government, unless there is a rival political authority that controls significant portions of the state's territory and population. (For instance, UN troops were invited into Bosnia by the recognized Sarajevo government in 1992, but since that government controlled less than half of the country's territory and population at the time, the international force deployment still counted as an intervention.)

The more specific purpose for which force is used is secondary to the definition. Thus, an intervention might aim to provide humanitarian protection by deterring attacks on the local population, end a civil war by imposing a settlement, neutralize a specific threat emanating from within the target state, install a more democratic/malleable/congenial political regime, or simply compel the target state's government to change its policies in conformity with the intervener's demands. That said, the nature of an intervention has to be "finite and transitory"—it requires a clear beginning and end (Rosenau 1969: 161; see also Vincent 1974: 8). An intervention cannot seek to permanently erase a state's sovereignty, even if only over parts of its territory. Traditional wars of conquest or colonial submission thus go beyond any plausible understanding of intervention. Hitler's occupation of Poland in 1939 and Saddam Hussein's invasion and annexation of Kuwait in 1990 were classic interstate wars, not interventions. Likewise, the cross-border use of force aimed at repelling an external attack against oneself or one's allies, or at liberating a foreign country from what most members of international society regard as illegitimate foreign rule, exceeds any plausible definition of intervention. Thus, Allied combat operations against German forces in France during World War II and U.S.-led coalition operations against Iraqi forces in Kuwait in 1991 were not interventions but traditional wars of collective self-defense.

Finally, against one possible understanding of intervention as "limited war," the scale or intensity of military operations should not matter to the definition. An intervention may be very limited in time and scope, consisting of just a single air strike against a specific target, or it may involve a full-scale invasion aimed at changing a state's political regime through a prolonged occupation involving hundreds of thousands of troops deployed for several years. Central to the definition of intervention espoused here, once again, is that the use of force be aimed at influencing the behavior and/or changing the internal politics of the target state but without seeking to permanently erase the target state's sovereignty. Consequently, U.S. military operations over Kosovo in 1999 and the 2003 invasion of Iraq both count as military interventions, even though they involved fairly large-scale combat and resulted in protracted stabilization missions.

[9]

Table I.2 Definition of intervention versus war

Intervention	Traditional interstate war
• Cross-border deployment of armed forces, involving actual or anticipated combat	• Cross-border deployment of armed forces, involving actual or anticipated combat
• Seeks to influence behavior/change internal politics of the target state	• Seeks to annex foreign territory (conquest) or repel an attack/undo
• Does not seek to permanently erase the target state's sovereignty (no conquest)	an occupation (individual and collective self-defense)
• E.g., U.S. interventions in Haiti (1994), Kosovo (1999), and Iraq (2003), also limited incursions and air strikes	• E.g. Iraq's invasion of Kuwait in 1990 but also 1991 Gulf War

Coalitions-Based versus Institutions-Based Multilateralism

Scholars generally distinguish between two types of multilateralism, *coalitions-based* and *institutions-based* (or "quantitative" and "qualitative"). The former involves cooperation through improvised multinational coalitions, or "the practice of coordinating national policies in groups of three or more states" (Keohane 1990: 731). The latter is more demanding and involves the sanction of standing IOs that coordinate "relations among three or more states on the basis of 'generalized' principles of conduct—that is, principles which specify appropriate conduct for a class of actions, without regard to the particularistic interests of the parties" (Ruggie 1992: 571; see also Finnemore 2003: 80–81).

According to the quantitative definition, almost all U.S. military interventions beyond limited air strikes carried out since the end of World War II have been multilateral. For instance, U.S. interventions in Vietnam during the 1960s and in Lebanon and Grenada in the 1980s all involved the support and participation of improvised coalitions of states (Fisher 2013: 135–37, 159–63). The 2003 invasion of Iraq, as well, was multilateral according to the quantitative definition: it enjoyed the political support of a "coalition of the willing" made up of over thirty states, even though most of them were small developing countries dependent on U.S. economic aid, and only two major allies (Britain and Australia) contributed significant numbers of troops to the initial combat phase.[6]

For the purpose of this book, I adopt the qualitative definition of multilateralism. Hence for a military intervention to be considered multilateral, it must be explicitly approved by a standing IO with a mandate in the field of international security. Relevant IOs include first and foremost the

---

6. On coalition contributions to the Iraq War, see Davidson 2011: chap. 6; Weitsman 2014: chap. 6.

United Nations. The UNSC has primary responsibility for international peace and security under the UN Charter and remains the sole body that can authorize military intervention under international law. Regional organizations such as NATO, the Organization of American States (OAS), and the African Union (AU) also qualify, since they have mandates in the field of international security and coordinate state behavior according to generalized principles of conduct. The approval of such regional IOs, to be valid, must be granted by the organ designated for that purpose in the organization's charter: NATO's NAC, the OAS Permanent Council, or the AU's Assembly of Heads of State and Government, on the basis of consensus in the first case and by two-thirds majorities in the latter two cases.[7]

The decision to focus on qualitative rather than quantitative multilateralism is driven by a concern with explaining puzzling, or theoretically interesting, state behavior. The United States, with its superior economic resources and unparalleled diplomatic leverage, can quite easily cobble together a nominal multinational coalition in order to manage public perceptions and increase U.S. domestic support for the use of force. As Marc Grossman, who served as a senior State Department official under several presidents, laconically explains, "Some coalition is always available."[8] Furthermore, the political backing of improvised coalitions does not meaningfully affect U.S. freedom of maneuver, as the United States can first decide on a course of action and then seek coalition support without having to adapt its policy. Therefore, Washington's frequent reliance on quantitative multilateralism, or ad hoc coalitions, is hardly surprising. Such an option is both low-cost and low-risk, encouraging U.S. policymakers to pursue it whenever they anticipate that it might be the least bit beneficial.

By contrast, securing the approval of a standing IO such as the UN or NATO is usually more costly. As previously noted, it may require protracted diplomacy, involving side payments and logrolling, and may significantly constrain U.S. freedom of action. When working through standing IOs, the United States cannot simply cherry-pick the most pliable international partners who are particularly susceptible to American pressure or inducements. Instead, it must persuade a set group of member states, several of which are usually regional powers with their own interests and priorities that might conflict with Washington's. Therefore, U.S. qualitative or institutions-based multilateralism is likely to be more

---

7. See NATO, "Consensus Decision-Making at NATO," http://www.nato.int; OAS, "Rules of Procedure of the Permanent Council," OEA/Ser.GCP/doc.1112/80 rev. 4 corr. 1, Aug. 27, 2003; African Union, "Constitutive Act of the African Union," adopted on July 11, 2000, art. 7.1.

8. Author interview with Marc Grossman, AssistSecState for European Affairs, 1997–2001, and UnderSecState for Political Affairs, 2001–5 (Jan. 13, 2011).

than just window dressing: it involves significant tradeoffs, and the motivations behind it are worth studying in detail.

THE BOOK'S POST–COLD WAR FOCUS

This book focuses on post–Cold War military interventions. The primary reason for this choice is that the UN Security Council was deadlocked for most of the Cold War. The UNSC authorized the U.S.-led response in the Korean War in 1950, but during the subsequent four decades the bipolar standoff between the United States and the Soviet Union, and the resulting mutual vetoes at the Security Council, made its approval practically unavailable. Only in the late 1980s did this political deadlock begin to be overcome. Soviet president Mikhail Gorbachev's announcement in 1987 that Moscow was prepared to reengage with the UN marked the beginning of a new era, and over the following three years, the council became actively involved in managing political transitions and establishing multilateral peace missions in Angola, Namibia, and Central America (Russett 1994: 192–93). After the fall of the Berlin Wall in 1989, UNSC approval for coercive military operations was again within reach—as demonstrated by the council's authorization of "all necessary means" to expel Iraqi forces from Kuwait in November 1990 (Malone 2006: 58–70).

In addition, several scholars have argued that since the early 1990s, and especially as a result of the precedent set by the 1991 Gulf War, new international norms have emerged and progressively become consolidated that require IO approval as a condition for legitimate intervention (Russett 1994; Voeten 2005: 527–57; Hurd 2007). It may be that American leaders have internalized those norms and therefore seek IO approval before intervening out of "an internal sense of moral obligation" (Hurd 1999: 387; see also Risse-Kappen 1997). Alternatively, U.S. policymakers might want to reassure foreign audiences who value those norms, in order to avert potentially costly international opposition in the form of negative issue linkage, or "soft balancing" against the United States across various policy domains (Voeten 2005; Thompson 2009). Finally, it may be that, as I hypothesize, pro-intervention U.S. policymakers seek IO approval and the resulting legitimacy to maximize the prospect of sustained burden sharing in completing the mission, thereby mollifying the American military and other domestic opponents of intervention.

In short, by focusing on the post–Cold War period, I am able to compare and contrast my argument centered on burden sharing and civil-military relations with two prominent alternative explanations based on norm internalization and concerns about issue linkage. I recognize that a normative shift may indeed have occurred since the end of the Cold War and that IO approval may accordingly have become more valuable to legitimate international intervention. However, explanations based on norm internalization and on concerns about issue linkage are for the most part alternative to my own. In my argument, legitimacy norms matter primarily insofar as norm-compliant behavior, as certified by IO approval, facilitates the sustained burden sharing that the military and others in the U.S. government demand.

In the book's empirical chapters, I evaluate each of those explanations. I conclude that the principal existing explanations, based on the norm-internalization and issue-linkage hypotheses, lack strong empirical support and are therefore by themselves insufficient to account for post–Cold War U.S. efforts to secure multilateral approval ahead of intervention. Likewise, explanations that recognize the value of multilateralism as a catalyst for burden sharing but treat the United States as a unitary actor (e.g., Kreps 2010) are incomplete. They cannot account for why the United States generally seeks IO approval for coercive humanitarian missions and other wars of choice aimed at internal political change *even when*, as is frequently the case, some of the most influential U.S. civilian leaders at first advocate a unilateral course of action.

CASE SELECTION AND OUTLINE

The next chapter discusses in greater detail how UN or NATO approval, obtained ahead of intervention, facilitates sustained international burden sharing and thereby helps maintain U.S. domestic support for open-ended deployments. Chapter 2 constitutes the core theory chapter of this book: it more fully develops the argument that civil-military bargaining can steer U.S. intervention policy toward the UN or NATO, especially for interventions aimed at internal political change where IO approval is usually difficult to obtain. The chapter also specifies observable implications of the argument in order to facilitate empirical testing. The four subsequent chapters investigate U.S. decision making in the run-up to military interventions in Haiti (1994), Bosnia (1995), Kosovo (1999), and Iraq (2003). These case studies highlight the costs of securing IO approval and evaluate my argument as well as alternative explanations.

I have chosen to focus on U.S. policy debates in the run-up to the Haiti, Bosnia, Kosovo, and Iraq interventions, primarily because securing IO approval was unusually time-consuming and difficult in those cases. Indeed, the 2003 Iraq effort was ultimately unsuccessful. In other cases in which the United States secured multilateral approval before intervening—such as Somalia 1992, Afghanistan 2001, Liberia 2003, and Haiti 2004—other IO member states supported Washington's goals (providing humanitarian protection without forcibly changing the internal political structure or, in the Afghanistan case, fighting terrorist organizations) from the outset; consequently, securing IO approval was neither time-consuming nor otherwise particularly difficult.[9] In the Afghanistan case, the United States did not even seek IO approval for the initial intervention, although NATO had invoked article 5 of the Washington Treaty on September 12, 2001, offering to support the United States in its response to the 9/11 terrorist attacks.[10]

Furthermore, the four selected cases allow me to study U.S. policy vis-à-vis different IOs—namely the UN (for Haiti, Bosnia, and Iraq), NATO (for Bosnia and Kosovo), and the OAS (for Haiti). In principle, U.S. policymakers may view each of those IOs as offering distinct benefits, although in practice they will often engage in "forum shopping" and work with the IO whose approval appears most realistically achievable.

Finally, the selected cases occurred long enough ago that relevant government documents have begun to be declassified, and key individuals involved in policymaking at the time are willing to be interviewed on the record and speak candidly about their motivations and concerns. Consequently, we can reconstruct the U.S. decision-making process with a higher degree of confidence than would be possible for more recent interventions. My initial analysis was not focused on civil-military relations but rather more conventionally on executive-legislative relations. Only in the course of the empirical investigation did it occur to me that civil-military bargaining played a central role in steering U.S. policy toward relevant multilateral bodies.[11]

Chapters 3 (Haiti), 4 (Bosnia), and 5 (Kosovo) begin with a discussion of the diplomatic, political, and financial costs to the United States of securing IO approval. The chapters' central parts then trace the decision-making process in the run-up to those interventions, in order to evaluate the hypothesis that when securing IO approval is difficult, civil-military bargaining can steer U.S. policy toward multilateralism. In all three cases, I find that some of the most influential civilian policymakers were

9. On Somalia see Boutros-Ghali 1999: 55–59. On Liberia see Kuperman 2008. On the 2004 Haiti intervention see Sablière 2013: 237–39.

10. On the Afghanistan intervention, see also Kreps 2011: chap. 6; Weitsman 2014: chap. 5.

11. Hence I did not select "most likely" cases that I knew would support my argument. I simply selected four cases in which it was clear that securing IO approval would be difficult but Washington nevertheless made the effort.

initially inclined to bypass relevant IOs. The uniformed leaders, however, were reluctant to intervene and altogether opposed to doing so unilaterally; consequently, the civilian interventionists realized that they needed to secure IO approval in order to avert a military veto. Each chapter concludes with an evaluation of prominent alternative hypotheses on why the United States seeks IO approval for its interventions.

The 2003 Iraq case, discussed in chapter 6, is more complex. In the run-up to the Iraq War, most senior military officers had significant reservations about using force, worrying that the invasion would result in a costly and open-ended U.S. commitment. However, America's top-ranking generals, JCS chairman Richard Myers, his deputy Peter Pace, and Tommy Franks, the commander of Central Command, failed to adequately highlight the invasion's likely costs and to challenge the optimistic expectations of civilian interventionist hawks. The civilian interventionists' relentless insistence that the goal of regime change in Iraq was a central component of the administration's "war on terror" made it difficult for other senior military officers to speak out without appearing disloyal, unpatriotic, or dangerously naive. Consequently, in the months leading up to the Iraq War, the bureaucratic political dynamics that had made IO approval all but necessary for other wars of choice aimed at internal political change were not activated, with the result that the United States made only a limited, and ultimately unsuccessful, effort to obtain UN approval before intervening.

The concluding chapter summarizes the book's main findings and then briefly analyzes U.S. decision making in the run-up to the 2003 Liberia and 2011 Libya interventions. Although securing IO approval was not particularly difficult in those two cases, the available evidence indicates that the military's reluctance to intervene and staunch insistence on burden sharing again shaped U.S. policy in consequential ways, making multilateral sanction a sine qua non condition for intervention. The conclusion also discusses various implications of the book's argument for theory and policy.

[1]

The Value of Multilateral Legitimacy

Why did international audiences for the most part support the 1991 Persian Gulf War as a legitimate endeavor, while the 2003 Iraq War was widely condemned as illegitimate? One important reason, apart from the change in U.S. policy objectives (countering Iraqi aggression vs. imposing regime change), was that the United States secured explicit UN approval in the first case but not in the latter. The approval of multilateral bodies such as the UNSC and NATO's NAC can enhance the perceived legitimacy of military intervention by signaling that the use of force is not narrowly self-serving but instead follows established international rules and procedures. In the broadest sense, this legitimation effect appears to be the principal reason why U.S. policymakers typically seek IO approval for major military interventions. As General Colin Powell, who served as national security adviser, JCS chairman, and secretary of state in various administrations explains, "If you can get multilateral support for a planned intervention, then you should seek it, in order to have the greatest possible legitimacy for the action."[1]

The argument that military interventions that are not obviously in self-defense enjoy greater legitimacy when endorsed by the UNSC or regional IOs is compelling, as is the claim that expectations of greater legitimacy are, generally speaking, what motivate even powerful states to seek IO approval (see, e.g., Claude 1966; Finnemore 2003; Coleman 2007). But those arguments are not particularly controversial. Even Hans Morgenthau, one of the founders of modern political realism, acknowledged the UN's ability to legitimate states' exercise of power beyond national

---

1. Author interview with Gen. Colin L. Powell (Feb. 2, 2011).

borders. "Legitimate power," he wrote, is "power which can invoke a moral or legal justification in its exercise," and in international politics this typically means "power exercised in self-defense or in the name of the United Nations" (Morgenthau 2005: 32). A more interesting question is: Why do powerful countries and their leaders covet the legitimacy resulting from IO approval? Or, put differently, what is the *value* of multilateral legitimacy to powerful countries like the United States?

Existing scholarship offers three distinct answers. First, policymakers have internalized new international norms of appropriate behavior and consequently desire IO approval and the resulting legitimacy out of a deep sense of moral obligation. Second, policymakers seek IO approval in order to signal benign intentions to third-party states and reduce the risk of costly retaliation in the form of negative issue linkage. Third, policymakers value IO approval as a means of bolstering domestic support for intervention and reducing the ability of Congress to veto an intervention altogether. This chapter begins by reviewing each of the three aforementioned explanations. I identify observable implications that can be tested empirically and conclude that those explanations, by themselves, cannot account for U.S. efforts to secure multilateral approval. Thereafter, I build on research about the role of domestic politics in U.S. military intervention decision making to develop an alternative set of hypotheses.

My argument is that policymakers seek UN or NATO approval and the resulting legitimacy as a domestic insurance strategy: their goal is to facilitate sustained military and financial burden sharing on the intervention at hand, in the expectation that this will help maintain congressional support for potentially open-ended troop deployments, especially in the absence of clear threats to American security. The chapter, however, ends with a caveat. Policymakers frequently disagree among themselves as to whether a foreign crisis threatens American security and whether armed intervention is likely to yield an open-ended deployment, as well as more generally about how difficult it will be to maintain U.S. domestic support. Consequently, a more complete explanation of when and why the United States is likely to seek IO approval requires us to look at intra-administration bargaining involving civilian and military leaders. That is the focus of chapter 2.

COMPLYING WITH INTERNALIZED NORMS

One prominent explanation of why policymakers seek IO approval, associated with the social constructivist research program in international relations, relies on the assumption that over time states and their leaders internalize prevailing norms of international legitimacy. Once

[17]

internalized by states, norms acquire a taken-for-granted quality and are no longer a matter of broad debate among policymakers. Compliance is then perceived as a matter of duty and is motivated "by an internal sense of moral obligation" (Hurd 1999: 387–88). Put differently, norms influence policymakers' behavior by fundamentally altering their preferences instead of merely affecting their strategic calculus. The "logic of appropriateness" trumps the "logic of expected consequences" (March and Olsen 2009).[2]

The modern international sovereignty regime entails a strong prima facie rule of nonintervention in states' internal affairs. According to constructivist scholars, this "Grundnorm" of international society has been internalized by the vast majority of states, which explains why it is "very rarely challenged in a profound way" (Hurd 1999: 393; see also Biersteker and Weber 1996). The nonintervention rule can be violated only on exceptional grounds: either one has to be acting in self-defense, or the intervention has to be authorized by standing IOs and preferably by the UN Security Council. As Christian Reus-Smit (2005: 71) sums it up, "a set of principles have evolved internationally" and become widely accepted, according to which "in situations other than self-defense, decisions to use force must be made multilaterally." Thomas Risse-Kappen (1997: 288) takes the argument to its logical conclusion, claiming that "it is more and more inconceivable that any of the Western great powers will intervene militarily to pursue unilaterally defined strategic interests," and consequently, "unilateral military interventions for whatever purpose appear to belong increasingly to the past." These arguments yield the following hypothesis.

Hypothesis 1.1: Policymakers seek IO approval because they have internalized new legitimacy norms according to which, in situations other than self-defense, decisions to use force must be made multilaterally.

If norm internalization determines U.S. efforts to secure IO approval, then we should observe a high degree of consistency in American behavior across similar cases. Barring noncontroversial cases of self-defense (e.g., following an external act of aggression), the United States should intervene only after having secured resolutions of approval from the UNSC or from regional IOs with mandates in the field of international security, such as NATO or the OAS. At the very least, before intervening,

---

2. Weaker forms of constructivism (e.g., Finnemore 2003: 81–82) view norm compliance as instrumentally driven, but those arguments are virtually indistinguishable in their observable implications from rationalist arguments about IO approval as a means for increasing domestic or international support.

the United States should always make a genuine effort to secure the approval of relevant IOs, by engaging in sustained multilateral diplomacy and offering significant side payments to recalcitrant member states if needed. Since the early 1990s, the United States has in fact usually sought the approval of relevant IOs—at least before launching major interventions aimed at changing the internal authority structure of foreign countries. However, it would be wrong to conclude that norm internalization has occurred merely because state behavior can, by and large, be interpreted as consistent with the norm in question. Instead, we would need to observe evidence of norm internalization that is *independent* of the outcome being explained (see Cortell and Davis 2000).

The strongest proof of norm internalization by a particular state would be evidence that the norm has been translated into, or "nested" in, domestic law (Müller 1993: 385). For instance, most liberal democracies, including the United States, have internalized international human rights norms as enshrined in the 1948 Universal Declaration and the 1966 Covenant on Civil and Political Rights, by translating them into binding domestic law. But there is no evidence that the requirement of IO approval for military intervention has become similarly embedded in U.S. domestic law. The Constitution of the United States and related public laws embody a strong conception of national sovereignty, which entails that domestic authorities alone are to decide on the appropriateness of foreign military action without any kind of international scrutiny. This contrasts with the constitutional frameworks of other liberal democracies, which to varying degrees accept multilateral limitations on national sovereignty— and notably with the German, Italian, and Japanese constitutions, which outlaw offensive military action not approved by relevant IOs.[3]

Even in the absence of nesting in domestic law, international norms might have been internalized by American leaders, and consequently those leaders might feel a pull toward compliance based on a perceived sense of moral obligation. Policymakers who have internalized norms requiring IO approval should view unilateral military intervention as all but unthinkable, putting aside uncontroversial instances of self-defense, or at least should display a high threshold for violating related precepts. Furthermore, these policymakers, feeling that IO approval is a matter of obligation, should view it as intrinsically desirable—that is, as an end in

---

3. Although the post–World War II German constitution outlaws offensive war (articles 26, 87a), the country's constitutional court ruled in 1994 that national authorities are "at liberty to assign German armed forces in operations mounted by . . . NATO to implement resolutions of the UNSC." See Miller 2010. Similarly, while article 11 of the Italian constitution and article 9 of the Japanese outlaw offensive war, they have been interpreted as allowing for participation in multilateral peace operations.

itself and not merely as a useful tool to assuage domestic and international critics. The case studies in this book evaluate the norm internalization hypothesis precisely by investigating policymakers' beliefs about the value of multilateral approval.

Inferring policymakers' moral convictions and more generally their private policy preferences is fraught with difficulties. Analyzing public speeches and official documents is insufficient for this purpose because public statements either for or against multilateralism might be made instrumentally, to please various audiences. Hence "discourse analysis" suffers from a confirmatory bias when it comes to testing normative hypotheses, which makes it methodologically problematic. Nor should we uncritically rely on policymakers' own after-the-fact recollections of their motives, since such accounts can be expected to be biased in the respondent's favor. Nevertheless, by drawing on and cross-checking with a variety of different sources—such as interviews with officials from various agencies, declassified government memos, transcripts of originally secret conversations, memoirs, and contemporaneous newspaper reports—we can gain a fairly reliable picture of the private preferences and beliefs of senior policymakers in the run-up to specific interventions.

Relying on such a wide range of sources, the case studies in this book find no evidence that leading U.S. policymakers have internalized norms requiring multilateral approval. Those who appear farthest from norm internalization are civilian policymakers who passionately support armed intervention and, partially because of their commitment, are particularly influential in related debates—including, perhaps surprisingly, liberal Wilsonians who tend to publicly profess their principled attachment to multilateralism. I find that when confronted with serious human rights violations and perceived humanitarian emergencies abroad, liberal Wilsonians in senior policy positions usually push for quick military intervention and are often willing to bypass relevant IOs for the sake of maximizing U.S. freedom of action. In short, the evidence suggests that in situations marked by an overt conflict of norms, liberal Wilsonians usually prioritize norms of humanitarian intervention and democracy promotion over norms of multilateral legitimacy. If liberal Wilsonians, with their conspicuous multilateralist rhetoric, feel no intrinsic attachment to IO approval, it is unlikely that other U.S. policymakers of comparable status and influence do.

AVERTING NEGATIVE ISSUE LINKAGE

Another prominent explanation of why U.S. policymakers seek IO approval rests on the hypothesis that they fear negative issue linkage or "soft balancing" against the United States across various policy domains. Scholars associated with realist balance-of-threat theory claim that if the United States pursues unilateral military interventions that signal revisionist intentions, other powerful states such as Russia, China, India, or Brazil might retaliate through soft balancing across various issue areas. Specifically, those other states might reduce their cooperation with the United States on issues such as finance and trade, nuclear proliferation, and counterterrorism, thus imposing tangible costs on U.S. policy. As Robert Jervis writes, "Assertive hegemony erodes the willingness of [other states, including] allies, to cooperate [with the United States] on a wide range of endeavors" (Jervis 2005: 105; see also Pape 2005: 36–40; Walt 2005b: 126–29). Liberal institutionalists, although reasoning from different premises, similarly predict that if the United States acquires a reputation for noncompliance with the norms, rules, and procedures embedded in the UN Charter regime, other states might reciprocate through costly retaliation and negative issue linkage, by "form[ing] coalitions to balance American behavior in other areas such as trade or the environment" (Nye 2002: 17; see also Kupchan 2011).

Assuming that U.S. policymakers are aware of those risks, then fears of negative issue linkage or soft balancing across various policy domains might explain why the United States frequently seeks IO approval for its military interventions. Michael Mastanduno (1997: 61) was among the first to note that if "balancing is a response to threat, then . . . it is reasonable to assume that the dominant state in a unipolar setting will rely on multilateralism in its international undertakings. Multilateral decision-making procedures may be less efficient, [but] they are more reassuring to other states." More recently, without explicitly drawing on balance-of-threat theory but building on institutionalist arguments about issue linkage, Erik Voeten (2005) and Alexander Thompson (2006, 2009) have developed the argument further.

Voeten's (2005: 543) starting assumption is that if "the United States exercises force in the absence of SC authorization, other states [may] challenge it . . . for instance, by reducing cooperation elsewhere." That, he argues, creates incentives for U.S. policymakers to seek IO approval in order to uphold "cooperative efforts" across an array of issues, including on "economic issues [and] common security threats" (ibid., 541). Thompson (2009: 19) similarly assumes that interventions carried out without IO approval and in defiance of established norms are likely to result in "international political costs," which can involve "direct retaliation or countercoalitions" by third-party states as well as "long-term costs imposed . . . through negative issue linkage: the coercer finds its relations with other states suffering in other issue areas." This leads him to hypothesize that "powerful coercers" like the United States seek IO approval

[21]

strategically in order to signal benign intentions to potentially antagonistic third-party states and minimize international political costs (ibid., 24–33).[4] Those arguments leave us with a fairly clear-cut hypothesis.

> Hypothesis 1.2: Policymakers seek IO approval in order to reassure third-party states about U.S. intentions and thereby minimize the risk of negative issue linkage.

If concerns about negative issue linkage motivate U.S. leaders to seek IO approval, we should observe policymakers working hardest to secure such approval in cases in which there is a significant risk that powerful third-party states might otherwise interpret U.S. intentions as revisionist (e.g., when an intervention appears aimed at control of foreign territory or natural resources, political regime change, or straightforward retaliation—all goals that are prima facie incompatible with the UN Charter norms that underpin the international status quo). It is unclear that a consistent correlation exists between those variables. Even assuming that it did, however, it would not be sufficient for us to infer a causal effect. For causal inference to be warranted, policymakers would have to declare in interviews and published memoirs that when they sought IO approval, signaling benign intentions to avert negative issue linkage was in fact an important concern.

The four cases of U.S. military intervention decision making analyzed in this book are most-likely cases for the hypothesis that concerns about issue linkage motivate U.S. leaders to seek IO approval. The Haiti, Bosnia, Kosovo, and Iraq interventions were probably *the* most internationally controversial U.S. interventions of the post–Cold War period. First, they all entailed significant elements of internal political change. Second, American objectives were to be achieved through large-scale troop deployments and protracted occupations—raising the specter of "neo-imperialism" among foreign audiences, especially in the developing world. Most-likely cases can be considered easy test cases, and as such they are tailored to cast strong doubt on a theory and related hypotheses if the evidence does not fit (George and Bennett 2004: 122).

I find no evidence that U.S. policymakers who sought IO approval for the Haiti, Bosnia, Kosovo, and Iraq interventions were motivated by

---

4. Thompson (2006) was ambivalent or noncommittal as to whether IO approval is sought to avert negative issue linkage or merely to generate international support and burden sharing on the intervention at hand. However, he resolved much of this ambiguity in his subsequent book, putting the emphasis squarely on averting issue linkage and clarifying that for his argument to hold up, "other rationales, such as burden sharing must be ruled out as the primary motivators" (2009: 51).

concerns about issue linkage. Since those are most-likely cases for the hypothesis, we can doubt that concerns about issue linkage played a significant role in other cases in which Washington similarly sought IO approval although third-party states had fewer reasons to worry about American motives and costly resistance was therefore less likely to begin with. Perhaps one reason why American leaders in the post–Cold War period have generally been little concerned about costly international resistance in the form of issue linkage is that under unipolarity, "other states are generally much more dependent on [America] than it is on them" (Brooks and Wohlforth 2008: 99). If weaker states were to reduce their cooperation with the United States across various issue areas, notably in matters of finance and trade, they would primarily harm themselves. American leaders could conceivably become more concerned about issue linkage in the future, as emerging powers like China, India, and Brazil further increase their capabilities and acquire greater leeway to retaliate against the United States. However, recent scholarship indicates that unipolarity and with it the incentive for weaker countries to accommodate the United States might persist for several decades to come (Norrlof 2010; Beckley 2011).

Lack of evidence that fears of issue linkage motivate the United States to seek IO approval even when an intervention might a priori seem illegitimate does not necessarily lead to the conclusion that U.S. intervention policy is unaffected by international norms. American leaders might still view compliance with norms requiring multilateral approval as instrumentally valuable—first and foremost to ensure the necessary U.S. domestic support.

Ensuring Domestic Support

It may be that when U.S. policymakers seek IO approval, they are primarily motivated by concerns about domestic politics. Opinion polls in the United States asking people about possible future uses of force regularly find greater public support for multilateral than for unilateral military intervention (Kull 2002; CCGA 2012: 19–20). Some scholars accordingly hypothesize that policymakers seek IO approval in order to increase U.S. public support for intervention, by either validating their own claims about foreign crises (Wedgwood 2002: 168; Grieco et al. 2011), or reassuring the public about the likely consequences of military action (Fang 2008; Chapman 2011). One study even claims to have found concrete evidence that UNSC approval boosts U.S. public support by increasing the "rally-'round-the-flag" effect (Chapman and Reiter 2004). However, the coding of cases underlying this study is problematic, raising questions about the validity of the finding.[5] There is strong evidence that once U.S. troops are deployed in combat abroad, the public tends to rally around the flag and support the president, regardless of multilateral approval—at least so long as there is bipartisan *congressional backing* (Brody 1991; Baker and Oneal 2001; Baum and Groeling 2009). Therefore, also taking into account that Congress ultimately holds budgetary power over military intervention, it may be worth focusing in more detail on congressional attitudes.

As a former senior U.S. national security official puts it, "If you are looking for a kind of universal principle that explains multilateral action, the underlying thing is, what is it that makes an intervention legitimate in the eyes of the American electorate as expressed through the Congress."[6] To date, scholars theorizing the value of IO approval in terms of executive-legislative relations have largely viewed it as a means of increasing the president's freedom of action in the run-up to the use of force, claiming that it "ties the president's hands" and thus minimizes the risk that Congress might veto an intervention altogether (see esp. Schultz 2003; but also Cortell and Davis 1996; Tago 2005).

Yet a significant body of research indicates that regardless of multilateral approval, it is exceedingly difficult for legislators on Capitol Hill to prevent a determined administration from intervening militarily abroad. The 1973 War Powers Resolution, intended to constrain the executive branch in matters of military intervention, has been largely ineffectual. In the short run, legislators usually aim at "blame avoidance": they prefer to neither vote for military intervention, since that would involve ceding control entirely to the executive branch (while sharing the blame in case of failure), nor vote against it and risk being blamed for undermining U.S. coercive diplomacy (Lindsay 1995; Bennett 2001).

It would nevertheless be wrong to conclude that Congress is toothless when it comes to constraining U.S. policymakers on the use of force. Congressional opposition can become more of a problem in the long run, following the deployment of American troops, as combat and stabilization missions become protracted, resource costs rise, and success remains uncertain (Auerswald and Cowhey 1997; Howell and Pevehouse 2007:

5. Chapman and Reiter (2004: 897n28) code the Iraqi no-fly zones (no explicit SC authorization), the 1992 UNPROFOR deployment in Bosnia (no U.S. troop deployment), and the initial 2001 Afghanistan intervention (no explicit SC authorization) as UN-authorized, U.S. military interventions. Meanwhile they leave out the 1992 Somalia intervention, the Bosnian no-fly zone, and the 2003 Liberia intervention, which were all explicitly UN-authorized, U.S.-led interventions. See also Chapman 2011: 112.
6. Author interview with Leon Fuerth, NatSec Adviser to the VP, 1993–2001 (Mar. 9, 2010).

chap. 2). Support in Congress for open-ended deployments is likely to become increasingly brittle, making it difficult for policymakers to secure the necessary appropriations—especially when the mission is largely humanitarian and no clear threat to American security exists. Congressional opposition in turn can dramatically undermine U.S. public support for ongoing interventions, as the American news media generally "index" the slant of their coverage to reflect the range of opinion that exists within Congress (Zaller and Chiu 2000; Howell and Pevehouse 2007: 153–91). As an extreme measure, Congress might adopt binding legislation requiring the withdrawal of all U.S. troops, as it did for the Lebanon intervention in 1983 (Fisher 2013: 140–41), or cut off funding after a set deadline, as it did for Vietnam in 1973 and Somalia in 1993 (Grimmet 2007: 2–3).

Domestic Support through Sustained Burden Sharing

Research on congressional opinion finds strong bipartisan demand on Capitol Hill for international burden sharing and more generally for a cooperative approach to solving international problems (Busby et al. 2013). Consequently, when U.S. policymakers expect a resource-intensive commitment and congressional support appears lukewarm to begin with, they may seek advance approval from the UNSC or NATO's NAC in order to maximize the prospect of sustained international burden sharing and reduce the likelihood of future congressional backlash.

Scholars have long recognized that IOs facilitate burden sharing, or what David Lake (1999: chap 5) calls the creation of "joint production economies" in foreign affairs, reducing the cost to individual member states of achieving set objectives (see also Keohane and Nye 1985; Abbott and Snidal 1998). With specific regard to military intervention, advance IO approval, by legitimating the use of force, makes it easier for foreign partner states to actively cooperate with the intervener, offering landing and basing rights and contributing troops and resources (Wedgwood 2002; Thompson 2006; Chapman 2011: chap. 5). But it is unlikely that the United States, as the world's military superpower, values IO approval and the resulting legitimacy primarily for the purpose of capability aggregation during major combat. American combat operations are increasingly technology-intensive endeavors, carried out either exclusively from the air or on the ground by highly mobile, networked units that often cannot be effectively integrated with forces from international partners. The growing "capabilities gap" between the United States and even its principal allies, coming on top of doctrinal differences and domestic political constraints on the employment of non-American forces, limits the operational value of international coalition involvement for major combat (Weitsman 2014: chap. 2).

[25]

Advance approval from the UNSC or NAC is more likely to be valuable to the United States as a catalyst for sustained military and financial burden sharing *after major combat*, with the ultimate goal of ensuring U.S. domestic support for the mission's entire duration. While only a few major allies, particularly Britain and France, possess the ability to substantially contribute to U.S.-led combat operations in terms of advanced war-fighting capabilities, many more foreign partners possess the more basic capabilities required for postwar stabilization and reconstruction. As Richard Betts (2012: 211) explains, "Imperial policing, unconventional warfare, and the need for 'boots on the ground' in many places simultaneously . . . require manpower in quantity and get only a minimal boost from expensive, high-tech advantages in naval and air power." In certain areas, some allies even possess critical capabilities that the United States currently lacks, notably in terms of constabulary policing, establishing the rule of law, and local knowledge and intelligence networks in particular regions of the world (Rabasa et al. 2011: chap. 6).

Through what mechanisms, then, can advance IO approval function as a catalyst for sustained burden sharing after major combat? John Ikenberry (2001: 41) theorizes that by working through IOs, "states . . . lock in their commitments and relationships, to the extent that this can be done by sovereign states." This, he claims, facilitates sustained international cooperation in pursuit of set objectives. Although Ikenberry does not specifically focus on IO approval for military intervention, there are two ways in which UNSC or NAC approval can lock in international support in this context. First, the multilateral resolution of approval can contain assurances of a UN handoff by explicitly mandating a follow-on UN peacekeeping force led by other international partners. Second, the burden-sharing commitment can be less formal, based on the legitimation effect of IO approval and the reputational implications of public pledges of support.

Assurances of a UN Handoff

The strongest assurance of sustained burden sharing is obtained when the initial resolution authorizing military intervention, typically a UNSC mandate, also contains a formal commitment on the part of the multilateral body and its principal member states to set up a follow-on UN peacekeeping force led by other countries. For instance, SCR 940, which authorized the 1994 Haiti intervention, explicitly mandated the establishment of a follow-on UN force as soon as basic security had been restored. More recently, UN resolutions have become increasingly specific in this regard. SCR 1497, authorizing a U.S.-led intervention in Liberia in 2003, included a commitment on the part of the SC "to establish . . . a follow-on United Nations stabilization force" under regional leadership (i.e., led by countries other than the United States) within a maximum of two months. Similarly SCR 2085, authorizing a French intervention in Mali in 2012, mandated the deployment of an African-led stabilization mission that would gradually take over most of the stabilization burden.[7]

This mode of proceeding is particularly attractive for lower-stakes humanitarian missions, where a quick exit of most American (and other Western) forces may be politically desirable and where reliance on less proficient troops from developing countries appears acceptable for keeping the peace. Establishing a follow-on multilateral force under regional leadership does not necessarily mean that the United States can completely shift the longer-term burden onto others. The bargains negotiated with international partners may require that reduced contingents of U.S. troops continue to participate for some time in the follow-on UN force. In addition, Washington may have to offer technical, logistical, and intelligence support to other troop contributors. Nevertheless, once follow-on UN missions deploy (such as in Haiti or Liberia), most American forces can usually be withdrawn. Moreover, rather than having the United States directly cover the incremental costs of other states' troop contributions, follow-on UN missions are funded out of the assessed UN peacekeeping budget, thus ensuring significant financial burden sharing.[8]

Public Commitments and the Shadow of the Future

Even in the absence of an authorizing resolution that explicitly mandates a follow-on multilateral force, advance IO approval can facilitate sustained burden sharing—primarily through its legitimation effect. As a former senior U.S. defense official explains, "Many countries take the position that they won't participate in a peacekeeping, postconflict type operation unless the original intervention has been authorized by the UN."[9] The UN Security Council is generally regarded as best equipped to legitimate the international use of force, given that it is charged with this function under the UN Charter. Moreover the UNSC, in spite of its unrepresentative character, is not dominated by any of the great powers and has a restraining influence by virtue of its ability to withhold international sanction for self-serving interventions.

Besides the UNSC, regional IOs can also help legitimate U.S. interventions in the eyes of international audiences. Especially when one of the

---

7. SCR 1497 (Aug. 1, 2003), § 2; SCR 2085 (Dec. 20, 2012), §§ 9–11.
8. See Marjorie Ann Browne, "UN Peacekeeping: Issues for Congress," *CRS Report for Congress* (Feb. 11, 2011), 1–3.
9. Author interview with Walter Slocombe, UnderSecDef for Policy, 1994–2001, and Senior Adviser for Iraq Reconstruction, 2003 (Mar. 11, 2010).

[27]

organization's members is targeted by intervention, advance approval from that same organization (e.g., the Arab League or the African Union for interventions in the Middle East or Sub-Saharan Africa, respectively) signals some politically valuable form of local consent. Such regional approval undermines arguments about "American imperialism," facilitating the subsequent adoption of UNSC mandates. For instance, in the spring of 2011, the Gulf Cooperation Council and Arab League endorsed the imposition of a no-fly zone over Libya. That paved the way for the adoption of SCR 1973 on March 17, which authorized the United States and its allies "to take all necessary measures . . . to protect civilians and civilian populated areas under threat of attack . . . [and] to enforce compliance with . . . a ban on all flights" in Libya.[10]

Yet the legitimation effect of IO approval, while significant, may be insufficient to lock in international support and commit allies and partners to sustained burden sharing, especially in the face of mounting casualties. This is where the reputational implications of public pledges of support become relevant. A UNSC resolution authorizing the use of "all necessary means" involves a public, and therefore potentially costly, commitment to support U.S. policy on the part of all those SC members who have offered their affirmative vote. The same goes for approval from NATO's NAC, which requires a consensus among all members of the alliance. Once member states are thus committed to supporting U.S. policy, subsequent resistance by them to the establishment of UN or NATO stabilization missions becomes unlikely. (It would expose them to accusations of flip-flopping, harming their reputation as reliable international partners and straining their relationship with the United States— thus potentially precluding future cooperation benefits elsewhere.)

Countries other than the United States may also independently value multilateral institutions such as the UN and NATO for the security benefits they provide. Consequently, once a UN or NATO stabilization mission has been approved and the institution's reputation becomes linked to mission success, member states may be willing maintain significant troop contributions even in the face of mounting costs. Approval of a U.S.-led intervention by NATO's NAC, in particular, can be expected to substantially increase Washington's ability to extract significant and sustained burden-sharing contributions from its most militarily capable allies. As former NATO secretary-general Jaap de Hoop Scheffer explains (*Europe's World*, June 1, 2008), "The sense of keeping one's obligations and commitments to other allies upon whom one's own security ultimately depends, is a powerful driver towards equitable burden-sharing." There is indeed evidence that because of the awareness of

10. SCR 1973 (2011), §§ 4, 8. See also Bellamy and Williams 2012.

mutual security benefits from cooperation within NATO and the related long shadow of the future, non-U.S. member states continue contributing troops and resources to NATO-led stabilization missions long after those missions lose popularity at home (Kreps 2010).

Keeping Congress on Board

Members of Congress, as quintessential political players, may have other reasons beyond concerns about the military and financial burden for opposing a particular intervention. They may be opposed for parochial and ideological reasons (Schultz 2003; Hildebrandt et al. 2013), or because they are beholden to sectoral economic interests that have little to gain from an assertive foreign policy involving military intervention (Trubowitz 1998; Nazirny 2007). However, as subsequent chapters will show, whatever other reasons members of Congress may have to oppose an intervention, in public they tend to emphasize ostensibly nonpartisan issues such as the intervention's likely cost in terms of military and financial resources. By securing multilateral burden-sharing commitments, U.S. policymakers can address those criticisms, making it more difficult for Congress to continue to publicly oppose an intervention and especially to justify funding cut-offs once American troops are deployed.

In the Balkans, for instance, where the United States intervened in 1995 and again in 1999 only after securing IO approval, Washington's international partners subsequently took on most of the stabilization burden. In Bosnia, the U.S. contribution to the NATO-led stabilization force, initially at about 30 percent in late 1995, was steadily reduced until a European Union force took over entirely in 2004 (Cimbala and Forster 2010: 118–34; Recchia 2007). In Kosovo, after the 1999 NATO air campaign, the U.S. contribution to stabilization and reconstruction never exceeded 15 percent of the total to begin with. Such evidence of significant burden sharing helped forestall serious congressional opposition to Washington's military commitments (Woehrel 2009; Cimbala and Forster 2010: 123–39). Similarly, securing UN approval for the 1994 Haiti intervention allowed the United States to rapidly establish a follow-on UN peacekeeping force and shift most of the stabilization burden to other countries. That, as a former U.S. policymaker recalls, satisfied members of Congress who "were eager either to cut or restrict appropriations for Haiti" (Talbott 2008: 302).

By contrast, when the United States launches interventions that are not obviously in self-defense without IO approval, any international backing that it may be able to elicit from improvised coalitions of the willing is likely to be fickle and short-lived. The American experience in Iraq from 2003 to 2011 is an eloquent case in point. After the 2003 invasion, launched

[29]

by the United States and Britain without UN approval, Washington and London struggled to persuade other countries to contribute stabilization troops. Once the United States agreed to offset the financial costs of those contributions, in the short run it was able to recruit about 16,000 troops from other partners besides Britain, making up about 10 percent of the total international force (Richter, *LA Times*, June 22, 2003; see also Newnham 2008). However, the improvised coalition showed little staying power, disintegrating as the operation became protracted and casualties mounted. By May 2007, when America "surged" its own troops to more than 150,000 to control the Iraqi civil war, the non-U.S./UK component had shrunk to only about 7,000 troops, making up less than 5 percent of the total. This pointed lack of burden sharing resulted in growing congressional pressure to withdraw all American troops (Zeleny and Hulse, *NYT*, March 28, 2007).[11]

To some degree, U.S. decision makers are always likely to engage in forum shopping, seeking to work with the IO whose approval is most readily available and that offers the highest degree of flexibility. However, different IOs are not perfect functional equivalents in terms of the benefits they provide. Ideally, a prospective intervention would first be endorsed by non-Western regional IOs (e.g., the African Union or the Arab League), before being authorized by the UNSC. That would signal the broad legitimacy that U.S. partner states may require as a condition for contributing troops and resources. Finally, the NAC would also approve the intervention, and NATO would become actively involved by deploying the advanced capabilities of Washington's closest allies while allowing the United States to maintain significant control over the mission. As a former senior policymaker explains, "A UNSC resolution is always desirable, because it gives you the closest thing to legitimacy in the international system. But then you ought to have the opportunity to carry out the SC resolution through an organization that can carry it out, and NATO might best be able to do the job. In practice, you do the best you can in the circumstances."[12]

Decision makers might inherently value sustained burden sharing as facilitated by IO approval for its policy benefits. Yet in democracies like the United States, sustained burden sharing is likely to be valuable primarily as a means of assuaging domestic critics of open-ended military commitments. Former deputy secretary of state Strobe Talbott sums it up

11. On troop contributions, see Joseph A. Christoff, *Stabilizing and Rebuilding Iraq: Testimony Before the House Subcommittee on IOs, Human Rights, and Oversight*, 110th Cong. (May 9, 2007), 5–8; Christopher M. Blanchard and Catherine Marie Dale, "Iraq: Foreign Contributions to Stabilization and Reconstruction," *CRS Report for Congress* (Dec. 26, 2007), 11–18.
12. Author interview with Marc Grossman, AssistSecState for European Affairs, 1997–2000, and UnderSecState for Political Affairs, 2001–5 (Jan. 13, 2011).

as follows: "Particularly when it comes to intervening in civil wars or failed states and there is no clear threat to U.S. national security, it is much more sustainable if you have regional IOs and coalitions that are backed by global institutions to carry these things out, because you just can't have U.S. forces stay that long. It goes to our domestic politics."[13] That yields the following hypothesis as to why U.S. policymakers seek IO approval before intervening:

> Hypothesis 1.3: Policymakers seek IO approval to facilitate sustained burden sharing and thereby maintain congressional support for the mission's entire duration.

If concerns about burden sharing and congressional support motivate U.S. efforts to secure IO approval, we should observe policymakers working hardest to secure such approval for interventions anticipated to be resource-intensive and potentially open-ended, and more generally for (humanitarian) interventions in peripheral regions that are likely to enjoy only limited congressional support. Once again, however, a positive correlation would not be sufficient to infer causality. For causal inference to be warranted, policymakers should further declare in interviews and published memoirs that when they sought IO approval, ensuring sustained burden sharing with the ultimate goal of maintaining congressional support was in fact an important concern.

Policymakers' Differing Cost-Benefit Analyses

In an important contribution to theory, Sarah Kreps argues that two factors determine whether the United States seeks multilateral approval for military intervention: first, its time horizon, as determined by the overall sense of urgency, and second, the anticipated operational commitment, "which refers to the level of resources directed toward the particular intervention" (Kreps 2011: 31 and 28–33 more generally). When time horizons are long, reflecting low urgency, and the United States anticipates a significant operational commitment, multilateralism will seem attractive "as a way to reassure other states [and] share . . . costly burdens" (ibid., 35). Conversely, when time horizons are short, reflecting a strong sense of urgency (based on the perception that important American interests are threatened), and the United States "thinks it can win quickly or on the cheap, . . . there will be fewer incentives to aggregate resources" and we can expect a unilateral course of action (33). Kreps argues that time horizons as determined by the sense of urgency "tend to

13. Author interview with Strobe Talbott (July 9, 2009).

[31]

dominate" because a high sense of urgency reduces concerns about operational commitment (34). Although Kreps does not explicitly link U.S. demand for multilateralism to concerns about domestic support, her argument is compatible with the hypothesis that policymakers value multilateralism and the burden sharing it facilitates in order to ensure congressional support for open-ended military commitments.[14]

Sometimes the value of the variables that Kreps has identified may be so obvious that policymakers quickly reach a consensus on whether the longer-term burden sharing benefits of securing IO approval are likely to outweigh short-term freedom-of-action costs. Perhaps more often than not, however, policymakers debating the merits of intervention under the pressure of rapidly evolving circumstances differ significantly in their sense of urgency and their expectation of the likely operational commitment. For instance, as I will show in subsequent chapters, there was no consensus among U.S. policymakers as to whether the 1994 Haitian governance and refugee crisis, the large-scale ethnic violence in the Balkans following the breakup of Yugoslavia, or even Iraq's suspected WMD proliferation around the turn of the millennium, required urgent military action. In each of those cases, policymakers also fundamentally disagreed on the likely operational commitment and on how difficult it would be to maintain congressional support.

Policymakers who view armed intervention as urgent and anticipate a limited operational commitment can be expected to conclude that, unless IO approval can be obtained quickly without meaningfully constraining the United States, the short-term freedom-of-action costs of a multilateral course will exceed any longer-term benefits in terms of burden sharing and domestic support. Such interventionist hawks are consequently likely to have a low threshold for recommending that relevant IOs should be bypassed altogether. Meanwhile, more dovish officials, who view military action as less urgent and worry about potentially open-ended commitments, can be expected to be more favorably inclined toward seeking IO approval. As Stephen Brooks (2012: 7) notes, since the sense of urgency and consequently "the discount rate may vary from one policymaker to another in ways that cannot be explained simply by looking at the objective nature of the security environment," policymakers' cost-benefit analysis vis-à-vis multilateralism is also likely to vary. He concludes that "more research is needed on this topic" (ibid.). The discount

14. Interestingly, when identifying potential drivers of U.S. multilateralism, Kreps (2011: 37–40) views "domestic politics" and "burden sharing" as distinct, alternative hypotheses. She favors the latter, disregarding the possibility that domestic politics may motivate decision makers' interest in burden sharing and ultimately in multilateralism.

rate of senior U.S. officials and their cost-benefit analysis vis-à-vis multi-lateralism are likely to be influenced by several factors that will be analyzed further in chapter 2.

For now, the differences in policymakers' cost-benefit analysis vis-à-vis multilateralism can be captured in the form of two ceteris paribus hypotheses:

Hypothesis 1.4: U.S. officials who have a low sense of urgency are more likely to value the (long-term) burden sharing benefits of IO approval.

Hypothesis 1.5: U.S. officials who anticipate an open-ended commitment are more likely to value the (long-term) burden sharing benefits of IO approval.

Evaluating hypotheses 1.4 and 1.5 requires careful within-case analysis and process tracing to investigate the preferences, concerns, and resulting attitude vis-à-vis multilateralism of senior officials involved in military intervention decision making. Comparison across cases is also useful, in order to assess whether the hypothesized pattern is an empirical regularity. As sources of information, we can rely on declassified documents, interviews, published memoirs, and contemporaneous newspaper reports. Greater confidence in our findings can be achieved through triangulation between different sources.

It follows from hypotheses 1.4 and 1.5 that unless one group of like-minded officials is clearly dominant (or IO approval is readily available, in which case there is no puzzle), decisions to seek UN or NATO approval are likely to result from significant deliberations and bargaining between, on the one side, interventionist hawks who emphasize the payoffs of a prompt use of force and, on the other, more cautious doves who highlight its potential downsides and long-term costs. Thinking of foreign policy decisions as the outcome of bureaucratic politics and bargaining does not come naturally to international relations scholars, who have traditionally conceived of such decisions as the result of rational decision making by a unitary actor (the head of government representing "the State"). However, there is much evidence to indicate that unless the external environment is extremely compelling, foreign policy decisions typically result from the interaction of disparate individuals and organizations at the domestic political level, who often bargain hard to advance their parochial interests.[15]

15. Responding to criticism of her own unitary-actor approach, Kreps (2012: 22) has acknowledged that a fuller explanation of why the United States seeks IO approval "would include a theory of bureaucratic politics."

[33]

[2]

Institutions, Burden Sharing, and the American Military

Civil-military relations are central to U.S. decision making on armed intervention.[1] From a normative standpoint, democratically legitimated civilian authorities "have a right to be wrong," meaning that once senior military officers have presented their advice, the president and the cabinet should be able to set policy without undue military interference (Feaver 2003: 65). Yet the traditional model of civil-military relations, according to which policymaking should be left to civilians while uniformed leaders concentrate on the art and science of warfare, has never captured the *reality* of military intervention decision making in the United States. The country's top-ranking generals and admirals, as those responsible for managing military operations, inevitably influence related policy, and the military's high standing in American society further magnifies its leverage. "Beneath the surface," as historian Andrew Bacevich explains, the predominant pattern of U.S. civil-military relations in recent decades has been "not dialogue informed by mutual respect . . . but hard bargaining and mutual manipulation . . . driven as often by narrow self-interest as by concern for the common good" (Bacevich 2007: 210).

This chapter investigates how top-level military officers—the chairman and vice chairman of the Joint Chiefs of Staff, the combatant commanders, and senior officers on the Joint Staff who assist with planning and analysis—can influence U.S. decision making on armed intervention. Specifically, the chapter develops a theory that explains *when* and

1. The chapter is derived in part from my article, "Soldiers, Civilians, and Multilateral Humanitarian Intervention," published in *Security Studies* 24, no. 2 (2015): 1–33, available online at: http://www.tandfonline.com/10.1080/09636412.2015.1036626.

how, in what circumstances and through what mechanisms, civil-military bargaining can steer U.S. intervention policy toward the UNSC and NATO's NAC. In a nutshell, my argument is that the military's role in steering U.S. policy toward multilateralism is likely to be particularly salient when securing approval from the UNSC or NAC is difficult. The military's reluctance to intervene and its fears of costly quagmires can then motivate even hawkish civilian policymakers to make the extra effort needed to secure multilateral approval.

Multilateral approval is usually difficult to obtain for interventions aimed at changing the domestic authority structure of foreign countries, since other IO member states may view the objective as prima facie illegitimate and may thus be hesitant to offer their support. In such circumstances, strongly pro-intervention U.S. policymakers, including heavyweight presidential advisers, are initially likely to argue that relevant multilateral bodies should be bypassed for the sake of maximizing America's freedom of action. More dovish policymakers can be expected to put greater emphasis on multilateral approval as a source of legitimacy and catalyst for domestic and international support. Yet among U.S. civilian leaders, the interventionist hawks tend to carry disproportionate weight. That is where America's senior generals and admirals, as reluctant warriors who are skeptical of human-rights driven interventions and other wars of choice aimed at internal political change, play a central role.

Senior military officers typically worry that human rights-driven interventions and other wars of choice aimed at changing the domestic politics of foreign countries will result in costly quagmires that Congress may not support. When America's top-ranking uniformed leaders express strong concerns about the operational burden, then as long as civilian policymakers are divided over whether to intervene, which is likely absent clear threats to national security, the military can tilt the balance of power within the administration toward nonintervention. The military is thus likely to veto such interventions—*unless* pro-intervention policymakers can mollify the reluctant generals by securing UN or NATO approval combined with concrete burden-sharing commitments from international partners. By contrast, when top-level military leaders fail to express strong reservations about a prospective intervention, the administration's civilian hawks are empowered and the United States is more likely to bypass multilateral bodies.

AMERICA'S HAWKISH CIVILIAN INTERVENTIONISTS

Classical liberal internationalist, or Wilsonian, beliefs in individual freedom, self-government, and national self-determination have historically faced little ideological opposition in the United States. This has elicited a uniquely American impulse to assertively promote liberal values and institutions abroad or, in the words of one critic, to "impose Locke everywhere" (Hartz 1955: 13). America's liberal tradition has also made accommodation with nonliberal opponents difficult "by identifying the alien [i.e., the nonliberal] with the unintelligible" (ibid., 285; see also McDougall 1997). The result has been a tendency to magnify foreign threats, making nonliberal opponents appear more menacing than a dispassionate analysis of their capabilities to actually harm the United States would indicate—further increasing the desire to reshape foreign societies in America's own image (Desch 2009b: 46).[2] Since the end of the Cold War, the unipolar structure of world politics has emboldened U.S. policymakers to more readily act on that desire. Post–Cold War U.S. military interventions, as quintessential wars of choice rather than necessity, have indeed often sought to change the internal politics of foreign countries in a more liberal and democratic direction (Von Hippel 2000; Smith 2012).

But as Colin Dueck (2006) shows, a close examination of the history of U.S. foreign policy reveals that America's political culture has yielded two contradictory impulses: on the one hand, the aforementioned tendency toward hawkish interventionism, and on the other, a countervailing tendency toward risk-aversion, or limited liability. There is evidence that within the U.S. executive branch, different groups of individuals typically associated with different parts of the bureaucracy most clearly embody these countervailing tendencies toward hawkish interventionism and limited liability.

Individuals of liberal Wilsonian or neoconservative persuasion and without combat experience (who make up a significant portion of senior officials at the State Department and on the staff of the National Security Council) are usually the ones who push most strongly for military intervention to uphold American values and promote internal political change in foreign countries.[3] Liberal Wilsonians and neoconservatives also tend to believe in American exceptionalism and to display great confidence in the United States' ability to effectively deploy its formidable military power in pursuit of moral purposes abroad. As former secretary of state Madeleine Albright, a committed liberal interventionist, famously put it, "If we have to use force, it is because we are America. We are the

2. On how "liberal [foreign] policy . . . has often raised conflicts of interest into crusades," resulting in "fail[ures] to negotiate stable mutual accommodations of interest . . . with powerful states of a nonliberal character," see also Doyle 1983: 324.
3. For evidence of continuing high levels of support for hawkish liberalism among U.S. civilian policy elites, see Busby and Monten 2008. For evidence that policymakers with no combat experience tend to be more hawkish, see Horowitz and Stam 2014.

[36]

indispensable nation. We stand tall and we see further than other countries into the future" (interview on NBC-TV, Feb. 19, 1998). Meanwhile
for reasons explained below, high-ranking U.S. military officers and
other war veterans in senior administration positions tend to be reluctant
warriors, who question American exceptionalism and are skeptical about
using force for human rights-related purposes and more generally for
internal political change.

Incentives to Bypass Multilateral Bodies

In principle, liberal Wilsonianism has since its origins been sympathetic to international institutions (Recchia 2013; Slaughter 2008). Even
hawkish Wilsonian policymakers accordingly tend to profess their
attachment to international institutions, declaring that "multilateralism . . . has its place as a foreign policy tool" (Albright 2003: 176). Neoconservatives in contrast, usually emphasize the benefits of unfettered
American primacy and are more ideologically hostile to coordinating
policy with other countries through multilateral bodies (Halper and
Clarke 2004). Yet those principled differences between liberal Wilsonians and neoconservatives on the question of multilateralism frequently
disappear when it comes to concrete decision making on armed
intervention.

First, when confronted with systematic human rights violations
abroad involving mass atrocities, war crimes, or ethnic cleansing, liberal
Wilsonian and neoconservative policymakers alike usually view swift
military action as a moral necessity, leaving little room for consensus
building with international partners through multilateral institutions.
Similarly, both Wilsonians and neoconservatives tend to have little faith
in deterrence vis-à-vis nonliberal opponents who have a history of
international aggression and/or are thought to be developing weapons
of mass destruction. This can be expected to make them favorably
inclined toward preventive war aimed at removing the perceived threat
from such nonliberal regimes. For instance, Lee Feinstein and Anne-
Marie Slaughter (2004: 137), two Wilsonian intellectuals and former
senior State Department officials, advocate U.S. military intervention
not only to stop massive human rights violations but also to "prevent
nations run by rulers without internal checks on their power from
acquiring or using WMD." The authors explicitly indicate that, "given
the Security Council's propensity for paralysis," the United States
should not shy away from relying on "unilateral action or coalitions of
the willing" in the pursuit of its objectives (ibid., 148–49; see also Slaughter, *NYT*, Mar. 18, 2003). In short, if left to their own devices, liberal
Wilsonians and neoconservatives who view military intervention as

[37]

urgent to defend and promote American values are likely to have a low threshold for bypassing relevant multilateral bodies to maximize U.S. freedom of maneuver.

Furthermore, as subsequent chapters in this book will illustrate, Wilsonians, neoconservatives, and other interventionist hawks in senior policy positions tend to display great confidence in the ability of military action to quickly achieve desirable outcomes at limited cost to the United States. Focusing on the anticipated short-term payoffs of military intervention, such hawkish policymakers usually downplay attendant risks and (long-term) operational costs. As former secretary of defense Robert Gates (2014: 519) writes, pro-intervention civilian leaders "virtually never consider the [longer-term] cost" (see also Kupchan 1992: 243–56; Rapport 2012). That presumably makes the burden-sharing benefits of IO approval less appealing in their eyes.

Finally, in terms of generating and sustaining U.S. domestic support for intervention, hawkish policymakers tend to highlight the importance of decisive leadership and bold initiatives rather than multilateral backing. For instance, in the run-up to the 2003 Iraq War, Secretary of Defense Donald Rumsfeld and his neoconservative collaborators emphasized that "if public support [for military action] is weak at the outset, U.S. leadership must be willing to invest the political capital to marshal support to sustain the effort for whatever period of time may be required" (quoted in E. Cohen 2003: 229). Subsequent chapters of the book will demonstrate that during earlier policy debates about U.S. intervention in the 1990s, Secretary Albright and other interventionist hawks similarly never worried much about domestic support and believed that congressional misgivings about the use of force could be overcome through presidential leadership.

The most hawkish policymakers may go so far as to believe that even if on a specific occasion a multilateral mandate could be obtained with relative ease, it would be unwise for the United States to actually request it, as this might reinforce norms requiring IO approval and could thus potentially constrain U.S. actions in the future. Albright (2003: 384) indicates that she would have opposed efforts to obtain a UNSC mandate for the Kosovo intervention, even assuming it could have been obtained at little cost. "If a UN resolution passed," she argues, "we would have set a precedent . . . giv[ing] Russia, not to mention China, a veto" over America's use of force. For similar reasons, in 2001 the George W. Bush administration stopped short of requesting an explicit SC authorization under chapter VII of the UN Charter for its military intervention in Afghanistan, even though such approval could most likely have been obtained with limited effort. The Bush administration was determined to maximize America's freedom of action and did not want to reinforce the

[38]

expectation that IO approval is always required to legitimate U.S. intervention.[4]

Liberal and neoconservative interventionist hawks tend to carry great weight in U.S. administration debates about national security. Partially, this may simply reflect their steadfast commitment to their cause and the amount of personal time and energy they are willing to invest in its advancement. However, arguments in favor of armed intervention on humanitarian grounds, and more generally in the cause of freedom and democracy, also mesh well with America's sense of exceptionalism and liberal political culture, which can be expected to further empower the hawks (Hoffmann 2005). For all of the aforementioned reasons, the hawks can be expected to argue that unless multilateral support is readily available in particular crises that they believe require a strong American response, the United Nations and NATO should be bypassed to allow for quick military action.

More dovish civilian officials, who view military action as less urgent and tend to emphasize its (long-term) costs, can be expected to advocate caution and to be more favorably inclined toward seeking IO approval. However, confronted with a worsening humanitarian situation abroad, and/or with nonliberal opponents who assertively challenge American interests, the interventionist hawks are likely to be able to effectively draw on common morality, shocking imagery, and historical analogies (for example, the Holocaust, or the more recent genocide in Rwanda) to push the United States toward military action. Dovish civilian officials, on their own, may lack the technical expertise to credibly challenge the hawks' feasibility studies and optimistic assessments about the risks and likely operational costs of armed intervention. It is in this context that the U.S. military, with its acknowledged professional expertise, its consistent skepticism about wars of choice aimed at internal political change, and its high standing in American society, can play an important and hitherto underappreciated restraining role, steering U.S. policy toward multilateralism.

The Military's Skepticism about Interventions for Internal Political Change

The traditional view on the radical left is that America's uniformed leaders, in an unholy alliance with the U.S. arms industry, put strong and persistent pressure on the country's political authorities to intervene

4. Author interviews with William B. Wood, Acting AssistSecState for IO Affairs, 1998–2002 (Jan. 25, 2011), and John D. Negroponte, U.S. PermRep to UNSC, 2001–4 (Feb. 15, 2011). See also Rawski and Miller 2004: 370.

militarily abroad (see, e.g., Chomsky 1993). The evidence, however, over-whelmingly points in the opposite direction. Top-level military officers, with the chairman and vice chairman of the JCS at the forefront, are con-sistently among the most reluctant doves in U.S. policy debates about armed intervention. The senior generals and admirals worry more than most civilian leaders about operational costs and future quagmires. The military's dovish attitude appears to be the result of a combination of ideological preferences, organizational interests, and lessons learned from history.

Samuel Huntington (1957: 59–65) famously noted that senior military officers tend to be conservative political realists in foreign affairs. That insight has been confirmed with regard to the United States by survey research carried out under the auspices of the Triangle Institute for Secu-rity Studies (TISS). According to TISS data, America's military leaders usually conceive of national security in terms of traditional realpolitik goals (control of territory, maintenance of geostrategic access and posi-tion, and defense of major allies) and are more skeptical of humanitarian and other human rights-driven policies than most civilian leaders—especially those without military experience.[5] Fewer than 5 percent of uniformed leaders view the use of force "to address humanitarian needs abroad" as a "very important" role for the U.S. military, compared with almost 20 percent of nonveteran civilian leaders who view that same goal as "very important."[6]

Furthermore, as political realists, America's senior military officers tend to evaluate the seriousness of external threats primarily on the basis of the capabilities rather than the perceived intentions of foreign oppo-nents, and they believe that even nonliberal countries can usually be deterred (Huntington 1957: 66–67; Betts 1991: 37). As a consequence, the senior officers are likely to have generally lower threat perceptions than civilian policymakers, who, partially because of their liberal ideology, tend to give more weight to an opponent's perceived intentions and to have broader conceptions of America's national interest (Desch 2009a). The senior officers' lower threat perception, especially when they are faced with middle power states, can in turn be expected to make them skeptical of arguments about preventive self-defense by means of

5. TISS data indicates that 34 percent of civilian leaders with no military experience view "promoting and defending human rights in other countries" as a "very impor-tant" U.S. policy goal, while only 13 percent of active-duty military officers agree. Holsti 2001: 35; Feaver and Gelpi 2004: 37–38; Szayna et al. 2007: 86.
6. The views of civilian leaders with military experience are closer to those of active-duty military officers: only about 10 percent of them rate the goal as "very impor-tant." Holsti 2001: 46; Feaver and Gelpi 2004: 46–47.

forcible regime change. Survey evidence confirms that members of the U.S. armed services are generally suspicious of claims about American exceptionalism and significantly less likely than nonveteran civilians to support armed intervention aimed at changing the internal authority structure of foreign countries (Pew Research Center 2011: 22–26).

Parochial organizational interests further magnify the military's reluctance about interventions aimed at internal political change. Top-level military officers who regularly participate in policy debates about armed intervention—the JCS chairman and vice chairman, the combatant commanders, and senior officers on the Joint Staff (especially the J-3 director for operations and the J-5 director for strategic plans and policy)—rise to their position through the ranks of their services; consequently, they tend to be more parochial in outlook than civilian appointees who may join an administration from the private sector or civil society (Betts 2001: 126–32; Szayna et al. 2007: 680). As parochial career officials, the generals and admirals want to preserve the health, vitality, and social prestige of their organization. Thus, if the United States has to intervene militarily, they prefer narrowly targeted missions with a high likelihood of success.

A former senior Pentagon official explains it as follows: "The war fighters want clear military objectives—capture this hill, occupy this city"—but when it comes to humanitarian interventions and liberal wars of regime change, they ask, "What is my mission?"[7] They worry that changing the internal authority structure of foreign countries in a more liberal and democratic direction will require open-ended and resource-intensive commitments aimed at peace enforcement and stabilization, without any ultimate guarantee of success. Perhaps their greatest concern is that since the military objectives of such nontraditional missions are vague, beyond the initial coercive phase, the exit strategy, too, is often unclear (Betts 2012: chap. 9). If the United States intervenes out of a momentary urge to "do something," without a national consensus that important American interests are threatened, it may be difficult to maintain domestic support for such open-ended commitments, with potentially high long-term costs for the armed services and their troops. As General David Petraeus (1989: 498) notes, "It is, after all, the senior military's institutions—the services to which the officers have devoted their lives—that have the most to risk in foreign intervention." The most consistently cautious about interventions aimed at internal political change have been generals in the army and the Marine Corps, given that their services typically bear the greatest burden in terms of ground combat,

7. Author interview with John Veroneau, AssistSecDef for Legislative Affairs, 1999–2001 (Apr. 7, 2010).

logistics, and long-term stabilization (Betts 1991: 116–22; Petraeus 1989: 497).

Finally, the senior officers' cautious views on intervention and their concerns about maintaining domestic support for potentially open-ended commitments reflect the traumatic experience of America's war in Vietnam. As that war became protracted, Congress eventually cut off funding for all American troops after a set deadline, forcing a humiliating withdrawal (Grimmett 2007: 2–3). The antiwar movement resulting from the perceived failure in Vietnam gave birth to broader U.S. antimilitarism, which harmed the armed services and their institutional standing in American society until well into the 1980s. Only the perceived success of the 1991 Gulf War fully reestablished the public's confidence in the military, providing the occasion when, as Colin Powell (1995: 532) explains, "the American people fell in love again with their armed forces" (see also Bacevich 2007: 238).

The military's "lessons of Vietnam" are concisely summarized in what has become known as the Weinberger-Powell Doctrine on the use of American force. The doctrine, which continues to enjoy widespread support among senior military officers, holds that the United States should intervene only as a last resort when "vital" American interests are threatened, when there is "reasonable assurance" that Congress and the American public will be supportive, and when policymakers have identified clear political and military objectives, as well as an exit strategy for U.S. troops. Furthermore, the doctrine holds that if the United States chooses to intervene, uniformed leaders should be allowed to use "decisive force" in order to quickly achieve the mission's military objectives and then withdraw all U.S. forces within a short time frame (LaFeber 2009).[8]

Hawkish civilian policymakers, by contrast, have long viewed the Weinberger-Powell Doctrine as an expression of exaggerated caution and an impediment to American leadership. Albright (2003: 182) remembers that in the early 1990s, she challenged Powell's argument that U.S. military intervention in Bosnia might result in a quagmire: "What are we saving this superb military for, Colin, if we can't use it?" More recently, neoconservative hardliners in the George W. Bush administration insisted that the United States invade Iraq with only a small force, in part because they wanted to prove that the Powell doctrine and notably its requirement of overwhelming force was outdated.[9]

---

8. For evidence of the doctrine's continuing popularity among senior military officers, see Feaver and Gelpi 2004: 50–53; Szayna et al. 2007: 141–45.

9. Author interview with Marc Grossman, UnderSec State for Political Affairs, 2001–5 (Jan. 13, 2011). See also chap. 6 in this book.

The Military's Concerns about Congress

The armed services, like most specialized bureaucracies, approach planning for their activities according to standard procedures, which involve the elaboration of detailed operational maps that are reviewed at various levels in the organization's hierarchy. Those procedures, combined with the ideological and organizational factors mentioned above, make the uniformed leaders extremely risk-averse in matters of armed intervention and unlikely to discount the longer-term costs of ambitious military missions aimed at internal political change (Betts 1991: 153–60). This tendency is in line with the finding in psychological research that individuals who focus on *how* an action should be implemented usually consider questions of feasibility very closely and examine possible implications at a concrete operational level. Meanwhile, individuals who focus on *why* a specific course of action should be followed (such as interventionist civilian officials) typically consider the implications from a more abstract viewpoint and think primarily about the desirability of the expected payoffs (Trope and Liberman 2010).

Given the uniformed leaders' focus on how to implement complex military operations and their parochial concerns for the well-being of the services, they are typically quite anxious about the issue of congressional

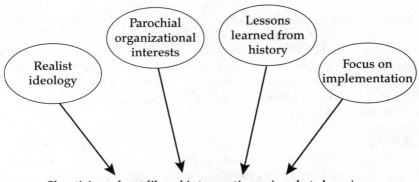

Skepticism about liberal interventions aimed at changing the internal authority structure of foreign countries.

Concerns about open-ended commitments and ability to maintain congressional support.

Figure 2.1 Understanding the military's reluctance

[43]

support—or rather, about the *dissolution* of such support in the face of open-ended commitments of dubious relevance to American interests and without clear evidence of success. The generals and admirals are aware that after the launch of offensive operations, in the short run, Congress and the American public can be expected to support the president and the troops (Petraeus 1989: 492). However, the uniformed leaders worry that unless the public perceives important national interests to be at stake, domestic support might evaporate in the face of mounting U.S. casualties and expenditures. As General Joseph Ralston, a former JCS vice chairman and commander of allied troops in Europe, explains, senior military officers don't "want to find themselves in a situation where we get started [with an intervention] and then suddenly the Congress says, 'Well wait a minute, we're not going to support that!'— because then you don't have a way to succeed."[10]

The political scientists William Howell and Jon Pevehouse (2007) find that U.S. presidents intervene militarily more often when they enjoy strong political support in Congress. According to Howell and Pevehouse, this indicates that "early congressional discussions about impending military action sen[d] valuable signals" to civilian policymakers about the likelihood of domestic political support for potentially "protracted or costly" interventions (ibid., 21, 26). Yet the authors provide no process-tracing evidence to support this inference. As noted, civilian policymakers who are favorably disposed toward armed intervention frequently do not worry much about the possibility that an operation might become protracted and that Congress and the American public might withdraw their support. As a former senior State Department official who dealt extensively with executive-legislative relations explains, the optimistic assumption of pro-intervention policymakers tends to be that once American troops are deployed, "there isn't a lot that Congress can do to stop what an administration is doing."[11]

The case studies in this book will demonstrate that senior military officers are the ones who usually alert civilian authorities to the likelihood of an open-ended commitment, involving the possibility of significant U.S. casualties with attendant risks of congressional backlash. Put differently, civilian authorities (including the president and senior White House officials) often become aware of the probability of a protracted troop deployment, which raises obvious questions of domestic support,

10. Author interview with Gen. Joseph Ralston, JCS Vice Chairman, 1996–2000, and SACEUR, 2000–3 (Mar. 17, 2010). On the military's concerns about congressional support, see also Avant 1996; Clark 2001: 137–38, 165.
11. Author interview with Barbara Larkin, AssistSecState for Legislative Affairs, 1996–99 (Apr. 2, 2010).

only *after* the military makes it clear that limited air strikes or a quick in-and-out mission are unlikely to achieve the objectives laid out by the national political leadership. Therefore, to the extent that concerns about future congressional opposition affect U.S. policymaking on armed intervention, the military leaders are likely to constitute a crucial transmission belt.

Demand for Burden Sharing and Exit Strategies

Another lesson that the military establishment drew from Vietnam was that in the future, top-level military officers should more assertively communicate to civilian authorities their concerns about the risks and likely costs of armed intervention (Powell 1995: 144; Bacevich 2007: 239–41). Therefore, assuming that America's senior generals and admirals act as politically independent professionals, they can be expected to acquiesce in coercive humanitarian missions and other human rights-driven interventions aimed at internal political change *only if* they believe that: first, the risk to American forces will be minimized (e.g., by relying exclusively on airpower during the active combat phase), and second, American forces will not carry the main burden—especially for "post-combat" stabilization missions in which success is notoriously elusive.

Walter Slocombe, former undersecretary of defense for policy, emphasizes that "in fact, the military wants to have as little of the burden as possible."[12] The senior officers' preference for international burden sharing on peacekeeping and stabilization follows naturally from their concerns about the (long-term) operational costs of intervention and related worries about maintaining U.S. domestic support. Deploying highly skilled American troops in protracted stabilization missions also has significant opportunity costs, since those troops will not be available for potentially more serious contingencies elsewhere. In the U.S. Army, the deployment of one combat soldier ("tooth") requires up to five additional military personnel ("tail") dealing with logistics and other support tasks (Priest 2003: 47).

The military's preference for burden sharing with foreign allies and partners is rarely articulated in officially sanctioned publications by the armed services or the Joint Staff, given that international cooperation is a matter of policy and therefore in principle reserved for civilian decision making. Nevertheless, since the end of the Cold War, the view that stabilization missions in the aftermath of major combat ought to be progressively internationalized seems to have taken hold within the services, to

12. Author interview with Walter Slocombe, UnderSecDef for Policy, 1994–2001, and Senior Adviser for Iraq Reconstruction, 2003 (Mar. 11, 2010).

the point where, as a former senior defense official explains, it is now "practically a doctrinal assumption."[13] America's generals and admirals understand that cooperating with international partners can constrain U.S. freedom of action; but the case studies in this book indicate that they usually view the resulting legitimacy and burden-sharing benefits as outweighing attendant coordination and flexibility costs.

The military's preference for international burden sharing on peace-keeping and stabilization was elevated into U.S. government doctrine as early as 1994, when President Clinton signed an executive order known as Presidential Decision Directive 25 (PDD 25).[14] The document reem-phasizes several core elements of the Weinberger-Powell Doctrine—notably the need for well-defined objectives, congressional support, and availability of an exit strategy. It also insists that postcombat stabilization tasks, especially in the aftermath of humanitarian interventions, should be carried out with allies and partners through "UN and other multilat-eral peace operations," because "in such cases, the U.S. benefits from having to bear only a share of the burden."[15]

Although "burden sharing" became somewhat of a buzzword in the 1990s, the military's preference for sharing operational costs and liabili-ties internationally was not merely an idiosyncrasy of the immediate post–Cold War period. Undoubtedly, as a result of recent experiences in Afghanistan and Iraq, the armed services now devote greater resources to training and capabilities development for counterinsurgency and sta-bilization missions overseas.[16] Furthermore, a majority of veterans now recognize that nation building is an appropriate role for the military (Pew Research Center 2011: 25). However, the experience of open-ended deployments in Afghanistan and Iraq appears if anything to have fur-ther convinced the uniformed leaders that the United States cannot bear the burdens of postwar stabilization all by itself. General John Abizaid, who oversaw U.S. military operations in Iraq between 2003 and 2007, sums up the senior officers' view as follows: "As combat operations are over and you move toward stabilization, the force structure should be robust and it should be increasingly international. American troops are best employed when decisive military force needs to be applied, but

13. Author interview with Frank Wisner, UnderSecState for International Security, 1992–93, and UnderSecDef for Policy, 1993–94 (July 16, 2009).
14. Several former officials interviewed for this book confirmed the military's influ-ence on PDD 25.
15. White House, "The Clinton Administration's Policy on Reforming Multilateral Peace Operations," PDD 25 (May 6, 1994), 2.
16. Author interview with Col. William Flavin, Director of Doctrine, Concepts, and Training, U.S. Army Peacekeeping and Stability Operations Institute, 1999–2013 (Jan. 18, 2011).

tying down U.S. troops in long-term occupations is not in the national interest."[17] The Pentagon's 2012 strategic guidance document and the 2014 Quadrennial Defense Review, reflecting the military's concerns, put strong emphasis on international burden sharing for peacekeeping and stability operations overseas.[18]

Related to the generals' and admirals' demand for burden sharing is their concern that civilian policymakers devise a clear exit strategy for American troops *before* ordering their deployment. A majority of U.S. military officers believe it is appropriate for top-level uniformed leaders to "insist" on the need for an exit strategy vis-à-vis civilian authorities (Holsti 2001: 87). General Powell, with whom the notion of an exit strategy is now commonly associated, interprets it as meaning that before American troops are committed abroad, "you better think through how it ends and what happens at the end."[19] Particularly in the context of humanitarian intervention, the U.S. exit strategy has increasingly consisted in handing off longer-term peacekeeping and stabilization tasks to follow-on UN or NATO missions, with the majority of troops contributed by other international partners. A recent U.S. Army field manual accordingly notes that officers planning a humanitarian intervention should aim to "accomplish transfer of authority [to follow-on multilateral missions] as early as possible. The timing of the transfer [ought to be] part of the initial negotiations."[20]

Traditionally, the U.S. military has been reluctant to deploy American troops as part of blue-helmeted UN peace operations unless one of its own officers commanded the mission. But in recent years, creative arrangements have been devised, especially for lower-stakes missions such as the peacekeeping operations in Liberia since 2003 and Haiti since 2004, whereby U.S. troops have effectively served under the operational control of foreign UN commanders.[21] For higher-stakes missions, in which the possibility of protracted combat and counterinsurgency is anticipated, such as in Kosovo or Afghanistan, the military's preference has been to entrust stabilization tasks to NATO instead of the UN, given

17. Author interview with Gen. John P. Abizaid, Director, Joint Staff, 2001–3, and CENTCOM Commander, 2003–7 (Jan. 27, 2011).
18. DOD, "Sustaining U.S. Global Leadership: Priorities for the 21st Century," Jan. 5, 2012; DOD, "Quadrennial Defense Review," Mar. 4, 2014.
19. Author interview with Gen. Colin L. Powell, JCS Chairman, 1989–93, and Sec-State, 2001–5 (Feb. 2, 2011).
20. Department of the Army, "The Army in Multinational Operations," FM 3–16 (Apr. 8, 2014), chap. 5, § 14.
21. Marjorie Ann Browne, "UN Peacekeeping: Issues for Congress," *CRS Report for Congress* (Feb. 11, 2011), 18–19.

the Atlantic alliance's more advanced capabilities and Washington's higher degree of control over NATO operations.[22]

The American military clearly understands that IO involvement can help legitimate the use of force and facilitate burden sharing, as evidenced by the fact that close to 80 percent of U.S. military officers emphasize the need to enlist the cooperation of the UN in settling international disputes (Holsti 2001: 36–38; see also Szayna et al. 2007: 101–3). That said, top-level generals and admirals are unlikely to explicitly recommend that the United States obtain the approval of relevant IOs before intervening abroad. The standard view among senior military officers, as General Powell explains, is that whether the United States seeks IO approval "is a political matter, and it is up to the political leadership to ultimately decide it."[23] What the generals and admirals are likely to request—with insistence in the case of humanitarian missions—is some reassurance *before* intervening that the longer-term burden will be shared with and shifted as much as possible to international partners so that large numbers of American troops won't get bogged down for the indefinite future.[24]

IO APPROVAL TO REASSURE THE RELUCTANT WARRIORS

America's generals and admirals are not the only senior U.S. national security officials who can be expected to emphasize the likely operational costs and potential pitfalls of armed intervention. Risk-averse doves among the civilian leadership, especially war veterans and others with significant exposure to the armed services, may express similar concerns. Indeed, civilian Pentagon officials—and the secretary of defense in particular—usually underscore the military's concerns in the interagency debate. However, the uniformed leaders, because of their acknowledged professional expertise and preeminent role in the planning and execution of military operations, have a unique ability to influence civilian policymaking on the use of force. The military's high standing in American society further magnifies the senior officers' leverage.

22. Author interviews with LTG David Weisman, Vice Director for Strategic Plans (J-5), Joint Staff, 1995–98, and U.S. Mil-Rep to NATO, 1998–2001 (Feb. 10, 2011); and William B. Wood, Acting AssistSecState for IO Affairs, 1998–2002 (Jan. 25, 2011).
23. Powell, author interview, confirmed by Abizaid, author interview.
24. At a lower level, military planners on the Joint Staff and at the combatant commands (especially the J-5 directors for strategy and policy) might go further, de facto advising that the United States intervene only with IO approval when they explicitly foresee such approval in their recommended options for the president.

The Generals' Leverage

The influence of high-ranking military officers in policy debates about armed intervention is largely negative, in the sense that while they can rarely set the agenda and successfully push a particular policy through the bureaucracy, they may be able to *veto* military options they decidedly oppose. Confronted with a foreign crisis that does not clearly threaten American security, civilian authorities are usually divided over whether to intervene. In such circumstances, senior generals and admirals have the ability to tilt the balance of power within the administration toward nonintervention and thus "exercise a veto over the use of American force, or if not a veto, the ability to [significantly] shape the character of American intervention" (Kohn 2002: 15; see also Avant 1996; Desch 1999: 22–33; Bacevich 2007: 248–49).

When the possibility of armed intervention is seriously considered by the national political leadership, military planners at the relevant combatant command are usually asked to develop an operations plan with several different options that provide some flexibility to adapt to changing circumstances. The various options with their underlying assumptions are then debated by senior members of the national security bureaucracy. "Of course, people reflect their backgrounds, and [the interests and perspective of] the agency they come from," explains a former senior Pentagon official.[25]

Even without explicitly opposing a particular policy, senior military officers can rely on their professional expertise and related informational advantage to portray some solutions as impractical. If the generals and admirals disagree with a specific use-of-force option, they can artificially inflate the required troop numbers and anticipated casualties so as to make it appear politically unfeasible. As Anthony Lake, former national security adviser, explains, when the "senior military guys are saying, 'This mission can't be done,' it's hard to say, 'Listen, you professionals, here's an amateur's view of how and why it can be done'" (quoted in Power 2003: 316). Beyond the JCS chairman and vice chairman and the combatant commanders, senior officers on the Joint Staff, who typically review all the war plans, are important players in this bureaucratic political game. "If the military discount an option, it will not be resourced," explains a former director of the Joint Staff. "If it is not resourced, it quickly dies."[26] The senior officers' informational advantage and related ability to quietly influence decision making on

25. Slocombe, author interview.
26. Author interview with LTG Walter Kross, Director, Joint Staff, 1994–96 (Feb. 11, 2011). See also Betts 1991: 154–55; Feaver 2003: 68–70.

armed intervention have probably never been greater, given that the number of civilian government officials with military experience has been steadily declining.[27]

But top-level military leaders can also act as more straightforwardly political players. At a time of generally diminishing popular support for public institutions in the United States, including Congress and the presidency, Americans continue to express high levels of confidence in the armed services.[28] Consequently, by opposing a particular policy in private and even just hinting at the possibility that they might openly voice their disagreements with the civilian leadership, the senior generals and admirals can wield extraordinary influence over military intervention decision making—particularly when the policy is already domestically controversial. John Hamre, a former deputy secretary of defense, explains that when the generals and admirals disagree with civilian authorities, they tend to "bring excruciating detail to the internal deliberations about why a specific course of action is perilous, and that usually signals to the civilian leaders that they can anticipate a political fight if it does go public."[29]

To further increase their bargaining leverage, the uniformed leaders might surreptitiously leak their reservations to the media, openly express their concerns about the risks and likely operational costs of intervention during press conferences and public congressional hearings, and even threaten their resignation as a last resort (Brooks 2009: 219–20; Betts 1991: 43–45). So long as the civilian principals are divided (and particularly as long as the secretary of defense sides with the uniformed leaders), a JCS chairman or combatant commander who openly expresses the military's concerns has a low probability of being punished by the president for speaking out (Avant 1996: 56–59; Feaver 2003: 87–90). Even if the generals and admirals don't aim to undermine administration policy, their public expressions of concern in response to questions from journalists or members of Congress are likely to have that effect in practice: recent survey research indicates that perceived military opposition to proposed uses of force has a significant negative effect on U.S. public support for

27. On the lack of military experience among civilian officials, see Thompson, *Time*, Nov. 21, 2011, 34–39.
28. According to a 2014 Gallup poll, 74 percent of Americans have confidence in the military, 29 percent in the presidency, and a record low 7 percent in Congress. Gallup, "Confidence in Institutions," June 5–8, 2014.
29. John Hamre, e-mail to author (Feb. 17, 2010). See also Brooks 2009: 232–33; Bacevich 2007: 247–49.

intervention, reducing it by seven percentage points on average (Golby, Dropp, and Feaver 2013).

The uniformed leaders' relationship with Congress can be especially useful for magnifying their influence vis-à-vis civilian policymakers. The 1947 National Security Act ensures the military's access to Congress, and congressional committees regularly encourage representatives of the armed services who are called to testify on Capitol Hill to inform the legislative branch of the military's disagreements with civilian administration officials (Betts 1991: 45; Feaver 2003: 81–82). Apart from using public and classified congressional hearings to pressure civilian policymakers, the military can also rely on personal contacts with members of Congress to convey its concerns. Such lobbying of Congress by elements of the bureaucracy is technically illegal; however, the senior officers may influence the legislative branch without leaving their fingerprints by relying on informal channels (Priest 2003: 47). The president also often needs the military's active cooperation in order to build up support for particular use-of-force policies in Congress, which further increases the senior officers' leverage.[30]

In short, through their professional expertise, threats of public opposition, and use of various expedients to convey their concerns to Congress and occasionally to the public, America's uniformed leaders can exert an extraordinary amount of influence over decision making about armed intervention. Once the president takes a final decision to intervene, the U.S. military "salutes and obeys"—meaning it can be relied upon to carry out civilian orders and complete the mission to the best of its abilities. But unless there is a clear and present danger to the security of the United States, U.S. citizens, or key U.S. allies, the president is unlikely to quickly decide on the use of force, seeking instead to keep his options open for as long as possible. As a former senior defense official explains, *until* the president, as commander in chief, takes a final decision, "the generals have plenty of capacity to sabotage things, if they want to."[31] That yields the following hypothesis about the military's influence over decisions on armed intervention:

> Hypothesis 2.1: When there is no clear threat to U.S. national security and policymakers consequently disagree about the merits of intervention, a determined military leadership can veto the use of American force.

---

30. Author interview with Adm. William Owens, JCS Vice Chairman, 1994–96 (Jan. 27, 2011). See also Holbrooke 1998: 219.
31. Slocombe, author interview.

Table 2.1 How the generals can influence military intervention decision making

A) Professional expertise

– Alert civilian policymakers to risks and likely operational costs

– Present some options as unfeasible

– Artificially inflate troop requirements

B) Threaten public opposition

– Strongly oppose particular policy in intramural debates

– Selectively leak reservations to the press (threaten further opposition)

– Hint at possible resignation

C) Speak out

– Background interviews

– Public statements to the press

– Open congressional hearings

Overcoming the Generals' Veto

Confronted with a military veto, whether actual or merely threatened, pro-intervention policymakers face an uphill bureaucratic battle. Especially for humanitarian crises and civil conflicts abroad that do not clearly threaten American security, the debate is at first structured against intervention. In such circumstances, the civilian interventionists need to be able to reassure the military leaders, or at least show that the military's concerns have been adequately addressed, in order to keep the use of force on the agenda and gradually pave the way to a presidential decision to intervene. Generally, the goal of a skilled bureaucratic player is to reassure one's principal opponents with the aim of reducing their obstructionism while at the same time persuading other influential players—especially fence-sitters who might tip the balance of power inside the administration—that the skeptics' concerns are either overblown or have been adequately addressed (Halperin and Clapp 2006: 214–18).

To address the military's concerns, the civilian interventionists, who are likely to have initially focused primarily on the (short-term) payoffs of the use of force, need to grapple with operational details to a much greater degree. "The military are very good at making the civilian leadership think all the way down the line in the interagency discussions and helping them understand the implications of their actions," explains Donald Kerrick, a former deputy national security adviser and former assistant to the JCS chairman.[32]

32. Author interview with Donald L. Kerrick (Mar. 22, 2010).

In the course of the resulting back-and-forth debate between senior military officers and civilian leaders, even the most hawkish civilians may acknowledge that a resource-intensive and potentially open-ended troop commitment is likely to be needed to achieve U.S. objectives and that maintaining congressional support will be difficult. One possibility, then, is that the civilian interventionists simply end up persuaded of the importance of securing advance IO approval combined with concrete pledges of international burden sharing. In such cases, the military's bargaining power stays latent and shapes the debate as a powerful background force. "If it works right," remarks a former senior Pentagon official, "it is quite a collegial and interactive process."[33]

However, when hawkish civilian policymakers and senior military officers start out from radically different assessments of a particular situation, the opposing players in the bureaucratic game may fail to persuade each other. Their positions can then only be reconciled through bargaining, and the ultimate policy outcome will reflect "the pulling and hauling that is politics" (Allison and Zelikow 1999: 255). If the interventionist hawks simply attempt to disregard the military's concerns and sideline representatives from the armed services in the intramural debates, the senior officers can form bureaucratic alliances with more dovish civilian officials and resort to all the aforementioned expedients in order to derail the interventionists' agenda. Therefore, as long as civilian authorities remain divided about the merits of military action, interventionist policymakers are likely to have to take the military's concerns into account, regardless of whether they end up personally persuaded by those concerns. Specifically, the interventionists are likely to have to modify their original proposal, make various concessions, and engage in logrolling in order to mollify the uniformed leaders and ultimately convince the president to approve the use of force.

One time-tested bargaining strategy aimed at securing the support of key participants for a controversial proposal, particularly when simple efforts at persuasion have failed, is to "alter the consequences to them of the proposal" (Halperin and Clapp 2006: 219). In the context of civil-military bargaining over armed intervention, this means that interventionist policymakers intent on securing the support or at least the acquiescence of a reluctant military leadership may need to alter the policy's consequences in such a way that the armed services' liability will be limited as much as possible. Concretely, the interventionists are likely to have to make a persuasive case that the use of force is a last resort, the objectives of military action are clearly and narrowly defined, there is a viable exit strategy for U.S. troops, and major international partners support the

---

33. Slocombe, author interview.

[53]

policy and are willing to shoulder a significant portion of the (long-term) operational burden.

Ultimately, therefore, when confronted with a military veto, even the most hawkish civilian interventionists can be expected to update their cost-benefit analysis vis-à-vis multilateralism. Even though at a personal level the interventionists may continue to have doubts about the policy benefits of securing IO approval, they can be expected to recognize its value for mollifying the reluctant warriors. The intervention advocates are thus likely to come to agree with the doves that delaying U.S. military action, accepting potentially cumbersome multilateral coordination, and even offering side payments to the most recalcitrant IO member states may be worthwhile and perhaps necessary to secure UN or NATO approval. Securing IO approval by itself is unlikely to reassure a reluctant military leadership; but such approval, *combined with* a narrowly defined mission and concrete pledges of operational support from key international partners, can be expected to reduce the military's opposition to a point where the president may feel comfortable taking a final decision to intervene.

Securing IO approval can thus be seen as part of a broader bargaining strategy on the part of interventionist policymakers, aimed at mollifying a reluctant military leadership and reassuring it that the armed services' liability will be limited. The specific hypothesis can be expressed as follows:

Hypothesis 2.2: When policymakers disagree about the merits of intervention and top-level military officers express strong concerns about the operational burden, IO approval is likely to be necessary to avert a military veto.

Circumstances that Magnify the Military's Role

So far the argument has addressed primarily the *demand* side of multilateralism, but the *supply* side also matters. The more internationally controversial a prospective military intervention, the less likely other IO member states are to "supply" multilateral approval and the higher the cost to the United States of obtaining it. Interventions that seek to forcibly change the internal authority structure of foreign countries are among the most internationally controversial—regardless of whether the ultimate goal is promoting democracy, resolving a humanitarian crisis at its roots, or simply removing a hostile regime. Such interventions violate the principle of noninterference in states' domestic affairs, as enshrined in article 2 of the UN Charter, and are thus prima facie incompatible with one of the constitutive norms of modern international

[54]

society. Consequently, there are good grounds to expect that not only emerging powers such as China, Russia, India, and Brazil (who are attached to traditionalist interpretations of state sovereignty) but also America's closest European allies (whose domestic audiences attach great value to compliance with UN Charter law) will be reluctant to offer their affirmative vote at the UNSC or NAC.[34]

As the difficulties of securing multilateral approval for such interventions become apparent, U.S. policymakers who strongly advocate the use of force for internal political change are at first likely to be especially inclined to bypass relevant IOs for the sake of maximizing U.S. freedom of action. Yet those are also the types of intervention about which the American military has the greatest reservations, given the probability of open-ended stabilization missions with dwindling congressional support. The military's role is therefore likely to be central in multilateralizing those particular types of interventions: absent clear threats to American security that might reduce the military's urge to limit its liability, securing IO approval and more specific burden-sharing commitments becomes essential to avert a military veto. Summing up, the centrality of the uniformed leaders' role in steering U.S. intervention policy toward the UN or NATO can be expected to be related to the ultimate goals of U.S. policy and the difficulty of securing IO approval. The following hypothesis captures this logic:

> Hypothesis 2.3: When securing IO approval is difficult because an intervention aims at internal political change, the military's role in steering U.S. policy toward a multilateral track is likely to be especially salient. When securing IO approval is easy, the military's role is likely to be minor.

Securing IO approval was very time-consuming and difficult in the four cases of U.S. intervention discussed in detail in this book (Haiti 1994, Bosnia 1995, Kosovo 1999, and Iraq 2003). Indeed, in the Iraq case, the effort ultimately failed. Each of those cases involved significant elements of internal political change, and heavyweight interventionist policymakers were at first inclined to bypass relevant IOs altogether.

For instance, during the 1998–99 Kosovo crisis, Secretary of State Albright and her hawkish civilian collaborators initially advocated unilateral military action against Yugoslavia without any international sanction in order to maximize U.S. flexibility. But securing NATO's approval became essential, after the Joint Chiefs made it clear that stabilizing Kosovo would require an open-ended deployment, and the president

---

34. On emerging powers' traditionalist interpretation of sovereignty norms see Brown 2010. On the Europeans' attachment to UN Charter law see Krause 2004.

indicated that he was unwilling to authorize U.S. intervention as long as the military had significant reservations. As Albright's former executive assistant explains, "To the extent that the secretary could reject the Pentagon's argument," by locking in NATO's support and making a persuasive case that the costs of stabilizing Kosovo would be shouldered largely by the Western European allies, "that certainly helped us in the interagency debate."[35] Morton Halperin, the State Department's head of policy planning at the time, is more explicit: "Getting NATO on board and knowing that NATO forces were going to go in later made it easier to sell the policy to the U.S. government—and particularly to the Joint Chiefs."[36]

By contrast, other post–Cold War interventions for which the United States also sought IO approval—such as Somalia 1992, Bosnia 1993 (defense of UN "safe areas"), Liberia 2003, and Haiti 2004—enjoyed significant international support a priori. Those were limited missions aimed at protecting civilian populations under threat of attack and facilitating the delivery of humanitarian assistance without seeking to forcibly change the internal authority structure of the target state. For Somalia, several regional powers and the UN secretary-general had called on Washington to take the lead in a humanitarian rescue mission, thus signaling widespread international support, well before the SC authorized military action (Boutros-Ghali 1999: 55–59; Wheeler 2000: 184–85). The same was true for Liberia in 2003 (Stevenson and Marquis, *NYT*, July 23, 2003). Similarly on Bosnia, in the early 1990s the Organization of the Islamic Conference (OIC) and several UNSC members had called for the United States and its allies to intervene in order to deter attacks on the civilian population, before the SC adopted Resolution 836 authorizing the defense of UN-designated safe areas (Murphy, *LA Times*, Dec. 1, 1992; Steinberg 1993: 46–47; Chollet 2005: 71). Finally in the 2004 Haiti case, after a turbulent domestic political transition, it took a favorably inclined UNSC less than twenty-four hours to adopt a resolution authorizing armed intervention to facilitate the delivery of humanitarian aid and stabilize the situation (Sablière 2013: 237–39).

In those latter cases, it was clear that securing UN approval would not be particularly difficult. Consequently, it appears that U.S. policymakers readily agreed that the limited negotiations required to that effect would be worthwhile, and the military's role in steering U.S. policy toward a multilateral track was probably less central.[37] Even in those cases,

---

35. Author interview with Alejandro Wolff (Mar. 31, 2010).
36. Author interview with Morton H. Halperin (Mar. 10, 2010).
37. On U.S. decision making on the 1992 Somalia, 1993 Bosnia, and 2003 Liberia interventions, see, respectively, H. Cohen 2000: 210–14; Daalder 2000: 17–21; and Kuperman 2008.

however, to the extent that civilian leaders agreed from an early stage on the value of securing IO approval, that may have partially reflected the U.S. military's repeated insistence on the risks and likely operational costs of intervention during the months and weeks *before* the issue was seriously debated at top levels of the national security bureaucracy.

Evaluating hypotheses 2.1, 2.2, and 2.3 requires both within-case and across-case observations. Comparison across cases is useful to assess whether the relevant independent and dependent variables are correlated. However, given that the primary purpose of this book is theory building and that I am primarily interested in theorizing the military's role in steering U.S. intervention policy toward multilateralism, three of my four principal cases (Haiti, Bosnia, Kosovo) display only limited variation on the main dependent variable—U.S. efforts to secure multilateral approval. I thus rely primarily on within-case analysis and causal process tracing to illustrate my argument and probe related hypotheses.

The aforementioned hypotheses would be strongly corroborated, if key policymakers who were initially willing to bypass relevant IOs for interventions aimed at internal political change acknowledged that the military's veto threat was, indeed, what persuaded them to work hard to secure UN or NATO approval. Policymakers, however, tend to downplay the importance of bureaucratic compromises forced upon them by others, presumably because they dislike giving credit to their opponents and instead prefer to emphasize their own leadership and initiative. As research by Etel Solingen (2007: 13, 16) shows, in the field of national security "leaders and state officials have incentives to justify decisions in terms of 'reasons of state' [or] by appealing to norms [rather] than by wielding parochial political considerations." Only rarely will senior officials acknowledge the importance of intragovernmental bargaining as a driver of national security decisions. It follows that the causal impact of such bargaining is hard to substantiate and "even partial substantiation . . . gains particular significance" (ibid., 5).

Table 2.2 Hypotheses

Hypothesis 2.1.: When there is no clear threat to U.S. national security and policymakers consequently disagree about the merits of intervention, a determined military leadership can veto the use of American force.

Hypothesis 2.2.: When policymakers disagree about the merits of intervention and top-level military officers express strong concerns about the operational burden, IO approval is likely to be necessary to avert a military veto.

Hypothesis 2.3.: When securing IO approval is difficult because an intervention aims at internal political change, the military's role in steering U.S. policy toward a multilateral track is likely to be especially salient. When securing IO approval is easy, the military's role is likely to be minor.

Scenario A: Military's role central

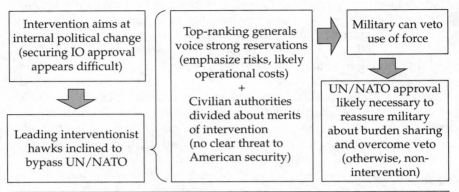

Scenario B: Military's role secondary

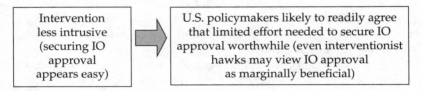

Figure 2.2 Schematic summary of the argument

The case studies in subsequent chapters present significant direct evidence from interviews and other sources indicating that civil-military bargaining indeed played a central role in steering U.S. intervention policy toward the UNSC or NAC. Even where such direct evidence is limited or unavailable, however, the motives that led to the adoption of particular policies can be established indirectly by carefully tracing the decision making process. If hawkish civilian leaders were initially willing to bypass the UNSC and NAC, but senior military officers were able to block U.S. intervention *until* the civilian leadership secured IO approval as well as more specific burden-sharing commitments, it can be inferred that the military played a central role in multilateralizing U.S. policy.

NONINTERVENTION AND UNILATERAL INTERVENTION

Absent clear threats to American security, I have argued, civilian officials who support armed intervention for internal political change can greatly increase the likelihood of such interventions occurring by securing UN or NATO approval combined with concrete pledges of burden sharing from international partners. If the interventionists are successful, the outcome is then likely to be *multilateral intervention*. However, the argument developed in this book can also help us better understand instances of U.S. *nonintervention* and straightforwardly *unilateral intervention*.

U.S. Nonintervention

When a foreign crisis does not clearly threaten American security, civilian authorities are consequently divided over whether to intervene, and policymakers who support the use of force aimed at internal political change cannot secure multilateral backing, the U.S. military is likely to veto the use of force. Thus, the most likely outcome is U.S. nonintervention. There are probably numerous instances in which the possibility of such interventions was debated at lower levels in the U.S. national security bureaucracy but ultimately no military action was taken. Unless the use of force was debated among the president's principal advisers, there may be no public record of those deliberations. Yet on several occasions in the post–Cold War period, the possibility of coercive humanitarian missions and other interventions aimed at internal political change was seriously debated at the highest levels of the national security bureaucracy, and the option was either temporarily or permanently shelved, given staunch military opposition and the lack of solid multilateral support.

For instance, in 2005 and 2006, senior civilian officials advocated the deployment of American combat troops on a humanitarian mission to Darfur aimed at stabilizing the local political situation. President George W. Bush was reportedly sympathetic to the idea. Members of the JCS, however, were adamantly opposed: they estimated that the mission would require up to 120,000 U.S. troops and emphasized the risk of a costly, open-ended commitment.[38] Seeking to address some of the military's concerns, the president, together with Secretary of State Condoleezza Rice, advanced the idea of "NATO stewardship" for Darfur.[39] But the administration was unable to obtain NATO's support, and the generals' objections eventually persuaded the civilian leadership that direct U.S. military intervention without solid multilateral

---

38. For a useful discussion see Hamilton 2011: chap. 6.
39. Author interview with Jendayi Frazer, AssistSecState for African Affairs, 2005–9 (Jan. 27, 2011). See also Graham and Lynch, *WashPo*, Apr. 10, 2006.

backing was unfeasible.[40] Similarly, as of spring 2015, America's military leaders had vetoed any humanitarian intervention in Syria aimed at weakening the local political regime, given the anticipated risk of an open-ended commitment and lack of solid international backing. President Barack Obama, with support from the JCS, authorized limited air strikes against Islamist militants in Syria in the fall of 2014; but the unspoken goal of those targeted strikes was to remove a threat to, rather than overturn, the regional political status quo (Landler, *NYT*, Sept. 10, 2014).

The uniformed leaders' opposition also played a key role in keeping the United States on a path of nonintervention as a genocide occurred in Rwanda in the spring of 1994. In late April 1994, reacting to reports of spiraling ethnic violence, midlevel officials from the NSC staff and the State Department floated the possibility of a U.S. humanitarian intervention in Rwanda (Power 2003: 364–70). Yet declassified documents show that their uniformed counterparts on the Joint Staff were "in stiff opposition," emphasizing the risks of intervention and "strongly object[ing] to signing up for open-ended missions that could lead to . . . troops being in life-threatening situations."[41] Given the highly volatile situation on the ground and the fact that there was little enthusiasm among other members of the UNSC for authorizing a peace-enforcement operation and contributing troops, no high-ranking U.S. official was willing to challenge the military and push for intervention (Power 2003: 370–73).[42] Only in late July 1994, after the ethnic violence in Rwanda had abated, did the JCS consent to the deployment of U.S. troops to the region as part of a UN-sponsored relief effort, having obtained credible assurances that a follow-on multilateral mission would soon take over.[43]

Unilateral Intervention

When America's top-level military officers agree with civilian policymakers that the operational costs of intervention will be limited, the United States is likely to bypass multilateral bodies and intervene on its own or with only ad hoc coalitions of allies. Limited U.S. air strikes and

---

40. Frazer, author interview. See also Hamilton 2011: 77–79.
41. OSD, "Rwanda Interagency Telcon," memorandum of conversation, May 11, 1994. See also OSD, "Discussion Paper: Rwanda," May 1, 1994. Both documents available at http://www.nsarchive.org.
42. On the lack of international support for peace enforcement in Rwanda, see also Wheeler 2000: 223–28.
43. Kross, author interview. See also Power 2003: 380–81.

commando raids with narrowly defined objectives that do not involve changing the domestic authority structure of the target state are in fact usually implemented without IO approval. In such instances the United States does not significantly benefit from burden sharing, and multilateral negotiations at the UN or NATO may unacceptably delay military action while eliminating the element of surprise.

But more ambitious military interventions may also be carried out unilaterally, after a direct attack on the American homeland or in the face of a foreign crisis that clearly threatens the security of American citizens or close allies.[44] When senior generals and admirals agree that U.S. national security is imminently threatened, their thinking is likely to increasingly resemble that of the civilian hawks they usually oppose: they are likely to become more risk acceptant, focusing primarily on the perceived threat and worrying less about the longer-term costs of intervention. Even though the senior officers may be aware that armed intervention might result in an open-ended commitment, they can be expected to conclude, again agreeing with their hawkish civilian colleagues, that the short-term costs of multilateral consensus building at the UN or NATO would outweigh any longer-term burden-sharing benefits. In any event, in such circumstances civilian authorities are typically united in favor of intervention, which can be expected to reduce the military's ability to influence related policy. Consequently, U.S. unilateralism is likely to be overdetermined. As General Powell laconically sums it up, "When you are invoking your inherent right of self-defense you don't need the international community, and frankly you don't have time to round them up."[45]

Perhaps the clearest example of this is the decision making process in the run-up to the 2001 Afghanistan intervention. After the terrorist attacks on the World Trade Center and the Pentagon on 9/11, U.S. policymakers rapidly agreed to intervene militarily in Afghanistan, with the twofold objective of killing or capturing individuals involved in planning the attacks and of helping local Afghan forces topple the Taliban regime that had offered the terrorists sanctuary (Bush 2010: 183–95; Woodward 2002: 75–90). Focusing on short-term security challenges, the president and his senior advisers did not dwell on the possibility that once the Taliban regime fell, the United States might end up with primary responsibility for Afghanistan's long-term stabilization. As Stephen Hadley, then the deputy national security adviser, explains, "It was widely predicted that this [9/11] was the first of a series of attacks that might involve weapons

44. For a similar argument see Kreps 2011: 7.
45. Powell, author interview.

of mass destruction. So the priority was to eliminate the threat. We did not anticipate that we would still be in Afghanistan ten years later."[46] Reportedly, during debates preceding the intervention some senior military planners raised concerns about a potentially open-ended commitment. However, given the sense of national emergency and strong domestic support for military action, the JCS had no fundamental objections to an intervention aimed at internal political change.[47]

After the 9/11 attacks there was widespread international solidarity with the United States. On September 12, the UNSC unanimously adopted Resolution 1368, which, without formally authorizing armed intervention, implicitly recognized that the traditional right of self-defense enshrined in article 51 of the UN Charter could be invoked against terrorist organizations. On that same day, NATO activated article 5 of the Washington Treaty, which states that an attack against any member of the alliance "shall be considered an attack against them all," thus offering the United States broad political and military support (Cimbala and Forster 2010: 149; Weitsman 2014: 100). Yet American leaders did not solicit any of those endorsements and stopped short of requesting an explicit SC authorization of military action under chapter VII of the UN Charter.[48] Furthermore, U.S. leaders declined to employ NATO assets during the initial combat phase (Kreps 2011: 95–97). As a senior State Department official in charge of U.S.-UN relations at the time recalls, "We felt that we had been attacked and wanted to conduct the operation under the mandate and ground rules that we were setting for ourselves. We didn't want this to be consultative."[49]

One final scenario needs to be discussed regarding the impact of civil-military relations on U.S. decision making about armed intervention. There may be situations in which, although civilian authorities are divided about the merits of intervention and the broader military establishment has strong reservations, America's top-ranking generals and admirals stop short of clearly conveying those reservations to the president. Such behavior on the part of top-level uniformed leaders is likely to be rare, not least because it contravenes an ingrained desire to limit the armed services' liability in the absence of major threats to American security. But should it occur, the military leadership's silence can be expected to empower the administration's civilian hawks, reducing any incentive for them to secure multilateral support.

---

46. Author interview with Stephen J. Hadley (Jan. 24, 2011). See also Feith 2008: chap. 5.
47. Flavin, author interview. See also Shelton 2010: 436–45.
48. Negroponte, author interview. See also Rawski and Miller 2004: 370.
49. Wood, author interview.

To a significant degree, as I explain in chapter 6, this is what happened during the period leading up to the 2003 Iraq War. Top-ranking generals, notably JCS chairman Richard Myers, Deputy Chairman Peter Pace, and General Tommy Franks, the commander of U.S. Central Command, were exceedingly deferential to civilian authorities and failed to effectively challenge the civilian hard-liners' highly optimistic assumptions about the war and its aftermath. In the absence of vigorous pushback from those generals, the bureaucratic political dynamics that had made UN or NATO approval all but necessary for other wars of choice aimed at forcibly changing the internal authority structure of foreign countries were not activated. The military's silence, combined with the civilian hawks' relentless insistence that invading Iraq was a central component of the administration's "war on terror," goes a long way toward explaining why the United States made only a limited effort to secure UNSC approval in 2002–3 and ultimately chose to bypass the United Nations.

Methodology and Data Sources

This book develops a new explanation of U.S. efforts to secure IO approval for military intervention in circumstances when such approval is difficult to obtain. Hence the goal is theory development more than theory testing. I rely on the method of structured-focused comparison, studying recent history in a way that is conducive to the development of general causal hypotheses. The analysis is structured in that I ask similar questions of each case to standardize data collection for the purpose of comparative analysis; it is focused in that I deal only with specific aspects of the cases examined that are relevant for investigating the phenomenon of interest. In addition, to gain further insights about causal relationships, I rely on process tracing—that is, I reconstruct the sequence of decisions and events that led to the outcome of interest in each particular case. Process tracing increases the number of theoretically relevant observations and can help uncover the motivations of different actors.[50]

The combination of methods I use is well suited for investigating complex causal relationships involving numerous variables with multiple interaction effects (especially when there are only a few empirical cases available). My comparative case study approach further allows me to account for the possibility of individual and organizational learning, whereby the lessons of past experiences are applied to subsequent decision making. For instance, U.S. decision makers may have learned

50. On process tracing and the method of structured-focused comparison, see George and Bennett 2004: 67–72, 205–16.

several lessons from military interventions in the early 1990s about the ability of advance IO approval to facilitate sustained international burden sharing, and those lessons may be relevant for understanding more recent U.S. policy. The methods I employ allow me to incorporate such causal feedback from the dependent variable in earlier cases to explanatory variables in subsequent cases—all this while satisfying the criterion of conditional independence between causal variables and outcome.[51]

I have gathered the information, or data, for this study from numerous sources in several languages. The most important data source consists of roughly one hundred on-the-record interviews that I conducted with senior foreign policy and defense officials, predominantly from the United States. Further primary sources include recently declassified transcripts and summaries of NSC debates and U.S. diplomatic cables. The Clinton Presidential Library has released hundreds of pages of previously classified NSC documents pursuant to several Mandatory Declassification Reviews (MDRs) that I requested.[52] Additional data sources include records of congressional hearings, published memoirs, transcripts of debates at the UNSC and other multilateral bodies, and contemporaneous newspaper reports—mainly from the *New York Times* and the *Washington Post* but also from several other newspapers including the *Los Angeles Times*, the *Guardian*, and *Le Monde*.

The interviews have been especially helpful in terms of reconstructing the motivations of, and bargaining between, senior U.S. officials. I have interviewed senior officials (typically at the level of assistant secretary or above) from different agencies and departments who were directly involved in the adoption of relevant decisions or were present at meetings where relevant decisions were taken. For instance, I have interviewed three former national security advisers (Brent Scowcroft, Anthony Lake, and Stephen Hadley), one former secretary of state (Colin Powell), three former vice chairmen of the Joint Chiefs of Staff (David Jeremiah, William Owens, and Joseph Ralston), three former deputy secretaries of state (Strobe Talbott, Richard Armitage, and John Negroponte), and one former NATO secretary-general (Javier Solana). All interviews were semi-structured, in that I asked each interviewee specific questions aimed at evaluating various hypotheses and reconstructing the causal process in the cases examined. Some questions were standard (i.e., I asked each interviewee a version of the same question), while others were targeted to the interviewee's particular government

51. On conditional independence see King, Keohane, and Verba 1994: 94–95.
52. MDR Requests 2009-0983-M; 2009-1289-M; 2009-1290-M; 2009-1291-M; and 2009-1292-M. All documents now available at http://clinton.presidentiallibraries.us/collections/show/36.

background and the role he or she played in developing the policy under consideration.

Admittedly, data gathered from interviews is sometimes unreliable, as memories may be clouded by hindsight and interviewees may exaggerate their own role in the policy process. Nevertheless, if interviewees from different agencies and departments offer similar conclusions, and their analyses are compatible with the written record, confidence in the findings increases. Official documents, assuming they are available, usually reflect a consensus view and consequently tend to be insufficient for the purpose of reconstructing the motives and bureaucratic bargains that lie behind particular policies. It is for this reason that Richard Neustadt concluded, after having studied American politics for several decades, "If I were forced to choose between the documents on the one hand, and late, limited, partial interviews with some of the principal participants on the other, I would be forced to discard the documents" (quoted in Allison and Zelikow 1999: 312).

[65]

[3]

Haiti, 1993–94: Multilateral Approval to Ensure a UN Handoff

In September 1994, about twenty thousand U.S. troops intervened in Haiti to put an end to systematic human rights violations and restore to office Jean-Bertrand Aristide, the country's democratically elected president who had been ousted in a coup three years earlier. During the summer preceding the intervention, the United States made an all-out diplomatic effort to secure UN approval for the use of force. Obtaining a UN mandate involved lengthy negotiations and constrained U.S. freedom of action in consequential ways. This chapter shows that America's top-ranking generals, who were extremely skeptical about intervening in Haiti and wanted to avoid an open-ended commitment, played a central role in steering U.S. policy toward the UNSC.

There is evidence that the most hawkish and influential civilian policymakers in Washington, led by National Security Adviser Anthony Lake and his staff, at first did not worry much about operational costs and were inclined to bypass the UNSC to ensure quick military action. However, top-ranking military officers made it clear that they would staunchly oppose any deployment of U.S. combat troops in the absence of a viable exit strategy. Specifically, the uniformed leaders demanded concrete assurances ahead of intervention that the longer-term stabilization burden would be shifted to international partners. Process tracing reveals that the civilian interventionists, faced with opposition from the JCS, began working hard to limit the military's liability: they did so by, among other things, seeking a UNSC resolution of approval that also explicitly foresaw the rapid establishment of a follow-on UN peacekeeping mission in which other countries would contribute the majority of troops. After the SC approved such a resolution on July 31, 1994, and international partners pledged their support, the U.S. military leaders fell in line and the United States intervened soon thereafter. Former civilian policymakers who were at first not especially concerned about multilateral support acknowledge the military's central role in alerting the administration to the importance of international burden sharing and driving U.S. policy toward the SC. The chapter also evaluates several alternative hypotheses as to why civilian policymakers might have sought UN approval, including norm internalization and concerns about issue linkage, but finds that those hypotheses are unsupported by the evidence.

Origins and Evolution of the Haitian Crisis

Jean-Bertrand Aristide, a leftist Catholic priest, was elected to the Haitian presidency in December 1990, with a staggering 67 percent of the popular vote certified by international observers. After decades of corrupt authoritarian rule, the Haitian people were eager for a radical break. The country's economic and military elites, however, had benefited from the old regime and feared that the new president would jeopardize their privileges and their wealth. Aristide fueled their anxieties through his populist rhetoric, his encouragement of violent street mobs, and his decision to fire the entire military high command soon after his inauguration. On September 29, 1991, he was overthrown in a military coup, after only eight months in power. The presidency was taken over by a junta headed by Lieutenant-General Raoul Cédras, whom Aristide himself had earlier appointed to the command of the Haitian army. Aristide left into exile and was granted political asylum in the United States (Pastor 2003: 120–22; Girard 2004: 14–19).

The Bush Administration's Hands-Off Approach, 1991–92

The United States, under President George H.W. Bush, initially condemned the coup in Haiti. On October 2, 1991, Secretary of State James Baker declared at an emergency meeting of the Organization of American States, "We do not and we will not recognize this outlaw regime. . . . Until President Aristide's government is restored, this junta will be treated as a pariah throughout this hemisphere" (Baker 1995: 601). Only days later, however, the administration began to back away from its support for Aristide, citing concerns over his human rights record and insisting that he "must publicly disavow mob violence and work toward sharing power with the Parliament" (quoted in Krauss, *NYT*, Oct. 7, 1991).

The U.S. military establishment, led by JCS chairman Colin Powell, was opposed to any armed intervention to restore democracy in Haiti. The top-ranking generals disputed that important American interests were at stake in Haiti and feared a repeat of 1915, when a planned short-term deployment of U.S. marines aimed at restoring political order in Haiti had turned into a protracted and costly occupation that lasted until 1934 (Powell 1995: 544). But there was generally little enthusiasm in the Bush administration for military options concerning Haiti. National Security Adviser Brent Scowcroft, Secretary of State Baker, and the president himself shared with the military a broadly realist approach to foreign affairs, which valued political stability over promoting and defending liberal values abroad.[1] The only senior administration official who persistently pushed for military intervention behind the scenes was Bernard "Bernie" Aronson, a liberal Wilsonian who at the time was serving as assistant secretary of state for Latin American affairs.[2]

The political situation in Haiti and its humanitarian implications became an important topic in the 1992 U.S. presidential election campaign. The Democratic challenger, Bill Clinton, chose to single out Haiti as one of the few foreign policy issues on which to criticize the incumbent administration. For most of 1992, President Bush's policy vis-à-vis Haiti had focused on intercepting boats of Haitian migrants headed for the United States and sending back all undocumented passengers. Clinton called the Bush administration's forced repatriation policy cruel and unacceptable and pledged that if elected, he would no longer be shipping those people back (Halberstam 2001: 269).

Washington's Missed Opportunity for a Negotiated Solution

Once Clinton was elected to the presidency, however, his engagement in favor of Haiti initially fell short of his lofty campaign rhetoric. Having been alerted by U.S. intelligence to the risk of a massive influx of Haitian migrants, the president-elect declared in January 1993 that the forced repatriation policy would temporarily remain in place (Holmes, *NYT*, Jan. 16, 1993). Thereafter, for much of 1993, the Clinton administration sought to bring the Haitian de facto rulers and Aristide together in a power-sharing arrangement. The administration was engaged in a difficult balancing act: on the one hand, to satisfy Aristide's backers within the U.S. human rights community and the Democratic Party, it wanted to restore him as quickly as possible; but on the other hand, to facilitate a political compromise among the Haitian factions and reassure influential Aristide skeptics at the Pentagon and among Republicans in Congress, it

1. Author interview with Adm. David Jeremiah, JCS Vice Chairman, 1990–94 (Jan. 28, 2011).
2. Author interview with John Christiansen, Pentagon Desk officer for the Caribbean, 1990–93, and Director, OSD Haiti Task Group, 1993–97 (July 15, 2009).

aimed to bring Aristide back "in some way that significantly reduced his role, in fact, ideally to that of a figurehead."[3]

In late June 1993, after the UNSC adopted a resolution that threatened to automatically impose international sanctions after a set deadline, the Haitian de facto rulers at last agreed to negotiations on a comprehensive political solution (Malone 1998: 84–85). A week of intense negotiations on Governor's Island in New York City, facilitated by the U.S. envoy, Lawrence Pezzullo, yielded a compromise agreement that foresaw Aristide's restoration to the presidency. In return Aristide would have to share power with a new prime minister, issue an amnesty decree, and engage in a political dialogue with his opponents (Malone 1998: 82–88; Pezzullo 2006: 86–106). The Governor's Island Agreement, as it came to be known, also foresaw the deployment of the United Nations Mission in Haiti (UNMIH), intended to provide assistance in "modernizing" Haiti's armed forces and establishing a new police force.[4] UNSC Resolution 867, adopted on September 23, accordingly authorized the deployment to Haiti of about six hundred international police monitors and seven hundred military trainers and engineers (Boutros-Ghali 1996: 46–47).

The UN mission, to be led by the United States, had no enforcement mandate, and the international trainers and monitors were to be only lightly armed. Nevertheless, the UN special representative for Haiti, Dante Caputo, publicly referred to the deployment as a "dissuasive force" (Pezzullo 2006: 182). Resolution 867 also referred to UNMIH as a "peace-keeping mission," thus making for a somewhat ambiguous mandate.[5] The U.S. military leaders had insisted on a limited training mandate for the UN mission, and they feared that Caputo was now trying to drag them into a more ambitious mission that would also include "stopping bad things from happening there."[6] The military's concerns about the Haiti deployment were greatly exacerbated after an ambush on American forces in Somalia on October 3, 1993, when eighteen U.S. Army Rangers were killed and seventy-five were wounded in the context of a UN-sanctioned mission.[7]

On October 11, the USS *Harlan County,* a navy ship carrying two hundred lightly armed American soldiers and twenty-five Canadian

---

3. Author interview with Lawrence Rossin, Haiti policy director on the NSC staff, 1993–94 (July 25, 2009), confirmed in author interview with Francesc Vendrell, senior adviser to the UN Special Envoy for Haiti, 1992–93 interview (June 27, 2009). For a detailed account of the U.S.-led mediation effort, see Pezzullo 2006: 61–67.
4. For the full text of the agreement see the UN Secretary-General's Report of July 12, 1993, UN Doc. A/47/975-S/26063, reprinted in Boutros-Ghali 1996.
5. SCR 687 (1993), § 5.
6. Author interview with Michael Kozak, Deputy U.S. Special Envoy for Haiti, 1993–94 (June 24, 2009).
7. Christiansen, author interview. See also Avant 1996: 72–73; Albright 2003: 156–57.

military trainers intended as the first sizable contribution to the UN mission, arrived in the harbor of the Haitian capital of Port-au-Prince. The ship was received at the pier by a mob of drunken Haitian thugs, some of them armed, who soon began to jump around wildly, waving their arms and screaming, "Somalia, Somalia!" The entire scene was broadcast live by U.S. television networks, which had arrived in Haiti to document the landing of American troops. There was no imminent threat to American lives, and the thugs might well have dispersed at the first sign of U.S. assertiveness. Nevertheless, President Clinton, under pressure from an extremely risk-averse Pentagon in the aftermath of the Somalia killings and following the recommendation of his closest political advisers, ordered the *Harlan County* pulled out of Haitian waters on October 12, thus bringing the mission abruptly to an end (A. Lake 2000: 260; Halberstam 2001: 271–72; Pezzullo 2006: 196–202).

The *Harlan County* incident was a serious blow to the Clinton administration's international credibility and domestic political standing. Nancy Soderberg, at the time the third highest-ranking official on the NSC staff, candidly admits as much: "That image came to symbolize the weakness of Clinton's foreign policy—it is an image that came to represent his early presidency" (Soderberg 2005: 44; see also Christopher 1998: 176). In Haiti itself, the image of American soldiers retreating at the first sign of resistance dramatically undermined Washington's political leverage. Pezzullo, then the U.S. special envoy for Haiti, recalls that as a result of the *Harlan County*'s withdrawal, the Haitian de facto rulers "had lost a great deal of respect for the United States."[8] His former deputy goes so far as to suggest that after the incident, "a negotiated solution to bring Aristide back to power had practically no chance of succeeding."[9]

Clinton's Decision to Intervene

Under the authoritarian rule of General Cédras, there was no room for political dissent in Haiti, and pro-democracy activists were routinely harassed and subjected to arbitrary arrests. According to the Inter-American Commission on Human Rights, an OAS body, political prisoners in Haiti were frequently subjected to torture, and 133 extrajudicial executions took place between February and May 1994.[10] However, there was no large-scale government-sponsored violence involving war crimes or crimes against humanity, which is conventionally viewed as

8. Author interview with Lawrence Pezzullo (June 24, 2009).
9. Kozak, author interview.
10. Presentation by Michael Reisman, president of the IACHR, at OAS foreign ministers' meeting on June 6, 1994, later published in OAS/OEA, "Acta de la séptima

the threshold for justifying humanitarian military intervention. Nor was Haiti, a resource-poor and economically backward country, of major strategic importance to the United States. Why, then, did President Clinton decide to intervene militarily in September 1994?

For several weeks between late 1993 and early 1994, with diplomacy at a standstill after the *Harlan County*'s withdrawal, policymakers in Washington discussed the possibility of restoring democracy in Haiti without Aristide. As a former official who was responsible for Haiti policy on the NSC staff recalls, "The dynamic was becoming get rid of Cédras, get rid of his military dictatorship, and then hold national elections without Aristide."[11] However, Aristide moved to the political offensive in the spring of 1994, confident of his backing by important liberal constituencies in the United States. On February 8, 1994, he publicly criticized the ongoing U.S. practice of forcibly repatriating Haitian migrants, comparing it to a "floating Berlin Wall" (quoted in Greenhouse, *NYT*, Feb. 10, 1994). The pro-Aristide lobby in the United States also mobilized: beginning in March, Aristide supporters from human rights nongovernmental organizations, the Hollywood community, and the U.S. Congress began to openly criticize the administration's policy on Haiti. Members of the Congressional Black Caucus, in particular, turned up the heat on the president by suggesting that there was racial prejudice in the forced repatriation of black Haitian migrants.[12]

Reacting to the growing political pressure, on May 8 President Clinton announced that henceforth, no Haitian migrants would be repatriated without first being given a chance to make the case for asylum (Devroy, *WashPo*, May 8, 1994). The consequences of that pledge were dramatic, as the numbers of Haitian boat people seeking to reach the United States exploded over the next several weeks. From mid-June to early July 1994, tens of thousands of Haitian migrants were picked up by the U.S. Coast Guard. The processing center at the U.S. naval base in Guantanamo, Cuba, was soon overwhelmed (Gordon, *NYT*, July 7, 1994; Pezzullo 2006: 259). The boat people crisis strengthened the hand of those in the administration who argued that the Haitian problem had to be resolved through military intervention. Strobe Talbott, then the deputy secretary of state, acknowledges that the Haitian migrants were "a big driver here—the refugee issue was getting totally out of control, and where we didn't want them coming was Florida."[13]

sesión," Réunion ad hoc de ministros de relaciones exteriores (Belém, Brazil, June 6, 1994), 20–21.
11. Rossin, author interview. See also Soderberg 2005: 46.
12. Author interview with Major Owens, head of the Haiti task force, Congressional Black Caucus, 1993–94 (July 12, 2009). See also Greenhouse, *NYT*, April 15, 1994.
13. Author interview with Strobe Talbott (July 9, 2009), confirmed by Pezzullo, author interview.

By the summer of 1994, the Clinton administration's generally lack-luster performance in foreign affairs was increasingly harming the president's political standing. U.S. policy toward Bosnia was at an embarrassing standstill, there had been the disaster in Somalia, and this was followed by the *Harlan County* incident in Haiti. Meanwhile, relations with North Korea over its alleged nuclear program had reached a crisis point after the breakdown of negotiations in April 1994, and perhaps most damningly, there had just been a genocide in Rwanda which the United States had done virtually nothing to stop. These images of American weakness, aloofness, and incompetence in the face of large-scale human rights violations and threatening developments abroad were particularly costly for a Democratic administration that was perceived as soft on national security and had abundantly relied on values-based internationalist rhetoric to legitimize its foreign policy.[14] With congressional midterm elections scheduled for November 1994, national security heavyweights associated with the Republican Party, such as Henry Kissinger, James Baker, and Richard Cheney, were openly questioning the administration's competence (Devroy and Williams, *WashPo*, July 28, 1994).

Compared with the situations in North Korea, Bosnia, and Rwanda, the Haitian problem appeared to be one of the most tractable foreign policy conundrums that the administration was facing. In short, this seemed to be a case in which the administration might be able to act decisively at limited cost, restoring Aristide and solving the refugee crisis, thereby also improving its own political fortunes. Richard Feinberg, at the time a senior NSC staffer dealing with inter-American affairs, offers a candid assessment of the administration's political calculus:

> Looking strategically around the world, in 1993–94, what did we see? Frustration in Somalia, frustration in Bosnia, North Korea being difficult, and we couldn't bring any of these difficult problems to a solution. We were frustrated everywhere, and there were the upcoming midterm elections. So the White House was thinking: we need at a minimum to show that we can remove one of these frustrations from the table.[15]

14. By the time the Haitian boat people issue began to reach crisis proportions, a majority of Americans rated Clinton's foreign policy a "failure." Balz and Morin, *WashPo*, May 17, 1994.
15. Author interview with Richard Feinberg, senior director for Inter-American affairs on the NSC staff, 1993–96 (June 22, 2009).

The 1994 Haiti intervention was thus largely driven by U.S. domestic politics (see also Stephanopoulos 1999: 218–19; Halberstam 2001: 278–79). The absence of a pressing strategic imperative resulted in a strong urge to limit America's liability. Indeed, President Clinton hesitated for most of the summer before taking a final decision. His senior advisers vehemently disagreed on the merits of intervention, with the Pentagon and the military leaders in particular remaining for a long time opposed. The president gave a green light for intervention only on August 26, after the UN Security Council had approved the use of force, international partners had pledged their support, and the administration had obtained credible assurances that a follow-on UN force led by other countries would take over within a short time (Devroy and Smith, *WashPo*, Sept. 25, 1994).

THE COSTS OF MULTILATERALISM

Securing multilateral approval for the use of force involved significant costs to the United States. First, it required considerable international arm-twisting, especially in the Western Hemisphere, and logrolling with Russia, which probably harmed Washington's international standing. Second, the sustained effort to secure UN approval delayed the intervention, limiting U.S. flexibility and preventing the administration from exploiting a momentary spike in domestic support for military action at the peak of the Haitian boat people crisis. Finally, by exposing the fragility of international support for U.S. intervention, the UNSC negotiations may have weakened U.S. coercive diplomacy, thus making a peaceful solution less likely.

Side Payments, Logrolling, and Questionable Legitimation

The United States had to engage in a sustained diplomatic effort before the SC adopted Resolution 940 on July 31, 1994, which authorized the use of force "to facilitate the departure from Haiti of the military leadership, [and] the prompt return of the legitimately elected President." Former president Clinton recalls that "it took months to build support . . . in our hemisphere [and] even longer to win the improbable 12–0 mandate from the UN Security Council" (quoted in Branch 2009: 186).[16] Talbott (2008:

---

16. Two countries, Brazil and China, abstained during the vote on SCR 940, and the representative of Rwanda was not present; hence the 12–0 outcome. Malone 1998: 109–10.

300) similarly remembers that the State Department "worked for two months on a resolution authorizing a military operation led by the U.S. to restore the democratically elected leadership of Haiti."

To facilitate UNSC approval, U.S. policymakers first sought some expression of support from the relevant regional multilateral body, the OAS.[17] Senior Clinton administration officials understood that it would have been virtually "unthinkable" to obtain an explicit OAS approval for the use of force and deploy peacekeepers under the OAS banner because in the Western Hemisphere "there is too much historical precedent of unwelcome [U.S.] intervention."[18] OAS approval for the use of force would have required a two-thirds majority in the organization's Permanent Council, an improbable threshold.[19] Nevertheless, declassified documents reveal that in May 1994 the Clinton administration, seeking to maximize its leverage vis-à-vis its Latin American partners, decided to explicitly link U.S. economic assistance in the hemisphere to support for its policy on Haiti.[20] Giving in to Washington's prodding, on June 9 the OAS went so far as to formally endorse a strengthened UN peacekeeping and training mission for Haiti—without, however, expressing any support for coercive military action.[21]

It took almost another two months after this OAS vote to secure UNSC approval for coercive intervention. The most recalcitrant SC members at the time were China, Brazil, and Russia. All three initially opposed a U.S. military intervention aimed at restoring Aristide, albeit for different reasons. Beijing was actively hostile to Aristide, who had recognized Taiwan during his short-lived presidency in 1991. Furthermore, China's opposition to intervention reflected its support for the principle of noninterference in states' internal affairs (Morris 1995: 391–412). Brazil was similarly opposed to U.S. intervention on principled grounds: at the aforementioned OAS meeting in June 1994, Brazil's representative declared his government's commitment to the search for a peaceful

---

17. The OAS had been involved in managing the Haitian crisis from the beginning, almost immediately condemning the Cédras coup in 1991 and subsequently calling for the imposition of multilateral sanctions. Boutros-Ghali 1996: 21–23.
18. Author interview with Harriett Babbitt, U.S. PermRep to the OAS, 1993–97 (July 7, 2009), confirmed in author interview with Alexander F. Watson, AssistSec-State for Inter-American Affairs, 1993–96 (June 23, 2009).
19. OAS, "Rules of Procedure of the Permanent Council," OEA/Ser.GCP/doc .1112/80 rev. 4 corr. 1, Aug. 27, 2003.
20. NSC-DC, Meeting on Haiti, Summary of Conclusions [henceforth: SumConcl], May 10, 1994 (released pursuant to MDR No. 2009-0983-M, requested by the author).
21. OAS Resolution, adopted by ad hoc foreign ministers' meeting in Belém, Brazil, June 9, 1994.

resolution to the crisis.[22] Russia, finally, had no intrinsic interest in either Haiti or U.S. policy in the Western Hemisphere. However, Moscow resented Washington's unwillingness to support a UN mandate for Russia's own military intervention in Georgia, and consequently Russian support for U.S. intervention in Haiti initially appeared uncertain (Malone 1998: 107–9; Morris 1995: 396–97).

China's stance at the SC was of particular concern to U.S. officials, who worried that Beijing might outright veto a resolution authorizing the use of force.[23] In the course of July 1994, under significant pressure from Washington, Beijing eventually signaled its willingness to abstain at the SC, provided that Russia voted in favor of the use of force and the UN's Latin American caucus was not opposed.[24] Chinese authorities had probably learned from the 1991 Gulf War experience that refraining from vetoing U.S. military action could pay off handsomely: back then, in exchange for China's abstention at the SC, Washington offered to lift all U.S. trade sanctions in place since the 1989 Tiananmen Square massacre and support a $114.3 million World Bank loan to Beijing (Pilger, *New Statesman*, Sept. 23, 2002; see also Baker 1995: 308–28). Furthermore, U.S. officials were able to allay Chinese concerns that Aristide's forcible restoration might set a precedent for pro-democracy intervention by inserting a passage in the draft UN resolution emphasizing the "unique character" of the situation in Haiti and its "extraordinary nature, requiring an exceptional response."[25]

After China made its own abstention contingent on Latin American acquiescence, Brazil's stance became central, given that Brazil—a nonpermanent member of the SC—represented the skeptical Latin American countries.[26] Seeking to persuade the Brazilian government to cooperate, high-ranking U.S. officials, including senior NSC staffer Richard Feinberg and Undersecretary of State Peter Tarnoff, traveled to Brasilia to deliver not-so-veiled threats that friendly relations with the United States and favorable economic treatment should not be taken for granted.[27] Eventually, Brazilian authorities agreed to abstain at the SC,

22. OAS/OEA, "Acta de la séptima sesión," 31.

23. Author interviews with James Dobbins, Special Haiti Coordinator, DOS, 1994–95 (July 10, 2009), and George F. Ward, Principal Deputy AssistSecState for IO Affairs, 1992–96 (Apr. 4, 2011). See also Branch 2009: 169.

24. Author interview with Leon Fuerth, NatSec Adviser to the VP, 1993–2000 (Mar. 9, 2010). See also Malone 1998: 109–16.

25. SCR 940 (1994), § 2. See also Pezzullo 2006: 75.

26. The other Latin American member of the SC at the time was Argentina, which broadly supported U.S. policy. See Malone 1998: 109–15.

27. Feinberg, author interview. See also LatinNews.com, "Another Two-Step from Washington," *Latin American Weekly Report*, June 23, 1994; and Malone 1998: 232n112.

provided that Aristide himself explicitly called for U.S. intervention. The exiled Haitian leader long remained reluctant to do so, fearing it might delegitimize him in the eyes of the Haitian people. As late as June 1994, he declared that he would "never, never, and never again" agree to be restored by a U.S. invasion (quoted in Albright 2003: 159). Nevertheless, U.S. officials at last persuaded Aristide to offer a vague endorsement of military intervention on July 29, only hours before the scheduled SC vote (Boutros-Ghali 1996: 62). That convinced Brazil, and by implication China, to abstain on the use-of-force resolution, although both countries also let it be publicly known that they continued to have reservations.[28]

Finally, the United States had to engage in a costly logrolling bargain to secure Moscow's cooperation. Madeleine Albright, then the U.S. permanent representative to the SC, recalls that the Russians "didn't care much about what we did in Haiti, but they were determined to play a little diplomatic poker" (Albright 2003: 158). Albright's Russian counterpart, Yuli Vorontsov, made it clear that Moscow's support on the Haiti issue would be contingent on Washington's supporting a UN mandate for Russian "peacekeepers" that had been deployed earlier that year in the Georgian breakaway region of Abkhazia. Moscow appeared determined to exploit its diplomatic leverage on this issue to the fullest.[29] After some intense backroom diplomacy, the United States and Russia agreed to accommodate their respective concerns. On July 21, Washington offered its support for a SC resolution that "welcome[d] the contribution made by the Russian Federation . . . of a peace-keeping force" in Georgia.[30] Ten days later, Russia reciprocated by voting in favor of Resolution 940, which authorized the U.S. intervention in Haiti (Malone 1998: 107).

The logrolling bargain between Washington and Moscow was quickly exposed, drawing intense public condemnation as a revival of classic spheres-of-influence diplomacy (Boone, *Times of London*, Aug. 1, 1994). That weakened the legitimation effect of UN approval for the Haiti intervention. Furthermore, the U.S. vote of support for Russia's military interference in the Caucasus arguably harmed Washington's broader strategic interests by undermining Western-oriented governments in the region. Finally, Russia's successful use of its diplomatic leverage at the SC on that occasion may have encouraged Moscow to advance its own interests more assertively in the future after an interlude of relative passivity in the early 1990s (Falk 1995).

28. UNSC, record of 3413th meeting, July 31, 1994 (Doc. S/PV.3413), 9.
29. Author interview with David Malone, Deputy PermRep of Canada to the UNSC, 1993–94 (Dec. 8, 2009), confirmed by Ward, author interview.
30. SCR 937 (1994), § 4.

Erosion of Domestic Support

The attempt in June and July 1994 to secure UN approval for the Haiti intervention significantly limited Washington's freedom of maneuver. Senior U.S. officials understood that once the effort became public in early July, the United States had to carry it through to a successful conclusion. Abandoning it halfway would have entailed a high reputational cost: a U.S. military intervention carried out after having sought and failed to secure UN approval would probably have attracted greater international condemnation than a straightforwardly unilateral intervention without any effort to involve the SC.[31]

The process of multilateral engagement, once begun, therefore prevented the administration from exploiting a momentary spike in U.S. domestic support for intervention at the height of the July 1994 Haitian refugee crisis. Support for intervening in Haiti was never high among the American people, but it momentarily reached almost 50 percent in July 1994 before falling back closer to 40 percent later in the summer (Larson and Savych 2005: 44–47). Former president Clinton acknowledged in subsequent conversations with the journalist Taylor Branch that the administration's multilateral engagement was paradoxically quite costly in terms of U.S. domestic support because it allowed the refugee crisis to be largely resolved by the time the invasion was launched in September. In Clinton's own words, "The exodus dried up, and public concern vanished in the United States. People didn't want to hear about Haiti anymore" (quoted in Branch 2009: 191).

Weakening of U.S. Coercive Leverage

Finally, the protracted negotiations at the UNSC and the OAS in the summer of 1994 exposed profound divisions within the international community. Policymakers and analysts sometimes suggest that UN approval for the use of force can increase Washington's coercive leverage by signaling that the international community stands united behind the United States (Christopher 1998: 176; Blechman and Cofman Wittes 1999: 16). In the case of Haiti, however, multilateral engagement appears to have rather muddied the message: there is evidence that the cacophony of voices during the multilateral negotiations undermined the effectiveness of U.S. coercive diplomacy vis-à-vis the Haitian de facto rulers.

Robert Malval, then Haiti's prime minister, notes that for most of the spring and early summer of 1994, the de facto rulers in Port-au-Prince drew comfort from China's well-known anti-Aristide stance and

31. Dobbins, author interview.

Russia's seeming opposition to armed intervention. In short, they concluded that America's threat of intervention should not be taken seriously (Malval 1996: 474; see also Pezzullo 2006: 75). The period from spring through early summer of 1994, however, is precisely when a credible threat of force would have stood the best chance of facilitating a power-sharing arrangement between Aristide and the Haitian rulers without a U.S. invasion. By the time the SC approved the use of force at the end of July, the Clinton administration, seeking to shore up domestic support for intervention, had already demonized the junta in Port-au-Prince to such a degree that a diplomatic compromise based on any kind of power-sharing arrangement had become impossible (Pastor 2003: 139).

Even as it became increasingly likely by late July that the SC would approve the use of force, most Latin American governments remained opposed to U.S. intervention, and several regional leaders said so in public. The representatives of Mexico, Colombia, Cuba, the Dominican Republic, Uruguay, and Nicaragua spoke out against the draft UNSC resolution shortly before the final vote. All those countries continued to oppose the use of force after the adoption of Resolution 940, and they were now joined by Peru and Bolivia in publicly condemning the prospective intervention (Malone 1998: 109).[32] This image of half-hearted international support seems to have persuaded the Haitian rulers that even after the SC's approval, U.S. military action was not in fact imminent (Malval 1996: 475; see also Bassir-Pour and Frachon, *Le Monde*, Aug. 2, 1994). Paradoxically, if the United States had clearly signaled its disregard for multilateralism from the outset by announcing its readiness to intervene without any kind of IO approval, the threat might have been more credible, and Washington could conceivably have brokered a power-sharing arrangement without having to deploy large numbers of American troops.

MULTILATERALISM AS THE RESULT OF CIVIL-MILITARY BARGAINING

The United States was willing to accept the high costs of multilateralism in this case because policymakers who supported the use of force realized that they needed UN approval to mollify the U.S. military, or at least address the military's principal concerns, and thereby pave the way

32. See also statement by the permanent mission of Peru to the chairman of the OAS Permanent Council, Aug. 4, 1994; and letter by the permanent mission of Bolivia to the OAS secretary-general, Aug. 5, 1994 (published in the same folder as OAS/OEA, "Acta de la séptima sesión").

to a presidential decision to intervene. The most hawkish and influential civilian policymakers were at first not particularly concerned about the possibility of an open-ended commitment. Hence, they were willing to bypass the UNSC for the sake of maximizing U.S. freedom of action. But after the top-ranking generals made it clear that they would veto a U.S. intervention in the absence of a clear exit strategy and credible assurances of international burden sharing, even the most heavyweight concluded that securing multilateral support through the SC was essential.

Bureaucratic Disagreements over the Use of Force

The principal U.S. national security officials in the run-up to the Haiti intervention were President Clinton, National Security Adviser Anthony Lake, Secretary of State Warren Christopher, Secretary of Defense William Perry (who replaced Les Aspin in February 1994), JCS Chairman John Shalikashvili (who replaced Colin Powell in October 1993), and CIA Director James Woolsey. As Boutros Boutros-Ghali, then the UN secretary-general, recalls, "The State Department, the Defense Department, and the CIA each seemed to have its own position and to be conducting its own policy in Haiti" (Boutros-Ghali 1999: 119). He should have added the NSC staff, which under Lake's guidance played a central role in U.S. policy on Haiti.

Lake, by his own definition a "neo-Wilsonian" (see Friedman, *NYT*, Oct. 31, 1993), was without doubt the Clinton administration's leading interventionist on Haiti. Soon after the administration took office, Lake raised the possibility of a military intervention to restore Aristide. As Pezzullo, then the special envoy for Haiti, remembers, "The first meeting I had with Tony Lake at his office [in March 1993], he said that we might have to use military force."[33] Over the following year, Lake and his deputies, Samuel Berger and Nancy Soderberg, as well as Lawrence Rossin, the Haiti policy director on the NSC staff, became increasingly convinced that no meaningful progress would be possible in Haiti without military intervention (Pezzullo 2006: 9; Devroy and Smith, *WashPo*, Sept. 25, 1994).

Focusing on the payoffs of military action and anticipating a limited commitment, Lake and his fellow civilian interventionists at first did not worry much about IO approval. "Dealing with Lake and Berger," Rossin explains, "I don't remember that they agonized over whether or not there was international approval for this intervention."[34] Lake confirms

---

33. Pezzullo, author interview. See also Soderberg 2005: 46.
34. Rossin, author interview, confirmed by Pezzullo, author interview.

that through most of the debate, he didn't view UN approval as essential, primarily because of his conviction that "Haiti is not Vietnam."[35] In October 1993, when the *Harlan County* was met by protesting Haitian thugs at the Port-au-Prince harbor, Lake was the only senior official in Washington who called for the use of force to disperse the protesters and land the American and Canadian peacekeepers.[36] The Pentagon staunchly opposed such a move, fearing it might result in a unilateral and potentially very costly U.S. occupation. Lake, however, bemoans in his memoirs that at the time "there was little—too little—debate in our meetings about whether to use force to compel Cédras' compliance" (A. Lake 2000: 131; see also Soderberg 2005: 46). From about March 1994 onward, Lake became increasingly outspoken in his advocacy of military intervention (Devroy and Smith, *NYT*, Sept. 25, 1994).

Policymakers at the State Department accepted that Aristide should be restored to the Haitian presidency. However, until April or May 1994, senior U.S. diplomats insisted that peaceful options had not yet been exhausted. "It's not like there was a great deal of enthusiasm for [military intervention] in the bureaucracy," Rossin recalls, "so the threat of force option was put on the table, but it wasn't yet picked up."[37] Secretary of State Christopher, a risk-averse World War II veteran, was skeptical of military intervention and had a strong preference for a negotiated political solution. Nevertheless, by the spring of 1994, as the domestic political pressure on the administration increased, the State Department gradually shifted toward a more interventionist stance. Talbott, who became deputy secretary of state in February 1994 and whose influence was magnified by his personal friendship with President Clinton, supported a force-based strategy. Albright, then the U.S. ambassador to the United Nations, was an avowed hawk on Haiti, as was James Dobbins, the State Department's new Haiti policy coordinator. Pezzullo remained opposed the use of force, but he became increasingly marginalized and resigned in late April (Devroy and Smith, *NYT*, Sept. 25, 1994; Albright 2003: 157; Branch 2009: 188).

During the spring of 1994, Talbott and Dobbins became the State Department's leading voices on Haiti, and they gradually brought the rest of the U.S. diplomatic community around to support a possible U.S. invasion. Some of the most hawkish State Department officials at first explicitly opposed the idea of seeking a UN mandate. Dobbins in particular

35. Author interview with Anthony D. Lake (June 26, 2009).
36. Christiansen, author interview. See also Halberstam 2001: 271–72; Pastor 2003: 125.
37. Rossin, author interview. See also A. Lake 2000: 132–34.

insisted that the United States should not even try to secure UN approval because the effort would be exceedingly costly, time-consuming, and unlikely to succeed. Washington, he argued, could live with the consequences of a unilateral invasion. The worst possible outcome in his view would be a failed American attempt at the SC (e.g., because of a Russian or Chinese veto), which by dramatically exposing the lack of international legitimacy, would empower those within the bureaucracy and Congress who opposed military action altogether.[38]

Meanwhile, within the U.S government, the Pentagon and the uniformed leaders in particular put up the strongest and most effective resistance to military intervention. The top-level generals and admirals disputed that important U.S. national interests were at stake in Haiti. They were skeptical about using force to restore democracy and protect human rights and worried about getting bogged down in an open-ended stabilization mission that Congress might not support.[39] Perhaps the strongest opponent of U.S. intervention in Haiti was General Powell, a Bush administration appointee who continued to serve as JCS chairman until October 1993. Powell's attitude had essentially remained unchanged since 1991: "We can take the place in an afternoon with a company or two of marines," he had declared back then, "but the problem will be getting out" (Powell 1995: 544; see also Halberstam 2001: 237–39).

Furthermore, the Pentagon leadership had serious reservations about Aristide, whom it saw as a firebrand politician likely to destabilize the country upon his return. "Most of us at the Pentagon actually thought that restoring Aristide was not a good idea," recalls Walter Slocombe, a former senior U.S. defense official.[40] The Pentagon's reservations about Aristide were fueled by U.S. intelligence reports that characterized the exiled Haitian leader as mentally unstable (Marquis, *WashPo*, Dec. 18, 1993). Slocombe, who largely shared the military's views on Haiti, declared at a party that he resented the idea of risking American lives "to put that psychopath back in power" (quoted in Sciolino, *NYT*, April 29, 1994). Such publicly expressed skepticism about Aristide on the part of senior defense officials, combined with frequent media reports highlighting the Pentagon's concerns about the risks and likely operational costs of intervention, made it difficult for the administration's civilian hawks to build up support for military action in Congress and among the American public (Halberstam 2001: 278–79).

---

38. Dobbins, author interview.
39. Author interview with Gen. Walter Kross, Director of the Joint Staff, 1994–96 (Feb. 11, 2011). See also Albright 2003: 157; Branch 2009: 86.
40. Author interview with Walter B. Slocombe, Deputy UnderSecDef, 1993–94, and UnderSecDef for Policy, 1994–2001 (Mar. 9, 2010).

[81]

The Pentagon's Insistence on the Exit Strategy

In 1994, under a new secretary of defense (Perry) and JCS chairman (Shalikashvili), the Pentagon was slowly brought around to the idea of restoring Aristide. But throughout the spring and early summer, the uniformed leaders disputed that the objective should be achieved through military intervention. They continued to insist that while invading the small Caribbean country, with its ragtag army of about five thousand poorly trained troops, would be easy, getting out would be a serious problem. Hence they recommended that a political compromise solution should be facilitated among the local parties, which would obviate a U.S. invasion.[41]

As the momentum toward military intervention increased, the Pentagon leadership emphasized the need to develop a clear exit strategy for American troops before launching offensive operations. During an NSC principals' meeting on May 7, 1994, Lake suggested that it would be "useful" to take a decision on the shift toward a force-based strategy. Thereupon General Shalikashvili informed the president and his foreign policy team that the military had plans to go in and neutralize the Haitian defense forces if needed. However, the military planners, on their own, could not "deliver . . . a plan on how to get out," and Shalikashvili made it clear that in the absence of a viable exit strategy, he would advise against intervention (quoted in Soderberg 2005: 49).

Lake and his fellow civilian interventionists on the NSC staff had primarily conceived of the threat of military force as a coercive instrument. There was little doubt in their mind that if the Haitian de facto rulers refused to step down voluntarily, the United States would have to follow through on its threat to oust them from power. Nevertheless, for over a year, the NSC staffers who most strongly advocated a force-based strategy had focused primarily on its anticipated (short-term) benefits, and they had not viewed the prospect of a protracted U.S. occupation as a major concern. "That was not a particular preoccupation," acknowledges Rossin, the former NSC staffer. "There was at one point a discussion about several different ways of restoring Aristide, ranging from a proper military intervention, to just putting special forces in to take him back to the place and leave. But the idea that we would somehow get stuck there and therefore needed to have an exit strategy before we got in was not something that was part of the discussion until pretty late in the day."[42]

41. Author interview with Frank Wisner, UnderSecDef for Policy, 1993–94 (July 16, 2009), confirmed by Kross, author interview.
42. Rossin, author interview.

This confirms that hawkish civilian policymakers with no combat experience usually focus primarily on the expected payoffs of armed intervention without adequately considering its potential downsides and longer-term costs. It was the military leaders who through their planning and advice forced other administration officials to come to terms with the fact that, given Haiti's volatile politics, implementing a force-based strategy would almost certainly result in an open-ended troop commitment to stabilize the country. Admiral William Owens, the JCS vice chairman at the time, recalls attending several NSC meetings on Haiti, "where the idealism of senior administration officials was running rampant" and the military was cautioning against the view that "everything was going to be rosy after [the United States] had gotten in and reestablished the leader."[43]

The predominant view among senior military planners was that if the United States had to intervene, its goals should be limited to restoring Aristide and maintaining basic stability for a short time thereafter. Longer-term nation building should be handed off to a follow-on UN mission as quickly as possible. That would relieve the burden on the armed services, allowing the bulk of American troops to be withdrawn as peacekeepers from other countries moved in. The uniformed leaders were adamant that the transition to a follow-on UN mission, which had been poorly planned and implemented in the case of Somalia in 1992–93, should be better prepared this time around. Hence the Joint Staff, under the coordination of Lieutenant General Wesley Clark, then the J-5 director for strategic plans and policy, working in cooperation with the U.S. Atlantic Command (USACOM), developed a matrix of specific tasks to be accomplished by American forces before longer-term stabilization and nation building could be handed off to the United Nations.[44]

The 1992 Somalia intervention had initially been conceived as a short in-and-out mission to assist embattled UN peacekeepers from other countries. American forces would limit themselves to opening up the food supply routes blocked by rebel militias, leaving longer-term nation building to a strengthened UN mission with only minimal U.S. participation.[45] In 1993, however, the intervention ended in a quagmire, after President Clinton, far from withdrawing American troops, gave in to a request from the UN secretary-general to change their mission to peace

---

43. Author interview with Adm. William Owens (Jan. 27, 2011).
44. Author interview with Col. William Flavin, Director of Doctrine, Concepts, and Training, U.S. Army Peacekeeping and Stability Operations Institute, 1999–2013 (Jan. 18, 2011). See also Ballard 1998: 62–66.
45. Jeremiah, author interview. For a useful discussion see also H. Cohen 2000: 210–14.

enforcement. A series of deadly clashes with Somali militias ensued, culminating in the killing of eighteen American soldiers during the Battle of Mogadishu (Bensahel 2002: 35–45).

American generals and admirals learned several lessons from the Somalia experience. First, U.S. objectives in humanitarian operations not only have to be limited but also need to be clearly defined in advance and should not be changed unless absolutely necessary. Second, before deploying American troops in humanitarian missions overseas, U.S leaders need to obtain a firm commitment from the UN or regional IOs, as well as from potential troop-contributing countries that there will be a rapid handoff to a follow-on multilateral mission led by other member states. Finally, the transition to follow-on multilateral missions has to be planned in much greater detail so as to avoid risky improvisation. Significantly, however, while civilian administration officials used the UN as a scapegoat for the failure in Somalia, the U.S. military blamed the haphazard strategy of the civilian leadership in Washington and remained convinced that the UN-handoff idea could represent a useful model for the future.[46]

The Military's Request for Assurances

The uniformed leaders, adamant that the burden for Haiti's long-term stabilization should be shifted to the international community, came close to explicitly requesting a UN mandate for the initial intervention. As Frank Wisner, former undersecretary of defense for policy, explains, there was "practically a doctrinal assumption" among the generals and admirals that the Haiti mission had to be internationalized from the beginning.[47] This was seen as essential to the U.S. exit strategy. Specifically, the Joint Chiefs requested concrete assurances that the UN mission for Haiti foreseen in the 1993 Governor's Island Agreement, with an adequately strengthened mandate, would take over all responsibility for maintaining political order soon after the invasion. As Admiral Owens, the JCS vice chairman, recalls, "We felt strongly that without that kind of commitment from the United Nations, one could not envision an American occupying force going in. There needed to be a United Nations force that would come in and have the size and texture to do this for the long term, because it wasn't going to get fixed in the short term."[48]

46. Flavin and Kross, author interviews; author interview with Adm. Frank L. Bowman, Director for Pol-Mil Affairs on the Joint Staff, 1992–94 (April 27, 2011).
47. Wisner, author interview.
48. Owens, author interview.

Such a commitment could best be obtained by securing a UN mandate up front that also included specific language about a follow-on multilateral mission. The military leaders, intent on shaping the policy in line with their own conception of the national interest and their parochial concerns, proceeded in close coordination with senior civilian officials from the Office of the Secretary of Defense (OSD). "The interagency coordination from the perspective of the Pentagon was done shoulder to shoulder between OSD and the Joint Staff," remembers General Walter Kross, who at the time directed the latter.[49] Indeed, civilian leaders at OSD helped the generals and admirals magnify their concerns vis-à-vis the rest of the administration. John Christiansen, who chaired the OSD Haiti task group in 1993–94, recalls how senior defense officials pushed back against the notion, advanced by some of their colleagues from the State Department, that it would be possible "to get the UN eventually to come in" without having obtained a UN mandate up front with explicit guarantees concerning the follow-on force: "That was absolutely critical. The Pentagon would have strenuously objected to going into Haiti by ourselves, without having the commitment of a follow-on [UN] force."[50] General Kross confirms that whenever the military planners briefed the president and the NSC, "the UN sanction up front would certainly be in the recommended option . . . [because] it was really a central element of our exit strategy."[51]

The JCS had been tasked with developing contingency plans for a U.S. invasion of Haiti in late 1993, after the *Harlan County* incident. Soon thereafter, a secret operational planning cell was set up at USACOM's headquarters in Norfolk, Virginia. Under the supervision of Major General Michael J. Byron, the cell developed a draft operations plan (code-named OPLAN 2370), which was completed in February 1994. The plan foresaw a twenty-four-day U.S. military operation in Haiti, after which longer-term stabilization tasks would be handed off to a multilateral (preferably UN) follow-on force (Kretchik, Baumann, and Fishel 1998: 48–49). The final plan approved by the Joint Staff and published on May 20, 1994, anticipated a forced entry by the Eighty-Second Airborne Division and explicitly foresaw that after an initial U.S.-led stabilization effort, "U.S. forces will be replaced as UNMIH forces arrive."[52] In the absence of clear presidential guidelines to the contrary, the Pentagon had planned for only a short U.S. troop deployment while making it clear

49. Kross, author interview.
50. Christiansen, author interview.
51. Kross, author interview.
52. USACOM Commander, message 131358Z, "Operation Uphold Democracy" (on file with the author).

that *some* form of longer-term constabulary presence would be needed to secure strategic objectives. That put significant pressure on the rest of the administration to achieve the highest possible level of multilateral buy-in from the UN and international partners.

Process tracing of the policy's development in the spring and summer of 1994 further clarifies the military's crucial role. On May 7, as noted, General Shalikashvili pointed out during an NSC principals' meeting that the military could not "deliver . . . a plan on how to get out." He also emphasized on that occasion that "we have to maintain order until . . . our forces are replaced by an international force or until the internal forces are rebuilt" (quoted in Soderberg 2005: 48). In previous days, high-ranking military officers had emphasized their concerns about the risk of an open-ended U.S. troop commitment in interviews with the press, publicly worrying about the absence of UN approval (Gellman and Marcus, *WashPo*, May 4, 1994). That was a clear signal that the military would remain opposed *until* the administration offered credible assurances about the exit strategy, preferably by securing an advance UN mandate that foresaw the establishment of a follow-on UN force within a relatively short timeframe.

By June 1994, senior uniformed planners at USACOM publicly announced that they "assumed" any military intervention in Haiti would be conducted under a UN mandate (Devroy and Gellmann, *WashPo*, July 2, 1994). Furthermore, through May and into June, Deputy Secretary of Defense John Deutch invited Strobe Talbott, his equal in rank from the State Department, and James Steinberg, the State Department's policy planning chief, to several informal conversations with the JCS and other high-ranking military officers. In the course of those meetings, Talbott in particular became much more aware of what the military planners viewed as the operation's principal risks (Devroy and Smith, *WashPo*, Sept. 25, 1994). It therefore appears that by sometime in June, U.S. defense leaders had convinced other senior figures within the administration that securing a UNSC mandate for the use of force would be essential, because that alone would effectively guarantee a quick handover to a follow-on UN mission. Albright in turn persuaded her State Department colleagues that a SC mandate was within reach. With support from fellow interventionists from across the U.S. government, she was then able to mobilize the necessary resources to secure a UN resolution of approval that explicitly foresaw a follow-on UN mission.[53]

In retrospect, former advocates of a force-based strategy on Haiti recognize the military's central role in alerting the administration to the need for an exit strategy and driving U.S. policy toward the United

53. Dobbins, author interview. See also Albright 2003: 157–59.

Nations. Lake reluctantly acknowledges that it was important to mollify the uniformed leaders, in order to build up intra-administration support for intervention: "Defining a mission that had an end point was something that it was certainly necessary to work on vis-à-vis the Pentagon."[54] Soderberg, one of Lake's former deputies, more explicitly recognizes that Chairman "Shali[kashvili] was the first to articulate" the link between the U.S. exit strategy and the idea of a UN handoff (Soderberg 2005: 48). Talbott goes further, acknowledging that the principal reason why the administration worked hard to obtain a SC mandate explicitly foreseeing a follow-on UN mission was to reassure skeptics at the Pentagon and notably the JCS: "Our principal reason for wanting to do a handoff to the UN as quickly as possible was that our military really wanted it. It was not so much about dealing with skeptics in Congress. It really had to do with Shalikashvili."[55] Finally, Morton Halperin, then a senior NSC staffer and strong advocate of U.S. intervention, confirms that "the deal that was brokered with the UN was very much to get the military to go in, [because] the generals were concerned about how quickly they could get out."[56]

Bringing the Pentagon on Board

UNSC Resolution 940, adopted on July 31, 1994, authorized the use of force in Haiti to restore the democratically elected leader while also committing the Security Council to establishing a follow-on UN mission that would "assume the full range of its functions" as soon as basic security had been restored. Senior U.S. military planners understood that international troops for the follow-on force would have to be recruited on an ad hoc basis, but what reassured them was "the commitment from the UN to start that process."[57] Once the uniformed leaders felt satisfied that the U.S. intervention would be limited in scope and duration, the Pentagon eventually fell in line. In mid-August 1994, Secretary of Defense Perry, who had previously been supportive of the military's concerns, reportedly told his staff, "That's it, we're not going to mess around anymore" by opposing armed intervention (quoted in Devroy and Smith, *WashPo*, Sept. 25, 1994). A few days later, on August 26, President Clinton finally authorized a U.S. invasion aimed at ousting the Cédras junta and restoring Aristide to office (ibid.).

54. Lake, author interview.
55. Talbott, author interview.
56. Author interview with Morton Halperin, senior director for democracy on the NSC staff, 1994–96 (Mar. 10, 2010).
57. Kross, author interview. See also Branch 2009: 188.

On September 15, the U.S. president issued a televised ultimatum to the Haitian de facto rulers: "Your time is up. Leave now, or we will force you from power." In his speech, Clinton also vowed that "the vast majority of our troops will come home in months, not years. . . . Then, in the second phase, a much smaller U.S. force will join forces from other members of the United Nations, and their mission will leave Haiti after elections are held next year."[58] Unnamed senior administration officials subsequently confirmed that "he [Clinton] waited until September to satisfy Pentagon reservations" (quoted in Devroy and Smith, *WashPo*, Sept. 25, 1994).

It should be noted that obtaining a SC mandate up front that explicitly foresaw a follow-on UN mission was only one, albeit crucial, dimension of a multipronged strategy aimed at reassuring skeptics of U.S. intervention at the Pentagon and especially in the armed forces. Other elements of that strategy included a CIA-led covert operation in the late summer of 1994 aimed at promoting an internal army coup in Haiti (McManus and Wright, *LA Times*, Sept. 16, 1994), systematic efforts to bribe the Haitian army leaders into exile by offering sizable financial incentives (Sciolino, *NYT*, Aug. 4, 1994), and a last-ditch diplomatic mission to Haiti on September 17 led by former president Jimmy Carter (Pastor 2003: 129–36). Ultimately, once Clinton had issued a clear coercive threat, Carter was able to persuade the Haitian rulers to agree to step down and consent to a peaceful deployment of American troops. That allowed a U.S. invasion force of twenty thousand to deploy without combat beginning on September 19.[59]

By the end of September, American troops were joined by a small contingent of 295 Caribbean soldiers. Over the following month, a Bangladeshi contingent of 1,100 peacekeepers, as well as roughly 200 international police monitors from Argentina, Jordan, and various Caribbean countries were added to the interim Multi-National Force (MNF) in Haiti.[60] General Cédras resigned from all his functions on October 10 and was granted political sanctuary in Panama. By October 15, the situation

---

58. Bill Clinton, Address to the Nation on Haiti, Sept. 15, 1994, http://www.presidency.ucsb.edu/ws/?pid=49093/.

59. Robert Pastor, at the time Carter's senior political adviser, informed Lake from Haiti that there was only an agreement to deploy a few hundred international troops. Yet retired General Colin Powell, who was a member of Carter's negotiating team, advised President Clinton to seize the opening and "go in hard" to neutralize the Haitian armed forces. See Papers of Anthony Lake, box 43 (handwritten notes, 1994), Manuscript Division, U.S. Library of Congress, Washington, DC.

60. A total of about two thousand non-U.S. troops and six hundred police monitors deployed as part of the MNF. See statement by UnderSecDef Walter Slocombe, *Hearing Before the House ArmedServ Committee*, 103rd Cong. (Oct. 7, 1994), 13–14.

had become sufficiently stable for Aristide to return to Haiti and resume the presidency (Boutros-Ghali 1996: 65). For several months, the United States had to shoulder virtually the entire cost of the MNF in Haiti.[61] By the end of March 1995, however, Washington was able to hand off peace-keeping responsibilities to a UN mission of six thousand, composed of a majority of non-U.S. troops and financed out of assessed UN peacekeeping funds. One year later, in March 1996, the United States turned over command of the peacekeeping force to Canada and withdrew all but a handful of American troops (Talbott 2008: 302). As Soderberg (2005: 50) notes, ultimately, "by getting UN support, [the administration] shifted much of the burden to America's allies."

Sources of the Generals' Influence

The uniformed leaders influenced U.S. policymaking on Haiti in two ways. First, they relied on their professional expertise and control over military planning to portray certain options as unfeasible and steer the policy process in their preferred direction. Since late 1993, USACOM had been developing contingency plans for a short-term U.S. military operation, with the expectation of a relatively quick handover of longer-term stabilization and reconstruction tasks to a follow-on UN mission. In the spring and summer of 1994, as the prospect of a U.S. intervention became increasingly real, those plans set the framework for Washington's policy toward Haiti. The uniformed leaders also persuaded several of their civilian counterparts—first and foremost their allies at OSD but also senior officials from other agencies such as Talbott and Lake—that devising an exit strategy for American troops in advance of any deployment was essential to ensure the operation's success. Lake was opposed to any protracted, neocolonial type of U.S. interference on principled grounds, and once the JCS persuaded him that a quick in-and-out mission would be impossible, he came to agree that the United States should aim for a rapid handoff to a follow-on multilateral mission.[62]

But top-ranking generals and admirals also acted as more straightfor-wardly political players. As long as the president remained undecided and did not commit the United States to intervention, the uniformed leaders, who could speak on the issue with great authority, had the ability to undermine public and congressional support for military action.

---

61. The United States covered all incremental costs resulting from the deployment of troops from non-OECD countries. See communication from Deputy SecDef John Deutch, *Hearing Before the Senate ArmedServ Committee*, 103rd Cong. (Sept. 28, 1994), 17–19.
62. Lake, author interview.

Without explicitly opposing the prospect of intervention, they could publicly highlight attendant risks and potential long-term costs by means of press leaks, statements to the media, and congressional hearings. Informal contacts with representatives on Capitol Hill further increased the military's leverage. Admiral Owens recalls that congressional leaders were "quite amenable to the kinds of arguments that [the military] brought up," including "on the need for UN authorization first."[63] The military's vigorous pushback created significant problems for civilian administration officials who advocated a force-based strategy and were trying to build momentum for a U.S. invasion.[64]

Frank Wisner insists that the lack of presidential leadership, which is typical for human rights crises abroad that do not threaten important American interests, magnified the military's leverage:

> If the president had decided that he wanted to go to Haiti and invade the country, then the Pentagon would have carried it out. In the face of a decision by the president that is clear, the Secretary of Defense is going to carry out the decision. The Pentagon will follow . . . provided that there is a clear mission that has been approved by the president. But here's the problem: the Haiti issue was a contested issue, and we were far from having an overwhelming and clear consensus.[65]

Finally, the recent traumatic experience in Somalia made the president himself quite risk-averse, notwithstanding the hawkish advice that he was getting from his top civilian policy advisers. Clinton was aware that in the aftermath of the Somalia debacle of October 1993, and with the impending November 1994 midterm elections, another botched military operation might be extremely costly in terms of U.S. domestic politics. "The deaths of thirteen American servicemen in Mogadishu led to a very sharp response in the public and the Congress," recalls a former high-ranking White House official. "As we debated the use of force elsewhere, there was a concern that a similar incident would be like an anaphylactic shock. The first bee sting you're OK, the second bee sting you're dead."[66] That undoubtedly magnified the military's influence over policymaking on the use of force. General Kross, who as director of the Joint Staff interacted with senior civilian policymakers on a regular basis, recalls that

63. Owens, author interview.
64. Numerous press leaks were attributed to the military, causing consternation among civilian leaders. Rossin, author interview.
65. Wisner, author interview.
66. Fuerth, author interview. On Clinton's awareness of the domestic political risks see also Branch 2009: 187–90.

"after Somalia, Clinton began paying a lot of attention to risk-averse military advice. There are numerous instances starting in Haiti where he was following all the advice about focusing on the exit strategy and all that. There are lots of examples where President Clinton actually over-rode a conclusion or an opinion by his NSC staff, in favor of the Pentagon."[67]

Alternative Hypotheses on U.S. Multilateralism

The remainder of this chapter evaluates alternative hypotheses for why the Clinton administration worked hard to secure UN approval in the run-up to the 1994 Haiti intervention. First, civilian policymakers might have sought UN approval in order to increase U.S. public support for intervention. Second, regardless of civil-military relations, they might have sought UN approval to reduce congressional opposition to the use of force. Third, administration officials might have been motivated by an internalized desire to comply with international norms. Finally, they might have aimed to avert potentially costly international retaliation in other policy domains.

Increasing Public Support

One prominent hypothesis for why U.S. policymakers seek IO approval is that they do so to increase support for armed intervention among the American public (Chapman and Reiter 2004; Grieco et al. 2011). With specific regard to the 1994 intervention, Sarah Kreps (2007: 467) argues that "perhaps the only way that the Clinton administration could execute the Haiti mission and not be punished by its domestic political audience was to conduct the mission multilaterally" (see also Schultz 2003: 121–23). If increasing U.S. public support was an important reason for seeking UN approval, senior officials involved in decision making at the time should acknowledge that, first, they were seriously concerned about public support and, second, they viewed multilateral backing through the SC as an effective means of dealing with the issue.

As noted in chapter 1, public opinion polls indeed generally suggest that the American people prefer multilateral to unilateral military inter-ventions. A closer examination of the polling evidence, however, reveals that what matters most to the American public is not so much IO approval

---

67. Kross, author interview.

per se as participation by other countries in multinational coalitions.[68] Opinion polls taken between July 1 and September 15, 1994, confirm this general finding. While baseline public support for military intervention in Haiti tended to be low, Americans were significantly more likely to support a multinational intervention with participation or at least political backing from allies and partners, than a straightforwardly unilateral one without any international support. Only 23 percent of Americans on average supported military intervention by the United States on its own. By contrast, an average of 45.5 percent supported a U.S.-led intervention with the endorsement or participation of international partners. Significantly, however, explicit references to UN approval did *not* further increase U.S. public support.[69]

Senior policymakers in Washington were aware during the period leading up to the Haiti intervention that UN approval would not be particularly helpful in terms of increasing U.S. public support. They understood that in the aftermath of the perceived UN failure in Somalia in 1993 and given the dismal performance of UN peacekeepers in the former Yugoslavia, the American public was at best ambivalent about U.S. participation in UN-sponsored missions abroad.[70] According to Lake, the president's foreign policy advisers interpreted public opinion polls as suggesting "support for the UN in principle," but it was clear to them that in terms of increasing public approval ratings, "the UN doesn't make a pivotal difference when considering interventions." In short, Lake and his colleagues correctly interpreted the polls as indicating that for increasing U.S. public support, "allies are more important than the UN."[71]

A UNSC mandate for the Haiti intervention might in principle have made it easier to forge a multinational coalition, which could then have helped with public support. However, there was no indication in the spring and summer of 1994 that IO approval would make a significant difference in terms of recruiting international partners for the initial intervention.

First, U.S. policymakers understood that even after the adoption of a UN mandate, it was extremely unlikely that countries in Latin America

68. Reviewing hundreds of public opinion polls on U.S. interventions in Somalia, Bosnia, Haiti, Kosovo, Iraq, and Liberia, Eichenberg (2005: 159–61) finds that on average, Americans are equally as supportive of interventions with UN or NATO approval as they are of interventions endorsed only by ad hoc multinational coalitions.
69. Data averaged from two dozen opinion polls by Gallup/CNN/USA Today; ABC News; CBS News/NYT; Times/CNN/Yankelovich Partners; ABC News/WashPo (July 1–Sept. 15, 1994). Source: iPOLL databank, http://www.ropercenter.uconn.edu.
70. On the U.S. public's reservations about UN performance see also Kull and Destler 1999: 67–69.
71. Lake, author interview.

and elsewhere that were skeptical of U.S. intervention would openly endorse it, let alone contribute troops to U.S.-led combat operations in Haiti.[72] Only the Argentine government, eager to improve relations with the United States, explicitly considered the possibility of contributing troops to the initial invasion, but it soon backed away in the face of strong opposition from its own parliament and domestic populace (Williams, *WashPo*, July 4, 1994).

Second, Haiti's immediate Caribbean neighbors, who feared a massive influx of Haitian refugees, had pledged their virtually unconditional support for U.S. military intervention, regardless of UN approval. The relevant subregional organization, the Community of Caribbean states (CARICOM), had called for the use of "all necessary means" to restore Aristide to office in 1991(Boutros-Ghali 1996: 205). In the spring of 1994, during private conversations with Albright, the principal Caribbean countries reiterated their support for military action, and CARICOM subsequently endorsed Washington's intervention plans *before* the UNSC voted on the matter (Albright 2003: 157; Branch 2009: 186). After the invasion, several Caribbean countries, led by Jamaica, were among the first to offer active support by deploying hundreds of peacekeepers within days of the American landing (Ballard 1998: 89). Therefore, for the purpose of bolstering short-term U.S. public approval, the Clinton administration could have relied on operational support from an ad hoc Caribbean coalition that would probably have been available regardless of UN approval.

Finally, senior U.S. officials who advocated the use of force expected that, regardless of international approval, there would be a rally-'round-the-flag effect once the invasion was launched. The Clinton administration had already benefited from this public rally effect once before: in June 1993, after a unilateral cruise-missile attack against Baghdad, the president's approval ratings had jumped by over ten points (Berke, *NYT*, June 29, 1993). Senior White House officials, in particular, predicted that a similar rally would again occur after the deployment of American combat troops to Haiti (Apple, *NYT*, Sept. 16, 1994; see also Girard 2004: 73). As early as May 1994, Dante Caputo, the UN representative for Haiti, reported in a confidential note to Boutros-Ghali, based on conversations with senior U.S. officials, that the predominant expectation in Washington was "that the current opposition of public opinion to an armed intervention will change radically, once it will have taken place."[73] In short, the administration expected that the benefits of UNSC approval in terms

72. Feinberg and Watson, author interviews.
73. Confidential note from SRSG Dante Caputo, May 23, 1994, leaked and published in *Congressional Record*, Sept. 29, 1994.

of bolstering U.S. public support would be limited at best. Hence concerns about public support can hardly explain why policymakers made such significant efforts to obtain a UN mandate and came to view it as practically necessary for U.S. intervention.

Reducing Congressional Opposition

It has also been suggested that concerns about congressional opposition persuaded the Clinton administration to seek UNSC approval for the 1994 Haiti intervention (see, e.g., Fisher 1997: 1270–71; Von Hippel 2000: 101; Schultz 2003). American legislators clearly had significant doubts about intervening in Haiti. If President Clinton had asked Congress to authorize the intervention at any point during the spring or summer of 1994, it is likely that a majority of legislators would have withheld their support. "We didn't have the votes, not even close," remembers George Stephanopoulos (1999: 307), then the White House communications director. Not only were Republicans on Capitol Hill almost unanimously opposed to intervention, but centrist Democrats, too, became increasingly outspoken in their criticism as the odds of military action increased significantly by July 1994 (Doherty, *CQ Weekly*, July 16, 1994).

Nevertheless, although Congress seemed unlikely to endorse the prospective intervention, it was equally unlikely to explicitly oppose it. Congressional leaders on both sides of the aisle understood that even nonbinding resolutions of disapproval would undermine Washington's coercive leverage and thereby make a peaceful resolution of the crisis less likely. Furthermore, Democrats controlled both branches of Congress in 1994, and they were unwilling to take the risk of constraining the president and embarrassing the administration on such a high-visibility issue shortly before the November midterm elections. The most likely scenario was that Congress would adopt a classic blame-avoidance strategy, shifting responsibility for the use of force more or less entirely to the executive branch.[74]

Between May and July 1994, Republicans in the House and Senate sponsored various resolutions and amendments opposing a U.S. intervention in Haiti. Yet all those efforts to limit the executive's freedom of maneuver prior to the intervention were rejected by the Democratic majority in Congress, often with support from senior Republicans who were reluctant to constrain the president on foreign policy (Hendrickson 2002: 51–56). On June 29, 1994, freshman Senator Judd Gregg (R-NH)

---

74. Author interview with Christopher Kojm, senior foreign policy staffer for Lee Hamilton, Chairman of the House Foreign Affairs Committee, 1993–94 (Aug. 9, 2009).

proposed an amendment to the 1995 foreign operations bill that would have required the president to seek congressional authorization before ordering American troops to Haiti. But the Gregg amendment was defeated 34–65, with several Republicans voting against it. Subsequently the Senate adopted (93–4) a much milder, nonbinding amendment that in general terms called on the president to seek congressional approval before committing troops to Haiti (Doherty, *CQ Weekly*, July 2, 1994). The Senate rejected two further Republican-inspired amendments intended to prevent Clinton from deploying troops in the absence of congressional authorization, on July 14 and August 5.[75] The House, for its part, voted 223–201 on May 24 in favor of a nonbinding amendment tabled by Congressman Porter Gross (R-FL), which urged President Clinton not to invade Haiti in the absence of a "clear and present danger" to U.S. citizens and interests. However, about two weeks later that same proposal was rejected in a second vote (195–226), after twenty-five House Democrats had switched their position under pressure from their party's leadership (Hendrickson 2002: 52).

On the basis of those votes on Capitol Hill during the spring and early summer of 1994, policymakers who favored U.S. intervention tended to believe that congressional opposition, while sometimes boisterous, would remain politically manageable.[76] Furthermore, they were confident that Congress would soften its stance once the president committed the nation's prestige to the operation and especially once U.S. combat troops were deployed (Doherty, *CQ Weekly*, Sept. 17, 1994). In fact, shortly after U.S. troops had landed in Haiti, House Democrats quite easily defeated (205–225) a resolution sponsored by Congressman Benjamin Gilman (R-NY) calling for the "immediate withdrawal of American troops." Subsequently, both the House and the Senate passed resolutions that, without approving the deployment, expressed support for the president and the troops (Doherty, *CQ Weekly*, Sept. 24, 1994; Hendrickson 2002: 60–62).

There is no evidence that senior policymakers viewed UN approval as particularly desirable, let alone essential, to limit congressional opposition in the run-up to the intervention. After the Clinton administration's debacle in Somalia and the ensuing scapegoating of the United Nations in U.S. foreign policy circles, senior White House officials came to the conclusion that "with a lot of the Congress, having a UN cover was not particularly useful."[77] For that reason, in the months leading up to the Haiti intervention, the White House sought to downplay reliance on the

75. "Special Legislative Outlook," *CQ Weekly*, Sept. 10, 1994.
76. Lake and Talbott, author interviews.
77. Lake, author interview.

UN in its relations with Congress. Lake remembers that "we were walk-ing away from the UN as much as we were wrapping ourselves in that mantle," and he insists that concerns about congressional opposition "were not an important consideration" in the decision to seek UN approval.[78] According to Talbott, at the State Department, too, the expec-tation was that UN approval would not be particularly helpful as a way of mollifying critics in Congress "because a lot of those critics weren't very crazy about the UN either."[79]

Policymakers might still have viewed advance UN approval, and the resulting greater likelihood of sustained international burden sharing, as advantageous in terms of maintaining congressional support *for the long run*. Yet as previously noted, civilian policymakers who called for a force-based strategy focused primarily on the anticipated short-term payoffs of intervention, and they initially did not envision an open-ended stabi-lization mission in Haiti. Consequently, they were not especially con-cerned about maintaining long-term congressional support. General Kross, who as director of the Joint Staff interacted frequently with civil-ian authorities, recalls that policy proposals developed by the NSC staff in particular reflected "superficial, wishful thinking—they were just not thinking through the risks of failure."[80] It was the military leadership that drew the administration's attention to the need for a protracted peacekeeping and stabilization effort in Haiti. The uniformed leaders also worried more than their civilian counterparts who advocated a force-based strategy about the administration's ability to maintain con-gressional support for an open-ended commitment of U.S. troops (Soder-berg 2005: 49). Therefore, to the extent that concerns about long-term congressional support influenced the administration's efforts to secure UN approval ahead of intervention, the military leaders functioned as a crucial transmission belt.

Complying with Internalized Norms

Another possibility is that U.S. policymakers seek IO approval because they have internalized relevant legal or moral norms that require such approval as a condition for legitimate intervention.[81] If senior Clinton administration officials sought UN approval for the Haiti intervention as a result of norm internalization, they should have displayed a high threshold for violating related precepts. Furthermore, they should have

---

78. Ibid.
79. Talbott, author interview.
80. Kross, author interview.
81. See chapter 1 for a more detailed discussion of this hypothesis.

viewed IO approval as intrinsically desirable—that is, as an end in itself, and not merely as a useful tool to facilitate burden sharing and assuage domestic or international critics.

The most widely accepted international norms of legitimate behavior are, almost by definition, those enshrined in formal legal conventions. According to the UN Charter, unless the international use of force is in self-defense, it must be authorized by the Security Council. The 1994 Haiti intervention was clearly not about self-defense, given that there was no imminent threat to U.S. citizens or the American homeland. Therefore, to assess the norm internalization hypothesis, we should first ask: To what extent did concerns about international legality determine the Clinton administration's efforts to obtain a SC mandate? The available evidence indicates that such concerns did not matter much. Lake candidly admits that "in the internal meetings, I don't recall us talking about international law."[82] Questioned about it during a congressional hearing at the time, William Gray, the U.S. special Haiti envoy, rejected the notion that the administration was feeling constrained by international law: "Ultimately the decision to use a military option must be made by the President of the United States, not by an international body . . . . So from a legal point of view the ultimate decision . . . would be up to the President . . . based upon what he believes are the best interests of the United States."[83]

The only senior U.S. officials who were genuinely concerned about compliance with international law were the administration's legal advisers. Secretary of State Christopher, himself a lawyer, also took some personal interest in the debate about the international legality of intervening in Haiti.[84] But overall, as a former NSC staffer who closely followed the debate recalls, concerns about international legality "never intruded into the main discussion."[85]

Even though senior administration officials were not motivated by concerns about international legality, they could still have internalized relevant *moral* norms requiring IO approval for offensive military operations. Planning for the Haiti intervention was driven largely by the White House and especially the NSC staff until midsummer of 1994, when a formal interagency planning cell was eventually set up.[86] It is therefore

82. Lake, author interview.
83. Statement of William Gray, *Hearing Before the House Foreign Affairs Committee*, 103rd Cong. (June 8, 1994), 15.
84. E-mail to the author by Michael Matheson, principal dep. legal adviser to the DOS, 1989–96 (July 30, 2009).
85. Rossin, author interview.
86. Ibid.

[97]

essential to establish, first and foremost, the moral convictions of President Clinton and his senior advisers on the NSC staff with regard to the question of IO approval for the use of force. Did those individuals view multilateral approval through the UN or the OAS as inherently desirable and perhaps necessary, quite apart from its instrumental value?

Rossin recalls that Lake and his collaborators were initially not particularly concerned "over whether or not there was international approval for this intervention."[87] In October 1993, when the USS *Harlan County* was met by a protesting Haitian mob at the Port-au-Prince harbor, Lake, as well as senior State Department officials, called for a unilateral use of force to disperse the Haitian thugs. Only when faced with strong opposition from the U.S. military leaders who feared being dragged into a costly invasion, did the civilian interventionists eventually back down.[88] Over the following months, Lake repeatedly made the case for moving toward a force-based strategy to restore Aristide to the Haitian presidency, long before there was any talk of securing UN approval (Devroy and Smith, *WashPo*, Sept. 25, 1994; Lake 2000: 131; Soderberg 2005: 46).

After the *Harlan County* incident, President Clinton himself reportedly came close to authorizing a U.S. unilateral invasion. Exhorted by David Gergen, one of his principal public relations advisers, Clinton came to believe that a vigorous display of military force might be beneficial to the administration's domestic political standing and its tarnished international reputation for resolve. Gergen and the president were extrapolating from Ronald Reagan's experience in 1983, when the latter had chosen to invade Grenada shortly after 250 U.S. Marines were killed in a terrorist attack in Beirut, Lebanon. "The Reagan people were much better at the politics of foreign policy than we are," Clinton told his national security team. "Look at Lebanon. They went into Grenada two days later and fixed it" (quoted in Stephanopoulos 1999: 217). Clinton was persuaded that the Grenada invasion had reduced the domestic political fallout from the Beirut killing. In the aftermath of the *Harlan County* incident and the humiliation in Somalia, he wondered whether a swift, unilateral invasion of Haiti might not similarly improve his administration's political fortunes (ibid.). In short, in late 1993 and early 1994, senior White House officials, including the president, were not particularly concerned about IO approval and certainly did not consider it a moral obligation.

Subsequently, in June 1994, Lake recommended that the United States should openly signal its willingness to use force unilaterally in order to minimize the likelihood that the most recalcitrant members of the UNSC

---

87. Ibid.
88. Christiansen and Kross, author interviews. See also Halberstam 2001: 271–72.

(Russia, China, and Brazil) would cast a negative vote.[89] The administration's principal advocates of intervention firmly believed that to maintain Washington's credibility at the SC into the future, that threat would have to be carried out if necessary. That is, in the event that the world body refused to authorize the use of force, the United States should have intervened without multilateral approval.[90] Soderberg confirms that if senior officials on the NSC staff could have independently set U.S. policy: "We would probably still have done it [without UN approval], because we had to do something. We were not going to let the UN dictate our policy—especially in Haiti! We would probably have cobbled together some coalition of the willing."[91]

Finally, as previously noted, senior officials at the State Department were skeptical of even attempting to secure UN approval. Dobbins, the department's Haiti policy coordinator, was opposed to any effort in that sense because he thought it would be exceedingly costly, time-consuming, and unlikely to succeed.[92] The administration's leading interventionists ultimately agreed that a serious effort should be made to secure UN approval, although obtaining a multilateral mandate would be difficult—but clearly the reason was not that they had internalized relevant international norms of legitimate behavior.

Averting Negative Issue Linkage

One final possibility is that American leaders seek IO approval for prospective interventions to reassure other states and thus avert costly international opposition in the form of negative issue linkage.[93] If averting issue linkage was an important motive for seeking UN approval in the Haiti case, senior officials involved in decision making at the time should first of all acknowledge that they were concerned about the possibility of reduced international cooperation with the United States in other issue areas as a consequence of U.S. unilateral intervention. Furthermore, they should affirm that preventing issue linkage was in fact a significant motive for seeking IO approval.

In the spring of 1994 it became apparent that international opposition to U.S. military intervention in Haiti would be concentrated in the Western Hemisphere, and specifically in Latin America. With the notable

---

89. Lake, author interview. See also Soderberg 2005: 48.
90. Talbott, author interview.
91. Author interview with Nancy Soderberg, Deputy NatSec Adviser, 1993–96 (July 29, 2009).
92. Dobbins, author interview.
93. See chapter 1 for a more detailed discussion of this hypothesis.

exceptions of France—the former colonial power in Haiti—and Russia, which appeared intent on using Haiti as a bargaining chip to increase its own leverage at the SC, political leaders and their followers outside the Western Hemisphere had little interest in Haiti or U.S. policy toward the impoverished Caribbean country. The Latin Americans, however, felt strongly about U.S. military intervention in the hemisphere. Moreover, although the Cédras junta had few supporters, most Latin American leaders felt uneasy about restoring Aristide, an unpredictable populist who had never taken liberal principles very seriously.

On the occasion of an ad hoc OAS foreign ministers meeting in June 1994, several Latin American governments went on the record as emphatically opposing the use of force to restore Aristide. The representatives of the Dominican Republic, Venezuela, Mexico, Paraguay, Uruguay, and Brazil denied that the situation in Haiti constituted a threat to international peace and security. Several of them further emphasized that the proposed U.S. military action would violate the hemispheric principle of nonintervention enshrined in the OAS Charter. Some Latin American countries, notably Paraguay, Uruguay, and Venezuela, went so far as to declare that they would oppose any U.S.-led intervention in Haiti, "no matter whether *unilateral* or *multilateral*."[94] A few weeks later, the Parlamento Latinoamericano, a regional assembly made up of representatives from eighteen national legislatures and largely unaffected by geopolitical calculations, came closest to expressing popular sentiment in the region. First, it objected to U.S. intervention in Haiti, and second, it called on Aristide to resign so that new presidential elections could be held.[95]

Such widespread Latin American skepticism about the prospective U.S. intervention in Haiti did not come as a surprise to senior Clinton administration officials. A majority of Latin American governments had condemned the two most recent U.S. interventions in the region—Grenada in 1983 and Panama in 1989. The Panama intervention was formally censured by the OAS in a 20–1 vote, pitting *all* the United States' regional partners against it.[96] That, combined with the long history of U.S. military interference in the hemisphere, led senior policymakers in Washington to expect significant Latin American protests against the

94. OAS/OEA, "Acta de la séptima sesión," 35 (Paraguay, emphasis added), 48–49 (Uruguay), 32 (Venezuela), 27 (Dominican Republic), 30–31 (Brazil), and 34 (Mexico).
95. LatinNews.com, "Setting the Scene for Military Action," *Latin American Weekly Report*, Aug. 4, 1994.
96. OAS Permanent Council, "Acta de la sesión extraordinaria," Dec. 20–22, 1989 (CP/ACTA 800/89), 110–11.

prospective Haiti intervention. Alexander Fletcher Watson, who led U.S. diplomacy vis-à-vis Latin America during the Clinton administration, was not in the least surprised at those protests as the possibility of intervention was being debated, because, as he puts it, "nobody on the planet has more experience with U.S. military intervention than the Latin Americans."[97]

However, it was equally clear to senior administration officials that Latin American governmental opposition was largely a matter of principle aimed at appeasing domestic audiences and had little to do with perceptions of threatening U.S. motives and fears of a revamped "Yankee imperialism." Richard Feinberg, then a senior NSC staffer dealing with inter-American affairs, candidly recalls that he and most of his colleagues saw Latin American hostility to U.S. intervention in Haiti as "just part of the background noise."[98] Put differently, there was never much doubt that hemispheric opposition would remain confined to the level of rhetoric and thus have no negative consequences for wider U.S.–Latin American relations.

For one thing, such optimism appeared warranted in light of previous experience. In 1989, Latin American governments had protested loudly against the unilateral U.S. invasion of Panama. However, several of them had also privately acknowledged that they had few qualms about the forcible removal from office of the Panamanian dictator, Manuel Noriega. Significantly, in the aftermath of the Panama intervention, nobody in the hemisphere took any retaliatory measures against the United States.[99] Quite the opposite. Latin American cooperation with Washington increased steadily in subsequent years. During the planning for the Haiti intervention, the Panama precedent was interpreted in Washington as suggesting that regardless of multilateral approval, Latin American countries were unlikely to react to a renewed U.S. pro-democracy intervention in the hemisphere by reducing their cooperation with the United States on other issues.[100]

Moreover, by the mid-1990s, most Latin American countries were deeply enmeshed in mutually beneficial relations with the United States. The Clinton administration had actively sought since 1993 to promote free trade agreements, liberal market reforms, and U.S. private investment in the region, while also increasing the overall amount of U.S.

97. Watson, author interview.
98. Feinberg, author interview.
99. Author interview with Michael Kozak, Acting AssistSecState for Western Hemisphere Affairs in 1989, and head of State Department's Haiti working group in 1994 (June 23, 2009). See also Baker 1995: 193.
100. Babbitt and Kozak, author interviews.

[101]

development assistance to its southern neighbors. The North American Free Trade Agreement (NAFTA) between the United States, Canada, and Mexico, had just come into force in January 1994. By calling for the first Summit of the Americas to be held in Miami in December 1994, the Clinton administration had announced its intention to further promote cross-border economic integration in the hemisphere. During related discussions with Latin American partners, senior U.S. officials never concealed the fact that the administration would "work a lot harder to get a trade agreement through Congress with a country that had cooperated with [the U.S. government] on issues that mattered to [the United States]."[101] In short, policymakers in Washington expected that their Latin American counterparts would be pragmatic enough to understand that their countries had the most to lose from a deterioration of bilateral relationships with the United States.[102]

Finally, there was no expectation among senior Clinton administration officials that securing UNSC approval would appease those Latin American countries that had most strongly condemned the prospect of U.S. intervention during the spring and early summer of 1994 (such as Mexico, Uruguay, and Venezuela) and induce them to moderate their rhetorical opposition. Lake recalls that he didn't "expect them, practically under any circumstances, to be in favor of an American intervention in the hemisphere, because of history."[103] Gray, the administration's Haiti adviser, similarly predicted during congressional testimony in early June 1994 that "under no circumstances would [some Latin American countries] favor military intervention."[104]

Lake and his colleagues were right in their expectation that securing a UN mandate for the use of force would have little impact on the level of rhetorical opposition in the hemisphere. As the negotiations at the SC entered their crucial phase, those Latin American countries that had most strongly opposed the prospect of U.S. intervention in previous weeks made it clear that they would inexorably remain opposed, regardless of whether or not there was UN approval. On July 31, 1994, during a SC debate immediately preceding the adoption of Resolution 940, the representatives of Mexico, Uruguay, Cuba, and Venezuela insisted that in their view, the situation in Haiti did not constitute a threat to international peace and security, which made it impossible for them to support military intervention. The Venezuelan representative, speaking more bluntly than several of his colleagues but seemingly capturing the mood

101. Babbitt, author interview.
102. Feinberg and Watson, author interviews.
103. Lake, author interview.
104. Gray statement (June 8, 1994), 9.

among Latin American governments, stated that his country could "not support *unilateral* or *multilateral* military actions in any nation of the hemisphere."[105]

Among the skeptical Latin American countries, Brazil was the only one represented on the SC. (Argentina, the other Latin American member of the SC at the time, broke with its regional partners in supporting the use of force and voted in favor of Resolution 940.) Ultimately Brazil, yielding to significant diplomatic pressure from Washington, abstained on the crucial vote. But the Brazilian representative nevertheless criticized the resolution's wording as "not felicitous" and explained that his government had "serious difficulties" with its content.[106] After the adoption of Resolution 940, the governments of Peru and Bolivia joined their aforementioned Latin American neighbors in publicly condemning the prospective U.S. intervention.[107]

Summing up, there is no evidence that the Clinton administration's efforts to secure UNSC approval for the Haiti intervention were motivated by concerns about costly international opposition in the form of negative issue linkage. U.S. policymakers anticipated that UN approval would do little to reduce the rhetorical opposition of most Latin American governments, but they were also quite sanguine that such opposition would be of little practical consequence. Countries outside the Western Hemisphere had no interest in upsetting their bilateral relationship with Washington by threatening retaliatory measures in opposition to an intervention to which the United States appeared increasingly committed.

Epilogue: The 2004 Intervention

Former deputy secretary of state Talbott (2008: 302) acknowledges that in the aftermath of the 1994 intervention, the United States "prematurely declared that [its] mission had been accomplished" and probably "underestimated the difficulty of establishing democracy in a country that had never really had such a thing." After Aristide's restoration to the presidency, his rule became increasingly arbitrary, encouraging the emergence

---

105. UNSC, record of 3413th meeting, July 31, 1994 (Doc. S/PV.3413), 8 (emphasis added).
106. Ibid, 9. On U.S. pressure toward Brazil, see LatinNews.com, "Another Two-Step from Washington."
107. Statements by the permanent missions of Peru and Bolivia to the OAS, respectively, on Aug 4 and 5, 1994 (published in the same folder as OAS/OEA, "Acta de la séptima sesión."). See also Bassir Pour and Frachon, *Le Monde*, Aug. 2, 1994.

of local paramilitary groups that sought to overthrow him. Violent clashes between progovernment and opposition forces first emerged around the year 2000. But the violence became more intense toward the end of 2003, and by February 2004, armed opposition groups had seized control of Haiti's second-largest city, Cap Haïtien (Polgreen, *NYT*, Feb. 23, 2004). That once again led to concerns in the United States about a potentially massive inflow of Haitian refugees to Florida. Furthermore, as in 1994, the Congressional Black Caucus put pressure on the U.S. president to intervene militarily and restore political stability (Howell and Barfield Berry, *South Florida Sun-Sentinel*, Feb. 27, 2004).

The Joint Chiefs and the Pentagon leadership more generally initially opposed any renewed commitment of American forces to Haiti, highlighting the risks of an open-ended mission that in their view was not justified given the limited U.S. interests at stake (Slevin and Graham, *WashPo*, Feb. 24, 2004). On this occasion, with hundreds of thousands of American troops already deployed in Afghanistan and Iraq, no senior policymaker in Washington appears to have advocated a U.S. intervention without IO approval. Nevertheless, the available evidence suggests that America's top-level military leaders again played an important role in making a UNSC mandate that also explicitly foresaw a follow-on UN mission a necessary condition for intervention. Colin Powell, now Secretary of State, initially sided with the Pentagon in seeking to prevent any renewed U.S. military involvement in Haiti. However, by late February 2004, Powell realized that unless the United States acted swiftly to facilitate a political compromise solution and restore stability, it might find itself dragged into a potentially much larger peace-enforcement mission down the road (Slevin, *WashPo*, March 2, 2004; Slevin, *WashPo*, March 15, 2004). As the situation in Haiti deteriorated further and the insurgents threatened to invade the country's capital, Port-au-Prince, President George W. Bush and his principal advisers agreed that the United States might have to intervene militarily. But they decided that U.S. troops would be deployed only as part of a UN authorized multinational force and only after the local parties had reached a negotiated political solution (Slevin and Graham, *WashPo*, Feb. 28, 2004).

On February 29, under strong pressure from Washington, Aristide resigned from the Haitian presidency and left the country, carried to the Central African Republic on a U.S. airplane (Polgreen and Weiner, *NYT*, Mar. 1, 2004; Miller and Curl, *WashTimes*, Mar. 2, 2004).[108] Later on that same day, the UNSC unanimously adopted Resolution 1529, authorizing the deployment of an interim multinational force led by the United

---

108. Aristide insisted that he was "kidnapped" by American forces.

States and France, "for a period of not more than three months," after which "a follow-on United Nations stabilization force [would take over responsibility for] the maintenance of a secure and stable environment."[109] On this occasion, securing a UN mandate was relatively straightforward. According to Jean-Marc de La Sablière (2013: 238), France's permanent representative to the SC at the time, he and his American counterpart received instructions to start negotiating a resolution authorizing the deployment of a multinational stabilization force only on the morning of February 29, after Aristide's resignation. By the late afternoon, the resolution was unanimously adopted, with even Brazil voting in its favor. Even conceding that informal negotiations on the resolution might have occurred at the ministerial level in previous days, securing UN approval was clearly much easier than it had been in 1994.

By early March 2004, about 1,900 peacekeepers from four countries (the United States, France, Canada, and Chile) had been deployed, with Washington initially contributing two-thirds of the UN force (Weiner and Polgreen, NYT, March 7, 2004). On June 1, in line with the original plan, stabilization tasks were handed over to a follow-on UN force of about 6,700 troops, led by Brazil, which allowed a gradual withdrawal of most American forces (Weiner, NYT, June 2, 2004). Although in 2004 securing a UN mandate was not particularly costly to the United States, it appears that as in 1994, the uniformed leaders' concerns about a potentially open-ended commitment resulted in a very risk-averse U.S. approach. The model established in terms of U.S.-UN cooperation ten years earlier served as a blueprint, and the prospect of a rapid UN hand-off once again facilitated the emergence of an intra-administration consensus in favor of intervention. In January 2010, the overall force levels of the UN stabilization mission in Haiti (MINUSTAH) were temporarily increased to facilitate the delivery of emergency humanitarian assistance after a devastating earthquake that killed an estimated 220,000 people (Sheridan and Booth, WashPo, Jan. 19, 2010). In the days and weeks that followed, more than ten thousand American troops were deployed to Haiti on a short-term humanitarian mission, code-named Operation Unified Response. However, virtually all those troops had left again by late May 2010, and while the United States continued to provide assistance through civilian agencies, UN forces from other countries were again left to deal with the longer-term stabilization and reconstruction burden (Cecchine et al. 2013: 39–43, 54–55).

As we have seen, civil-military bargaining played a key role in motivating the United States to seek UN approval for the 1994 Haiti

109. SCR 1529 (2004), §§ 2, 3.

intervention. It was clear from the outset that securing this approval would be costly to the United States, given the recalcitrance of key international partners such as Russia, China, and Brazil. The most hawkish U.S. civilian policymakers on the NSC staff and at the State Department at first downplayed the benefits of UN approval, and some of them explicitly recommended bypassing the SC to maximize U.S. freedom of action. However, America's top-level military leaders, by skillfully deploying their bureaucratic political influence and threatening to veto the intervention altogether, changed the cost-benefit calculus of even the most hawkish civilian policymakers and made UN approval practically a necessary condition for U.S. intervention.

Other factors often said to motivate the United States to seek IO approval played at best a secondary role. First, U.S. domestic politics affected decision making only indirectly. In particular, concerns about congressional support arose only after the JCS made it clear that once the United States intervened militarily, securing U.S. strategic objectives would almost certainly require a resource-intensive and open-ended stabilization mission. Hence to the extent that concerns about Congress mattered, the uniformed leaders functioned as a crucial transmission belt. Second, there is no evidence that an internalized desire to comply with international norms motivated U.S. IO approval, as the most influential policymakers never viewed such approval as intrinsically desirable, let alone necessary. Finally, policymakers were not motivated by concerns about negative issue linkage: senior Clinton administration officials were sanguine that even those countries that most strongly condemned the prospective intervention, notably in Latin America, would not reduce their cooperation with the United States in other policy domains, regardless of whether or not there was UN approval.

[4]

Bosnia, 1992–95: Keeping the
U.S. Military from "Owning" It

Soon after ethnic war broke out in Bosnia and Herzegovina in the spring of 1992, humanitarian activists in the United States—including senior civilian policymakers—began advocating coercive air strikes against Bosnian Serb military targets. Washington's Western European allies remained reluctant to openly take sides in the Bosnian conflict and contemplate coercive air strikes through NATO. Consequently, as the ethnic violence intensified from 1993 onward, U.S. ambassador to the UN Madeleine Albright and Assistant Secretary of State Richard Holbrooke began insisting that the United States should unilaterally bomb Bosnian Serb strongholds to roll back Serb territorial gains and facilitate a negotiated settlement. National Security Adviser Anthony Lake and several other U.S. policymakers were sympathetic to those hawkish proposals. Nevertheless, the United States clung to a multilateral course throughout the Bosnian War, seeking approval for even limited retaliatory air strikes from the United Nations Security Council and NATO's North Atlantic Council.

Proceeding multilaterally through the UNSC and NATO's NAC greatly constrained Washington's freedom of action. The first limited air strikes were not authorized until April 1994, and for over a year thereafter, the application of airpower remained highly ineffective, based on the lowest common denominator among NATO members. Moreover, the Clinton administration's hawkish rhetoric, combined with a hesitant multilateral approach in practice, sent mixed signals to the warring factions on the ground, making a negotiated solution less likely and exacerbating the humanitarian crisis. By late 1994, the visible contradiction between the administration's tough rhetoric and very hesitant action was seriously harming its domestic and international standing. Why, then, did President Clinton hold on to a cautious multilateral course throughout the conflict despite the clamor for a more muscular U.S. approach from his hawkish advisers and significant portions of the American public?

Process tracing based on primary evidence from interviews and declassified documents reveals that America's senior military leaders played a central role in keeping the United States on a multilateral track. The generals and admirals viewed American interests in the region as limited and expressed strong reservations about sending U.S. ground troops to Bosnia in the absence of a peace agreement, fearing that they might become embroiled in a Vietnam-style quagmire. Even limited air strikes, they cautioned, might lead the United States down a slippery slope toward a resource-intensive troop deployment that Congress might not support.

The uniformed leaders voiced particularly strong opposition to U.S. unilateral action, out of concern that it would leave the United States with primary responsibility for imposing and then policing a peace agreement in Bosnia. Specifically, they worried that unilateral air strikes without approval from NATO and the UN might prompt the Western European allies to withdraw their own troops, deployed as UN peacekeepers, leaving the United States to "own" the conflict in Bosnia without a viable exit strategy. Even when President Clinton decided after the Srebrenica massacre of July 1995 that heavier air strikes were necessary, the U.S. military leaders insisted on closely coordinating the bombing through NATO to avoid alienating the European allies and to ensure that the latter would subsequently shoulder most of the burden for Bosnia's stabilization.

The available evidence indicates that the Joint Chiefs were able to veto U.S. unilateral intervention by highlighting the high risks and likely operational costs of such a course of action and forging a blocking coalition with similarly minded civilian leaders (primarily Secretaries of Defense Les Aspin and William Perry but also Secretary of State Warren Christopher). More hawkish civilian policymakers such as Albright and Lake therefore needed to secure IO approval and specific assurances of multilateral burden sharing in order to mollify the reluctant generals and overcome their veto. The chapter also evaluates prominent alternative hypotheses that link U.S. efforts to secure IO approval to norm internalization and concerns about issue linkage, but finds them unsupported by the evidence.

LIMITING U.S. LIABILITY BY STAYING OUT OF IT, 1992–93

After the Yugoslav Federation began to unravel with the secession of Slovenia and Croatia in 1991, U.S. intelligence sources estimated that

"Bosnia-Herzegovina's prospects are dim," and they highlighted the risk of imminent ethnic violence "characterized by widespread and chaotic skirmishing."[1] In spite of such stark warnings, the international community adopted a largely hands-off approach, with only limited and belated mediation attempts. In 1992, fighting broke out in Bosnia-Herzegovina (henceforth Bosnia) between Bosnian Serb paramilitary units, supported by elements of the Serb-dominated Yugoslav National Army, and Bosnian Muslim and Bosnian Croat militias. By the fall of 1992, with assistance from the rump Yugoslav government under Slobodan Milosevic, the Bosnian Serbs (roughly one-third of Bosnia's total population) had gained control of about 70 percent of the country. The Bosnian Serb offensive soon culminated in the siege of Sarajevo, a formerly thriving multicultural city. The resulting humanitarian tragedy, broadcast live on television across the globe, generated increasing public pressure on Western governments to act to relieve the suffering (Burg and Shoup 1999: 128–80; Holbrooke 1998: 24–33).

The United States, under President George H. W. Bush, viewed the breakup of Yugoslavia as a regional, or European, problem that did not affect major U.S. strategic interests (Baker 1995: 636, 645–48; Halberstam 2001: 42–46). A few senior officials at the State Department, notably Assistant Secretary Robert Gallucci, raised the possibility of a U.S.-led humanitarian intervention—but the president and his principal foreign policy advisers showed little interest in such proposals.[2] In order to minimize its exposure without appearing indifferent to the suffering, the Bush administration supported the involvement of NATO and the United Nations. The Atlantic alliance began low-key naval operations in mid-1992 aimed at monitoring, and then enforcing, a UN arms and trade embargo on the Adriatic Sea, and it subsequently imposed a no-fly zone over Bosnia (Schulte 1997: 20–21; Leurdijk 1994: 24–35). In late 1992 the UN Security Council, acting under European initiative and with Washington's support, established a UN peacekeeping mission, known as the United Nations Protection Force (UNPROFOR), with a narrow mandate that was initially limited to facilitating the delivery of humanitarian assistance. The United States did not contribute any troops to UNPROFOR, reflecting the president's reluctance and the staunch opposition of the U.S. military establishment. As General Colin Powell, then the JCS

---

1. CIA, "Bosnia-Hercegovina: On the Edge of the Abyss," memorandum, Dec. 19, 1991. Most declassified documents cited in this chapter are available at http://www.foia.cia.gov.
2. Author interview with Robert Gallucci, AssistSecState for Pol-Mil Affairs, 1992–94 (Apr. 20, 2011). See also Halberstam 2001: 34.

chairman, recalls, "The U.S. military were not that anxious to get into what looked like a real swamp."[3]

During the 1992 U.S. presidential election campaign, candidate Bill Clinton strongly criticized the Bush administration's hands-off approach on Bosnia, insisting that Washington had to show "real leadership." While Clinton stopped short of advocating the deployment of American ground troops, he indicated that if elected, he would consider bombing Bosnian Serb military positions from the air. Furthermore, he demanded a lifting of the UN arms embargo, which had been imposed on the entire territory of the former Yugoslavia in 1991 and was now hitting the Bosnian Muslims hardest (Daalder 2000: 6; Chollet 2005: 4).[4]

Once in office, however, Clinton backtracked on his forceful campaign rhetoric. The president and his administration adopted a tough rhetorical stance, trying to appease various domestic constituencies that were calling for U.S. leadership on Bosnia while at the same time continuing to minimize America's involvement. The administration began by undermining the Vance-Owen peace plan—a European-backed proposal for the ethnic cantonization of Bosnia that would have required a significant contribution of U.S. troops for its effective enforcement—claiming that it was too favorable to the Bosnian Serbs (Burg and Shoup 1999: 233–51; Halberstam 2001: 197–98; Gibbs 2009: 142–47). During the spring of 1993, the president and his advisers then settled on an approach that became known as "lift and strike." They believed that through a combination of lifting the arms embargo and launching coercive air strikes against Bosnian Serb positions, they could (1) help roll back Serb territorial gains and (2) establish a more equal balance of power on the ground—thereby facilitating a negotiated settlement that would not simply ratify the results of ethnic cleansing (Drew 1995: 149–52; Burg and Shoup 1999: 251–53). The president, however, was unwilling to implement the policy unilaterally. Consequently, from May 1993 onward, the Clinton administration sought UN and NATO approval for air strikes and lifting the arms embargo (Halberstam 2001: 225–26; Daalder 2000: 15–17).

The Costs of Washington's Multilateral Approach

Seeking UN and NATO approval for military action entailed significant costs. First, it limited the United States' flexibility and undermined

3. Author interview with Gen. Colin Powell (Feb. 2, 2011). See also Baker 1995: 648–49; Halberstam 2001: 34–38.
4. The Bosnian Serbs and Bosnian Croats had their arsenals refueled through illicit arms transfers from Belgrade and Zagreb, respectively.

its coercive leverage, allowing the ethnic killing in Bosnia to continue largely unabated for over two years. Second, transatlantic disagreements over air strikes resulted in serious tensions between the United States and its Western European allies. NATO might have suffered permanent damage if changing circumstances on the ground had not eventually brought the alliance back together, allowing it to claim an important role in ending the war. Finally, by the spring of 1995, Washington's tough rhetoric, combined with a hesitant multilateral approach in practice, had left President Clinton open to accusations of inconsistency that greatly increased his domestic political vulnerability.

Limited and Ineffectual Air Strikes

The use of airpower first became an issue of contention between the United States and its Western European allies in the spring of 1993. Between April and May, the UNSC designated the (Muslim-majority) Bosnian towns of Srebrenica, Tuzla, Zepa, Gorazde, and Bihac, as well as the capital Sarajevo, as "safe areas." The ostensible goal was to prevent the Bosnian Serbs from taking control of those Muslim enclaves under siege (UNGA 1999: 16–17; Leurdijk 1994: 45). On June 4, under American prodding, the UNSC adopted Resolution 836, which authorized "member states, acting nationally or through regional organizations, . . . and subject to close coordination with the [UN] Secretary General and UNPROFOR," to take "all necessary measures, through the use of air power . . . in reply to bombardments against the safe areas." This provided the legal basis for NATO air strikes to defend the UN safe areas. As Gregory Schulte, then the director of NATO's Bosnia task force, remembers, "Our first involvement was really as a subcontractor to the United Nations."[5] Yet the UN did not provide a blank authorization for the use of force in defense of the safe areas—instead, it became deeply involved in managing many operational aspects of the air strikes.

In August 1993, as the Bosnian Serbs came close to encircling Sarajevo, the Western Europeans cautiously agreed to the use of NATO airpower in principle. Their acquiescence came at a heavy price: air strikes against specific targets would have to be authorized not only by NATO's Southern Command in Naples but also by the UN secretary-general or his designated representative in the Balkans. The cumbersome "dual key" arrangement was thus born, which allowed both NATO and the UN to veto American air strikes (Leurdijk 1994: 47–48; Sarooshi 2008: 236–37). The primary reason for this arrangement was that the Western Europeans were reluctant to openly take sides in the conflict and start bombing

5. Author interview with Gregory Schulte (Mar. 9, 2010).

the Bosnian Serbs. The British and French, in particular, had thousands of their own troops deployed in Bosnia as part of UNPROFOR, and they feared that NATO air strikes would lead to reprisals against their lightly armed peacekeepers (Burg and Shoup 1999: 253–55; Daalder 2000: 15–17).

Over the next two years, the British and French played what Robert Hunter, then the U.S. ambassador to NATO, calls a "double game." Under pressure from Washington, on several occasions London and Paris "would agree to turn NATO's key, but each time they were then going to [UN Secretary-General] Boutros-Ghali and telling him not to turn the UN key."[6] NATO did not actually launch its first limited air strikes until the spring of 1994. On April 10, 1994, seeking to deter Bosnian Serb forces from further advances against the Gorazde safe area, U.S. aircraft dropped a total of three bombs on a Serb artillery command facility, followed the next day by a NATO strike against a Serb tank and two armored personnel carriers (UNGA 1999: 34; Burg 2003: 61). Such "pinprick" air strikes, as they were derisively characterized in the media, had no strategic impact on the course of the war. Indeed, the Europeans' reluctance to shift to heavier bombing, combined with the Clinton administration's unwillingness to either beef up UNPROFOR by deploying American ground troops or implement air strikes unilaterally, signaled Western weakness and thus jeopardized the security of the safe areas that the allies had pledged to protect.

Mounting Transatlantic Tensions

Soon after NATO's bombing of Bosnian Serb military facilities near Gorazde in April 1994, the Serbs took about 150 UN peacekeepers hostage, initiating a pattern of tit-for-tat retaliation that would repeat itself several times over the next year (UNGA 1999: 34; Burg and Shoup 1999: 147–49). The danger to UNPROFOR as a result of Washington's insistence on air strikes was now no longer simply a theoretical possibility.

Tensions between the United States and its European allies who had troops in UNPROFOR came to a head in the fall of 1994. In October, Bosnian Muslim forces launched an offensive out of the Bihac safe area, but they were quickly repulsed by a Bosnian Serb counterattack, and Bihac came under heavy shelling. Britain and France at first publicly blamed the Bosnian Muslims, pointing out that they had initiated the fighting (Gordon, Jehl, and Sciolino, *NYT*, Dec. 4, 1994). Nevertheless, as Bihac risked being overrun by the Serb counteroffensive, London and Paris reluctantly agreed to NATO air strikes. Far from withdrawing, the Bosnian Serbs took about 250 UN peacekeepers hostage in a dramatic

---

6. Author interview with Robert Hunter (Mar. 11, 2010). See also Chollet 2005: 32.

escalation of the conflict. Radovan Karadzic, the Bosnian Serb leader, defiantly proclaimed that if NATO air strikes continued, UN peacekeepers would be dealt with as enemy forces (Daalder 2000: 31–32; Halberstam 2001: 284–85).

When in subsequent days Washington insisted on heavier bombing, Paris and London reacted furiously. "It's nice to say you want to help the victims against the aggressors, but it bears no relation to what is happening on the ground," a senior French military official told U.S. media, before adding, "The Americans say they know what is right and what we should do, but they don't even dare to put their troops on the line" (quoted in Drozdiak, *WashPo*, Nov. 23, 1994). The British defense minister concurred, pointing out that the United States should "match words [with] deeds and that doesn't include just a few aircraft" (quoted in Halberstam 2001: 285). British and French leaders increasingly saw U.S. behavior as reckless, and they began to openly question Washington's security commitment to Europe and thus ultimately the viability of NATO (Daalder 2000: 7, 33; Halberstam 2001: 285). Grasping the seriousness of the situation, President Clinton's principal foreign policy advisers concluded on November 28 that it would be "futile to attempt to win international support for a more robust air campaign" and decided to call off any further air strikes.[7]

In the aftermath of the November 1994 Bihac crisis, reducing tensions with the NATO allies became a key U.S. strategic imperative. The president's principal advisers decided that "priority must be given to ameliorating strains within NATO that have been exacerbated by recent Bosnia developments."[8] That further undermined Washington's ability to influence the course of the war on the ground, as it meant that for the time being, assertive American leadership and any recourse to coercive diplomacy were out of the question. As National Security Adviser Lake acknowledged in a secret memo for the president written shortly after the Bihac crisis, "the 'stick' of military pressure seems no longer viable."[9] The overall result was an even more reactive and seemingly directionless U.S. policy toward Bosnia.

NATO was essentially paralyzed for most of the spring of 1995. Not until July, after the massacre of seven thousand Bosnian Muslims at Srebrenica, did the alliance finally reach a consensus to use airpower more assertively in defense of the remaining safe areas (Burg and Shoup 1999: 344–50; Chollet 2005: 25–30). Yet even Operation Deliberate Force,

7. NSC/PC, "Meeting on Bosnia," memorandum for the record, Nov. 29, 1994.
8. Ibid.
9. Anthony Lake, "Bosnia Policy after the Fall of Bihac," memorandum for the Pres., Nov. 27, 1994.

[113]

NATO's more substantial air campaign in August and September 1995 (discussed in more detail below), remained highly constrained. Ambassador Hunter recalls "constant concerns" among European countries about the air strikes' legality. For that reason, tight "political control was maintained over the conduct of the air campaign" throughout.[10] The overarching goal of holding the alliance together narrowly limited NATO air strikes to military targets, while higher-impact dual-use targets always remained off-limits (Burg 2003: 67; Gibbs 2009: 166–67; Daalder 2000: 131–32). Notwithstanding allied rhetoric at the time about "decisive action," the contribution of Operation Deliberate Force to ending the war remains disputed. A secret CIA report concluded soon after the air campaign ended that its coercive success had been "moderate," although it had "greatly encouraged" the Bosnian Muslims and Croats, who were by then engaged in an all-out ground offensive against the Bosnian Serbs.[11]

Growing Political Trouble for the President

The Clinton administration's tentative approach between 1993 and 1995 in some respects made matters worse in Bosnia. On the one hand, the threat of force against the Bosnian Serbs emboldened the opposing Bosnian Muslim faction, making it more daring militarily and less willing to compromise at the negotiating table. At the same time, Washington's hesitations and its unwillingness to move beyond the lowest common multilateral denominator encouraged the Serbs to react to Muslim provocations in an increasingly brutal fashion, culminating in the Srebrenica massacre of July 1995. David Owen, the EU's chief Balkans envoy during the Bosnian conflict, bluntly writes that "from the spring of 1993 to the summer of 1995, . . . the effect of US policy . . . was to prolong the war" (quoted in Gibbs 2009: 148; see also Burg 2003: 62–63).

By the spring of 1995, the visible inconsistency between the Clinton administration's words and its deeds had become a serious domestic political liability, with the president's approval ratings on foreign policy on a downward slide (Woodward 1996: 255; Soderberg 2005: 81). The events at Srebrenica in July 1995 provoked further condemnation of Clinton's exceedingly timid approach in U.S. and international media (Power 2003: 430). Robert Dole, the Republican Senate majority leader and likely 1996 presidential candidate, had long been an outspoken activist on Bosnia. That positioned him well to make the massacre at Srebrenica a subject for American politics. For months, Dole had been advocating a

10. Hunter, author interview.
11. CIA, "Impact of the NATO Air Campaign in Bosnia," Sept. 19, 1995.

unilateral lifting of the international arms embargo. In late July 1995, under Dole's initiative, Congress approved a bill that in fact mandated an end to U.S. participation in the arms embargo—thus exposing the bankruptcy of the president's policy (Woodward 1996: 264–65; Daalder 2000: 61–64, 165; Power 2003: 422–29). As a former senior aide to President Clinton explains, in the aftermath of Srebrenica, "the political damage resulting from the portrayal of the president and the administration as being inept and allowing something like this to happen was no longer acceptable."[12]

Furthermore, in December 1994, seeking to soothe transatlantic tensions after the Bihac crisis, the U.S. president had made a costly pledge: if the peacekeepers of NATO allies in Bosnia came under fire and had to be withdrawn, the United States would be prepared to place up to twenty-five thousand of its own "ground forces at NATO's disposal to extricate UNPROFOR personnel."[13] As the situation in Bosnia deteriorated in subsequent months, the prospect became increasingly real that the United States might have to carry out that promise.[14] The president's senior policy advisers agreed that "politically, it would be extremely difficult to reject a call from a troop contributing state for . . . assistance in withdrawal."[15] Therefore, by the spring of 1995, the administration risked being drawn into precisely the situation it had doggedly sought to avoid for more than two years. U.S. ground troops might now end up in Bosnia, under the most dangerous of circumstances, with a concrete possibility of getting sucked into the conflict "and being unable to leave."[16] The prospect of having to carry out such a high-risk withdrawal operation in the middle of the presidential election campaign became a political nightmare for the president and his administration (Stephanopoulos 1999: 383; Power 2003: 424).

In short, it is evident that the Clinton administration's multilateral approach through NATO and the UN entailed significant costs. Had the president been willing to carry out air strikes unilaterally, without IO approval, the United States might have been able to end the war much sooner and save tens of thousands of Bosnian lives. Furthermore, if the

12. Author interview with Donald Kerrick, Director of European Affairs on the NSC staff, 1994–95 (Mar. 22, 2010).
13. NSC/PC, "Meeting on Bosnia," memorandum for the record, Nov. 29, 1994.
14. UNPROFOR withdrawal would be "a virtual certainty," U.S. intelligence predicted, if Washington unilaterally lifted the arms embargo. See National Intelligence Council, "Prospects for UNPROFOR Withdrawal," Dec. 1994.
15. NSC/PC, "Meeting on Bosnia," SumConcl, May 23, 1995. See also Anthony Lake, "Principals' Review of Bosnia," memorandum for the Pres., May 2, 1995.
16. Alexander Vershbow, "Bosnia: Strategic Choices," NSC staff discussion paper, May 17, 1995. See also Daalder 2000: 46–48; Holbrooke 1998: 65–67.

United States had stopped short of involving NATO, the Western Europeans could have publicly disassociated themselves from U.S. action,
making the Bosnian Serbs less likely to retaliate by targeting peacekeepers from NATO countries and sparing the alliance one of the worst crises
in its history during the Bihac fiasco. At the same time, had the United
States moved ahead unilaterally, it would probably have ended up owning primary responsibility for Bosnia for the indefinite future. As journalist Bob Woodward (1996: 254) notes, involving "the United Nations
and NATO . . . somewhat insulated the Clinton administration from full
responsibility in Bosnia." U.S. decision makers, however, disagreed as to
whether the United States should prioritize limiting its own liability or
instead take decisive action to help end the war, and between 1993 and
1995, the policy debate was often heated.

DEBATING THE (UNILATERAL) USE OF FORCE

Besides President Clinton himself, the principal officials who shaped
U.S. Bosnia policy from 1993 onward were National Security Adviser
Anthony Lake, Secretary of State Warren Christopher, Secretary of
Defense Les Aspin (replaced by William Perry in early 1994), U.S.
Ambassador to the United Nations Madeleine Albright, JCS Chairman
Colin Powell (replaced by John Shalikashvili at the end of 1993), and
Director of Central Intelligence (DCI) James Woolsey (replaced by John
Deutch in early 1995). Vice President Al Gore and his national security
adviser, Leon Fuerth, also played an important role in the debates about
Bosnia. It became apparent soon after the administration came to office
in early 1993 that there was no consensus among those top-ranking officials on greater U.S. involvement in the Balkans, and in the absence of
strong presidential leadership this resulted in intense bureaucratic
infighting.[17]

A Divided Administration

More than any other senior policy official in Washington, Albright,
who as U.S. ambassador to the UN enjoyed cabinet-level status, champi-
oned the use of force against the Bosnian Serbs. In 1993, she declared in
a memo distributed to her fellow NSC principals: "We have never tested
the proposition that American military intervention might intimidate the
Bosnian Serb militia and their patrons in Belgrade. That premise should

---

17. For good overviews see Halberstam 2001: 196–97; Drew 1995: 145–49.

be tested."[18] Albright viewed the Bosnian War as a straightforward tale of victimhood and aggression, and she felt genuine outrage at the humanitarian tragedy (Albright 2003: 177–80; see also Power 2003: 326). Moreover, having spent part of her childhood in Yugoslavia (her father was the Czechoslovak ambassador to Belgrade after World War II), she considered the Balkans an important U.S. strategic interest. "We are treating this area as of peripheral interest. History suggests it is more central," she asserted at an NSC meeting in February 1993.[19]

Lake, too, was an avowed activist on Bosnia. During an NSC meeting in April 1993, he "introduced" the option of "coming in with air power to support Muslim activities."[20] However, Lake initially stopped short of advocating a particular course of action and sought to proceed by means of a consensus with the other principals. As the administration's chief foreign policy coordinator, he took the views of his more reluctant colleagues seriously. He also understood that the Bosnian Muslims were attempting to lure the United States into the war on their side (Halberstam 2001: 196; Power 2003: 316). Fuerth was more forward-leaning and thought that the United States might have to use force to impose a settlement. "We should insist that the guns be silenced or we will try to silence them," he declared at an early NSC meeting.[21]

Secretary of State Christopher, a risk-averse individual and World War II veteran, clearly had reservations about using American force in Bosnia (Drew 1995: 159–60; Halberstam 2001: 333–34). The chief U.S. diplomat viewed the conflict there as a "morass" of deep distrust and ancient hatreds, and he pushed back against those who advocated military intervention in support of the Bosnian Muslims, pointing out that "there are atrocities on all sides" (quoted in Sciolino, *NYT*, May 19, 1993). Furthermore, as Christopher declared before the House Foreign Affairs Committee in the summer of 1993, he believed that Bosnia "does not involve [America's] vital interests," and "at heart, . . . this is a European problem" (quoted in Holmes, *NYT*, June 4, 1993). Below Christopher, however, many State Department officials were quite hawkish on Bosnia and deeply unhappy about what they viewed as an overly timid U.S. approach. Beginning in the summer of 1993, several lower-ranking U.S. diplomats went public with their discontent, and some of them resigned in protest (Power 2003: 313–14). The department's interventionists

18. Madeleine Albright, "Options for Bosnia," memorandum for the NatSec Adviser, Apr. 14, 1993.
19. Albright, "NSC/PC Meeting on Bosnia," minutes (Feb. 5, 1993), 1.
20. William Studeman, "CIA Debrief of PC Meeting on Bosnia," Apr. 9, 1993.
21. Leon Fuerth, "NSC/PC Meeting on Bosnia" (Feb. 5, 1993), 4. See also Albright 2003: 180.

gained a powerful ally in mid-1994 when Richard Holbrooke, an avowed humanitarian hawk, was appointed as assistant secretary of state for European affairs (Albright 2003: 184; Gibbs 2009: 149).

Albright and Fuerth were the administration's principal advocates of "lift and strike." The United States, they claimed, should lift the international arms embargo, thus enabling the Bosnian Muslims to better defend themselves, while striking Bosnian Serb strongholds from the air. As a former senior administration official who was himself skeptical of the policy recalls, they "wanted to end the fighting in Bosnia without having to send in ground troops, and believed that by using a combination of airpower and extra assistance to the Bosnian Muslims it could be done."[22] Albright (subsequently joined by Holbrooke) insisted on several occasions that if a multilateral consensus behind lift and strike could not be achieved at NATO and/or the UN, the United States should move ahead on its own. In a secret April 1993 memo, she explicitly raised the possibility of using airpower "unilateral[ly] . . . to demonstrate the commitment and will of the U.S."[23]

Meanwhile, senior officials at the Pentagon put up the staunchest and most effective resistance to U.S. intervention in Bosnia. America's senior military leaders viewed lift and strike as an ill-thought-out and potentially dangerous policy that might draw the United States into an open-ended commitment, and they vehemently opposed implementing it unilaterally. Civilian Pentagon officials unequivocally sided with the military: "There is no interest on the civilian side of this building in challenging the Joint Staff on issues like Bosnia," a senior Defense Department official remarked at the time (quoted in Quinn-Judge, *Boston Globe*, Apr. 20, 1994). General Powell, who continued to serve as JCS chairman until late 1993, was the most prominent and vocal of the opponents. The main lesson that Powell had learned from the Vietnam War, during which he had served as a junior officer, was that "limited war" and gradual escalation in the absence of clear objectives can lead to disastrous political outcomes (Powell 1995: 576; see also Drew 1995: 149; Halberstam 2001: 238–39). The reluctance of Powell and other U.S. military leaders to intervene in Bosnia was magnified after the Somalia debacle of October 1993, when eighteen U.S. Army Rangers were killed during clashes with local militias, resulting in a humiliating American withdrawal.[24]

---

22. Author interview with Walter Slocombe, Deputy UnderSecDef, 1993–94, and UnderSecDef for Policy, 1994–2001 (Mar. 11, 2010).
23. Albright, "Options for Bosnia." See also Daalder 2000: 13; Holbrooke 1998: 52.
24. Author interviews with Gen. Walter Kross, Director of the Joint Staff, 1994–96 (Feb. 11, 2011), and George Ward, Deputy AssistSecState for IO Affairs, 1992–96 (Apr. 4, 2011).

The Military's Skepticism about Air Strikes

The uniformed leaders were highly skeptical that limited air strikes could achieve U.S. strategic objectives. Walter Slocombe, undersecretary of defense for policy at the time, recalls the military's concerns as follows: "The military position was that there was no reason to believe that at the first whiff of gunpowder [Yugoslav president] Milosevic and [Bosnian Serb General Ratko] Mladic and [Bosnian Serb leader Radovan] Karadzic would cave. And we would have to explain [to those who advocated coercive air strikes] that there is no example of quickly bombing somebody into submission. And we needed to have a plan for what to do next."[25] In short, the uniformed leaders and their civilian allies at the Pentagon feared that even limited air strikes would put U.S. credibility on the line. In the absence of progress on the diplomatic front, the United States would then be under pressure to escalate further—until eventually, American combat troops might have to be deployed to impose and police a settlement (Avant 1996: 80–83).

General officers in the U.S. army and the Marine Corps were most skeptical of air strikes, wary of the burden that their services would have to bear during follow-on ground operations. As U.S. domestic pressure for air strikes increased in the spring of 1993, army General John Shalikashvili, Supreme Allied Commander (SACEUR) of NATO, publicly emphasized the risks of aerial bombing against Bosnian Serb military, pointing out that it would be largely ineffective, since the Serbs could easily reposition or hide their artillery (Williams, *WashPo*, Apr. 21, 1993). Marine Corps General John Sheehan, the director of operations (J-3) on the Joint Staff, told the media he could not fathom how the United States could possibly "declare victory and walk off the battlefield" after only launching air strikes (Williams, *WashPo*, Apr. 29, 1993). The only top-ranking military officer who was optimistic about what airpower on its own could achieve in Bosnia was, unsurprisingly, Air Force Chief of Staff General Merrill McPeak (Drew 1995: 279; Halberstam 2001: 39–41).

Powell and most other uniformed leaders acknowledged that in principle, the United States might rely exclusively on airpower to coerce the Bosnian Serbs into a negotiated settlement by engaging in "heavy bombing of the Serbs throughout the theater." But such a policy was deemed unfeasible because "it would be easy for the Serbs to respond by seizing UN humanitarian personnel as hostages" (Powell 1995: 576). Therefore, Powell informed his fellow NSC principals, airpower "solutions" wouldn't work to end the war: "we can use air power but ultimately

---

25. Slocombe, author interview.

must go in and separate the parties."[26] The only viable militarily solution would be a massive deployment of U.S. ground troops (estimated by the Joint Chiefs at seventy thousand) to impose a settlement by subduing the Bosnian Serbs through superior firepower, followed by a multiyear pacification campaign (Williams, *WashPo*, Apr. 24, 1993).[27] Ending the siege of Sarajevo alone, Powell advised, "would take a full infantry division [approximately twenty thousand troops] with air support."[28]

Senior Pentagon officials were convinced that, in view of America's limited interests in the region, the high risks and operational costs of deploying U.S. troops to Bosnia in a combat role were unwarranted. As Secretary of Defense Perry put it, "While Bosnia is in our interest, it is not in our vital interest and therefore it does not . . . warrant the risk of the lives of thousands of troops."[29] Civilian advocates of intervention such as Albright and Fuerth could point to high U.S. public support for air strikes, which remained above 50 percent (with spikes up to 70 percent) through most of the war (Sobel 2001: 184–90). Yet the military leaders, extrapolating from the Vietnam experience, feared that once American troops were deployed in combat, even a few casualties would cause domestic support to evaporate—and the 1993 Somalia debacle only reinforced this belief.[30] Secretary Perry, speaking for most of his Pentagon colleagues, judged that "there is no support either in the public or in the Congress for entering this war as a combatant."[31]

Hence the Pentagon's preferred course was for the United States to hold its nose and accept most Serb territorial gains while at the same time seeking to persuade the Bosnian Muslims to sign a permanent cease-fire along the existing lines of confrontation. Throughout the Bosnian War, the JCS and their civilian allies at the Pentagon argued that this would be an effective, relatively low-cost way of ending the fighting according to the principle of lesser evil.[32] In the eyes of the administration's humanitarian hawks, the Pentagon's suggestion to accept the results of ethnic cleansing as a means of stabilizing Bosnia was altogether unacceptable. The United States, Albright and her followers insisted, had a moral obligation "to resist evil" (Albright 2003: 177). Therefore,

26. Colin Powell, "NSC/PC Meeting on Bosnia" (Feb. 5, 1993), 2.
27. On the troop estimate see Drew 1995: 274.
28. Powell, "NSC/PC Meeting on Bosnia," 4.
29. William Perry, *U.S. Policy toward the Former Yugoslavia: Hearing Before the House NatSec Committee*, 104th Cong. (June 7, 1995), 5.
30. Kross and Slocombe, author interviews.
31. Perry, *U.S. Policy toward the Former Yugoslavia*.
32. Slocombe, author interview. See also Studeman, "CIA Debrief of PC Meeting on Bosnia"; Daalder 2000: 12, 105.

Washington should seek to reverse Serb territorial gains and deploy its formidable military muscle to help the Bosnian Muslims recover lost territory. For the humanitarian hawks, increasing America's commitment by intervening militarily—unilaterally if necessary—was highly desirable. "What are you saving this superb military for," Albright famously asked Powell, "if we can't use it?" (ibid., 182).

Clinging to Multilateralism: The Generals' Role

Between 1992 and 1995, the Joint Chiefs were able to keep the option of deploying U.S. ground troops to impose a settlement in Bosnia almost entirely off the table, primarily by highlighting its high risks and exorbitant costs. "We can perform this mission," Powell declared on one of the few occasions when the president's foreign policy team discussed the issue in early 1993. "But it will be expensive and could be open-ended with no promise of getting out."[33] For the most part, the uniformed leaders voiced their concerns privately in the intramural debates at the National Security Council and in various interagency meetings. Yet so long as civilian authorities remained divided over how to proceed, the JCS could also highlight the risks and likely operational costs in public, through press leaks, interviews, and open congressional hearings, thus weakening public support for intervention. As a senior civilian official affirmed, referring to the debate over armed intervention in Bosnia, "the Joint Chiefs of Staff exercise an incredible veto power over policies like this" (quoted in Quinn-Judge, *Boston Globe*, Apr. 20, 1994).

At the same time, the Joint Chiefs understood that the administration was under growing political pressure to react more forcefully to the ethnic violence in Bosnia. After Powell's retirement as JCS chairman in October 1993, General Shalikashvili and his deputy, Admiral William Owens, came to recognize that limited air strikes in response to Serb attacks might be acceptable—indeed, they could defuse calls for more serious U.S. military involvement. The military's view, Admiral Owens recalls, was that "if there were limited strikes, not strategic strikes, but limited strikes to teach them a lesson, that was a reasonable thing; [because] there was a lot of pressure to do something. But it would have to be very surgical, so as not to get us in deeper."[34]

Even limited air strikes, the JCS and the broader U.S. defense establishment insisted, should be approved by and channeled through NATO.

33. Powell, "NSC/PC Meeting on Bosnia," 7.
34. Author interview with Adm. William Owens (Jan. 27, 2011).

The uniformed leaders anticipated that keeping the Atlantic alliance fully involved would help spread the burden and socialize the risks of failure. If NATO airpower proved ineffective, others could be blamed, thus easing pressure on the United States to deploy ground troops in combat. By contrast, U.S. unilateral air strikes might prompt the European allies to withdraw their UNPROFOR peacekeepers from Bosnia, leaving the United States with full responsibility for the humanitarian and political situation on the ground. As General Walter Kross, then the director of the Joint Staff, recalls, "We didn't want UNPROFOR to leave. This was a potential quagmire, and we were briefing the NSC and the White House every week on this."[35]

So long as the Western European allies kept their UN peacekeepers in Bosnia, that would provide some buffer. Army Lieutenant General Donald Kerrick, then a senior NSC staffer for the Balkans, summarizes the U.S. military's outlook as follows: "UNPROFOR was there, the view was that they were ineffective, but at least they were trying to do something." The JCS, Kerrick explains, worried that if Washington implemented lift and strike unilaterally, "one, it could endanger UNPROFOR on the ground; two, it could cause UNPROFOR to withdraw—and then we would really own it."[36] Lieutenant General Wesley Clark, then the director for strategic plans and policy (J-5) on the Joint Staff, authored a study for the administration in which he insisted that conducting unilateral air strikes would "be very dangerous, in view of the prospect for UNPROFOR withdrawal" (Clark 2001: 41). In short, calls for U.S. unilateral intervention were anathema to the uniformed leaders: "Madeleine [Albright] was very aggressive in this area," remembers General Kross. "That was very concerning to us. We were very worried we were going to get stuck in there."[37]

The uniformed leaders pushed their civilian administration colleagues to more carefully consider the likely strategic implications of various courses of action, the ultimate goals they wanted to pursue, and the potential costs to the United States. "The military will do anything that is decided," Powell had explained back in 1993, "but we need to know what 'it' is that we are being asked to do."[38] By emphasizing that any U.S. military commitment toward Bosnia, even if initially limited to airpower, was likely to eventually result in a deployment of American ground troops (at least in a stabilization role), the generals also alerted their civilian colleagues to the question of the exit strategy. Fuerth acknowledges

35. Kross, author interview, confirmed by Slocombe, author interview.
36. Kerrick, author interview.
37. Kross, author interview.
38. Powell, "NSC/PC Meeting on Bosnia," 2.

with hindsight that the military's reluctance to intervene "was beneficial in the making of policy, because you couldn't make it sail unless you could make a case that would convince them that you knew why you were getting into this war and consequently you could define the circumstances under which you would get out."[39]

Restraining the Interventionist Hawks

Tracing the process of U.S. policymaking from the spring of 1993 onward further clarifies the military's role in keeping U.S. policy on a multilateral track. In May 1993, Secretary of State Christopher was dispatched across the Atlantic to seek to persuade the European allies to embrace lift and strike. But the allies, notably London and Paris, remained opposed (Drew 1995: 155–56; Daalder 2000: 16–17). Thereupon, Christopher told President Clinton that to persuade the Europeans, Washington would have "to tell them that we have firmly decided to go ahead . . . and that we expect them to support us" (Christopher 1998: 346–47; see also Halberstam 2001: 224–29). That however, would have required American willingness to carry out the air strikes unilaterally in case the Europeans continued to stall, because a hollow threat would have risked undermining Washington's credibility and future leverage.[40]

In July 1993, with Sarajevo under siege, the administration's humanitarian hawks, led by Albright, began insisting that the United States should in fact declare its willingness to implement air strikes unilaterally unless the Europeans came on board (Leurdijk 1994: 47-48; Drew 1995: 274–75; Daalder 2000: 19–21). By then, the administration was under strong domestic pressure from Congress to move ahead with air strikes (Fitchett, *NYT*, July 30, 1993). More than 60 percent of the American public also approved of air strikes at the time (Sobel 2001: 186). Consequently, as declassified documents show, in early August the administration was "considering air strikes in Bosnia without further international consultations."[41] However, given the administration's internal divisions, with the Pentagon and Secretary of State Christopher in opposition, the hawks were unable to forge a winning governmental coalition in favor of unilateral strikes. As Ambassador Hunter recalls, "That policy survived for about three days."[42]

---

39. Author interview with Leon Fuerth, NatSec Adviser to the VP, 1993–2001 (Mar. 9, 2010).
40. Lake, author interview.
41. Roger George and George Kolt, "Likely Allied Reactions to Unilateral US Actions in Bosnia," memorandum for the DCI, Aug. 5, 1993.
42. Hunter, author interview.

Secretary Christopher, although not opposed in principle to lift and strike, had been convinced by the military that any U.S. unilateral use of force would shift primary responsibility for Bosnia from the Western Europeans to the United States.[43] Already in the spring of 1993, Christopher had publicly echoed the generals' warning that rash unilateral initiatives might "well cause [the] allies to draw back, indeed maybe pull out their humanitarian efforts," with potentially disastrous consequences for the United States (quoted in Williams, *WashPo*, April 21, 1993). President Clinton himself appears to have been quite receptive to the military's arguments about the high risks and likely operational costs of implementing lift and strike without the European allies' consent. By the late summer of 1993, Clinton truncated the debate, making it clear that the United States would not intervene unilaterally: "I was reluctant to go [ahead with] unilaterally lifting the arms embargo," the former president recalls. "I also didn't want to divide the NATO alliance by unilaterally bombing Serb military positions, especially since there were European, but no American, soldiers on the ground" (Clinton 2004: 513; see also Daalder 2000: 17–18).

Changing circumstances on the ground subsequently led the humanitarian hawks to again push for more assertive action. NATO began to carry out a few limited bombing raids on Bosnian Serb military installations in the spring of 1994. For most of that year, as a former senior State Department official recalls, "it was really just the odd bomb here and there."[44] Then, in November, U.S. policymakers persuaded their reluctant Western European allies to support more substantial air strikes to defend the Bihac safe area. But as previously noted, after the Bosnian Serbs took about 250 peacekeepers hostage, spurring a serious transatlantic crisis, the Western Europeans were adamantly opposed to escalating the bombing. At that point, an intense bureaucratic debate unfolded among top-level U.S. national security officials.

On one side of the debate were the civilian hawks—Albright and Holbrooke, joined by Lake on this occasion—who insisted that Washington's credibility was on the line and that the air strikes should continue, unilaterally if necessary (Daalder 2000: 7–8, 31–33; Clark 2001: 42; Halberstam 2001: 285). On the other side were the risk-averse doves, notably senior Pentagon officials and Secretary of State Christopher. As the Western Europeans became more outspoken in their opposition to further air strikes in the final days of November 1994, Secretary of Defense Perry,

43. According to Admiral Owens, who was close to Christopher, "a fellow North Dakotan," the military had persuaded the Secretary of State to adopt a more "prudent" position on Bosnia. Owens, author interview. See also Christopher 1998: 345.
44. Hunter, author interview.

reflecting the generals' growing anxiety about a potential UNPROFOR withdrawal, seized the initiative. Perry publicly challenged his interventionist colleagues, declaring on national television that Washington should suspend the air strikes and accept the existing status quo on the ground—adding that anyway the Bosnian Muslims had "no prospect" of winning back lost territory (Marcus and Harris, *WashPo*, Dec. 5, 1994; see also Gordon, Jehl, and Sciolino, *NYT*, Dec. 4, 1994). Perry, supported by Christopher, ultimately convinced National Security Adviser Lake and President Clinton that the policy of using airpower to pressure the Bosnian Serbs should be abandoned. Lake, who had first backed the humanitarian hawks on this occasion before being outflanked by the Pentagon, seriously thought of resigning during those tense November days (Halberstam 2001: 285–86; Daalder 2000: 8).

In subsequent months, the Pentagon flexed its bureaucratic muscle once more over a similar issue. In the spring of 1995, the Bosnian Serbs again began shelling Sarajevo. Thereupon, following what had become a pattern, Albright, Holbrooke, and lower-ranking State Department officials began calling for air strikes. Now it was Albright who sought to outmaneuver her bureaucratic opponents by appealing to the American public and declaring to the media, "We do not understand why air power is not appropriate at this time" (Burg and Shoup 1999: 340; see also Albright 2003: 185). With U.S. public support for air strikes peaking at over 70 percent, the civilian interventionists won the first round of the debate.[45] Under American pressure, the European allies agreed to limited aerial bombings, and on May 25 NATO aircraft went into action, destroying two ammunition sites near the Bosnian Serb town of Pale. The Serbs, however, reacted swiftly, this time taking almost four hundred UN peacekeepers hostage, chaining several of them to telephone poles and using them as human shields. The spectacle, broadcast live on television networks across the globe, was deeply humiliating to UNPROFOR and the troop-contributing countries (Boutros-Ghali 1999: 234–36; Woodward 1996: 254).

Assistant Secretary of State Holbrooke at that point boldly recommended that Washington issue an ultimatum of forty-eight hours for the release of all hostages and threaten massive air strikes against Pale in case of noncompliance (Holbrooke 1998: 64; Burg and Shoup 1999: 329; Daalder 2000: 42). Because the Western European capitals were staunchly opposed to further air strikes, the bombing would almost certainly have been a U.S. unilateral affair, carried out by Washington on its own without IO approval. Yet Secretary of Defense Perry and JCS Chairman

---

45. For data on U.S. public support for air strikes, see Sobel 2001: 189–90.

Shalikashvili, supported by Christopher, vigorously pushed back against Holbrooke's suggestion and insisted in the intramural debates that any further discussion of air strikes should be "quietly" abandoned. The Pentagon's long-standing concerns about keeping American soldiers out of Bosnia were now heightened by the president's pledge, made in December 1994, to contribute up to twenty-five thousand U.S. troops to assist in any future withdrawal of UNPROFOR. President Clinton accepted the Pentagon's recommendation to call off further air strikes after the British prime minister, John Major, and the newly elected French president, Jacques Chirac, telephoned him and indicated that UNPROFOR's continued deployment was indeed on the line (Chollet 2005: 13; see also Daalder 2000: 42).

Endgame: The Military's Request for a European-Led Stabilization Force

While the Pentagon was able to prevent a further escalation after four hundred UN peacekeepers were taken hostage in May 1995, it now became apparent that Washington's reactive and hesitant approach had become untenable. The French government, by far the largest troop contributor to UNPROFOR, began to openly debate a withdrawal of all its 4,500 peacekeepers from Bosnia, and such a move would likely precipitate a collapse of the entire UN mission (Crossette, *NYT*, May 27, 1995; see also Nouzille 2010: 287–91). Over the next several weeks, Lake, Albright, and other proponents of a more assertive U.S. approach, seeking to exploit the changing political context to their advantage, began to argue that the United States should no longer aim to avoid UNPROFOR's withdrawal. They insisted that the UN mission had become an obstacle to effective coercive diplomacy; consequently, the United States should seek an orderly UNPROFOR withdrawal, while overall U.S. policy toward Bosnia had to be fundamentally rethought (Daalder 2000: 60; Lake 2001: 147; Chollet 2005: 20).

The overarching objectives of U.S. policy, as agreed upon by the NSC, remained to "obtain a political settlement that . . . rolls back some Serb aggression," while "avoid[ing] American entanglement in fighting on the ground in the Balkans."[46] Working within those parameters, in June 1995, Lake and his senior Balkans aide, Alexander Vershbow, in cooperation with Albright, began developing a comprehensive new policy proposal for Bosnia that became known as the "endgame strategy" (Woodward 1996: 257–59; Daalder 2000: 90–98; Soderberg 2005: 81–82).

---

46. Vershbow, "Bosnia: Strategic Choices."

The thrust of the new proposal was that the United States should launch a major diplomatic initiative, backed up by an array of carrots and sticks for all parties on the ground, to achieve a peace settlement before the end of the year that would preserve Bosnia as a viable state. If a negotiated settlement could be achieved, the United States would then deploy about twenty thousand troops as part of an international peace-implementation force. Conversely, if the final diplomatic effort failed, according to Lake and his collaborators Washington should adopt a more forceful approach in the short run, followed by general U.S. disengagement after a relatively short transitional period. Specifically, in this second scenario the United States should: (a) lift the arms embargo, (b) begin arming and training the Bosnian Muslims, and (c) "conduct aggressive air strikes against a broad range of Bosnian Serb military targets . . . during a one-year transition period, . . . [either] through NATO or . . . through a U.S.-led coalition of the willing."[47] In the absence of a negotiated settlement, the goal would be to enable the Bosnian Muslims to better defend themselves while also allowing them to recover some lost territory ahead of U.S. disengagement (Daalder 2000: 90–96; Woodward 1996: 258; Chollet 2005: 20).

By the late spring of 1995, with the Bosnian factions entrenched in their retrospective positions and unwilling to compromise, the prospects for a negotiated settlement appeared grim. Vershbow acknowledges that "we were rolling the dice a bit at that point."[48] Indeed, it appeared likely that by the end of 1995, the administration might have to implement its fallback option of "lift, arm, train, and strike." The Pentagon at first expressed strong concerns about that possibility. Secretary of Defense Perry and JCS Chairman Shalikashvili had come to support the use of airpower in Bosnia for clearly defined purposes, such as deterring further attacks on the safe areas. They also reluctantly accepted that in the event of the termination of UNPROFOR, the United States would contribute troops to a NATO extraction force.[49] However, they continued to think that U.S. interests were not sufficiently engaged for the United States to actively take sides in the conflict by offering strategic air support and other military assistance to the Bosnian Muslims (Daalder 2000: 105, 108).

47. Alexander Vershbow, "Bosnia Endgame Strategy," July 17, 1995.
48. Author interview with Alexander Vershbow, Senior Director for European Affairs on the NSC staff, 1994–97 (Apr. 2, 2010).
49. The JCS insisted that the extraction force should "remain completely neutral and impartial" toward the local conflict and have as its only objective "to conduct withdrawal operations and depart." OSD/JCS Paper, "Proposed US Policy Principles during NATO-Led UNPROFOR Withdrawal," May 12, 1995.

The military leaders and their civilian allies at the Pentagon firmly believed that even with the arms embargo lifted, it would take a long time before the Bosnian Muslims might be able to defend themselves. Therefore, U.S. air strikes were likely to result in incremental escalation: a demand to send in American trainers and air support liaison staff at first and then increasing numbers of combat troops to aid the Muslims. "There is no history of bombing by itself being effective, and we thought that once you did that, there was no turning back," Admiral Owens remembers.[50] During the initial discussions of the endgame strategy, U.S. defense leaders accordingly advocated "a more open posture of neutrality" while reiterating their long-standing preference for a de facto partition of Bosnia along the existing lines of confrontation.[51]

Changes in U.S. Policy after Srebrenica

Two dramatic events in Bosnia during the summer of 1995 changed the political landscape, facilitating a consensus on a more forceful approach both in Washington and within NATO and finally opening up the prospect of a negotiated settlement. First, in early July, the Bosnian Serb army overran the safe area of Srebrenica, making a mockery of the UN's and NATO's pledge to protect it. Second, later that summer, the Croatian army launched a cross-border offensive into Bosnia and, cooperating with the Bosnian Muslims, began to roll back Serb territorial gains, giving rise to a very fluid political situation on the ground.

Between July 6 and July 11, 1995, the Bosnian Serb army led by Ratko Mladic attacked and eventually overran the safe area of Srebrenica, slaughtering over seven thousand Bosnian Muslims—including women and children. The sense of shame resulting from the West's failure to stop the butchery at Srebrenica had a galvanizing effect on NATO member states. Chirac, the energetic new French president, offered to deploy a thousand French combat troops with robust rules of engagement to the threatened Muslim enclave of Gorazde, and he called for Washington's assistance. When President Clinton hesitated, Chirac, in a grandstanding move, noted that France stood "alone in wanting to take action" and compared the situation to the time in 1938 when the West had appeased Hitler (Burg and Shoup 1999: 326; Halberstam 2001: 316). Clinton, as his advisers recall, was visibly annoyed that Chirac had seized the initiative and the limelight (Woodward 1996: 261; Soderberg 2005: 67).

50. Owens, author interview.
51. Alexander Vershbow, "Former Yugoslavia Policy Review," discussion paper for NSC/PC, Mar. 16, 1995. See also Daalder 2000: 105, 108; Halberstam 2001: 326; Chollet 2005: 39–40.

Over the next several weeks, Lake exploited his physical proximity to the president to push the endgame strategy through the Washington bureaucracy. For the first time, Lake acted as a genuine policy entrepreneur and partially circumvented the formal interagency process, which had yielded an overly reactive and piecemeal approach on Bosnia. At a foreign policy team meeting on July 17, Lake laid out the complete endgame strategy to Christopher, Perry, Shalikashvili, and Albright. But the national security adviser had previously shown a draft to President Clinton, and since the president liked the proposal, Lake had asked him to drop by the meeting to voice his support (Woodward 1996: 261; Daalder 2000: 98–100). During the July 17 meeting, JCS Chairman Shalikashvili at first reiterated the military's reservations about lift, arm, train, and strike. However, toward the end of the meeting, Clinton appeared, as previously agreed with Lake: "I don't like where we are now," the president declared. "This policy is doing enormous damage to the United States and to our standing in the world." Without a change, he anticipated that the situation could "only get worse down the road" (quoted in Woodward 1996: 261; see also Daalder 2000: 101; Power 2003: 437–38).

The Pentagon was being outflanked in the bureaucratic political game by Lake, who together with Albright had persuaded the president of the need to adopt a more forceful U.S. approach. "You seek your allies, that's what was going on," Albright recalls.[52] In early August, Albright circulated a paper to her fellow NSC principals in which she passionately advocated "a modified lift and strike option." Washington's commitment to use U.S. ground troops to extract UNPROFOR, she began, "means that this conflict will be 'Americanized' sooner or later." Consequently, she argued, "our previous strategy—give primary responsibility to the Europeans, [and] help the Bosnians rhetorically . . . —is no longer sustainable." Albright insisted that "we must stop thinking of Bosnia as a 'tar baby.'" Her recommendation, consistent with her advocacy over the previous two years but now with a realistic possibility of being implemented, was "using our military forces, primarily through the air, to help the Bosnians by changing the balance of power."[53]

By early August, the Joint Chiefs, preferring to avoid a showdown with the president and sensing that in the aftermath of Srebrenica, the Europeans, too, were now coming on board, no longer explicitly opposed

52. DOS Dayton History Project, interview with Madeleine Albright, Oct. 28, 1996.
53. Madeleine Albright, "Why America Must Take the Lead," memorandum for the NatSec Adviser, Aug. 3, 1995.

the endgame strategy.[54] As Vershbow explains, the military continued to have reservations until the end, "but that was settled by the commander in chief."[55] On August 8, the entire foreign policy team met to discuss the endgame strategy one last time before taking a formal decision. The NSC staff again went through the details of the proposal: there would be a last-ditch effort to reach a settlement by the end of the year, but if diplomacy failed, the United States would lift the arms embargo, arm and train the Bosnian Muslims, and rely on air strikes during a transitional period of several months. After presidential approval of the new strategy, Lake would travel to Europe and simply inform the allies of the president's decision, making it clear that the United States was willing to move ahead unilaterally (Lake 2000: 149; Daalder 2000: 107–13; Chollet 2005: 41–44). But Vershbow recalls predicting that, by then, "the Europeans would breathe a sigh of relief at the sight of U.S. leadership and would come along."[56] Clinton himself mused during the August 8 meeting, shortly before approving the strategy, "We're not asking for something the Europeans won't like. This time we'll be pushing on an open door" (quoted in Woodward 1996: 266–67).

By the time the U.S. president formally approved the endgame strategy on August 8, the military balance in the Balkans had also begun to shift dramatically. Over the previous year, the United States had promoted an alliance between Bosnian Muslims and Bosnian Croats, which became known as the "Federation agreement." Washington had also facilitated covert arms transfers to Bosnia and Croatia from Eastern Europe and various Muslim countries, including Iran.[57] On July 25, 1995, Croatia's strengthened military forces launched a cross-border offensive into Bosnia near Bihac and, reinforced by Bosnian Muslim troops, easily overran Bosnian Serb positions, sending an estimated eight thousand Serb soldiers and civilians fleeing (Daalder 2000: 122; Chollet 2005: 35–36). On August 4 the Croats, emboldened by their success in Bihac and by Washington's tacit approval, launched a broader offensive (code-named Operation Storm) against the Serb-held Krajina region in Croatia, which resulted in the forcible expulsion of almost two hundred thousand Serb civilians (Holbrooke 1998: 72–73; Daalder 2000: 123).

---

54. In previous days, Shalikashvili had met with several European counterparts, and at a meeting in London on July 21, the allies expressed support for more vigorous air strikes. See Daalder 2000: 70, 74n96; Soderberg 2005: 82.
55. Vershbow, author interview.
56. Vershbow, author interview.
57. CIA, "Croatia: Using the Gray Market to Beat the UN Arms Embargo," intelligence report, May 1995; Weiner, *NYT*, Nov. 8, 1996.

The Pentagon and the U.S. intelligence community, like most of Washington's European allies, had long predicted that if the Croats attacked Serb strongholds either in Bosnia or in the Krajina region of Croatia, the Serbs would defeat them. As General Kerrick, the senior NSC staffer working on the Balkans, remembers, the U.S. defense community didn't have "a lot of confidence that the Croats could defeat the Serbs. I don't recall there being a sense that there was any real military solution to this."[58] But once it became clear that Yugoslav president Milosevic had written off the Kraijna Serbs, senior U.S. officials, including from the Pentagon, began to openly endorse the Croat move: "We hope that it is successful," Secretary Perry declared (quoted in Priest, *WashPo*, Aug. 5, 1995; see also Daalder 2000: 123). It was not until several weeks later that the Croatian army, again supported by Bosnian Muslim troops, launched a significant ground offensive into Bosnia that went much beyond Bihac and reversed most Serb territorial gains from the previous three years.[59] Yet when Clinton approved the endgame strategy on August 8, with Operation Storm already in full swing, there was a well-grounded expectation in Washington that the hitherto recalcitrant Serbs might become more amenable to negotiations (Holbrooke 1998: 86).

Planning for Peace Implementation

The endgame strategy developed by the NSC staff with Albright's support foresaw that successful negotiations on a peace agreement would result in the deployment of an international stabilization force, combined with significant economic assistance for postwar reconstruction.[60] By early August 1995, the prospect that the strategy could be implemented multilaterally through NATO significantly reduced the risk that the United States might get stuck shouldering a heavy stabilization burden largely on its own. This realization provided further ammunition to the administration's interventionists: "In response to the obvious charge of a 'slippery slope,' " Albright sought to reassure her colleagues, "we should point to Haiti, where we set a timetable for deployment and met the deadline. It is simply wrong to argue that a multinational force with a U.S. component spells an open-ended American commitment."[61]

---

58. Kerrick, author interview. See also Holbrooke 1998: 62; Daalder 2000: 120–22.
59. Croatian forces launched an all-out ground offensive into Bosnia on September 8. Burg and Shoup 1999: 331; Daalder 2000: xviii.
60. Vershbow, author interview. See also Daalder 2000: 100.
61. Albright, "Why America Must Take the Lead."

In the case of Haiti, as detailed in chapter 3, Washington secured international approval for the use of force and was able to hand off longer-term peacekeeping to a UN force. Fuerth, who supported Albright's approach throughout, recalls that the civilian interventionists had "learned a lot" about the military's concerns and how those could be effectively addressed "in the course of figuring out what to do about Haiti, and that was reapplied when thinking about what to do about Bosnia." In particular, he explains, "after Haiti, it occurred to us, yes you can actually work with others to get the stabilization part done"—an argument used extensively during the interagency debate about Bosnia.[62]

Yet the Joint Chiefs demanded concrete assurances that the American military would shoulder as little of the stabilization burden as possible. During the initial debates about peace implementation, the uniformed leaders recommended setting up a European Union stabilization force from the outset. The best solution from the military's standpoint, explains Admiral Owens, the former JCS vice chairman, would have been to deploy a "European peacekeeping force," or at any rate a predominantly "European presence supplemented by the United States on the edges."[63] However, the Western European allies as well as the Bosnian Muslims insisted on a sizable U.S. military contribution, at least for the initial implementation phase.[64] Consequently, the focus of U.S. military planners increasingly shifted to a NATO-led implementation force, in which the United States would play an initially significant but rapidly diminishing role. By late June 1995, Secretary of Defense Perry declared that the Pentagon was willing to countenance a sizable deployment of U.S. troops for a limited period of time, "as a part of a NATO force to help implement a peace settlement."[65]

The Joint Chiefs firmly recommended that U.S. troops be deployed in significant numbers only for a twelve-month period, with longer-term peacekeeping handed off to a largely European force. "We were pushing the Europeans as much as we could to get their commitment that they would take it from there," Admiral Owens recalls.[66] America's top-ranking generals and admirals were adamant that the administration

---

62. Fuerth, author interview.
63. Owens, author interview, confirmed by author interview with Edward Warner, AssistSecDef for Strategy and Requirements, 1993–97 (Apr. 12, 2011).
64. Warren Christopher, *U.S. Policy toward the Former Yugoslavia: Hearing Before the House NatSec Committee*, 104th Cong. (Oct. 18, 1995), 164.
65. Perry, *U.S. Policy toward the Former Yugoslavia*, 5.
66. Owens, author interview. Schulte confirms there was an "expectation that the United States would go in heavy up front, and the Europeans and other partners would take up more of the burden as the force went down." Author interview.

coordinate its policy with NATO at every step, in order to maximize Washington's leverage over its partners and ensure that the Western Europeans—who after all had a greater stake in a stable Bosnia—would take the lead on postwar stabilization. "This was a potential quagmire," remembers General Kross, the former Joint Staff director. "If we weren't going to get stuck in there, we needed to have something to hand it off to. So NATO was very important to the exit strategy."[67]

The military leaders made it clear that if diplomacy failed to produce a negotiated settlement, they would strenuously object to deploying American ground troops to train or defend the Bosnian Muslims. The Western Europeans, too, were unlikely to contribute troops for "train and strike" in a hostile environment. Consequently, the Clinton administration debated for some time the possibility of deploying a more robust successor force to UNPROFOR, composed of troops from moderate Muslim countries, as an alternative to a NATO force in case diplomacy failed. "We had some discussions with Indonesia and Turkey [about] a Muslim peacekeeping force," remembers Admiral Owens. "We could have provided intelligence to them and combined it with limited strikes to force the Serbs into compliance."[68]

Locking in the Allies: Operation Deliberate Force

After the Srebrenica massacre, Albright, Holbrooke, and Lake launched a concerted effort to persuade skeptics at the Pentagon and Secretary of State Christopher to back heavier bombing *in support of* the diplomatic track—something that the previously developed endgame strategy had not explicitly foreseen. Albright in particular saw an opening to push for "using military pressure to compel the [Bosnian] Serbs to negotiate a suitable peace settlement."[69]

The U.S. military leaders remained skeptical of moving toward a coercive bombing campaign.[70] After Srebrenica, serious disagreements over air strikes within NATO that might have created problems for subsequent burden sharing on peace implementation appeared less likely. Nevertheless, adamant about limiting the armed services' liability, the Joint Chiefs insisted on the need to carefully coordinate with the

---

67. Kross, author interview.
68. Owens, author interview. The possibility of replacing UNPROFOR with "forces from Islamic countries" was explicitly foreseen in Vershbow's "Bosnia Endgame Strategy" document of July 17, 1995.
69. Albright, "Why America Must Take the Lead." See also Burg and Shoup 1999: 349–50; Power 2003: 413.
70. Owens, author interview. See also Halberstam 2001: 326–30; Daalder 2000: 105.

European allies. "If you go into a combat situation it's nice to have somebody besides you bearing the risks," explains Slocombe, the former number three at DOD.[71] Furthermore, the JCS expected that by closely coordinating U.S. intervention policy with the Europeans through NATO, the United States could avoid alienating the allies and persuade them that European leadership on subsequent stabilization was warranted in the context of broader alliance burden sharing. "There is no doubt that the military wanted to lock in the allies—it was a European problem, and they wanted a strong European [stabilization] force," explains Edward Warner, then the assistant secretary in charge of peacekeeping at the Pentagon.[72]

Prodded by the United States, at a special conference held in London on July 21, 1995, NATO agreed to streamline the dual key authorization process for air strikes in order to facilitate the defense of the remaining safe areas (Boutros-Ghali 1999: 239–41; Power 2003: 417). When on August 28 an artillery shell launched from Serb-held territory landed on the crowded Sarajevo marketplace, France, Britain, and Germany joined the United States in calling for NATO air strikes (Daalder 2000: 129–31). The Clinton administration's interventionists clearly saw the ensuing air campaign, Operation Deliberate Force, as a coercive instrument that could support the shuttle diplomacy of which Ambassador Holbrooke had recently taken charge (Woodward 1996: 269–70; Burg and Shoup 1999: 352). President Clinton himself reportedly insisted, referring to the Bosnian Serbs, "We have to hit 'em hard" (quoted in Chollet 2005: 60).

Yet the principal European countries remained reluctant to move toward full-fledged strategic bombing (Priest, *WashPo*, July 25, 1995; see also Daalder 2000: 75–79). Holbrooke therefore wrote in a secret cable from Europe that although "the bombing . . . is an essential component of our negotiating strategy, I will continue to assert publicly that the bombing has not [been] designed for the negotiations, but is, rather, a necessary response to the outrageous attack in Sarajevo."[73] Such public ambivalence was intended to avoid ruffling the allies' feathers. Reflecting European sensitivities, NATO Secretary-General Willy Claes declared that the air campaign's objectives were merely "to reduce the threat to Sarajevo and to deter further attacks on any other safe area" (quoted in Cohen, *NYT*, Aug. 30, 1995).

To prevent the fragile NATO consensus on air strikes from falling apart, the bombing was narrowly limited to military targets, while

---

71. Slocombe, author interview.
72. Warner, author interview.
73. Richard Holbrooke, "Belgrade Talks," diplomatic cable, U.S. Embassy, Athens, Sept. 1995.

dual-use "Option Three" targets (such as power grids) always remained off-limits.[74] Indeed, under pressure from the JCS, the United States ended the bombing on September 14, several days earlier than initially planned and than the civilian hawks in Washington would have preferred, after "Option One" targets (Bosnian Serb military units) and "Option Two" targets (command-and-control facilities, radars, and ammunition depots) had been exhausted. This was deemed necessary to maintain a multilateral consensus with the European NATO allies, who were growing increasingly uneasy about the bombing and were clearly unwilling to move to Option Three targets (Holbrooke 1998: 146).

The Joint Chiefs had also strongly recommended that as many of the NATO allies as possible should participate in the bombing or otherwise be involved in campaign management and logistics, although it was understood that this would limit Washington's own freedom of maneuver: "We wanted to get their hands dirty in there so that they felt they had a real dog in the fight to keep that area stable," explains General Kross.[75] Operation Deliberate Force was a truly multinational enterprise. Seven European NATO members (the United Kingdom, France, the Netherlands, Spain, Turkey, Italy, and Germany) contributed fighter or reconnaissance aircraft.[76] "Almost all the other NATO countries in some capacity" shared in the effort, explains General Michael E. Ryan, then NATO's southern air forces commander.[77]

Alliance aircraft flew a total of 3,515 sorties and dropped 1,026 munitions against Bosnian Serb targets. The United States shouldered the lion's share of the combat burden, flying about 65 percent of all sorties and delivering the vast majority of precision-guided munitions (Daalder 2000: 131; Gibbs 2009: 166). What mattered most to the U.S. military leaders, however, was that the joint air campaign, by closely tying NATO's future credibility to success in Bosnia, locked in the European allies' support, thus maximizing the likelihood that they would take the lead on Bosnia's long-term stabilization. After all, the Europeans had benefited most from a strong NATO over the years. As Admiral Owens explains, "Our view was that the Europeans should be the ones to take it forward—that any peacekeeping activities on the ground would be dependent on the Europeans. So you really needed to have them as part of the air campaign, even though they were not adding frankly very much and it was hard to incorporate them in the plan."[78]

74. Hunter, author interview. See also Burg 2003: 67.
75. Kross, author interview.
76. NATO, "Operation Deliberate Force," *Fact Sheet* (Naples: AFSOUTH, Dec. 2002).
77. Quoted in John Tirpak, "Deliberate Force," *Air Force Magazine* 80 (10), 1997: 37–38.
78. Owens, author interview.

Concerns about Congress

By early September 1995, a negotiated settlement of the Bosnian War appeared increasingly likely.[79] Therefore, while Operation Deliberate Force was still ongoing, the Pentagon began to focus in greater detail on peace implementation.[80] The Joint Chiefs, influenced by the Powell Doctrine, recommended deploying an oversized stabilization mission with a robust enforcement capability that could quash any local resistance if needed and achieve its objectives within a limited time frame. Preliminary plans that had emerged by late August foresaw a NATO-led Implementation Force (IFOR) of sixty thousand with a prospective twelve-month deployment (Daalder 2000: 141). To increase the odds of a successful mission, the uniformed leaders also demanded that IFOR's mandate be narrowly circumscribed to military matters and exclude tasks such as humanitarian relief, refugee resettlement, and reconstruction. The generals held firm on this point, which resulted in significant friction with Holbrooke and other State Department officials who believed that IFOR should also take on broader reconstruction tasks. General George Joulwan, the commander of U.S. and allied troops in Europe, reportedly "felt that NATO was going to win or lose based on how they were going to come out of Bosnia, and his view was that if NATO stuck to the military part of the operation, they stood a good chance of succeeding."[81]

The uniformed leaders' insistence on burden sharing and a narrowly targeted mission with a clear exit strategy undoubtedly reflected, to some extent, their parochial organizational interests. Yet it also reflected, as Holbrooke (1998: 211) subsequently acknowledged, a "deeply held conviction of the Pentagon . . . that the American people would not support involvement in Bosnia without an 'exit strategy.'" The Joint Chiefs were in frequent communication with congressional leaders, especially members of the House and Senate Armed Services Committees who were responsible for military appropriations. As a result of those interactions, the JCS worried more than the administration's civilian interventionists about Congress's willingness to support a protracted U.S. troop deployment in Bosnia. (The civilian interventionists interacted predominately with members of the House Foreign Affairs and Senate Foreign

---

79. On September 8, the foreign ministers of Bosnia, Croatia, and Serbia agreed to a roughly equal division of Bosnia's territory between a Muslim-Croat "federation" and a Serb entity. See Holbrooke 1998: 133–41; Burg and Shoup 1999: 336.
80. Warner, author interview.
81. Author interview with Col. William Flavin, Deputy Director of SpecOps for the SACEUR, 1995–99 (Jan. 18, 2011).

Relations Committees, who tend to raise fewer questions about the costs of intervention.)[82]

Between 1993 and 1995, the mood on Capitol Hill was far from unequivocally hostile to greater U.S. involvement in the Balkans. Congressional leaders such as Senator Dole (R-KS) and Senator Joseph Biden (D-DE) strongly supported U.S. air strikes and encouraged President Clinton to do more (Hendrickson 2002: 74–87). Yet while such support energized the administration's civilian interventionists, the military had learned from Vietnam and Somalia that domestic support might rapidly evaporate in the face of mounting costs. As General Kerrick remembers, "Our Congress would say, 'yeah we should do something about it,' but they were very reluctant to want to commit U.S. military forces. So they would say, 'Who is going to pay for this? How long are they going to be there? What is the mission going to be?' It got to a point where there was a realization that well, we need to do this multilaterally."[83]

The Pentagon's recommendation was that to ensure congressional support, the president should declare that U.S. troops would remain in Bosnia for only one year as part of IFOR and then be almost completely withdrawn by the end of 1996. "We needed to convince Congress that we had an exit strategy," remembers General Kross. "And the final element of the exit strategy was, hand it over to NATO and the Europeans on the ground."[84] Ultimately, the generals obtained a narrow mandate for IFOR, limited to separating the former warring parties, deterring potential spoilers, and arming and training Muslim and Croat forces, so as to establish a more stable balance of power on the ground (Holbrooke 1998: 216–17; Daalder 2000: 146–47; Dobbins et al. 2003: 93–97). Furthermore, IFOR was given only a one-year mandate, with the expectation that a largely European force would take over thereafter.[85] From late summer of 1995 onward, the JCS developed all plans for postwar stabilization in close cooperation with European military representatives at NATO to ensure the maximum level of burden and risk sharing compatible with an effective operation (Daalder 2000: 142–43, esp. n. 59).

While the uniformed leaders were clearly concerned about Congress, the military's own backing for the president's policy was essential to ensure support on Capitol Hill, notably in the Armed Services Committees. That required the military leaders to walk a fine line; it was not in their interest to undermine congressional support for a policy that in

82. Author interview with Barbara Larkin, senior congressional aide on foreign affairs, 1986–1995 (April 2, 2010). See also Drew 1995: 273.
83. Kerrick, author interview.
84. Kross, author interview.
85. Schulte, author interview. See also Daalder 2000: 149–50; Holbrooke 1998: 210–11.

some form or another they would likely be ordered to execute, but it also vastly increased the generals' bargaining leverage. "The White House was understandably averse to a direct confrontation with the military," Holbrooke notes. "If the military openly opposed the deployment, our political difficulties would be vastly increased. We had to have their backing to get congressional and public support for the mission, which meant that they had the upper hand in the debate over what their mission would be" (Holbrooke 1998: 219; see also Daalder 2000: 146).

In short, the military, eager to limit its liability and ensure congressional support, insisted on (1) narrowly circumscribing IFOR's mandate; (2) developing a clear exit strategy before any deployment of American troops; and (3) locking in the European allies through NATO. Undoubtedly, the top-level uniformed leaders were not the only presidential advisers concerned about congressional support. Vice President Gore, for instance, himself a former U.S. senator and congressman, privately worried from 1993 onward that "the American people will not want to send our boys there."[86] Nevertheless, insofar as anticipated congressional opposition to a large-scale U.S. troop deployment contributed to keeping the United States on a steady multilateral track between 1993 and 1995, the uniformed leaders constituted an important transmission belt and magnifying factor.

IFOR deployed to Bosnia in December 1995, soon after the successful conclusion of the final peace negotiations held in Dayton, Ohio. The Pentagon, with support from the State Department, secured troop contributions from over thirty NATO and non-NATO countries (Cimbala and Forster 2010: 132, 147). However, by the end of 1996, the peace remained exceedingly fragile. The Western Europeans, while ready to step up their own contribution, were not yet willing to take over entirely. Given that a precipitous American withdrawal might have derailed the entire peace process, the JCS reluctantly agreed to an extension of the U.S. deployment, and they cooperated in securing congressional funding for the follow-on NATO-led Stabilization Force (SFOR).[87] The United States contributed 8,500 troops to SFOR (making up 30 percent of a total NATO force of slightly over 27,000), down from an initial U.S. contribution to IFOR of 20,000 troops (roughly 40 percent of the total NATO component).[88] Smaller and steadily decreasing contingents of U.S. forces remained in Bosnia until 2004, when a 6,000-strong European Union peacekeeping force (EUFOR) took over from NATO (Recchia 2007: 13–14).

---

86. Albert Gore, "NSC/PC Meeting on Bosnia" (Feb. 5, 1993), 6.
87. Schulte and Hunter, author interviews. See also Dobbins et al. 2003: 95.
88. Karen Donfried and Paul Gallis, "Bosnia and NATO: Allied Contributions to SFOR," *CRS Report for Congress* (May 18, 1998).

ALTERNATIVE HYPOTHESES ON U.S. MULTILATERALISM

To further clarify the importance of civil-military bargaining in steering U.S. policy on Bosnia toward NATO and the UN, it is worth evaluating prominent alternative hypotheses on why the United States generally seeks IO approval for its interventions. First, it may be that by 1993–94, U.S. civilian policymakers had internalized new legitimacy norms according to which, in situations other than self-defense, decisions to use force must be made multilaterally. Second, policymakers could have worried that U.S. unilateral intervention might result in costly international retaliation in the form of negative issue linkage.[89]

Norm Internalization

If policymakers have internalized legal and moral norms that require IO approval, they should display a high threshold for violating related precepts. Barring uncontroversial instances of self-defense (e.g., in the face of an armed attack on the homeland or U.S. citizens), armed intervention without such approval should be all but unthinkable to them. This should be evident not only from their public statements but also from arguments made privately during intramural debates. Furthermore, policymakers should view IO approval as intrinsically desirable and not merely as a tool to assuage domestic and international critics.

Samantha Power asserts in the Bosnia chapter of her acclaimed study of U.S. decision making on humanitarian intervention, *A Problem from Hell* (2003: 304), that "Clinton's foreign policy architects were committed multilateralists. [Consequently,] they would only act with the consent and active participation of their European partners." Such arguments resonate with the norm-internalization hypothesis. The Clinton administration, replete with self-proclaimed liberal Wilsonians who made ample use of multilateralist rhetoric, is indeed a most-likely case for that hypothesis. It follows that if the hypothesis does not hold up in this case, its broader applicability is called into question.[90]

A careful review of the public and private stances of foreign policy leaders in the Clinton administration reveals that few, if any, had internalized relevant norms requiring multilateral approval. The administration's most prominent liberal Wilsonians, who were also the strongest advocates of U.S. intervention in Bosnia (Albright, Lake, and Holbrooke) did not stand out for their attachment to multilateralism. In fact the

---

89. See chapter 1 for a more detailed discussion of those hypotheses.
90. On using most-likely cases for hypothesis testing see George and Bennett 2004: 120–22.

opposite was the case: the liberal Wilsonians, because of their hawkish attitude on Bosnia, felt that proceeding multilaterally through NATO and the UN was too constraining, and consequently they were more willing than others to violate international norms requiring IO approval. For the humanitarian hawks, the substantive obligation to fight genocide seems to have taken precedence over procedural norms on multilateral approval.

Albright, the Clinton administration's most vocal advocate of U.S. intervention in Bosnia, certainly did not view IO approval as a matter of obligation. By her own account, she merely viewed multilateralism instrumentally as "a foreign policy tool" that might help facilitate collective action and burden sharing (Albright 2003: 176). She was clearly willing to bypass multilateral bodies like the UN and NATO whenever she concluded that the costs of multilateralism outweighed attendant benefits, and she thus never viewed IO approval as a necessary, or near necessary, condition for legitimate intervention.

By the spring of 1993, Albright was deeply frustrated with the slow pace of the multilateral diplomacy on Bosnia. She thus wrote a secret memo calling for American leadership and advocating the use of "air power—unilateral[ly]" if necessary.[91] If UN or NATO approval could not be obtained within a short time frame, she argued, the United States should make the case "that sufficient authority already exists under Article 51 of the Charter . . . to strike at Bosnian Serb strategic targets."[92] Such an expansive interpretation of article 51 of the UN Charter, on individual and collective self-defense in cases of aggression, would hardly have increased the intervention's legitimacy in the eyes of skeptical audiences at home and abroad. It was also based on a controversial reading of local circumstances in Bosnia. Albright viewed the Balkan wars in somewhat Manichaean terms, clearly dividing the local parties into victims and aggressors, and the only norm she appears to have been firmly committed to complying with was the "obligation . . . to resist evil" as she saw it (Albright 2003: 177).

National Security Adviser Lake was more pragmatic and more receptive to arguments about the likely risks and costs of intervention (see, e.g., Drew 1995: 140–41; Power 2003: 316). To some extent, that may have been due to his institutional role as the administration's principal foreign policy coordinator, which required that he take the views of other top-ranking officials into account when formulating advice to the president. As early as August 1993, Lake acknowledged in a memo for the president that "the need . . . [for] reconstruction assistance to Bosnia . . . will be vast," and he echoed the Pentagon's view that the "West Europeans

91. Albright, "Options for Bosnia."
92. Ibid.

should shoulder most of the burden."[93] Lake's overall preference for multilateralism on Bosnia thus appears to have been less the reflection of an inherent normative conviction than the result of contingent cost-benefit calculations. He concluded that multilateral approval was desirable as long as it could be secured within a reasonable time frame and at an acceptable cost because "the more you involve others, the more you reduce the burden on the United States."[94]

At the same time, Lake clearly had a lower threshold than the military leaders and their civilian allies at the Pentagon for concluding that the costs of multilateralism outweighed attendant benefits. For instance, when the Bihac safe area risked being overrun by the Bosnian Serb army in November 1994, as previously noted, Lake initially advocated heavier U.S. air strikes against the Serbs. Those strikes would almost certainly have been carried out unilaterally by the United States since, as Lake himself (2000: 144–45) acknowledges, the European "allies were somewhere between strongly opposed and apoplectic . . . about heavier bombing."

After the Srebrenica massacre of July 1995, the national security adviser again concluded that the costs of continued multilateralism might be unsustainable, and he made the case for striking Bosnian Serb targets unilaterally unless the NATO allies rapidly came on board. Lake believed "it had to be made clear to the allies that they had no veto over our approach; we would act with or without them" (ibid., 147). Vershbow, Lake's senior Balkans aide, remembers that, had the Europeans not supported coercive air strikes, "We were prepared to do it [i.e., bomb] unilaterally. The risk of a rift in NATO was seen, but our credibility was on the line and we had to act."[95] Recently declassified documents further reveal that with the president's pollsters suggesting that coercive bombing would be popular among the U.S. public, Lake and Vershbow went so far as to recommend that the United States threaten and possibly launch unilateral "strikes against military targets *inside Serbia*."[96]

Finally, Assistant Secretary of State Holbrooke appears to have been the least attached to multilateralism as a matter of obligation. As early as 1993, he had come to the conclusion that bombing "Serbia proper" would be a useful tool of coercive diplomacy that might allow Washington to "send the proper message" (Holbrooke 1998: 52). Ambassador Hunter, the former U.S. representative to NATO, explains that such a policy

---

93. Anthony Lake, "Bosnian End-Game Strategy," memorandum for the Pres., Aug. 25, 1993.
94. Lake, author interview.
95. Vershbow, author interview.
96. Vershbow, "Bosnia Endgame Strategy" (emphasis added). On the pollsters' advice see Stephanopoulos 1999: 381–82.

would have been "utterly unacceptable to the allies" (French President Chirac said it was "out of the question"), and it could therefore only have been carried out unilaterally by the United States.[97] Similarly, in May 1995, after the Bosnian Serbs had taken hundreds of UN peacekeepers hostage, Holbrooke insisted that Washington issue a forty-eight-hour ultimatum for the release of all hostages and then bomb the Bosnian Serb headquarters at Pale in case of noncompliance. Aware that "the Europeans will oppose this," he recommended that the United States proceed unilaterally (Holbrooke 1998: 64).[98] Not until the late summer of 1995, after Holbrooke became chief U.S. negotiator for the Balkans and after tense interactions with the JCS, did he begin to acknowledge the strategic imperative of proceeding by means of consensus with the NATO allies to maximize postwar burden sharing (ibid., 84).

In short, the Clinton administration's most prominent liberal interventionists felt no distinctive attachment to multilateralism as a matter of obligation. Instead, they saw it as a tool whose usefulness depended on the circumstances—and the more hawkish the individual, the lower the threshold at which he or she was willing to bypass relevant IOs. President Clinton, too, appears to have viewed multilateralism as having contingent rather than absolute value. In the aftermath of Srebrenica, when Lake and Albright argued that the United States might have to intervene unilaterally to reassert American leadership and credibility, the president reportedly "did not balk at the proposal to go it alone" (Woodward 1996: 259). The Bosnia experience therefore reveals that even those U.S. leaders who, judging from their public rhetoric and general ideological orientation, might be expected to have a strong attachment to multilateralism are far from having internalized relevant norms requiring IO approval as a condition for legitimate intervention.

Averting Issue Linkage

Another prominent hypothesis is that U.S. policymakers seek IO approval in order to signal benign intentions to third-party states and thereby avert negative issue linkage, or reduced international cooperation with the United States across various policy domains such as finance and trade, counterterrorism, or nonproliferation. For the hypothesis to be corroborated, there should be evidence that American leaders involved in decision making during the Bosnia crisis were in fact concerned about

97. Hunter, author interview. On the French president's stance see Nouzille 2010: 255.
98. Holbrooke had also joined Lake in advocating further U.S. bombing, in spite of strong European objections, during the November 1994 Bihac crisis. See Clark 2001: 42.

negative issue linkage. Furthermore, those leaders should acknowledge that reassuring third-party states with the ultimate goal of averting issue linkage was an important reason for seeking IO approval.

Third-party states across the globe were quite supportive of U.S. intervention in Bosnia. That included most of the world's Muslim countries, which are usually suspicious of American intentions and tend to view U.S. military operations with skepticism. The Organization of the Islamic Conference (OIC), a grouping of more than fifty states from North Africa, Central and Southeast Asia, and the Middle East, had urged the United States to adopt a tougher stance on Bosnia from late 1992 onward. On numerous occasions, the leaders of Muslim countries called on the Clinton administration to use military force in support of the Bosnian Muslims, without much concern for UN or NATO approval (Murphy, *LA Times*, Dec. 1, 1992; see also Steinberg 1993: 46–47; Albright 2003: 180).

There were only a few states that remained opposed for a long time to the coercive use of American airpower over Bosnia. First were Washington's principal NATO allies, notably Britain and France: as noted, they had deployed thousands of their own lightly armed soldiers as peacekeepers in Bosnia and feared that heavy aerial bombing of Serb positions would result in costly retaliation. Second was the Russian Federation, which for ethnic, religious, and historical reasons was closely aligned with the Serbs. By definition, the European NATO countries were not third-party states, given their close alliance with the United States and deep involvement in Bosnia. Even after a U.S. unilateral bombing campaign, the Western Europeans would have been highly unlikely to retaliate against the United States on issues such as international trade or nonproliferation. Therefore, the Russian Federation was the only genuine third-party state whose opposition might have been of concern to American leaders, in view of possible repercussions for broader relations between Washington and Moscow.

Russia was a cosponsor of SCR 836, adopted in June 1993, which authorized the use of airpower to protect UNPROFOR and deter attacks against the safe areas (UNGA 1999: 24). However, Moscow favored a narrow interpretation of the resolution and, over the subsequent two years, Russian officials repeatedly denounced what they felt was an unwarranted use of airpower by NATO. In the spring of 1994, Moscow disputed NATO's authority to establish a weapons-exclusion zone in and around Sarajevo and threaten air strikes in case of Serb noncompliance, insisting that those measures were not authorized under existing UN resolutions (Leurdijk 1994: 55; Talbott 2002: 121–22; Sarooshi 2008: 237). At the London conference held in the aftermath of the Srebrenica massacre, the Russian foreign minister, Andrej Kozyrev, and the defense minister, Pavel Grachev, still rejected heavier air strikes against the

[143]

Bosnian Serbs and refused to sign the final communiqué streamlining the dual key authorization process (Burg and Shoup 1999: 344; Daalder 2000: 76). Finally, in September 1995, after NATO launched Operation Deliberate Force, the Russians furiously denounced the air campaign as illegal in a number of public statements (Holbrooke 1998: 144).[99]

Yet Russia's public protests over Bosnia never stopped the United States from carrying out air strikes whenever there was a consensus within NATO. Former secretary of defense Perry and Ashton Carter, then the Pentagon's assistant secretary for global strategy, remember that to most American officials dealing with Bosnia, Russia's antagonistic stance seemed at worst "like an unnecessary complication" with little potential for harming broader U.S. interests (Carter and Perry 1999: 36). From the spring of 1993 onward, the Clinton administration viewed Moscow's public opposition to air strikes largely as an attempt by President Boris Yeltsin to defuse "domestic political pressure" from lawmakers and the general public.[100] Russian officials were not nearly as vehement in private conversations with U.S. policymakers as they were in public. Fuerth, who was closely involved in managing U.S.-Russian relations, remembers that in private "the Russians were willing to extend themselves—maybe they didn't feel that they had much choice, given their economics and internal position."[101] In short, Washington took seriously Moscow's objections to heavier air strikes out of concerns that Russia might undermine U.S. diplomacy in the region, but the Yeltsin government never came close to having a veto over U.S. decisions concerning Bosnia, given its inability to harm broader U.S. interests.[102]

In 1994 and 1995, U.S. policymakers understood that channeling the use of force through NATO would be anything but reassuring to Moscow. The Atlantic alliance, far from legitimating U.S. intervention in Russian eyes, was viewed in Moscow as an instrument of American hegemony that threatened Russia's strategic interests. President Clinton's announcement in late 1994 that NATO would expand eastward had created a storm in Moscow, and the Russian nationalist leader Vladimir Zhirinovsky warned that he and his parliamentary allies would consider any military action by NATO against the Bosnian Serbs akin to a declaration of war

---

99. Moscow even sponsored a UNSC resolution calling for an immediate cessation of the bombing but was not able to secure its adoption. Burg and Shoup 1999: 357.

100. Daniel Wagner, "Memo for the NSC staff," DCI Balkan Task Force, Feb. 19, 1993. See also Hockstader and Atkinson, *WashPo*, Sept. 8, 1995.

101. Fuerth, author interview. See also Talbott 2002: 124–28; Daalder 2000: 76n.; Chollet 2005: 45.

102. In September 1995, when Russia strongly condemned Operation Deliberate Force, Clinton dispatched an emissary to Moscow without in any way changing U.S. policy. Talbott 2002: 172–73; Holbrooke 1998: 144.

against Russia (Williams, *WashPo*, Dec. 2, 1994; Carter and Perry 1999: 28–31). Former deputy secretary of state Talbott (2002: 77) recalls that even mainstream Russian elites feared at the time that the Balkans might become "a staging area for the expansion of American power right up to the border of Russia itself" (see also Clark 2001: 57). Schulte, a U.S. official who directed NATO's Balkans task force at the time, goes so far as to speculate that "the Russians would probably have been happier if the United States just did it unilaterally because with the Warsaw Pact gone, the first threat to Russia was the expansion of NATO."[103]

The fact that NATO's repeated use of airpower in Bosnia, up to and including Operation Deliberate Force, was ostensibly authorized under existing UNSC resolutions also seems to have had little reassuring effect on Moscow. Russian officials consistently argued that there was no SC authorization for offensive military action in Bosnia. In Moscow's eyes, the United States and its NATO allies had stretched SCR 770 (of August 1992, which authorized limited force to facilitate the provision of humanitarian assistance) and SCR 836 (of June 1993, on the defense of the safe areas) beyond recognition, in blatant disregard of the council's original intent (Sarooshi 2008: 241).[104] The UNSC was one of the few international platforms that still allowed Russia to interact with the world's other major powers on an equal footing, and the ability of the Western allies to largely disregard Russia's opposition to the use of force at the SC was deeply troubling to Moscow (Talbott 2002: 123). It was not until Russian forces were given a visible role in the NATO-led peace-implementation force (IFOR) after difficult negotiations between Secretary of Defense Perry and his Russian counterpart, Grachev, that Moscow adopted a more cooperative attitude.[105]

Ultimately, there is no evidence that U.S. policymakers sought IO approval for the use of force over Bosnia in order to reassure antagonistic third-party states, and Russia in particular, about American intentions. Securing NATO's approval, far from reassuring Russia, further increased Moscow's worries. That raises serious doubts about the ability of regional IOs—especially those that are dominated by one of the intervening powers—to legitimate the use of force in the eyes of antagonistic non-member states. The Bosnia case also demonstrates that the mere fact that a UNSC resolution mentions "all necessary means," as was the case for both 770 and 836, does not mean that all council members will

---

103. Schulte, author interview.
104. Former UN secretary-general Boutros-Ghali (1999: 86) agrees that SCR 770, in particular, merely authorized using force for the "protection of UN troops under attack."
105. On the inclusion of Russian troops in IFOR see Carter and Perry 1999: 33–44.

automatically interpret it as authorizing *coercive* military action. Indeed, an expansive interpretation on the part of the United States of a SCR originally approved to authorize only limited force may signal anything but "benign" U.S. intentions. The disagreements between Russia and the West over what kind of military action was authorized by UN Resolutions 770 and 836, far from being unique, foreshadowed subsequent Russia-NATO disputes over the interpretation of relevant UN resolutions on Kosovo in 1999 and especially Libya in 2011.[106]

The reluctance of U.S. military leaders to intervene in Bosnia between 1992 and 1995 played a crucial and hitherto neglected role in keeping American policy on a steady multilateral track. As this chapter has shown, proceeding by multilateral consensus through NATO came at considerable cost, limiting U.S. freedom of action, emboldening local warring factions, and harming the Clinton administration's domestic and international standing. Senior civilian policymakers such as Albright and Holbrooke repeatedly advocated striking Bosnian Serb strongholds unilaterally to reassert U.S. credibility and facilitate a resolution of the war that would not simply ratify the results of ethnic cleansing. Yet civilian interventionists were rebuffed by a risk-averse Pentagon that worried about large numbers of American soldiers "getting stuck" with primary responsibility for Bosnia's stabilization. In the long run, Washington's multilateral approach paid off, at least to the extent that it limited U.S. liability. Proceeding by consensus with the European allies at every step and channeling the use of force through NATO, the United States was able to link the alliance's future credibility to success in Bosnia. That locked in European support and made it possible to shift most of the stabilization and reconstruction burden to EU member states after Dayton.

Other factors, like norm internalization and concerns about negative issue linkage, cannot account for Washington's steady multilateral course. There is no evidence that U.S. policymakers had internalized international norms requiring IO approval as a condition for legitimate intervention. The most influential civilian policymakers, notably Albright and Lake, were clearly willing to bypass relevant IOs whenever they believed that the costs of multilateralism outweighed its benefits. Nor can concerns about issue linkage, or costly retaliation in other policy domains by antagonistic states such as Russia, have motivated U.S. efforts to secure IO approval. U.S. policymakers understood that NATO's approval would do little to reassure Russia, and predictably, Washington's expansive interpretation of existing UNSC resolutions intensified frictions with Moscow.

106. On Kosovo, see chapter 5. On Libya see the conclusion of this book.

[5]

Kosovo, 1998–99: Reassuring the Generals With NATO's Buy-In

On March 24, 1999, NATO member states began a coercive bombing campaign against the Federal Republic of Yugoslavia. Allied aircraft from fourteen countries pounded Yugoslavia for seventy-eight consecutive days in an effort to persuade President Slobodan Milosevic to stop his systematic oppression and mass expulsion of the Kosovar Albanian population. The United States contributed the lion's share of the military hardware and technological capabilities to the air campaign, Operation Allied Force. However, all the most important decisions, including those to threaten air strikes, initiate air strikes, and approve increasingly controversial targets, were taken by the allies collectively through an integrated NATO command structure. That arguably made the Kosovo air war "the most multilateral campaign ever" (Betts 2001: 126).

Proceeding by multilateral consensus through NATO came at significant cost to the United States. First, securing the North Atlantic Council's endorsement for air strikes required months of intense transatlantic negotiations, undermining Washington's coercive leverage while the situation in Kosovo continued to deteriorate. Second, even after NATO endorsed air strikes and commenced military action, allied disagreements over target selection and tactics made for an ineffective use of airpower, allowing Yugoslav authorities to escalate their ethnic cleansing campaign and bringing the U.S.-led intervention close to failure. Yet without NATO's approval "it is pretty clear that it [the intervention] would not have happened," explains Walter Slocombe, U.S. undersecretary of defense for policy at the time.[1] The freedom-of-action costs of

---

1. Author interview with Walter B. Slocombe (June 9, 2011).

working through NATO were largely foreseeable, given the previous experience over Bosnia. Why, then, did U.S. policymakers come to view NATO's approval as practically necessary for military intervention?

When long-simmering ethnic tensions in Kosovo broke out into open violence in the spring of 1998, Secretary of State Madeleine Albright and several of her hawkish collaborators, seeing NATO's reluctance to intervene, initially made an impassioned plea for U.S. unilateral air strikes. What followed was a year-long bureaucratic struggle in Washington between Albright and other humanitarian interventionists on the one side and America's reluctant military leaders on the other. The Joint Chiefs doubted that limited air strikes could resolve the Kosovo problem, and they were determined to avoid a situation in which the United States might have to introduce ground troops to impose a settlement. Furthermore, the top-ranking generals were adamant that any long-term stabilization of Kosovo should be left to the European allies.

Process tracing reveals that Albright and her fellow interventionists recognized, only after being rebuffed by the Pentagon, that securing the NAC's approval and channeling the use of force through NATO would be necessary in order to lock in allied support and reassure the U.S. military about postwar burden sharing. Several of Albright's former collaborators interviewed for this chapter indeed acknowledge that they came to view NATO's approval as central to winning their bureaucratic struggle with the Pentagon. The chapter finds no support for alternative arguments that explain policymakers' efforts to secure IO approval as the result of norm internalization or concerns about negative issue linkage.

BACKGROUND TO THE CRISIS

The Serbs have long viewed Kosovo as the historical birthplace of their nation and the site of the most important event in their national history, the 1389 battle of Kosovo Polje (Field of the Blackbirds), which resulted in nearly five centuries of Ottoman Muslim rule. At the same time, Kosovo has for centuries been inhabited by a substantial ethnic Albanian population (over two-thirds of total residents in recent decades) that considers the region a natural part of greater Albania. Those incompatible nationalist claims have resulted in long-standing ethnic tensions (Phillips 2012: 3–6).

By the time NATO launched Operation Allied Force in late March 1999, Kosovo had already been on the international community's radar for roughly a decade. In 1989 Milosevic, seeking to consolidate his power as president of Serbia, stripped Kosovo of its regional autonomy. He then encouraged unemployed Serbs to move to Kosovo, guaranteeing them local employment in an effort to change the province's demographics. After the outbreak of ethnic war in neighboring Bosnia in 1992, Kosovo risked being engulfed by sectarian violence. The United States, under President George H. W. Bush, concluded at the time that only a credible threat of U.S. military action could prevent a violent Serb crackdown in Kosovo.[2] Consequently, on Christmas Eve 1992, Secretary of State Lawrence Eagleburger sent the following explicit warning to Belgrade in a classified cable: "In the event of conflict in Kosovo caused by Serbian action, the U.S. will be prepared to employ military force against Serbians in Kosovo and in Serbia proper" (quoted in Gellman, *WashPo*, Apr. 18, 1999). After President Bill Clinton came to office, the new secretary of state, Warren Christopher, reissued the "Christmas warning" to Milosevic twice—in February and July 1993 (ibid.).

In 1995, however, U.S. authorities chose to leave the Kosovo issue out of the negotiations with Milosevic at Dayton in order to avoid further complicating the diplomacy over Bosnia. Many Kosovar Albanians subsequently concluded that only violent resistance would bring sufficient international attention to their cause. In 1996 a previously unknown group, the Kosovo Liberation Army (KLA), emerged in the province and began to engage in sporadic attacks against Serb policemen and other central government representatives. The KLA's violent tactics aimed to provoke Serb authorities in the hope that Serb retaliation would bring about increased international attention and ideally trigger a foreign military intervention. Even Albright, who by her own account "sympathized with their [the KLA's] opposition to Milosevic," has acknowledged that "they seemed intent on provoking a massive Serb response so that international intervention would be unavoidable" (2003: 386). Hashim Thaci, one of the group's leaders who became the first prime minister of independent Kosovo in 2008, declared in a BBC interview shortly after the U.S.-led intervention that the KLA knew "any armed action we undertook would bring retaliation against civilians," but that was seen as a price worth paying.[3]

After a series of brazen KLA attacks in February 1998, Serb paramilitary and police forces launched a brutal counterinsurgency campaign that intentionally targeted civilians in an effort to persuade the Kosovar Albanian population to withdraw its support from the insurgents. The violence reached a critical threshold at the beginning of March, when Serb security forces killed fifty-eight ethnic Albanians in the Drenice

2. Robert Frowick, the U.S. envoy to the region, recommended issuing a unilateral threat, which, however, involved some bluffing. Author interview with James O'Brien, DOS adviser on Balkans policy, 1992–2000 (Mar. 9, 2010).
3. In "Moral Combat: NATO at War," *BBC 2 Special Report*, Mar. 12, 2000.

region of Kosovo (Daalder and O'Hanlon 2000: 10–11; IICK 2000: 67–71; Petritsch and Pichler 2004: 104–6). Secretary Albright, who had been deeply involved in shaping U.S. policy over Bosnia, was determined to avert humanitarian tragedy over Kosovo. That inclined her to support a preventive display of American force, before the violence reached potentially genocidal proportions. One lesson that Albright had learned from Bosnia was that Milosevic was a schoolyard bully—a boisterous and ruthless individual who nevertheless "responds to strength. . . . He needs to see the U.S. as a major power."[4]

The Costs of Multilateral Action

In the spring of 1998, prior to NATO's active involvement over Kosovo, Washington relied on the Balkans Contact Group, a diplomatic forum made up of the United States, Great Britain, France, Germany, Italy, and Russia, to coordinate the international response to the crisis. This group, Albright (2003: 383) recalls, was generally ineffective and "agreed on essentially nothing." To begin with, it included Russia, which was openly aligned with the Serbs. But Washington's principal Western European allies, too, were suspicious of the KLA and its brazen tactics. Through the first part of 1998, most Contact Group members insisted on impartial mediation between the conflicting parties, and it took the group several weeks to agree to impose even limited economic sanctions on Yugoslavia (Daalder and O'Hanlon 2000: 28–29; Burg 2003: 76).[5]

Confronted with a worsening humanitarian situation in Kosovo, Washington's principal European allies, including the United Kingdom, France, Italy, and Germany, at first insisted that any threat of force, let alone its actual use, had to be authorized by the UN Security Council (Clark 2001: 125; Bellamy 2002: 86–89). In early June 1998, London even circulated a draft UNSC resolution intended to authorize the use of "all necessary means" against Yugoslavia under chapter VII of the UN Charter (Smith, *WashPo*, June 6, 1998; Bellamy 2002: 88). The Russians, however, persuaded Washington and London to refrain from putting the draft resolution to a vote, making it clear that Moscow would veto any straightforward SC authorization of military action.[6] By mid-July 1998, the United States concluded that given Russia opposition, "efforts to

4. DOS Dayton History Project, interview with Madeleine Albright, Oct. 28, 1996.
5. During this period, Yugoslavia consisted of two constituent republics, Serbia and Montenegro.
6. Author interview with Peter Burleigh, Acting U.S. PermRep to the UN, 1998–99 (Apr. 3, 2010).

achieve a United Nations Security Council Resolution under Chapter VII would be counterproductive."[7] During subsequent months, Washington focused its multilateral diplomatic efforts almost exclusively on the Atlantic alliance, with the goal of securing an endorsement of military action from NATO's supreme political organ, the North Atlantic Council.

Technically, NATO had already become involved in the Kosovo crisis in late May 1998. Meeting in Luxembourg on May 28–29, NATO's foreign ministers agreed to initiate planning for preventive military deployments into Albania and Macedonia, aimed at avoiding a regional spillover of the crisis. A few weeks later, NATO's defense ministers directed their military planners to develop a full range of options to halt the campaign of violent repression and expulsion in Kosovo (Daalder and O'Hanlon 2000: 32; Cordesman 2001: 10). For several more months, however, NATO remained far from a consensus on threatening—let alone using—military force against Serbia. As former deputy secretary of state Strobe Talbott (2002: 301) recalls, "through the summer and into the early fall of 1998 . . . NATO was paralyzed by the West Europeans' unwillingness to contemplate military action without authorization from the UN Security Council."

Spiraling Ethnic Violence

There is evidence that NATO's (but especially Washington's) belligerent rhetoric during this period, combined with the alliance's unwillingness to follow through on its threats of military action, made matters in Kosovo worse. While NATO's threats appear to have rapidly lost credibility in Milosevic's eyes, the Kosovar Albanians were emboldened by the alliance's tough-sounding rhetoric—and the result was a spiral of ethnic violence on the ground.

The first concrete indications of possible NATO military action in June 1998 (the alliance held a major aerial exercise in nearby Albania and Macedonia), combined with pressure from Moscow, initially persuaded Milosevic to scale down counterinsurgency activities in Kosovo (Daalder and O'Hanlon 2000: 32–35; Petritsch and Pichler 2004: 119–22). The KLA, however, promptly took advantage of the Yugoslav authorities' restraint to launch a significant military offensive of its own: by mid-July, the rebel group had set up numerous checkpoints in the province and claimed

7. NSC/Principals Committee (hereafter PC), "Meeting on Kosovo," SumConcl, July 15, 1998. Most declassified documents cited in this chapter have been released pursuant to MDR No. 2009-0983-M, requested by the author, and are now available at http://clinton.presidentiallibraries.us/collections/show/36.

exclusive control of as much as 40 percent of Kosovo's territory (Burg 2003: 79; Petritsch and Pichler 2004: 116–17). Thereupon even moderate ethnic Albanian leaders, aware that the KLA could not defeat Yugoslav security forces on its own, openly began to call for U.S. or NATO military intervention in the hope that it might pave the way for Kosovo's independence (Harris, *WashPo*, May 30, 1998; Bellamy 2002: 83). Yet by the end of July, as a former high-ranking NATO official explains, "Milosevic who was never unaware of NATO deliberations rightly concluded that the NATO threat was a bluff," and consequently he ordered his security forces to crush the KLA.[8] Over the next month, fearing Serb reprisals, more than two hundred thousand ethnic Albanians either fled to neighboring countries or became internally displaced (Halberstam 2001: 398–99; Petritsch and Pichler 2004: 122).

Roughly the same pattern repeated itself later that year. On September 23, the UNSC adopted Resolution 1199, which, while not authorizing the use of force, condemned the Serb crackdown and demanded that Belgrade end military operations in Kosovo and facilitate the return of all Kosovar Albanians to their homes. By mid-October, after intense negotiations led by U.S. envoy Richard Holbrooke and now under the explicit threat of NATO air strikes, Milosevic agreed to stop military operations in Kosovo, commence direct talks with the Kosovar Albanians, and accept the deployment of unarmed international monitors to the province (Daalder and O'Hanlon 2000: 45–48; Clark 2001: 145–47).[9] Yugoslav authorities at first appeared fairly cooperative—indeed, senior U.S. officials privately acknowledged in late October that "there exists very substantial FRY [Federal Republic of Yugoslavia] compliance with UNSCR 1199."[10]

The October agreement, however, focused entirely on Serb compliance and placed no concrete demands on the Kosovar Albanian side (Daalder and O'Hanlon 2000: 57–59; IICK 2000: 150; Burg 2003: 104). In subsequent weeks, the KLA once again took advantage of Serb restraint to reorganize itself and regain control of parts of Kosovo from which it had recently been expelled. By mid-November, the KLA was engaged in systematic attacks against Serb targets in Kosovo. According to Wolfgang Petritsch, then the EU's special envoy for Kosovo, those attacks were clearly intended to bring about Serb retaliation with the goal of triggering a U.S.

8. Gen. Klaus Naumann, *Kosovo After-Action Review: Statement Before the Senate ArmedServ Committee*, 106th Cong. (Nov. 3, 1999), 3.
9. On the terms of the October agreement see also Weller 2009: 100–102.
10. NSC/Deputies Committee (hereafter DC), "Meeting on Kosovo," SumConcl, Oct. 27, 1998.

or NATO military intervention (Petritsch and Pichler 2004: 148).[11] The ensuing Serb crackdown, launched in December, was particularly harsh this time around (O'Connor, *NYT*, Dec. 24, 1998). NATO, however, was still not ready to use military force. Javier Solana, NATO's secretary-general at the time, acknowledges that in late 1998, NATO was still "very far away from action."[12] That became fully apparent toward the end of the year, when several European countries publicly hinted that the KLA had brought the Serb crackdown upon itself (Daalder and O'Hanlon 2000: 61; Petritsch and Pichler 2004: 155).

By early 1999, the violence in Kosovo risked spiraling out of control. On January 15, Serb paramilitary forces killed forty-five ethnic Albanians, most of them civilians, near the village of Racak in southern Kosovo (Daalder and O'Hanlon 2000: 63; Halberstam 2001: 409–10). The United States advocated a forceful response to the massacre. Policymakers in Washington briefly discussed two possible courses of action: first, immediately launch limited NATO air strikes "to degrade Belgrade's ability to conduct repressive security operations in Kosovo";[13] or, alternatively, issue an ultimatum for Milosevic to accept an interim political agreement within ninety-six hours and in case of noncompliance launch a phased NATO air campaign to impose the agreement.[14] Even after Racak, however, the principal Western European allies remained hesitant to initiate military action against Belgrade. "The key allies weren't ready," remembers Alexander Vershbow, then the U.S. ambassador to NATO.[15]

The Western Europeans insisted on a further round of negotiations. Hence military action was again postponed while representatives of Yugoslavia and the Kosovar Albanians were summoned to Rambouillet, France, for negotiations on a comprehensive political settlement. Belgrade was asked to withdraw most of its security forces from Kosovo, grant substantial autonomy to the province, and accept the presence of armed international peacekeepers. Meanwhile, the Kosovar Albanians were asked to dismantle the KLA and renounce their claim for independent statehood. For several weeks, neither of the parties appeared willing to compromise. But after Secretary Albright signed a secret side letter, promising that Kosovo could hold a referendum on independence after a three-year period, the Kosovar Albanians accepted the Rambouillet agreement on March 18, 1999. Yugoslav authorities continued to reject it.

---

11. For a similar conclusion see also Naumann, *Kosovo After-Action Review*, 2.
12. Author interview with Javier Solana (Mar. 24, 2011).
13. NSC/DC, "Meeting on Kosovo," SumConcl, Jan. 16, 1999.
14. NSC/DC, "Meeting on Kosovo," SumConcl, Jan. 20, 1999.
15. Author interview with Alexander Vershbow (Apr. 5, 2010).

That finally prompted NATO to reach a consensus on commencing air strikes to achieve Yugoslav compliance (Weller 2009: 152–55; see also Albright 2003: 402–30).

NATO began bombing Yugoslavia on March 24. Milosevic must have known that he had no chance of prevailing militarily against the most powerful alliance in history. Why, then, did he choose to stand up to NATO instead of yielding at Rambouillet? Undoubtedly his choice reflected the fear of losing Kosovo, a region of great symbolic importance to his core Serb nationalist constituency (Halberstam 2001: 387–88; Weller 2009: 136–48).[16] But it also appears likely that Milosevic, having observed NATO's divisions over the previous year, did not take the threat of military action very seriously and expected at worst a few limited air strikes. General Klaus Naumann, who chaired NATO's military committee at the time, suggests that by early 1999, NATO's "stick had been transformed into a rubber baton" because the allies "had threatened too often and had not done anything."[17] Albright, too, acknowledges "it is possible Milosevic thought that we were bluffing" (2003: 406)

Compromised Military Effectiveness

The consensus on using military force that had emerged within NATO after the breakdown of the Rambouillet negotiations remained exceedingly tenuous. The predominant assumption, or hope, was that the alliance would fight a short, limited war. The goal was not to *compel* the Serbs to leave Kosovo by crushing them militarily but rather to employ moderate amounts of force to *persuade* Milosevic to return to the negotiating table. When the air strikes began, NATO leaders told UN Secretary-General Kofi Annan that it "would be a matter of three or four days of bombing and then it would be over" (Annan 2012: 97). The alliance had initially not even developed plans for more than two weeks of air strikes—a far cry from the seventy-eight days, or two and a half months, that it ultimately took to break Milosevic's will to resist (Cordesman 2001: 21; see also Burg 2003: 93; Shelton 2010: 370–71).

The NATO coalition used force only in limited and incremental amounts. American defense leaders would have preferred to hit Milosevic hard from the beginning, applying overwhelming force to swiftly defeat the Yugoslav military. "That's what air force doctrine calls for— figure out where your opponent's center of gravity is and knock the hell

16. Gibbs (2009: 188–89) argues that Yugoslav authorities primarily rejected the idea of a NATO-led implementation force.
17. Klaus Naumann, *US Policy and NATO Military Operations in Kosovo: Hearing Before the Senate ArmedServ Committee*, 106th Cong. (Nov. 3, 1999), 466.

out of it," explains Colonel Gregory Kaufmann, who headed the Pentagon's Balkans task force at the time.[18] But the political imperative of holding together a fractious multinational coalition outweighed immediate considerations of military effectiveness. Secretary of Defense William Cohen, asked at the time why NATO did not launch a more robust air campaign from the beginning, admitted as much: "Acting unilaterally, . . . that's precisely the kind of air campaign that you'd want—hit fast and hard, and cripple Milosevic's forces as soon as possible. The difference here, of course, is that we're acting as an alliance."[19]

Concerns among the Western European allies about bombing sensitive facilities resulted in a cumbersome and micromanaged targeting process. Many European NATO members, unlike the United States, had signed the 1977 additional protocol to the 1949 Geneva Conventions, which bars attacks on "objects indispensable to the survival of the civilian population" (Coleman 2007: 234). As a result, those countries were reluctant to strike dual-use infrastructure, such as electrical power grids, bridges, and fuel-storage facilities. The principal European allies, notably Britain and France, wanted to have a say in the selection of particular targets (Daalder and O'Hanlon 2000: 123). Meanwhile, the Italians, Germans, and Greeks complained that moving ahead too quickly on controversial targets might trigger domestic political crises in their respective capitals (Schnabel and Thakur 2000: chap. 9; see also Clark 2001: 213). By early June, an exasperated JCS chairman, General Hugh Shelton, complained to President Clinton that "after months of bombing we have still not been allowed to hit some of the more strategic targets near Belgrade" (Shelton 2010: 384).

The thirteen allies other than the United States that actually participated in the air campaign (twelve European countries plus Canada) dropped only 20 percent of all bombs, launched barely 10 percent of all cruise missiles, and conducted fewer than 10 percent of the crucial electronic warfare and reconnaissance missions (Daalder and O'Hanlon 2000: 14; Cordesman 2001: 22, 64). As John Hamre, the deputy secretary of defense at the time, explains, the United States "had 600 aircraft in the theater that could sustain night-time combat operations, whereas the total contribution of the [other] NATO allies was only twelve aircraft that could fly fully at night."[20] In terms of military capabilities, the United States could thus easily have conducted the campaign unilaterally. It

18. Author interview with Col. Gregory Kaufmann, chief of staff, 1997–98, and director, 1999–2001, OSD Balkans task force (Mar. 10, 2010).
19. William Cohen, interview for "War in Europe," *Frontline*, PBS, Feb. 2000, http://www.pbs.org/wgbh/pages/frontline/shows/kosovo.
20. John Hamre, e-mail to author (Feb. 17, 2010).

might also have done so more effectively as there would have been fewer coordination problems and fewer limitations on striking dual-use infrastructure. Albright came close to admitting as much when she declared after the first month of ineffective bombing that "not everything may be moving as rapidly as it would unilaterally."[21]

In addition, the multinational coalition was extremely risk-averse. To avoid Yugoslav air defenses, alliance aircraft generally flew at an altitude of about fifteen thousand feet. As a consequence, the pilots' ability to reliably identify and hit Serb military targets, especially in Kosovo's mountainous and forested terrain as well as generally in bad weather, was significantly curtailed (Roberts 1999: 115–16; Daalder and O'Hanlon 2000: 122). Bombing from this altitude also increased the risk of "collateral damage," such as when NATO hit a passenger train crossing a bridge and mistook a convoy of Kosovar Albanian refugees for an armored column. According to a report by the NGO Human Rights Watch, at least five hundred Serb and ethnic Albanian civilians died as a result of the NATO bombing.[22]

Finally, European sensitivities were one important reason why at the beginning of the air campaign, NATO publicly ruled out the possibility of a ground invasion of Kosovo. As Gregory Schulte, then a senior NSC staffer working on the Balkans, explains, "Getting the decision on air strikes was hard for NATO, and there was a real concern that if you added to that the possibility of ground troops being introduced, you wouldn't even get air strikes."[23] Ruling out a ground offensive from the beginning, however, almost certainly further undermined the alliance's coercive leverage, since Milosevic was essentially being told that he would not have to bear the full brunt of U.S. and allied military power.

The discord within the alliance and NATO's constant hesitations may well have convinced Milosevic that he might be able to ride it out. "You want to hold the group together," explains a former senior State Department official. "But it's a perverse, or at any rate a very difficult situation. You had a very savvy interlocutor, who knew nothing really bad was going to happen [to Serbia], and so that meant he wasn't going to be intimidated."[24] Air Force General Charles Wald, who was closely

21. Madeleine Albright, *The War in Kosovo: Hearing Before the Senate Foreign Relations Committee*, 106th Cong. (Apr. 20, 1999), 18.
22. Human Rights Watch, "Civilian Deaths in the NATO Air Campaign," Feb. 2000, http://www.hrw.org/legacy/reports/2000/nato/. See also Weitsman 2014: 82.
23. Author interview with Gregory Schulte, Special Assist. to the Pres. for Balkans Policy, NSC staff, 1998–99 (Mar. 9, 2010). See also Clark 2001: 166–67; Weitsman 2014: 90.
24. Author interview with James O'Brien, Dep. Dir. of Policy Planning and Special Balkans Envoy, DOS, 1997–2001 (Mar. 9, 2010). See also Cordesman 2001: 17; Burg 2003: 94.

involved in planning the air campaign, has few doubts that NATO's tentative and incremental approach to war fighting "prolonged the problem."[25]

Serbs Emboldened after Launch of Pinprick Air Strikes

In October 1998, President Clinton told U.S. senators that if force was going to be used against Milosevic, "there will be no pinprick strikes" (quoted in Sciolino, *NYT*, Apr. 18, 1999). The president was referring to the limited air strikes over Bosnia earlier that decade, which for a long time had allowed the genocide there to continue unabated. However, once the air strikes over Kosovo began, they remained highly restricted, conjuring up uncomfortable memories of the Bosnia pinpricks. Following standard practice, the initial package of air strikes that the NAC approved in late March 1999 was "focused primarily on the [Yugoslav] integrated air defense system in Serbia"—however, NATO commenced hostilities without even having finalized and approved "contingency response options for follow-on strikes . . . intended to respond to renewed violent aggression against the Kosovar Albanians."[26] The alliance's hesitations allowed the Yugoslav leader to step up his ethnic cleansing campaign in Kosovo virtually unimpeded and may well have emboldened him to do so. During the first ten days of air strikes, Serbian security forces forcibly expelled half a million Kosovars across the border into Albania and Macedonia, creating a massive humanitarian emergency that overshadowed anything seen over the previous year. By the end of NATO's bombing campaign, approximately 860,000 Kosovar civilians had been expelled from the country and another 590,000 were internally displaced, out of a total population of less than 2 million (IICK 2000: 90; Moskovitz and Lantis 2004: 264).

NATO's intelligence analysts had not fully predicted the scale of Milosevic's ethnic cleansing in response to an allied air war—according to one source, the alliance anticipated "only" 200,000 new Kosovar refugees (Garton Ash, *NYRB*, Sept. 21, 2000). Nevertheless, NATO leaders clearly anticipated that Yugoslav security forces would dramatically step up their assault on the ethnic Albanian population of Kosovo. The following dialogue, which took place on March 6, 1999, between U.S. General

---

25. Author interview with Gen. Charles Wald, Dir. Strategic Plans and Policy, USAF headquarters, Jan.–Oct. 1998, and Vice Dir. Strategic Plans and Policy, Joint Staff, Oct. 1998–2000 (Mar. 8, 2010).

26. Samuel Berger, "Meeting on Kosovo Military Options," memorandum for the president, Mar. 20, 1999.

[157]

Wesley Clark, NATO's supreme allied commander, and Secretary of State Albright is illustrative in this regard:

> Albright: "If we commence the strikes, will the Serbs attack the population?"
> Clark: "Almost certainly they will attack the civilian population. This is what they are promising to do."
> Albright: "So what should we do? How can we prevent their striking the civilians?"
> Clark: "We can't. . . . It's not going to be pleasant."
> Albright: "But you think we should go ahead?"
> Clark: "Yes, we have to. . . . We have to follow through and make it work."
> Albright: "Yes, I think so, too" (quoted in Clark 2001: 171).

NATO's official line was that there was little the alliance could have done to prevent the ethnic cleansing anyway. A few days after the launch of the air campaign, German intelligence claimed to have found evidence of preexisting plans for a Serbian Operation Horseshoe, allegedly approved by Milosevic in late 1998, to cleanse Kosovo of virtually the entire ethnic Albanian population regardless of NATO actions (Daalder and O'Hanlon 2000: 58). But after the war, it emerged that the Horseshoe allegations were based on thin evidence and may have been fabricated from run-of-the-mill Bulgarian intelligence reports (Gibbs 2009: 192). The Serbs almost certainly had planned for a possible large-scale expulsion of Kosovar Albanians—otherwise they could not have implemented it so quickly after the start of the air strikes. Yet one cannot infer from the existence of a plan, especially a contingency plan, the firm intention to actually carry it out. Indeed, had Milosevic been confronted with the credible threat of a ground invasion of Kosovo or substantial air strikes against strategic targets in Belgrade, he might well have been deterred from authorizing such a massive population expulsion.

As one critic pointedly notes, "NATO was willing to bomb but not . . . to take the kinds of military action that might have prevented the ethnic cleansing of almost the entire Kosovar population" (Rieff 1999: 7). Given the alliance's professed goal of humanitarian protection and the fact that the risk of large-scale ethnic cleansing was clearly anticipated, NATO's war planning and subsequent combat behavior verge on the irresponsible. While most refugees were able to return to their former homes after the end of hostilities, an estimated ten thousand Kosovar Albanians perished at the hands of Serb security forces during the NATO bombings (IICK 2000: 2).

Not until late April 1999, as European leaders became aware that NATO's failure over Kosovo might call into question the alliance's future viability, did they agree to step up the bombing campaign by deploying additional aircraft and significantly expanding the target set (Cordesman 2001: 27; Power 2003: 456–57). Those moves, combined with a Russian diplomatic initiative in early June and growing indications that in spite of earlier declarations a U.S.-led ground combat option was now being seriously considered, eventually broke Milosevic's will to resist.[27] But the multinational coalition could easily have broken apart had Belgrade held out for another few weeks and had NATO been confronted with the choice of actually having to implement a ground offensive. Talbott candidly sums it up as follows: "Milosevic could have beaten us. Could we have kept the thing going for eighty-five days? One hundred? . . . I think if he had held out for another couple of weeks, the coalition might well have collapsed. And we might have had to accept some half-baked compromise. It ended OK, but it could have ended disastrously, and we were acutely aware of that."[28]

The United States could have chosen a different approach in order to maximize its coercive leverage vis-à-vis Milosevic. First, in the spring of 1998, U.S. authorities could have threatened to use force unilaterally, reviving the Christmas warning first issued by Secretary Eagleburger in 1992, and they might even have unilaterally launched a few missiles against strategic targets in Belgrade. Second, once the NAC had approved the use of force in the spring of 1999, Washington could have chosen to carry out a larger bombing campaign on its own or with only a loose coalition of the willing (e.g., Britain and Canada), instead of relying on the alliance's formal and cumbersome institutional structure to manage the war. Proceeding in such a way would have made it easier to hit strategic targets in Serbia from early on, which in turn might have forced Milosevic's capitulation within a matter of days. All that assumes, of course, that the continental European allies' reluctance was the only obstacle to a more decisive U.S. approach. But there were powerful players in Washington who were staunchly opposed to U.S. unilateral intervention.

ALBRIGHT'S PUSH FOR UNILATERAL AIR STRIKES

President Clinton's principal advisers in the policy debate over Kosovo were National Security Adviser Samuel Berger, Secretary of

27. Clinton (2004: 855) writes that "by late May, [he] was ready to send troops in if necessary." See also Daalder and O'Hanlon 2000: 155–60.
28. Author interview with Strobe Talbott, DepSecState, 1994–2000 (July 9, 2009).

State Albright, Secretary of Defense Cohen, and JCS Chairman Shelton. In the spring of 1998, when the deteriorating situation in Kosovo became a matter of growing international concern, Secretary Albright emerged as the administration's leading advocate of military intervention. As one of her former aides recalls, "Albright believed very early on that the lessons of Bosnia were that Milosevic would respond only to the use of force, and she began to talk about that—publicly. In the middle of 1998, the State Department was certainly the only department considering the use of force."[29]

During the previous crisis over Bosnia, Albright's influence in Washington had been limited, given her junior cabinet position as U.S. ambassador to the United Nations. Now, however, she was the administration's top foreign policy official, and she effectively used her new bully pulpit to advocate a decisive response to Milosevic's crackdown. Throughout 1998, President Clinton focused much of his energies on deflecting accusations that he had engaged in sexual misconduct with Monica Lewinsky, a young White House intern. Albright skillfully took advantage of the resulting power vacuum in the administration to advance her cause (Halberstam 2001: 386; Burg 2003: 84).

The secretary of state not only pushed her own views assertively during internal debates—she also publicly went out ahead of her fellow cabinet members, using tough rhetoric in an effort to commit the administration to resolving the crisis. Thus, as early as March 1998 she declared at a news conference in Rome, "We are not going to stand by and watch the Serbian authorities do in Kosovo what they can no longer get away with doing in Bosnia" (quoted in Gellman, *WashPo*, Apr. 18, 1999). Apart from Bosnia, the relevant historical analogy for Albright was Munich: there could be no appeasement in the face of aggression and attempted genocide (Albright 2003: 19; Power 2003: 326). Ronald Asmus, then a senior State Department official working on European affairs, is convinced that the Kosovo intervention "never would have happened without Albright."[30] He remembers that as soon as the first images of ethnic massacres in Kosovo began to emerge, "she said, 'it reminds me of the Holocaust. This is unacceptable.' She had made up her mind when she looked at those pictures and said: 'This is evil.'"[31]

During the first half of 1998, most of Washington's key European allies—including France, Italy, and Germany—were reluctant to

29. Author interview with James Rubin, AssistSecState for Public Affairs, 1997–2000 (Apr. 9, 2010). See also Bellamy 2002: 72–73; Moskovitz and Lantis 2004: 256.
30. Ronald Asmus, Dep. AssistSecState for European Affairs, 1997–2000, e-mail to author (Apr. 5, 2010).
31. Ibid.

countenance the use of force (Bellamy 2002: 86–87; Albright 2003: 380–83). In light of that, Albright and several of her hawkish State Department advisers became convinced that U.S. unilateral strikes might be necessary. Robert Gelbard, the administration's Balkans envoy, and U.S. ambassador to Macedonia Christopher Hill, an influential voice on policy toward the region, insisted from early 1998 onward that Washington publicly reemphasize the threat of U.S. unilateral intervention first issued in 1992.[32] Toward the middle of April, Gelbard went further in a meeting with Albright, where he argued that the United States might have to actually carry out unilateral air strikes. Gelbard's specific proposal was that a high-level emissary, ideally the secretary of state or her deputy, be dispatched to Belgrade with a letter from the president. Milosevic should be given an ultimatum of between three and five days to remove most of his security forces from Kosovo, and in case of noncompliance the United States should "use Tomahawk missiles, and in the middle of the night destroy the [Yugoslav] ministry of defense and the ministry of interior."[33] Thereafter, U.S. diplomats would go back to Belgrade and resume negotiations with Milosevic. Asked about the role of NATO and the European allies, Gelbard concedes, "I am not even sure we ever thought about the other allies at the time."[34]

Albright herself was deeply dissatisfied with the slow pace of multilateral diplomacy in the Balkans Contact Group. "I am sick and tired of going to meeting after meeting. Now I can see how Bosnia happened," she privately vented her frustration as early as March 1998 (quoted in Rubin, *FT*, Sept. 30, 2000). Over the next several weeks, the secretary of state came to agree with Gelbard that U.S. unilateral military action might be necessary. A former senior State Department official further clarifies Albright's thinking: "Because of where Secretary Albright was coming from, she thought there are some times when you need to do it regardless of multilateral support. And partially because of her own personal background, she had very strong feelings about what was happening in the Balkans and the role the U.S. could and should play."[35]

On April 23, 1998, Albright and Gelbard went to the White House, where they made the case for a U.S. unilateral ultimatum and potential air strike to National Security Adviser Berger and his deputy, Donald

---

32. Author interview with Robert Gelbard, U.S. Special Balkans Envoy, 1996–99 (Mar. 22, 2010). See also Clark 2001: 108.
33. Gelbard, author interview.
34. Ibid.
35. Author interview with Barbara Larkin, AssistSecState for Legisl. Affairs, 1996–99 (Apr. 2, 2010).

Kerrick.[36] Berger, however, summarily rejected the idea of bombing Serb infrastructure or administrative facilities as ill conceived. Eventually he lost his temper: "So you want to bomb some goddamn bridge!" Berger reportedly shouted. "Well, what if that doesn't work? Do you bomb another goddamn bridge?"[37] Berger was wary about publicly threatening force and absolutely opposed to doing so unilaterally. Once issued, the threat might have to be carried out. Then, assuming that a limited strike would not break Milosevic's resolve, the administration would have to escalate further, and ultimately American ground combat troops might have to be introduced.[38] The president himself, Albright recalls, subsequently made it "very clear that . . . we had to work with the allies, that we weren't going to do this unilaterally."[39]

Berger's and the president's skepticism about unilateral air strikes appears to have been influenced to a considerable degree by their frequent interactions with representatives of the JCS. Prior to the aforementioned meeting at the White House on April 23, America's defense leaders, aware of the State Department's planning behind the scenes, had made it clear that they strongly opposed any unilateral U.S. military action in the Balkans. "We used to talk to Sandy [Berger] a lot," remembers Lieutenant General David Weisman, who at the time played a key liaison role between military leaders and civilian authorities as the deputy head of policy and strategy on the Joint Staff. "Bob Gelbard had no idea about how to deploy military force."[40] As a senior U.S. military officer confirmed to the press shortly after NATO commenced hostilities, "We were not prepared for unilateral action" (quoted in Gellman, *WashPo*, Apr. 18, 1999).

SEEKING NATO'S SUPPORT TO MOLLIFY THE GENERALS

If Albright's preferred analogy was Munich, for the uniformed leaders the more relevant precedent was the quagmire in Vietnam. The Joint Chiefs doubted that airpower alone could persuade Milosevic to yield to Washington's demands, and they strongly opposed sending in U.S. ground troops to compel him to comply. Furthermore, they worried that even if a negotiated solution to the crisis could be found, an open-ended

36. Author interview with Donald Kerrick (Mar. 22, 2010). See also Albright 2003; Sciolino and Bronner, *NYT*, Apr. 18, 1999.
37. Gelbard, author interview. See also Daalder and O'Hanlon 2000: 30.
38. Gelbard, author interview. See also Halberstam 2001: 376.
39. Madeleine Albright, interview for "War in Europe."
40. Author interview with LTG David Weisman (Feb. 16, 2011).

peacekeeping mission would be needed that Congress and the American people might not support.[41] Berger, persuaded by the Joint Chiefs of the dangers of armed intervention, began to express concerns in the intramural debates that closely echoed those of the uniformed leadership: "This will be our Vietnam," he reportedly told Albright and her collaborators. "This will destroy the Clinton administration and we will not let you do that."[42] Over the following weeks, the secretary of state and her fellow advocates of intervention gradually realized that to achieve an administration consensus on the use of force, the European allies first had to be brought on board. Berger himself had hinted as much during the April 23 meeting. His view was that the administration should "avoid empty rhetoric as [it] tried to multilateralize the threat of force" (quoted in Daalder and O'Hanlon 2000: 30).

The Military's Concerns

The Joint Chiefs, led by Army General Shelton and his deputy, Air Force General Joseph Ralston, disputed that there were major U.S. strategic interests at stake in Kosovo that warranted the risks and high operational costs of armed intervention. Secretary of Defense Cohen tended to agree with the chiefs: he viewed Kosovo as an obscure place, and he questioned whether U.S. troops ought to be deployed to promote domestic political change in foreign countries. He also believed that the pure humanitarian argument proved too much—it would quickly lead the United States to overextend itself militarily.[43] Hence one fundamental question that Pentagon leaders repeatedly raised in the interagency debate was, "Do we really think Kosovo is so important that we should intervene militarily?"[44]

Shelton and Ralston saw lots of potential pitfalls, and Secretary Cohen reflected and magnified the generals' concerns in debates at the National Security Council. "We weren't totally opposed [to air strikes], but we were very reluctant," recalls a former senior military planner on the Joint Staff, before clarifying that there was in fact complete "opposition to a ground combat role to force the Serbs out of Kosovo."[45] The uniformed leaders' principal concern regarding airpower was that it might be

41. Wald, author interview. See also Clark 2001: 137, 165; Albright 2003: 395; Halberstam 2001: 411–16.
42. Author interview with Ronald Asmus (Apr. 21, 2010). See also Harris, *WashPo*, May 16, 1999.
43. Slocombe, author interview. See also Halberstam 2001: 441.
44. Kaufmann, author interview. See also Clark 2001: 120; Moskovitz and Lantis 2004: 259.
45. Weisman, author interview.

insufficient to persuade Milosevic to accede to Washington's demands, and they feared it would put the United States on a slippery slope toward a full-scale ground invasion. "People would say, 'OK just the threat of air strikes will work,'" General Ralston recalls. "Well, then we'd ask, what if it doesn't? 'OK,' they replied, 'then, if you drop one or two bombs, it will solve the problem.' Well, we continued, what if it doesn't? Then you'd have to go to the next step. Ultimately, you'd have to be prepared to introduce ground forces, or do whatever was needed."[46]

The uniformed leaders pushed back against those at the State Department and elsewhere who argued that since limited air strikes had succeeded in Bosnia, the same pattern could be expected to repeat itself over Kosovo. First, the generals reminded their hawkish civilian colleagues that in the case of Bosnia, the combined Croat-Muslim ground offensive of August and September 1995 had played a central role in persuading the Serbs to accept a negotiated solution. The ragtag KLA was not even close to posing a comparable military challenge to Milosevic. Furthermore, Kosovo, unlike Bosnia, was central to Milosevic's own political survival, which was bound to make him less amenable to compromise this time around.[47]

The Joint Chiefs were also fundamentally skeptical about using force in the pursuit of goals like ethnic minority protection and regional autonomy, which appeared eminently political in nature and could not be linked to precise military objectives. As a former senior Pentagon official explains, "The warfighters want clear military objectives—capture this hill, occupy this city. But with regard to Kosovo, they were asking, 'What is my mission?'"[48] The uniformed leaders worried that because military objectives were vague, the exit strategy could not be clearly defined. They feared becoming embroiled in protracted peacekeeping or counterinsurgency operations with dwindling U.S. domestic support, raising the specter of a Vietnam-like quagmire. Consequently, one question the military asked over and over again was, "How do we define success here?"[49]

The generals worried that even if air strikes persuaded Milosevic to accept Washington's demands, using airpower would inevitably escalate the situation on the ground in Kosovo. Therefore, in the aftermath of air strikes, ultimate success would almost certainly require an open-ended international military commitment to maintain peace and stability in the

---

46. Author interview with Gen. Joseph Ralston (Mar. 17, 2009). See also Clark 2001: 119.
47. Slocombe and Weisman, author interviews.
48. Author interview with John Veroneau, AssistSecDef for Legisl. Affairs, 1999–2001 (Apr. 7, 2010).
49. Ibid.

region. Planners at the Pentagon "were very much looking at SFOR [i.e., the international stabilization force in Bosnia]," explains Kaufmann, the former head of the Balkans task force in the Office of the Secretary of Defense. "Our thought was that we would have to deploy a similar kind of force in Kosovo. Certainly that was the first way that people at OSD were looking at this—that any eventual mission if the coercive diplomacy worked would be more like a peacekeeping or peace-enforcement mission."[50]

Through 1998 and into early 1999, the JCS and senior OSD officials expressed significant concerns in the interagency debates about the potential lack of congressional support for another protracted U.S. troop deployment to the Balkans in addition to the one in Bosnia. As General Ralston recalls, "The Congress was pretty skeptical about involvement in the Balkans and in Kosovo. The military didn't want to find themselves in a situation where we get started in this and then suddenly the Congress says, 'Well, wait a minute, we're not going to support that!' Because then you don't have a way to succeed."[51]

Worries about Congressional Support

The senior military officers had learned from Vietnam and the more recent experience in Somalia that maintaining domestic support for the mission's entire duration is critical to its success. They feared that given the limited U.S. interests at stake in Kosovo, even a few U.S. casualties might cause domestic support to evaporate, resulting in a precipitous withdrawal of American troops that might harm the military as an institution.[52] As General Clark (2001: 119), who was personally more supportive of intervention than his Pentagon superiors, remembers: "the top military officials wanted to protect their people and their resources." The generals' awareness of their organizational interests, combined with their ideological skepticism about humanitarian intervention, made them acutely concerned about operational costs and the related issue of domestic support. Secretary of Defense Cohen, a former congressman who had joined the House of Representatives at the end of the Vietnam War, was less parochial in outlook but nevertheless harbored similar concerns about the lack of support on Capitol Hill for another protracted troop commitment to the Balkans.[53]

---

50. Kaufmann, author interview. See also Clark 2001: 307; Daalder and O'Hanlon 2000: 65.
51. Ralston, author interview. See also Albright 2003: 395; Clark 2001: 137–38.
52. Veroneau, author interview.
53. Cohen, interview for "War in Europe." See also Daalder and O'Hanlon 2000: 53–54; Halberstam 2001: 440–42.

[165]

Former senior officials from the State Department confirm that, compared with their Pentagon colleagues, during the run-up to the Kosovo intervention they were less worried about congressional support.[54] In part, that may simply have reflected the departments' different congressional constituencies. The State Department deals primarily with the Senate Foreign Relations Committee, whose members are typically quite internationalist in outlook. Meanwhile, the Pentagon interacts primarily with members of the House and Senate Armed Services Committees, who play a key role in the defense appropriations and authorization process and are traditionally more reluctant to commit U.S. forces abroad. (Secretary Cohen had long been a member of the Senate Armed Services Committee, and consequently he understood the concerns of its members particularly well.)[55] Fundamentally, however, senior State Department officials tended to be significantly more optimistic than their Pentagon colleagues that, provided the right incentives were brought to the table (e.g., through a short display of American airpower), Milosevic would become more cooperative, and a largely self-sustaining autonomy arrangement for Kosovo could be achieved.

The prevailing view at the State Department for most of 1998 was that while *some* external presence would probably be needed to build confidence and maintain stability in Kosovo after a political settlement, that presence could be limited to aid workers, observers, and perhaps a small international police mission—without having to deploy a large international military force. Indeed, for some time, senior U.S. diplomats thought that renouncing a military deployment might be essential to make any political solution acceptable in Milosevic's eyes.[56] So long as senior State Department officials remained hopeful that an open-ended troop commitment would not be necessary, there was no reason for them to be particularly concerned about the issue of congressional support. Barbara Larkin, then the assistant secretary of state for relations with Capitol Hill, confirms that during the interagency debates, "it was the military and Secretary Cohen who raised those concerns [about congressional support] and caused those conversations to happen."[57]

Not until August 1998 did a senior State Department official, Ambassador to NATO Alexander Vershbow, make the case in a classified cable to Washington that the "only way" of stabilizing Kosovo would be "by putting an armed NATO peacekeeping force on the ground, as we did in

54. Larkin, Rubin, and Halperin, author interviews.
55. Larkin, author interview.
56. O'Brien and Burleigh, author interviews. See also Bellamy 2002: 82–84; Phillips 2012: 100–101.
57. Larkin, author interview.

Bosnia."[58] By contrast, the JCS expected from early on that air strikes would have to be followed by an open-ended deployment of external peacekeepers. For that reason, the uniformed leaders were adamant that airpower should be used only as a last resort, and for several months they insisted that alternative avenues of resolving the problem had not yet been exhausted.[59] So long as it appeared that air strikes could be avoided, the military leaders were happy to agree with their State Department colleagues that the administration should envision only a "civil implementation" mission for Kosovo, with specific emphasis given to "local police development and quick-impact civil reconstruction projects."[60] As a consequence, the administration as a whole persisted until late 1998 in the unrealistic assumption that "there will not be a NATO-led military force deployed to Kosovo to assist in implementing a settlement."[61]

It soon became clear that the U.S. military was determined to veto a strategy based on air strikes unless it was given credible assurances that Washington's European allies would carry the primary burden for maintaining long-term stability. The uniformed leaders believed that after air strikes, "the only way you could have a deal which would be real was if there was, effectively, an occupation," explains Slocombe, then the third highest-ranking Pentagon official. "So there had to be an international force, and the U.S. military was very anxious that we not have the main burden—in fact, we wanted to have as little of the burden as we could possibly have."[62]

In September 1998, National Security Adviser Berger acknowledged in a memo for the president that "using air power now could also commit us later to playing a role in implementing a settlement once one is agreed."[63] Berger noted with concern that "NATO has conducted neither the detailed planning nor the force generation for this option, and it is questionable whether allied countries . . . would be willing to make the necessary contributions."[64] During subsequent weeks, as Milosevic intensified his campaign of violent repression and the State Department stepped up its advocacy of military intervention, the Pentagon, which had found a sympathetic ear in Berger, became more assertive in its

---

58. Vershbow, author interview. See also Daalder and O'Hanlon 2001: 54–55.
59. Ralston, author interview.
60. NSC/DC, "Meeting on Kosovo," SumConcl, Oct. 28, 1998.
61. NSC/DC, "Meeting on Kosovo," SumConcl, Oct. 30, 1998.
62. Slocombe, author interview.
63. Samuel Berger, "Kosovo: Preparing for an Ultimatum," memorandum for the president, Sept. 24, 1998.
64. Ibid.

argument that the European allies would have to bear primary responsibility for any postwar stabilization.

Secretary of Defense Cohen declared in early October, "It is my recommendation and my—I would almost say insistence—that [the stabilization force] be largely, if not wholly, European in nature, given [that U.S. forces] will be carrying the bulk of the load" in any air campaign. He added that congressional unhappiness with the prolonged U.S. presence in Bosnia and the high costs of that mission dictated against "a significant presence of [U.S.] combat forces on the ground in Kosovo" (quoted in Graham and Droziak, *WashPo*, Oct. 7, 1998). The perceived need for international burden sharing as a way of maintaining U.S. domestic support made Cohen and the JCS "absolutely convinced that the United States could not afford to take any kind of unilateral action from a political point of view."[65]

NATO's Role in Reassuring the Generals

Berger and Clinton understood that overt opposition from the military could have had disastrous implications in terms of public and congressional support for the administration's Kosovo policy (Halberstam 2001: 375). In the period leading up to the intervention, the top-level uniformed officers for the most part voiced their disagreements privately in the intramural debates, but they clearly signaled to civilian authorities that there would be a political fight unless their concerns were taken seriously.[66] The military, of course, could also seek to persuade the more cautious civilian leaders of the validity of its views. By the fall of 1998, Berger had come to share the Joint Chiefs' worry that "Congress will be concerned about any military action that is seen as putting U.S. forces at risk or leading to a long-term military commitment." He thus warned the president that the administration might run into trouble on Capitol Hill "if it appears that the United States has a stronger commitment . . . than do its European allies."[67]

The JCS could further attempt to shape the attitudes of congressional leaders and establish informal coalitions with sympathetic legislators, particularly from the Armed Services Committees. "Do the military have back channels to the Congress? Of course they do," explains a former senior Pentagon official who was deeply involved in shaping U.S.-Kosovo policy.[68] For example, as the humanitarian crisis worsened in the

65. Cohen, interview for "War in Europe."
66. Hamre, e-mail to author. See also Halberstam 2001: 415.
67. Berger, "Kosovo: Preparing for an Ultimatum."
68. Kaufmann, author interview.

fall of 1998, legislators on Capitol Hill initially pressed the administration to carry out air strikes against Milosevic; but after being briefed by skeptical members of the JCS, previously hawkish members of Congress became more aware of the risks involved in such a course of action and consequently displayed greater hesitation (Pomper, *CQ Weekly*, Sept. 26 and Oct. 10, 1998).

From the perspective of Secretary Albright and her fellow advocates of armed intervention, the goal was not so much to persuade the JCS and OSD to wholeheartedly support a force-based strategy. Instead, the crucial challenge was to get the Pentagon leadership to a point at which it was no longer explicitly opposed to the use of force. That in turn could be expected to make it easier to mollify Berger and ultimately persuade President Clinton to authorize military action.[69] To that end, the civilian interventionists needed to take the generals' concerns very seriously. Put differently, as a result of the bureaucratic struggle over air strikes, in the course of 1998 the civilian interventionists had to more systematically consider the likely implications and potential downsides of their preferred course of action. James Rubin, one of Albright's closest collaborators, acknowledges that the interventionists at first "didn't want to spend a lot of time thinking about what would happen if it [i.e. the bombing] didn't work—that's true."[70] This is consistent with the argument presented in chapter 2, that hawkish civilian leaders initially rarely focus on questions of feasibility and costs when debating the use of force.

Undoubtedly, in this case the military's leverage was somewhat reduced by the fact that General Clark, the commander of U.S. troops in Europe and NATO's chief military official, was himself quite hawkish on Kosovo. "That made a huge difference in terms of how the internal debate unfolded," Rubin explains.[71] Clark had been a member of Holbrooke's negotiating team at Dayton in 1995, and like Albright he had been profoundly affected by his firsthand experience of dealing with Milosevic over Bosnia. As early as March 1998, Clark began to argue in the intramural debates that coercive air strikes might be needed to prevent a humanitarian disaster in Kosovo (Clark 2001: 109–13; Halberstam 2001: 396). Over the next several months, Clark became a close ally of Secretary Albright in the policy debate. As a senior State Department official who accompanied Albright on several trips to Europe recalls, "We would often fly to [NATO headquarters in] Brussels and Wes [Clark] and Madeleine [Albright] would go off in the corner one-on-one and talk for a

---

69. Asmus, author interview.
70. Author interview with James Rubin (Apr. 9, 2010).
71. Rubin, author interview. See also Halberstam 2001: 436.

very long time with no note takers and no one present. We all suspected they were talking about how to outmaneuver various opponents in the bureaucratic process who were opposed to what they wanted to do."[72]

However, Clark's close relationship with the State Department resulted in serious frictions with the JCS and Secretary Cohen. As General Weisman, the former deputy head of strategic planning on the Joint Staff explains, "Wes Clark was pushing to go to war. He would sometimes call Albright and not consult with the Pentagon at all. . . . [Consequently,] Secretary Cohen became suspicious of Wes. Secretary Cohen would never do anything without taking into account the recommendation of Hugh Shelton as chairman of the JCS."[73] It soon became clear that Clark did not speak for other Pentagon leaders on matters regarding Kosovo, and for most of 1998 the Joint Chiefs quite effectively curtailed his access to the president and the NSC (Clark 2001: 109, 126–27; Halberstam 2001: 436; Power 2003: 455).

Albright (2003: 383) recalls that regardless of Clark's support for intervention, in the face of a Pentagon leadership that was somewhere between very skeptical and outright opposed, "to forge a consensus within my own government [was] not an easy task." One of Albright's former collaborators confirms that "almost everyone in the U.S. government opposed her in the beginning. She had to first convince Berger, then Clinton. She convinced them through her tenacity."[74] The secretary's tenacity and commitment played an important role. However, in order to overcome the Pentagon's veto of military action, Albright and her fellow interventionists also needed to persuade the JCS and Secretary Cohen, as well as Berger and ultimately the president, that the United States' contribution to any stabilization force for Kosovo could be kept to a minimum. As a former senior adviser to Secretary Albright explains, "Our assumption was that we had to find ways to minimize the percentage of American troops . . . if there was any hope of getting the Pentagon . . . to buy it" (quoted in Gellman, *WashPo*, Apr. 18, 1999).

The only way of minimizing America's contribution to postwar stabilization without jeopardizing the overall policy was to maximize the contribution of the European allies. "That's why there was a lot of emphasis on making sure that the European allies came along on this thing—the uniformed pounded on it," explains a former senior U.S. defense official.[75] Albright's former executive assistant agrees that securing broad international support as well as concrete assurances of

72. Asmus, author interview.
73. Weisman, author interview.
74. Asmus, author interview.
75. Kaufmann, author interview.

postwar burden sharing became essential components of the State Department's strategy for winning the bureaucratic struggle in Washington: "To the extent that the secretary could reject the Pentagon's argument" about the costs of intervention by making a persuasive case that the stabilization burden would be shouldered largely by the European allies, "that certainly helped us in the interagency debate."[76]

In the top-level policy meetings, the uniformed leaders did not explicitly demand a NATO endorsement of the use of force, but nevertheless made their preference clearly known. Extrapolating from the previous experience in Bosnia, the JCS expected that securing NAC approval and involving the alliance in all aspects of policy planning and implementation would lock in alliance support for completing the mission. Tying the alliance's credibility to success in Kosovo would help commit NATO and its principal member states to sustained burden sharing. "If there was going to be a military solution, we wanted to make sure that the allies were on board," recalls General Weisman. "We needed the NATO endorsement, and NATO had to take the lead, so that everybody would be involved, not only with the operation, but also with the peace afterwards—in fact, that was the most important part."[77]

Senior State Department officials came to appreciate by the summer of 1998 that they needed to "secure multilateral approval," preferably through NATO, "in order to win the policy argument internally."[78] Initially, they also considered the possibility of seeking a UNSC mandate as a complement to NAC approval. As Morton Halperin, then the State Department's head of policy planning, explains, "From our point of view, if we had had a UN Security Council resolution to do it [use force], getting the Europeans involved would have been much easier."[79] However, by July 1998 senior U.S. diplomats understood that it would be very difficult to persuade Russia to abstain on a use-of-force resolution at the SC.[80] Consequently, in subsequent months the State Department worked hard to convince the European allies that NATO might have to use force without UN approval.

In late August 1998, the NSC Deputies Committee, where senior officials below cabinet rank typically work out the details of U.S. national security policy, concluded that "the first round of air strikes should not be launched without agreement in principle on a substantial follow-on

76. Author interview with Alejandro Wolff (Mar. 31, 2010).
77. Weisman, author interview.
78. Author interview with William Wood, Acting AssistSecState for IO Affairs, 1998–2002 (Jan. 25, 2011).
79. Author interview with Morton Halperin (Mar. 10, 2010).
80. Burleigh, author interview.

package. With this in mind, [it was decided that] Secretaries Albright and Cohen . . . will contact their [NATO] counterparts to . . . build consensus for substantial air operations."[81] State Department officials with experience in the field of transatlantic relations were confident that by involving NATO, the United States could trigger the "pull" of alliance solidarity and ensure European leadership on Kosovo's postwar stabilization—after all, the Europeans had greatly benefited from a strong Atlantic alliance over the years.[82] Halperin, who played a key role in developing the State Department's Kosovo policy, explicitly acknowledges the role of civil-military relations in steering U.S. policy toward NATO: "We wanted this as a shared burden, and we wanted the U.S. forces to get out as quickly as possible. Getting NATO on board and knowing that NATO forces were going to go in later made it easier to sell the policy to the U.S. government—and particularly to the Joint Chiefs."[83]

The JCS and Secretary Cohen would not have been satisfied with just *some* European participation in the peacekeeping, which might have been achieved without securing NATO's approval from the outset. The Pentagon wanted the Western European allies to contribute the *vast majority* of troops and material resources for Kosovo's long-term stabilization—ideally, following air strikes, the stabilization burden should be shifted entirely to the Europeans. General Clark (2001: 142) remembers that throughout the fall of 1998, "there had been continuing questions from the Pentagon about . . . whether there could be a NATO ground force without [any] United States participation."

The administration concluded that to maximize the postcombat contribution of the European allies, it would not be enough for the NAC to merely approve the use of force. Instead, any air strikes should be carried out by a fully integrated NATO coalition, with a unified command structure and the largest possible multinational participation from the outset.[84] Talbott (in foreword to Norris 2005: xii) confirms that the goal was to enlist "as much participation in the war as possible from allies and ad hoc partners *in order to* ensure their participation in the reconstruction." In the summer of 1998, the State Department briefly considered implementing air strikes with only an ad hoc coalition of the willing, possibly with the NAC's political blessing but without using NATO's integrated

---

81. NSC/DC, "Meeting on Kosovo," SumConcl, Aug. 26, 1998.
82. Author interviews with James Dobbins, U.S. PermRep to the EU, 1991–93, and Special Envoy for Kosovo, 1998–99 (July 10, 2009); Marc Grossman, AssistSecState for European Affairs, 1997–2000 (Jan. 13, 2011).
83. Halperin, author interview.
84. Grossman and Slocombe, author interviews.

command structure, yet that option was subsequently discarded.[85] Senior
military planners on the Joint Staff made it clear that they preferred to
rely on NATO's integrated command structure and have as many of the
allies as possible participate in the air campaign to ensure that they
would have "a stake in the outcome"—even though it was anticipated
that their "combat contribution would be negligible, with the exception
of France and Great Britain," and that managing the multinational coalition would be cumbersome.[86]

January 1999: Bringing the Pentagon on Board

The Joint Chiefs and OSD gradually reduced their opposition to the
use of force between late 1998 and early 1999 as the outlines of a consensus on air strikes emerged within NATO and the European allies agreed
to take on most of the stabilization burden. At the end of September 1998,
President Clinton approved a recommendation by his principal foreign
policy advisers that the United States begin "pressing NATO to issue an
ultimatum demanding that Milosevic take concrete steps to resolve the
humanitarian and political crisis, or face a military response."[87] The U.S.
military reluctantly supported that recommendation at the time, partially because it understood that even though NATO might threaten the
use of force, military action was not in fact imminent.[88]

Rubin, Albright's former right-hand man, acknowledges that "we
could never have issued threats [of military action] in 1998 if the Pentagon had been opposed to it."[89] In mid-October, NATO formally threatened air strikes against Yugoslavia, seeking to persuade Milosevic to
comply with the terms of the agreement that he had just reached with
Holbrooke on the withdrawal of Serb security forces from Kosovo. The
NAC issued an Activation Order (ACTORD) for air strikes October 12,
which was publicly portrayed at the time as a NATO "endorsement" of
military action (see, e.g., Cohen, *NYT*, Oct. 13, 1998).[90] However, declassified documents show that several of the European allies, including
France and Italy, had supported the ACTORD only with the understanding that a further NAC decision would be necessary before moving to the

---

85. O'Brien, author interview.
86. Weisman, author interview.
87. Berger, "Preparing for an Ultimatum." (Berger's memorandum, summarizing a
consensus among the principals, was approved by Clinton on Sept. 28, 1998.)
88. Kaufmann, author interview.
89. Rubin, author interview.
90. On the ACTORD see also Daalder and O'Hanlon 2000: 45–48.

implementation stage.[91] Therefore, "the October ACTORD involved an element of bluff," as then U.S. ambassador to NATO Vershbow candidly admits.[92]

The bureaucratic balance of power in Washington more clearly shifted in favor of the interventionists in early 1999, after the January 15 massacre of forty-five ethnic Albanians near the village of Racak in southern Kosovo. Rubin recalls that "it wasn't until Racak in 1999 that the use of force became real—before that it was very notional, it was the beginning of the discussions and the different positions were being laid out."[93] There had been worse civilian massacres in Kosovo over the previous year. Yet the events at Racak produced a hitherto unseen sense of outrage in the West, in large part due to the vivid scenes of the killing shown in the media (Daalder and O'Hanlon 2000: 63–64; Halberstam 2001: 409–10). Furthermore, NATO had explicitly threatened to use force if Milosevic reneged on the October agreement, and consequently there was now a widespread perception, increasingly shared by the Pentagon, that the alliance's credibility was on the line.[94]

During the days immediately following the Racak massacre, Albright and her staff developed a comprehensive policy proposal. Laid out on January 19, it foresaw that the conflicting parties on the ground—the authorities in Belgrade and the Kosovar Albanians—should be given an ultimatum to accept an interim settlement by a specific date. If both parties agreed to the settlement, "NATO [would] deploy a military force to assist" in implementation. If Belgrade agreed and the Kosovars didn't, the United States and its allies might reassess their support for the latter. But if only the Kosovars agreed, NATO would launch a phased air campaign in order "to impose an interim settlement."[95]

After the State Department presented the new proposal, Secretary of Defense Cohen and Chairman Shelton at first continued to argue against U.S. participation in any peacekeeping force for Kosovo. They expressed concerns about getting caught in the middle of a civil war and once again emphasized that Congress might not support another significant U.S. troop commitment to the region (Albright 2003: 394–95; Moskovitz and Lantis 2004: 261). However, the political tide had clearly shifted in favor of those who advocated intervention, and nobody could come up with a compelling alternative to Albright's proposal. "We were sitting at the

91. NSC/DC, "Meeting on Kosovo," SumConcl, Oct. 12, 1998.
92. Vershbow, author interview.
93. Rubin, author interview.
94. Hamre, e-mail to author. See also Albright 2003: 391; Moskovitz and Lantis 2004: 263.
95. NSC/DC, "Meeting on Kosovo," SumConcl, Jan. 19, 1999.

table," remembers a former senior Pentagon official, "and at some point we realized, well we're going to lose this argument, we need to start thinking about the next step. And change occurred because of that process."[96]

With Berger and the president signaling their support for the State Department's proposal, the Pentagon, increasingly isolated and unwilling to force a public showdown with the rest of the administration, reluctantly came on board. On January 23, Secretary Cohen and the JCS expressed their support for a strategy of direct negotiations backed by the threat of force. It was clear that if diplomacy failed, air strikes would be carried out—contingent on NATO's final approval. The Pentagon leaders now also accepted the principle of a NATO-led peacekeeping force and recognized that U.S. participation in such a force was "possible," meaning they no longer explicitly opposed it (Albright 2003: 395; see also Daalder and O'Hanlon 2000: 72; Soderberg 2005: 89–90).

Albright and her collaborators repeatedly insisted in the internal debates that NATO's credibility was at stake in the belief that such arguments "favored those who wanted to see military intervention."[97] The perception after Racak that NATO's credibility was on the line also helped mobilize support for Albright's proposal among Republicans on Capitol Hill (who had hitherto been skeptical)—and that in turn reduced the Pentagon's concerns about congressional support.[98] Richard Lugar (R-IN), a senior member of the Senate Foreign Relations Committee, spoke for several of his colleagues when he suggested that, while purely humanitarian concerns such as might exist about African crises would not necessarily warrant military intervention, NATO's credibility did: "We have a special responsibility of leadership in NATO. We don't have NATO in Africa" (quoted in Pomper, *CQ Weekly*, Mar. 20, 1999).

What finally persuaded the Pentagon and especially the JCS to agree to Albright's proposal, however, was their understanding that NATO was now locked in and the United States would not be left with a heavy postwar stabilization burden. After the latest Contact Group meeting on January 22, the Joint Chiefs were reasonably confident that the Western Europeans fully supported the strategy and could be relied upon to generate the majority of troops for Kosovo's long-term stabilization.[99] European policymakers were aware that a bureaucratic struggle had been going on for months in Washington between a hawkish State

96. Kaufmann, author interview.
97. Wolff, author interview. See also Gibbs 2009: 194–95.
98. Author interview with Leon Fuerth, NatSec Adviser to the VP, 1993–2000 (Mar. 9, 2010).
99. Weisman, author interview. See also Moseley, *Chicago Tribune*, Jan. 23, 1999.

Department and a risk-averse Pentagon that opposed any large-scale U.S. troop commitment (see, e.g., Scognamiglio 2002: 153–54). Therefore, by the time the Clinton administration adopted Albright's proposal on January 23, it was apparent to the European NATO allies that if force was going to be used, there would be a division of tasks. "People understood," recalls a former senior State Department official, "the United States clearly had the bulk of the military hardware" and would lead on the air campaign—but "this was a European problem, so there was going to be a balance."[100]

On January 30, the NAC then agreed to "take whatever measures are necessary in the light of both parties' compliance."[101] Detailed transatlantic discussions on the size and shape of a NATO-led stabilization force for Kosovo (KFOR) began soon thereafter. On February 1, Secretary Cohen once again publicly emphasized that the "European allies must bear a substantial burden in terms of dealing with Kosovo and that any participation by the United States should be as small as it could be" (quoted in Priest, *WashPo*, Feb. 2, 1999). Furthermore, the U.S. military leaders made it clear that they wanted to keep KFOR's mandate narrowly focused on security and deterrence, with policing, law enforcement, and reconstruction left to UN and European civilian agencies.[102]

Over the next several weeks, the Pentagon exploited its ties to Capitol Hill to gain additional leverage over both the administration and the NATO allies. General Shelton, meeting with the Senate Armed Services Committee on February 3, pointed out that the Joint Chiefs aimed at a U.S. contribution of between two thousand and four thousand troops, out of an anticipated force of about thirty thousand (Graham, *WashPo*, Feb. 4, 1999). Roughly that proportion of American troops—a maximum 15 percent of the total force—then became part of an informal agreement that Secretary Cohen and JCS Vice Chairman Ralston negotiated with congressional leaders.[103] Ralston insists that the agreement aimed to ensure there would be sufficient congressional support for any U.S. deployment: "If we had gone above that threshold, I think there would have been great reluctance in the Congress to support the operation."[104] But Cohen and Ralston's agreement with congressional leaders was also

100. O'Brien, author interview.
101. NAC, "Statement on Kosovo," Jan. 30, 1999, http://nato.int/docu/pr/1999/p99-012e.htm.
102. Kaufmann, author interview. See also Drozdiak and Priest, *WashPo*, Feb. 11, 1999.
103. The existence of such an agreement was acknowledged by Deputy Secretary of Defense Hamre. See *Kosovo Operations Supplemental Appropriations: Hearing Before the Senate Committee on Appropriations*, 106th Cong. (Apr. 27, 1999), 66, 72.
104. Ralston, author interview.

a convenient way of increasing the Pentagon's bargaining leverage vis-à-vis the rest of the administration. As a former senior defense official points out, opponents of a larger U.S. contribution "at the Pentagon, including Ralston, Shelton, and Cohen, could use it to say, 'Look, we can't go further, this is the end of our political rope.'"[105] With NATO effectively locked in, the agreement became a useful tool that U.S. diplomats could subsequently use in a classic two-level game to extract the maximum possible contribution from the European allies.[106]

After the failure of a last-ditch diplomatic effort in Rambouillet, France, NATO launched its air campaign on March 24. Washington's pursuit of a consistently multilateral approach over Kosovo bore the intended fruits. On June 3, after seventy-eight days of bombing, Milosevic yielded to NATO's demands as presented by the European and Russian envoys, Martti Ahtisaari and Victor Chernomyrdin (Daalder and O'Hanlon 2000: 173–74). One day later, the European NATO allies publicly reconfirmed their willingness to take the lead in stabilizing Kosovo and laid out an ambitious agenda for postwar reconstruction (Swardson and Trueheart, *WashPo*, June 5, 1999). KFOR reached its full strength of roughly fifty thousand troops by late 1999, with the United States contributing a mere seven thousand (Moskovitz and Lantis 2004: 265). Over the next decade, reflecting the Pentagon's agreement with congressional leaders, the U.S. troop contribution to KFOR, as well as to postwar reconstruction more generally, never exceeded 15 percent of the total (Woehrel 2009: 11; Cimbala and Forster 2010: 134).

Alternative Hypotheses on U.S. Multilateralism

As is clear from the preceding discussion, civil-military bargaining played an important role in steering U.S. intervention policy on Kosovo toward NATO. The centrality of that role becomes even more apparent if we can rule out other prima facie plausible explanations for Washington's multilateral course of action. Specifically, it might be that regardless of civil-military bargaining, policymakers sought multilateral approval through NATO because they (1) had internalized new norms of legitimate behavior, (2) wanted to provide NATO with a new strategic purpose, and (3) worried about potential negative issue linkage by antagonistic states.

---

105. Veroneau, author interview.
106. O'Brien, author interview.

Norm Internalization

One prominent hypothesis, presented in chapter 1, is that policy-makers have internalized international norms requiring IO approval as a condition for legitimate military intervention. If policymakers have internalized such norms, they should display a high threshold for violating related precepts and, setting apart self-defense, intervention without IO approval should be all but unthinkable to them. Furthermore, policymakers, feeling that such approval is a matter of obligation, should view it as intrinsically and not just instrumentally desirable.

Since the support for multilateralism is frequently associated with liberal Wilsonianism as a political doctrine, policymakers of liberal Wilsonian persuasion should be most likely to value UN or NATO approval for intrinsic normative reasons. Senior foreign policy officials in the Clinton administration, especially those who were sympathetic to humanitarian intervention, were convinced liberal Wilsonians (Smith 2012: 358–60). Yet there is no evidence that they viewed IO approval as a necessary, or near necessary, condition for the use of force. Even straightforwardly unilateral intervention without any kind of international sanction was anything but unthinkable to them, as Albright's advocacy of U.S. unilateral air strikes over Kosovo in the spring of 1998 clearly demonstrates. Nor is there evidence that when those policymakers sought multilateral approval, they did so for intrinsic normative reasons.

To begin with, the leading U.S. interventionists were not greatly concerned about compliance with international *legal* norms concerning the use of force. Under international law, the Kosovo intervention would have required explicit UNSC approval since no plausible argument could be made for individual or collective self-defense (IICK 2000: 166–73). Secretary Albright, however, displayed a lack of concern for international law bordering on contempt. When the British foreign secretary, Robin Cook, cited "problems with our lawyers" over using force against Yugoslavia without UN authorization, Albright bluntly told him, "Get new lawyers" (quoted in Rubin, *FT*, Sept. 30, 2000).

Furthermore, Albright suggests in her memoir that she viewed the Kosovo case as an opportunity to establish the principle that NATO could intervene without UN approval. Even if U.S. policymakers had been confident that a UN mandate could be secured—for instance, by offering side payments to Russia—it is not clear that Albright would have viewed the effort as worthwhile: "If a UN resolution passed," she explains, "we would have set a precedent that NATO required Security Council authorization before it could act. This would give Russia, not to mention China, a veto" over future U.S. military interventions (Albright 2003: 384). The secretary of state may have convinced other senior U.S.

officials that NATO ought to be free to intervene without prior UN approval. Thus, by the fall of 1998, the NSC Principals Committee collectively decided that "the United States should *discourage* [the other NATO] allies from seeking a further UN resolution specifically authorizing the use of force."[107]

For General Clark, another committed advocate of U.S. intervention over Kosovo, international legal norms appear to have mattered only insofar as they were of concern to the European leaders with whom he interacted on a frequent basis. Beyond that, Clark takes striking liberties of interpretation when it comes to assessing the Kosovo intervention's international legality. In his memoir, *Waging Modern War* (2001: 134), he writes that SCR 1199, adopted on September 23, 1998, effectively "authorize[ed] member nations to use . . . force if necessary." However, the resolution, though adopted under chapter VII of the UN Charter, did not ipso facto approve military intervention and nowhere authorized the "use of all necessary means." Indeed, National Security Adviser Berger clearly noted in a memo for the president at the time that "the UN resolution helps . . . many of our Allies, but it does not explicitly authorize the use of force."[108] Sergey Lavrov, Russia's UN ambassador, had emphasized before voting for the resolution that "no use of force and no sanctions are being imposed by the Council at the present stage."[109]

The State Department's legal advisers at first privately indicated in 1998 that UNSC approval would be necessary, but following instructions by Albright, they abandoned any suggestion that the use of force without prior UN approval would be illegal and remained agnostic on the matter.[110] Once it became clear that NATO's endorsement was within reach even without a UN mandate, compliance with international law dropped almost entirely off the administration's radar. The matter was viewed as inconsequential in terms of building up U.S. domestic support for military intervention: "The American public doesn't care much about international legality," explains James O'Brien, then the State Department's deputy head of policy planning. "The American public wants to see Americans fight a good fight. Certainly self-defense is one of the best fights. Beating down a bully is another great fight. The legal is merely a proxy for the first two."[111]

---

107. NSC/PC, "Meeting on Kosovo," SumConcl, Oct. 5, 1998 (emphasis added).
108. Berger, "Preparing for an Ultimatum."
109. UNSC, record of 3930th meeting, Sept. 23, 1998 (Doc. S/PV.3930), 3.
110. Halperin, author interview.
111. O'Brien, author interview.

According to a former senior White House official, the only legal matter that seriously concerned the administration's lawyers leading up to the Kosovo intervention was whether President Clinton had the domestic constitutional authority to initiate military action in the absence of explicit congressional support: "When the White House, DOD, and State lawyers got together, they weren't focused on whether or not there was a Security Council resolution. That didn't matter to them. They were focused on whether the U.S. president had the authority to order U.S. troops into combat under the U.S. constitution."[112]

Even if senior U.S. policymakers did not worry much about compliance with international legal norms, they might still have internalized relevant *moral* norms requiring IO approval as a condition for legitimate intervention. However, the evidence does not support this hypothesis. Albright, the Clinton administration's leading interventionist, never thought that multilateral approval through NATO or the UN would be necessary or strongly desirable on moral grounds. In her eyes, the intervention's humanitarian purpose appears to have been a sufficient source of moral legitimacy. Put differently, she seems to have thought that the duty to use all available means to prevent genocide and ethnic cleansing trumps international norms requiring multilateral approval. As the former secretary of state subsequently wrote in her memoir, multilateralism, far from being a matter of obligation, is merely a "tool" of foreign policy and as such has no intrinsic value (Albright 2003: 176).

While Albright was certainly the most hawkish among the administration's top-level policy officials, she was hardly alone in her views. In the spring of 1998, as previously noted, several other senior State Department officials, notably U.S. Balkans envoy Robert Gelbard and Ambassador Christopher Hill, also advocated the threat and potential implementation of U.S. unilateral air strikes. So long as senior State Department officials expected that limited air strikes would be sufficient for resolving the Kosovo crisis, with no need for a costly and potentially open-ended troop commitment, they believed the United States could do without IO approval. The State Department's humanitarian hawks changed course and began working hard to secure NATO's approval only after they were rebuffed by the military leaders and it became clear that President Clinton would not authorize a unilateral intervention. That is incompatible with the argument that policymakers sought IO approval out of feelings of moral obligation.

112. Schulte, author interview.

Revitalizing NATO

Another prima facie plausible explanation of America's efforts to secure IO approval, specific to the Kosovo case, takes as its point of departure Washington's commitment to NATO as a privileged instrument for dealing with security crises on the European continent and more generally for exerting influence over European affairs. One scholar, for instance, asserts that "the principal motivations for the war [over Kosovo] were to establish a new basis for U.S. hegemony in Europe and a new rationale for the primary institutional embodiment of that hegemony—the North Atlantic Treaty Organization" (Gibbs 2009: 172). In short, it might be that NATO itself was the primary reason for the intervention, and U.S. policymakers channeled the use of force through NATO in order to provide the alliance with a new sense of purpose and consolidate U.S. hegemony over the North Atlantic. For the hypothesis to be corroborated, we should find that senior officials who played a key role in shaping U.S. policy over Kosovo worried about providing NATO with a new strategic purpose. Furthermore, those same officials should acknowledge in interviews and memoirs that revitalizing NATO was in fact a primary reason for involving the alliance over Kosovo.

NATO was established in 1949 as a traditional military alliance to deter and, if necessary, defend Western Europe against a Soviet attack. With the end of the Cold War and the breakup of the Soviet Union, however, NATO had lost its principal raison d'être. Consequently, in the 1990s, U.S. policymakers sought to redefine NATO's strategic purpose, from a traditional instrument of collective defense to a new instrument for projecting stability and democracy (as well as U.S. influence) into Central and Eastern Europe. As part of that project, the Clinton administration decided in 1994 to make NATO's eastern enlargement one of its top foreign policy priorities (Goldgeier 1999: 45–76). In July 1997, three former Communist countries—Hungary, the Czech Republic, and Poland—were formally invited to join the organization, and their accession was planned for April 1999.[113]

In light of the administration's efforts to revitalize NATO and provide it with a new strategic purpose for the post–Cold War period, it might seem obvious that U.S. policymakers wanted to involve the alliance over Kosovo. NATO's latest "strategic concept," finalized in the months immediately preceding the Kosovo air campaign, explicitly foresaw the alliance's involvement in humanitarian emergencies and "crisis response

---

113. NAC, "Madrid Declaration on Euro-Atlantic Security," July 8, 1997, http:// www.nato.int/docu/pr/1997/p97-081e.htm.

operations" on the European periphery.[114] As one former senior State Department official explains, "The big project of the Clinton administration in Europe was the renovation of NATO for the twenty-first century. New members, new missions, going out of area. And our goal was to transform NATO into a different kind of alliance that unified Europe and could go beyond its borders to deal with these issues. Those decisions were made well before Kosovo."[115] Furthermore, because NATO had played an important role in resolving a similar crisis over Bosnia that involved several of the same individuals in Washington, Belgrade, and Western European capitals, the Atlantic alliance might have seemed the default institution through which to channel the coercive diplomacy over Kosovo.

These factors undoubtedly must be taken into account in trying to understand Washington's multilateral approach in the Kosovo case. The overarching goal of preserving NATO as the central pillar of Euro-American security and preventing the emergence of a separate EU defense community (the foundations of which were laid at a Franco-British summit held in Saint Malo, France, in 1998) made involving the alliance over Kosovo all but imperative in the eyes of the administration's most committed Atlanticists.[116] As Marc Grossman, then the assistant secretary of state for European affairs, explains:

> We were also simultaneously, don't forget, trying to revolutionize NATO. And so to have the allies operate with us, and fly with us, and participate with us was part of the whole argument about what the future of NATO should be like. If you look at the strategic concept of 1999, everything that went around that—expansion, new roles and missions, new capabilities—all these things come together in Kosovo.[117]

Yet these motives are insufficient by themselves to explain the outcome of interest. Those officials at the State Department and elsewhere who were most closely involved in reforming the Atlantic alliance were not necessarily the same individuals who were driving U.S. policy on Kosovo. Albright herself, as noted, was initially willing to sideline NATO altogether when she pushed for U.S. unilateral intervention in the spring of 1998. She was supported by several senior State Department officials, most of them experts in Balkans regional diplomacy, who initially

114. NATO Strategic Concept, Apr. 24, 1999, http://www.nato.int/cps/en/nato live/official_texts_27433.htm.
115. Asmus, author interview.
116. Kerrick, author interview.
117. Grossman, author interview.

believed that the freedom-of-action costs of forging a multilateral consensus through NATO would outweigh attendant benefits.

In the eyes of Albright and her hawkish Balkans advisers, NATO's hesitations over Bosnia, where a genocide was carried out over nearly three years while the United States squabbled over limited air strikes with its Western European partners, taught a sobering lesson: if President Clinton wanted to stop Milosevic before he triggered another massive humanitarian crisis, the administration would have to consider acting unilaterally.[118] Albright and her fellow humanitarian hawks eventually changed course, agreeing that NATO had to endorse any military action over Kosovo. However, the primary reason for this change was not that they were persuaded by the State Department's in-house Atlanticists (although that may have played an important subsidiary role)—instead, they realized that the reluctant warriors at the Pentagon would probably veto a U.S. unilateral intervention without NATO approval.

Preventing Negative Issue Linkage

Yet another hypothesis is that U.S. policymakers sought IO approval as a means of signaling benign intentions to antagonistic third-party states that might otherwise have reduced their cooperation with Washington across an array of issue areas. The political scientist Katharina Coleman (2007: 237–38), for instance, claims that the United States sought NATO's approval for the Kosovo intervention because it "recognized that both its reputation as a relatively benign superpower and its leadership position in the post–Cold War world would be damaged if it was intentionally perceived as engaged in illegitimate aggression." Involving NATO and securing NATO's approval, she argues, "provided an excellent base" for signaling benign U.S. intentions and minimizing potentially costly opposition from non-NATO states (ibid., 221).

For this hypothesis to be corroborated, there should be evidence that U.S. policymakers actually worried that intervening without IO approval might result in reduced international cooperation with the United States across various issue areas, such as counterterrorism, nonproliferation, and economic affairs. Furthermore, senior officials involved in decision making at the time should acknowledge that averting such negative issue linkage was an important motive for seeking IO approval.

The broader international community of non-NATO states was divided over the Kosovo intervention. At one end of the spectrum there were global and regional powers such as Russia, China, India, and South Africa that strongly opposed what they perceived as an instance of

---

118. Gelbard, Kerrick, and Larkin, author interviews.

illegitimate aggression against a sovereign state (Schnabel and Thakur 2000). On the day that Operation Allied Force began, Russian President Boris Yeltsin declared that "Russia is profoundly outraged by NATO's military action against sovereign Yugoslavia, which is nothing less than an act of open aggression."[119] The Chinese ambassador to the UNSC similarly condemned NATO's intervention as "a blatant violation of the United Nations Charter and of the accepted norms of international law."[120] Russia and China had their own unresolved secessionist conflicts in places such as Chechnya, Tibet, and Xinjiang. Leaders in Moscow and Beijing were alarmed that the world's most powerful alliance was asserting a right to intervene militarily on behalf of oppressed ethnic minorities abroad. As Strobe Talbott recalls, "The Chinese did not like the idea of NATO bombing a capital of a country on behalf of a Muslim minority, and the Russians could not have been more explicit about analogies to Chechnya."[121]

The Non-Aligned Movement (NAM), an association of developing countries known for their attachment to national sovereignty, issued a declaration while the air campaign was ongoing that reiterated the movement's principled opposition to humanitarian intervention in the absence of UN approval: "We reject the so-called 'right' of humanitarian intervention, which has no legal basis in the UN Charter or in the general principles of international law."[122] While rejecting humanitarian intervention as a matter of principle, however, the NAM's 114 members were in fact divided over the particular Kosovo intervention. The reason was not that NATO's endorsement reassured developing country leaders about U.S. intentions and legitimized the use of force in their eyes. Instead, Arab and Islamic countries within the NAM were simply unwilling to condemn the use of force in support of an oppressed Muslim population.[123]

In the run-up to the use of force, senior Clinton administration officials never worried that those states that rhetorically opposed the intervention would care enough to actually retaliate by reducing their cooperation with the United States in other issue areas. James Dobbins, then the State Department's special Kosovo envoy, offers a particularly candid

---

119. UNSC, record of 3988th meeting, Mar. 24, 1999 (Doc. S/PV.3988), 3.
120. Ibid., 12. India's representative to the SC called the intervention an "arbitrary, unauthorized, and illegal military action [that] should be stopped immediately." Ibid., 16.
121. Talbott, author interview.
122. NAM, "Final Document: XIII Ministerial Conference," Cartagena, Colombia, Apr. 8–9, 2000, http://www.nam.gov.za/xiiiminconf/minconf.pdf/.
123. Author interview with Ian Johnstone, senior political officer, UN secretary-general's office, 1997–2000 (Apr. 2, 2010).

assessment: "The only state outside NATO that was of serious concern was Russia. The assumption was that the Chinese would go along with whatever the Russians would go along with. So the pivotal state was Russia. As to the NAM, there wasn't anything they could do to help Serbia or harm us."[124] Morton Halperin confirms that in all the departmental and interagency meetings in which he took part, the possibility of costly retaliation by third-party states beyond Russia "was not on the screen at all."[125] For the U.S. military, as well, the possibility of costly international opposition "was a fairly marginal factor."[126]

It remains to be ascertained how much U.S. policymakers were concerned about specifically Russian opposition and whether they expected that NATO's approval would reassure Russian authorities. Moscow had long maintained a close political relationship with Belgrade, based on strong ties of ethnic and religious kinship. Thus, when NATO launched its air campaign in March 1999, Russian leaders issued public statements vehemently condemning the bombing. However, in Washington the boisterous rhetoric from Moscow was largely interpreted as an attempt by the Russian leadership to placate its restive domestic public (Daalder and O'Hanlon 2000: 127; Albright 2003: 413). In private, throughout the crisis Russian authorities proved quite cooperative.

In the fall of 1998, Foreign Minister Igor Ivanov let it be known to his Western counterparts that Russia was willing to tacitly support an ultimatum to Milosevic (Bellamy 2002: 93; Talbott 2002: 302). Several weeks later, on January 27, 1999, Secretary Albright and several of her advisers met with Ivanov in Moscow. Albright had joined Ivanov for an opera performance at the Bolshoi Theater, and during the intermission, the U.S. delegation made Washington's intentions with regard to Kosovo unmistakably clear. Unless the planned last-ditch negotiating effort was going to yield concrete results, the United States and its allies would start bombing Yugoslavia and continue until Serb troops withdrew from Kosovo and international peacekeepers were let in. "We were very explicit," remembers Halperin, who was part of the U.S. delegation at the Bolshoi. "The Russians' response was, 'We can't endorse this.' But there was not any hint of a threat that they would be on the other side. They knew what we were doing. They accepted that it was the only way to stop Milosevic."[127]

At the time, Russia was recovering from a serious financial crisis that had hit the country in 1998, and Moscow's political leaders were aware

124. Dobbins, author interview.
125. Halperin, author interview.
126. Ralston, author interview.
127. Halperin, author interview. See also Albright 2003: 396–97.

of their country's dependence on Western economic aid. Consequently, the Russian government was trying to walk a fine line, opposing the use of force in public while acquiescing to NATO's strategy in private. The United States had offered $5.4 billion in bilateral economic assistance to Russia between 1992 and 1998, in addition to significant U.S. contributions to multilateral assistance programs aimed at Russia for a total of more than $100 billion.[128] In late 1998 and early 1999, as the Kosovo crisis reached its climax, Russia was engaged in delicate negotiations with the IMF over a major economic loan.[129] Given Washington's preponderant influence over IMF loan disbursements, political authorities in Moscow had strong incentives to privately cooperate with the United States (see also Halberstam 2001: 473; Norris 2005: 31).

Senior Clinton administration officials, cognizant of the dire economic straits in which Russia found itself, viewed Moscow's public opposition to the use of force as a problem that could be managed through skillful diplomacy. "Nobody in the U.S. government argued against intervention out of concern for Russia's reaction," remembers Stephen Sestanovich, then the secretary of state's special adviser for the former Soviet Union. "The Russians did not like the way in which the U.S. and the West had established a kind of hegemony in the Balkans. Everybody expected them to be difficult. But that just meant, we have a problem— we have to deal with it, we have to work on it patiently through our diplomacy."[130]

U.S. policymakers understood that NATO's involvement would do little to reassure the Russians—in fact, quite the opposite. In late December 1998, President Yeltsin personally told President Clinton during a private telephone conversation, "We are very seriously concerned over plans under way to expand the theater of NATO activity."[131] The Atlantic alliance was viewed in Moscow as the primary tool of Washington's new hegemony over the Balkans and Eastern Europe more generally. As a former senior State Department official who was involved in high-level negotiations with Russian diplomats explains, "NATO was expanding at the time into their former sphere of influence. They would certainly have liked NATO to fail in its effort over Kosovo."[132]

---

128. Stephen Sestanovich, *Russia's Foreign Policy Objectives: What Are They? Hearing Before the House Committee on International Relations*, 106th Cong. (May 12, 1999), 78.
129. Ibid., 13.
130. Author interview with Stephen Sestanovich (Mar. 4, 2010).
131. Memorandum of telephone conversation between Presidents Clinton and Yeltsin, White House, Dec. 30, 1998 (released pursuant to MDR No. 2009-1292-M).
132. Burleigh, author interview. Confirmed by Norris and Schulte, author interviews.

Most senior members of Russia's national security apparatus were former cold warriors who throughout their careers had been taught to oppose NATO "aggression." It was hard to imagine that suddenly those same individuals could perceive NATO as signaling benign American intentions. Therefore, in its efforts to reassure Moscow, the Clinton administration for the most part relied on bilateral diplomacy rather than on the Euro-Atlantic Partnership Council, a NATO body established in 1997 to smooth relations with the alliance's eastern neighbors. Shortly after NATO launched its air campaign, President Clinton thought it wise to send a private letter to Yeltsin through U.S. diplomatic channels: "Let me assure you," Clinton emphasized, "that none of our actions in the Balkans are aimed against Russia."[133] In short, although Russia's public opposition to the intervention was concerning to the United States, U.S. policymakers clearly did not seek NATO approval to reassure authorities in Moscow about U.S. intentions.

Ultimately, neither norm internalization nor concerns about NATO's future nor fears of costly international opposition can explain Washington's multilateral approach over Kosovo. Detailed process tracing, building on evidence from interviews and declassified documents, indicates that the Clinton administration's efforts to secure NAC approval for the use of force and to channel U.S. policy through NATO were primarily the result of civil-military bargaining in Washington. America's top-ranking generals and admirals, fearing an open-ended U.S. troop commitment that Congress might not support, threatened to veto the use of force. Senior civilian policymakers who advocated armed intervention, seeking to tilt the bureaucratic balance of power in their own favor, therefore sought NATO's approval and buy-in, in order to reassure the reluctant warriors at the Pentagon that the operational costs would be limited and that European allies would shoulder most of the longer-term stabilization burden.

133. Bill Clinton, "Message to President Yeltsin regarding the Situation in Kosovo," diplomatic cable, U.S. embassy Moscow, week of Apr. 5, 1999, exact date unknown (released pursuant to MDR 2009-1290-M).

[6]

Iraq, 2002–3: Silence from the Generals

On March 19, 2003, American and British forces launched Operation Iraqi Freedom, the invasion aimed at disarming Iraq of its presumed weapons of mass destruction (WMD) and changing the country's political regime.[1] For more than a decade, the United States had sought to weaken Saddam Hussein, the Iraqi dictator, by relying on a combination of economic sanctions, occasional bombing raids, and financial support for various opposition groups. But soon after the terrorist attacks of September 11, 2001, the George W. Bush administration decided that Saddam Hussein had to be forcibly removed. In a climate of heightened American vulnerability, the administration concluded that Saddam, believed to be amassing weapons of mass destruction, constituted a serious threat to U.S. national security. Hard-liners like Vice President Richard Cheney and Secretary of Defense Donald Rumsfeld also expected that toppling the Iraqi dictator would send a powerful signal of U.S. resolve to other actual or potential WMD proliferators. Finally, President Bush himself and several of his neoconservative advisers viewed the invasion of Iraq as a unique opportunity to advance the cause of democracy and human rights in the Middle East.

The Bush administration's most ardent proponents of a war for regime change, notably senior civilian officials at the Department of Defense, believed that toppling Saddam and stabilizing Iraq thereafter would be easy—a "cakewalk," in the words of the neoconservative political commentator Kenneth Adelman (Adelman, *WashPo*, Feb. 13, 2002). The war

---

1. About two thousand Australian troops and two hundred Polish special forces also took part in the initial invasion. Woodward 2004: 382, 401.

advocates' optimistic assumptions led them to conclude that a small number of American troops would suffice to quickly stabilize Iraq after the invasion. As a result, they did not see any compelling reason to secure advance UN approval aimed at legitimating the war and facilitating sustained international burden sharing. As a former senior military officer who interacted closely with hawkish civilians in the Office of the Secretary of Defense (OSD) explains, "The civilians at OSD believed strongly that it was going to be a cakewalk; we had proven it in Afghanistan, it was going to be simple and it wasn't going to cost very much. You didn't need allies or the UN for this."[2]

Senior U.S. military officers in the services, on the Joint Staff, and at the combatant commands doubted that the Iraqi regime constituted an imminent threat to U.S. national security and believed that Iraq, weakened by a decade of international sanctions, could continue to be contained. Furthermore, most senior uniformed officers viewed the civilian hard-liners' optimistic assumptions as naive and worried that invading Iraq would result in a significant and open-ended U.S. troop commitment. The U.S. military, in short, had serious reservations about a war for regime change. The prevailing belief among America's generals and admirals was that at the very least, before invading Iraq, the United States should devote the necessary time and resources to building up solid multilateral support so as to maximize the likelihood of sustained burden sharing with international partners.

However, in the months leading up to the 2003 Iraq War, civil-military relations did not follow the standard pattern described in previous chapters of this book. The top-ranking generals, notably JCS chairman Richard Myers, vice chairman Peter Pace, and CENTCOM commander Tommy Franks, were exceedingly deferential to the civilians at OSD and never assertively conveyed the military establishment's concerns about postcombat stabilization to the president or the NSC. The civilian hard-liners' relentless insistence that toppling the Iraqi regime was integral to the administration's war on terror also made it difficult for senior military officers to push back effectively. As a consequence, the bureaucratic political dynamics that had made UN or NATO approval all but essential for previous U.S. interventions aimed at internal political change in Haiti and the Balkans were not activated during the run-up to the Iraq War.

In the late summer of 2002, Secretary of State Colin Powell, who shared many of the military's concerns, nevertheless persuaded President Bush that involving the UNSC would be helpful. That resulted in the adoption

2. Author interview with Gen. Charles Wald, Commander of CENTCOM Air Forces, 2000–2001, and Deputy Commander, EUCOM, 2002–6 (Mar. 8, 2010).

of SCR 1441 in November 2002, which established a new UN weapons inspections regime and warned of "serious consequences" in case of further Iraqi noncompliance with its international obligations. Once 1441 was adopted, however, the Bush administration showed little interest in a further UN resolution explicitly authorizing the use of force. Ultimately, the United States chose to bypass the Security Council and went to war without UN approval. The Iraq War was consequently considered illegitimate by global audiences, there was only limited international burden sharing, and the United States and Britain had to shoulder most of the cost of a nearly decade-long stabilization effort on their own.

Prologue: The Desert Fox Air Strikes

After the 1991 Persian Gulf War, which undid Iraq's invasion of Kuwait, the United States and its international partners embarked on an ambitious policy of containment vis-à-vis Iraq. The policy consisted of stringent economic sanctions, a UN inspections regime aimed at identifying and destroying Iraqi weapons of mass destruction, two no-fly zones imposed over the Kurdish north and Shiite south of the country, and a stepped-up military aid program to Iraq's regional neighbors intended to build up their defensive capabilities. From Washington's perspective this approach had a twofold objective: first, to reduce the Iraqi threat to regional stability, and second, to undermine Saddam Hussein's rule, fomenting internal political change. The assumption was that the Iraqi dictator, weakened domestically by his crushing military defeat in 1991, would not survive politically for long. But the goal of regime change enjoyed little international support, and consequently U.S. authorities, seeking to keep the UNSC united on Iraqi sanctions, downplayed that goal in public for several years.[3]

The 1990s: Disarmament versus Regime Change

To disarm Iraq of its chemical and biological weapons, the UNSC set up a special organ in 1991, the United Nations Special Commission (UNSCOM). Responsibility for Iraqi nuclear capabilities fell to the International Atomic Energy Agency (IAEA). As an incentive for Iraq to cooperate with the UN inspectors and conform to its disarmament obligations, SCR 687, adopted at the end of the 1991 Gulf War, envisaged that

3. Author interview with Bruce Riedel, Director for Gulf Affairs, 1991–93, and Senior Director for Near East Affairs, 1997–2002, on the NSC staff (Dec. 15, 2010). See also Albright 2003: 272; Haass 2009: 158.

economic sanctions would be lifted in return for "Iraq's compliance . . . and general progress toward the control of armaments in the region." Iraq's cooperation over the next several years was mixed at best, and on numerous occasions Iraqi authorities prevented the UN inspectors from accessing suspected illicit weapons sites (Malone 2006: 155–56; Thompson 2009: 97–100). Nevertheless, by the mid-1990s, Iraq's nuclear and chemical weapons capabilities had been largely eliminated. After General Hussein Kamel Hassan, the Iraqi dictator's son-in-law, defected to Jordan in August 1995 and revealed extensive details of Iraq's biological weapons program, most of those capabilities were also destroyed (Haass 2009: 160–61; ElBaradei 2011: 31–32).

By the middle of the decade, growing international opposition to the economic sanctions had materialized. Russia, France, and several other European countries began to advocate a policy change. Iraq, they argued partially out of economic self-interest, no longer posed a serious military threat. The sanctions were hurting primarily Iraqi civilians and would never achieve Saddam's full cooperation, let alone his overthrow. Thus the only viable long-term solution was to gradually reintegrate Iraq into the community of nations through trade, investment, and a normalization of diplomatic relations (Malone 2006: 116–20; Thompson 2009: 101–5). UN Secretary-General Kofi Annan privately shared the goal of lifting the sanctions and gradually ending Iraq's isolation (Goshko, *WashPo*, Feb. 23, 1999). Meanwhile, the United States claimed that the sanctions should stay in place so long as Saddam remained in power. In the spring of 1997, then Secretary of State Madeleine Albright declared in a speech at Georgetown University, "We do not agree with the nations who argue that if Iraq complies with its obligations concerning weapons of mass destruction, sanctions should be lifted" (quoted in Wright, *LA Times*, Mar. 27, 1997). Lest there be any doubts about the U.S. position, President Bill Clinton later insisted that "the sanctions will be there until the end of time or as long as he lasts."[4]

Since Iraq's invasion of Kuwait in 1990, American leaders had demonized Saddam as another Hitler, making Iraq's straightforward reintegration into the international community a political nonstarter in Washington—especially given Iraq's less than forthright cooperation with UNSCOM.[5] In the fall of 1998 the Clinton administration, under pressure from a hawkish Congress and neoconservatives such as William Kristol, Richard Perle, and Paul Wolfowitz—who had recently

4. Bill Clinton, Remarks in meeting with President Zedillo of Mexico, Nov. 14, 1997, http://clinton6.nara.gov/1997/.
5. On the comparison between Saddam and Hitler, see Dowd, *Fortune*, Feb. 11, 1991; Dickey and Thomas, *Newsweek*, Sept. 23, 2002; Hendrickson 2002: 157–58.

launched a new advocacy group aimed at promoting a more muscular U.S. foreign policy, the Project for the New American Century (PNAC)—took the next logical step. The administration adopted the Iraq Liberation Act, which elevated regime change into an official U.S. policy goal and authorized $97 million to provide military support to the Iraqi opposition (Gordon and Shapiro 2004: 43; Haass 2009: 164–66). This explicit embrace of regime change put the United States on an increasing path of collision with its international and especially European partners, and it removed any incentive for the Iraqi dictator to cooperate with the UN inspectors.

A Game of Cat and Mouse

On November 3, 1997, seeking to exploit growing divisions at the Security Council, Iraqi authorities blocked an UNSCOM inspection team from accessing a suspicious missile site. Soon thereafter, the Iraqi government expelled six inspectors of U.S. nationality. The Iraqis claimed that the Americans working for UNSCOM were undercover CIA spies—a claim that, incidentally, was subsequently confirmed by independent sources (Woodward 2004: 245; ElBaradei 2011: 32–33). In response, on November 14, President Clinton dispatched an aircraft carrier to the region and threatened military action. Further escalation was averted on this occasion after the Russian prime minister, Yevgeny Primakov, brokered an agreement that allowed all UNSCOM inspectors to return (Albright 2003: 277–80; Malone 2006: 157–58).

Another, similar crisis ensued in January 1998 when Iraq again blocked several UN inspection teams. This time, after renewed U.S. saber rattling, the UN secretary-general stepped in, extracting an agreement from Iraqi authorities to fully cooperate with UNSCOM and comply with existing Security Council resolutions (Albright 2003: 281–83; Malone 2006: 159). On March 2, 1998, the SC then unanimously adopted Resolution 1154, which threatened the "severest consequences" in case Iraq failed to honor its commitments. The resolution did not authorize an automatic military response, given that most of the council's members (including Russia, France, and China) were increasingly at odds with Washington's hawkish attitude. Nevertheless, in a way that foreshadowed the Bush administration's behavior following the adoption of Resolution 1441, senior U.S. officials asserted that they had obtained a "green light" for military action in case of renewed Iraqi noncooperation (Thompson 2009: 113).

On September 9, 1998, the SC took further action on Iraq, adopting Resolution 1194, which called for a "comprehensive review" of the country's compliance with all relevant resolutions. The idea, first proposed by

Secretary-General Annan, was for UNSCOM to report to the council on the state of each weapons file (nuclear, chemical, biological, and missile) with the goal of providing a detailed account of Iraq's cooperation, or lack thereof, based on specific benchmarks.[6] Yet after the Clinton administration adopted the Iraq Liberation Act on September 19, Iraqi authorities ceased all cooperation with UNSCOM (Albright 2003: 284; Thompson 2009: 115–16). Thereupon the U.S. president, warned by his advisers that American credibility risked being undermined, ordered a substantial bombing campaign on November 14. Once again, virtually at the last minute, Iraqi authorities pledged in a letter to Annan that they would resume cooperation with UNSCOM. Senior U.S. officials, including Secretary of Defense William Cohen and Albright, were adamant that the bombing proceed anyway (Woodward 2000: 492; Halberstam 2001: 375). The British, however, who had been closely aligned with Washington up to that point, made it clear that they would no longer participate in the air strikes. Consequently, the U.S. president decided to call off the bombing. Clinton was willing to order military action without explicit UN approval, but like his successor George W. Bush, he was reluctant to use significant force without at least Britain's participation.[7]

By mid-December, the cat-and-mouse game between Iraq and the United States had run its course. On December 15, the chief UN weapons inspector, Richard Butler, reported to the SC that Iraqi authorities had continued to obstruct inspections and failed to turn over documents pertaining to their chemical and biological weapons programs (Malone 2006: 160). President Clinton had approved revised plans for a substantial U.S.-UK aerial attack already in early December, and several days *before* the Butler report was issued, Clinton's national security team recommended that the president authorize the air strikes (Clinton 2004: 833; Shelton 2010: 366). Nevertheless, in consultation with Tony Blair, the British prime minister, Clinton decided to wait until after the publication of Butler's report. As Jeremy Greenstock, at the time Britain's ambassador to the SC, explains, "We were trying to show that the action was justified under the [UN] resolutions, which President Clinton hadn't been particularly concerned about in November or earlier."[8] The air campaign, code-named Operation Desert Fox, started on December 16. The

---

6. Jeremy Greenstock, "Developments at the UN," written statement to UK Iraq Inquiry, Nov. 27, 2009. All UK Iraq Inquiry documents cited in this chapter are available at http://www.iraqinquiry.org.uk.
7. Author interviews with Walter Slocombe, UnderSecDef for Policy, 1994–2001 (Mar. 10, 2010), and Jeremy Greenstock, UK PermRep to the UN, 1998–2003 (Mar. 30, 2011).
8. Greenstock, author interview.

bombing lasted only four days, but it was the most robust military action against Iraq since 1991. More than four hundred cruise missiles and six hundred bombs hit a total of ninety-seven Iraqi targets, most of them military command centers, missile factories, and airfields (Ricks 2006: 19).

There was no illusion in Washington that a four-day air campaign would dramatically set back Iraq's weapons programs or produce fundamental political change in Baghdad. Bruce Riedel, then a senior NSC staffer working on the Middle East, explains the Clinton administration's calculus as follows: "I would describe the Desert Fox air strikes as providing a pivot point for the administration to put an end to the endless cat-and-mouse game with the Iraqis. Because it was draining American foreign policy, it was a constant irritant, which frequently made the administration look weak."[9] The bombings, and the subsequent decision to terminate UNSCOM given Iraq's now-unbridled obstructionism, resolved the inherent contradiction of calling for Saddam to comply with international demands (with the promise of lifting economic sanctions if he did so) while at the same time calling for his ouster. By ending the inspections, however, the Desert Fox campaign left the United States and its allies unable to monitor suspected WMD developments inside Iraq, thereby contributing to a distorted and inflated picture of Iraq's capabilities in subsequent years.[10]

UN Approval Deemed Unnecessary in 1998

America's top-ranking generals expressed some reluctance but no fundamental opposition in the period leading up to the Desert Fox air strikes. The campaign's military objectives, as General Joseph Ralston, then the JCS vice chairman, recalls, were narrowly defined as "disrupting and degrading Iraq's missile capability for some period of time."[11] Hence the uniformed leaders understood that there was no risk of a costly, open-ended troop commitment and the military's liability would be limited.[12] Even Albright, the Clinton administration's chief interventionist, acknowledges that "no serious consideration was given to actually invading Iraq" (2003: 277). The senior military officers were further reassured by indications of solid domestic support for the bombing in Congress and among the American public.[13] In the days preceding the

---

9. Riedel, author interview.
10. I am grateful to series editor Stephen Walt for encouraging me to highlight this.
11. Author interview with Gen. Joseph Ralston (Mar. 17, 2009). See also Shelton 2010: 365.
12. Slocombe and Wald, author interviews.
13. John Hamre, Deputy SecDef, 1997–2000, e-mail to author (Feb. 17, 2010).

campaign, General Anthony Zinni, the commander of U.S. Central Command, and JCS chairman Hugh Shelton expressed some reservations in the intramural debates about the timing of the bombing and its likely impact on the ground. But Secretary of Defense Cohen strongly supported the prospective air campaign, and in a series of private meetings he was able to assuage the generals' concerns (Woodward 2000: 492–93).

In the run-up to Desert Fox, neither the JCS nor any other national security leader in Washington raised significant concerns about the absence of an explicit multilateral endorsement through the UN or NATO. It appears that, given the expectation of a limited operational commitment, U.S. policymakers were simply unwilling to engage in lengthy negotiations and offer significant side payments to other IO member states in order to obtain an explicit multilateral mandate. Thus the evidence does not support the argument, made by policy analysts close to the Clinton administration, that "in 1997 and 1998, the United States was unwilling to use force in Iraq without broad international support" (Gordon and Shapiro 2004: 45). Senior U.S. officials argued at the time that there was "continuing authority" for military action under existing UN resolutions, notably SCR 678 and SCR 687 on the 1991 Gulf War—but the argument was rejected by most other members of the UNSC.[14] Once the Desert Fox air strikes began, they were condemned as a blatant violation of international law by governments throughout the Middle East, as well as by Russia, China, and the 113 members of the Non-Aligned Movement.[15]

The Clinton administration wanted to act quickly, seizing the window of opportunity between the publication of Butler's report on December 15 and the beginning of the Muslim holy month of Ramadan a few days later (Woodward 2000: 493). Obtaining an explicit SC authorization for the use of "all necessary means" would undoubtedly have taken longer. It would have required significant side payments to Moscow aimed at preventing a Russian veto. (A French abstention at the SC might have been easier to secure, since Paris had privately consented to military action.)[16] According to Greenstock, the British ambassador, it would

14. See Roberts 2003: 42. SCR 687, adopted at the end of the 1991 Gulf War, makes clear in its final paragraph that the Council (as opposed to individual member states) "will take such further steps as may be required for the implementation of the present resolution and to secure peace and security in the region."
15. "Non-Aligned Movement Deplores U.S. Air Strikes on Iraq," Xinhua News Agency, Dec. 18, 1998; Cornwell, *Independent* (London), Dec. 19, 1998; Williams, *WashPo*, Dec. 20, 1998.
16. The French military even secretly helped Washington and London select suitable targets. See Webster, *Guardian* (London), Dec. 23, 1998.

[195]

have been almost unthinkable for Moscow to go along with a use-of-force resolution in November or December 1998. However, he believes there was a reasonable chance of securing a Russian abstention at a later stage—especially if the SC, in cooperation with UNSCOM, had carried out the comprehensive review of Iraq's compliance called for in Resolution 1194, which would have involved "look[ing] at the performance of Iraq against the benchmarks set in the resolutions to date." But the Americans, he adds "cut through that with the bombing in December."[17]

Stephen Sestanovich, at the time a senior U.S. diplomat dealing with Russian affairs, concurs that Moscow might have been persuaded to abstain on an "all necessary means" resolution, but he notes that the Clinton administration "never explored the question of what the Russians' price might be."[18] No senior U.S. official ever offered a serious quid pro quo for Russian support. "The most obvious economic inducements that Russia sought," Sestanovich (2002: 155) explains, "were those associated with an end to sanctions"—given that Russian oil companies in particular had significant economic interests in Iraq. In short, if the United States had sufficiently valued UNSC approval for air strikes, it could conceivably have obtained it within a matter of months through an intense diplomatic effort culminating in the following grand bargain: full multilateral approval for military action aimed at signaling resolve and degrading Iraq's weapons capabilities in exchange for a gradual lifting of economic sanctions. However, lifting the sanctions, which symbolized the administration's tough policy vis-à-vis Iraq and enjoyed widespread U.S. domestic support, was too high a price for President Clinton to pay, especially given the limited expected payoffs of securing UN approval for the bombing.

The administration's approach in 1998, whereby the United States was unwilling to postpone the operation or make other meaningful concessions to obtain an explicit SC mandate, while claiming that military action was justified under existing UN resolutions, set a precedent that was seized four years later by President Bush and his advisers. After the terrorist attacks of September 11, 2001, Bush became willing to more wholeheartedly embrace the policy of regime change that Clinton had somewhat tentatively endorsed as a matter of principle. The means that the United States was willing to employ to topple Saddam Hussein changed radically after 9/11. But the U.S. modus operandi on Iraq vis-à-vis the SC remained the same.

17. Greenstock, author interview.
18. Author interview with Stephen Sestanovich, ambassador-at-large for the states of the former Soviet Union, 1997–2001 (Mar. 4, 2010).

THE BUSH ADMINISTRATION: IRAQ AS A VITAL THREAT

President George W. Bush took up office in January 2001 having promised during his election campaign that he would pursue a "humble" foreign policy that would eschew military interventions and "nation building" abroad (Malone 2006: 185; Ricks 2006: 24–25). His principal foreign policy advisers were Secretary of State Colin Powell, Secretary of Defense Donald Rumsfeld, Vice President Richard Cheney, National Security Adviser Condoleezza Rice, and JCS chairman Richard Myers (who replaced Shelton in October 2001). The administration's leading neoconservatives, notably Deputy Secretary of Defense Paul Wolfowitz and Lewis "Scooter" Libby, the national security adviser to the vice president, had argued for much of the 1990s that America should use its military muscle more assertively to change Iraq's political regime. From the spring of 2001 onward, those individuals insistently repeated that same argument in internal policy meetings (Woodward 2004: 21–22; Feith 2008: 203–8).

Before the terrorist attacks on the World Trade Center and the Pentagon on September 11, the neoconservative hard-liners were unable to convince the Bush administration as a whole that Iraq warranted urgent military action. During the administration's first eight months in office, its Iraq policy focused on reviving the international sanctions regime. The goal was to "narrow the sanctions, easing the pressure on the civilian population, and thereby save the sanctions regime," explains Stephen Hadley, then the deputy U.S. national security adviser.[19] Yet after the 9/11 terrorist attacks, the administration's advocates of forcible regime change found themselves suddenly empowered.

During an emergency meeting of the administration's national security team on September 12, 2001, Secretary of Defense Rumsfeld asked whether the terrorist attacks might not represent an "opportunity" to launch military action against Iraq (Woodward 2004: 25; Shelton 2010: 441). Three days later, Wolfowitz and Libby insisted during a foreign policy team meeting at Camp David that the administration should forcibly topple Saddam Hussein in the first round of the newly proclaimed "war on terror." Secretary of State Powell and Chairman Shelton pushed back against those proposals, arguing that the broad international coalition that had emerged in support of the United States after 9/11 would unravel if the administration were to invade Iraq (DeYoung 2006: 352; Shelton 2010: 442–44). With CIA director George Tenet and Vice

---

19. Author interview with Stephen J. Hadley (Jan. 24, 2011). See also Malone 2006: 122–23; Haass 2009: 174.

President Cheney also cautioning against an immediate attack on Iraq, President Bush decided that the time was not yet ripe to go after Saddam Hussein. As a former senior Pentagon aide recalls, "We knew they [the terrorists] were in Afghanistan, not in Iraq. And even though Dr. Wolfowitz made a very forceful case that we should take this opportunity to get rid of Saddam, the decision was made by the president, with the support of Secretary Powell, that no, this is not the time to do it."[20]

However, although President Bush was unwilling to immediately go after Saddam Hussein, he concluded in the weeks after September 11 that "keeping Saddam in a box looked less and less feasible" (quoted in Woodward 2004: 27). According to Riedel, a Clinton appointee who continued to serve as a senior national security official in the new administration for almost a year, "the Bush-Cheney decision to invade Iraq was made shortly after 9/11, and the goal was to invade Iraq and remove Saddam Hussein, not to disarm Iraq."[21] General Shelton similarly writes in his memoir (2010: 479) that President Bush "had so much as indicated" to him during the aforementioned Camp David meeting that he intended to take out Saddam before the end of his first term in office.[22] On November 21, 2001, shortly after the U.S.-backed Northern Alliance took the Afghan capital, Kabul, formally sealing the fall of the Taliban regime, Bush instructed Secretary Rumsfeld to secretly start working on an updated invasion plan for Iraq (Woodward 2004: 1–3, 30; Rumsfeld 2011: 425).

Over the next several months, the U.S. president, while denying that any decision had been taken on military action against Iraq, began to prepare the American people for war. In his State of the Union address on January 29, 2002, Bush identified an "axis of evil" made up of North Korea, Iran, and Iraq, three ostensibly hostile regimes that were pursuing weapons of mass destruction and could hand them over to terrorist groups. The president also indicated in his address that the United States, facing a heightened international threat environment, might take military action soon. "Time is not on our side," he declared. "I will not wait on events, while dangers gather. . . . The United States of America will not permit the world's most dangerous regimes to threaten us with the world's most dangerous weapons."[23]

20. Author interview with Col. Stephen P. Bucci, Military Assist. to SecDef, 2001–5 (Jan. 19, 2011). See also Shelton 2010: 444; Cheney 2011: 334.
21. Riedel, author interview.
22. For similar conclusions see also Haass 2009: 169; Gordon and Shapiro 2004: 163.
23. George W. Bush, "Address on the State of the Union," Jan. 29, 2002, http://www.presidency.ucsb.edu/ws/index.php?pid-29644.

Limited Patience for Multilateral Diplomacy

In a climate of deep uncertainty about Iraq's WMD programs (Saddam had ceased all cooperation with UN inspectors after the 1998 Desert Fox strikes), U.S. officials widely believed that Iraq had resumed its WMD development.[24] Those conclusions involved significant extrapolation, relying on indeterminate human and signals intelligence (mainly reports from Iraqi opposition figures and interceptions of communications), since no anthrax or chemical weapons samples had recently been discovered inside Iraq.[25] Yet America's heightened sense of vulnerability after 9/11 significantly lowered the administration's threshold of tolerance for Iraq's putative WMD proliferation. As Condoleezza Rice (2011: 198) subsequently put it, "Saddam had shown a willingness to act recklessly before. We didn't believe that we had the luxury of inaction."

In the aftermath of 9/11, Vice President Cheney became one of the administration's strongest advocates of forcibly toppling the Iraqi regime. Emphasizing the possibility of a "nexus" between Iraq's WMD and radical Islamic terrorism, the vice president insisted that "containment is not possible when dictators obtain weapons of mass destruction, and are prepared to share them with terrorists."[26] Cheney, like several of the administration's other hard-liners, was probably to some extent engaging in threat inflation to build up public support for the war.[27] Yet in private conversations, too, Cheney and other hawkish officials seemed personally convinced that the threat stemming from Iraq's presumed WMD proliferation was mortal and real (Woodward 2004: 30, 175, 292, 429; Gellman 2008: 215–27). British prime minister Blair, who loyally followed the Bush administration in its headlong march to war, concluded from his interactions with senior U.S. officials after 9/11 that "the U.S. attitude to risk had been turned upside down"—America's leaders were now willing to sacrifice their nation's blood and treasure to tackle a perceived vital threat (Blair 2010: 398).

24. Author interview with Robert G. Joseph, senior NSC director for counterproliferation and homeland defense, 2001–5 (Feb. 2, 2011). On the perceived Iraqi WMD threat, see also Bush 2010: 242; Rice 2011: 167–70. The October 2002 National Intelligence Estimate (NIE) concluded that "Baghdad has chemical and biological weapons; [and] if left unchecked, it will probably have a nuclear weapon during this decade." NIE, "Iraq's Continuing Programs for WMD" (Oct. 2002), 5.
25. Bucci, author interview. See also Woodward 2004: 245–46.
26. Richard Cheney, speech to the Veterans of Foreign Wars national convention, Nashville, Aug. 26, 2002.
27. Haass (2009: 218), who as the State Department's head of policy planning had access to much of the intelligence on Iraq, writes that "the vice president's speech [of August 26] badly overstated the Iraqi threat." On the politicization of U.S. intelligence in the period leading up to the war, see also Pillar 2011: 13–95.

The vice president and his staff believed that although there were other hostile countries known to be developing WMD—such as North Korea, Libya, and Iran—effectively dealing with one of them could have a significant "demonstration effect," sending a powerful message to other actual or potential proliferators (Gellman 2008: 231). Rumsfeld, Wolfowitz, and Douglas Feith, the Pentagon's hawkish undersecretary for policy, agreed with Cheney that a bold military initiative was required to enhance U.S. deterrence vis-à-vis terrorists and WMD proliferators (Rumsfeld 2011: 342–43).[28] The prevailing view among the administration's hard-liners was that the threat stemming from Iraq's WMD proliferation had to be dealt with sooner rather than later, through a policy of preventive war that left little room for multilateral consensus building with foreign partners (Woodward 2004: 132–33; Rumsfeld 2011: 423).

In June 2002, the president himself first mentioned the possibility of unilateral "preemption" in a speech at West Point, where he emphasized that containment was no longer a viable strategy in the face of rogue states with WMD that could secretly provide those weapons to terrorists.[29] The argument was then fleshed out in a secret memo authored by Feith: in a world where hostile regimes might covertly use terrorist groups to deliver WMD "in an unattributable, and hence undeterrable, manner," the United States should not have to wait until it is attacked before launching military action in self-defense, nor should it feel constrained "by a requirement for international approval of some kind (e.g., from the UN)."[30] Finally, in September 2002, the new U.S. National Security Strategy elevated unilateral "preemption" to the level of official government doctrine.[31]

UNDERESTIMATING THE NEED FOR BURDEN SHARING

The administration's chief advocates of military intervention, perceiving an imminent threat to U.S. national security, focused in detail only on the short-term challenges of toppling Saddam's regime and neglected to adequately plan for, or indeed foresee, the challenges of stabilizing Iraq after the invasion. Their longer-term thinking, as is typical for the most hawkish policymakers, was based on abstract scenarios and a set of

28. Confirmed by Simon Webb, policy director at the British MoD, 2001–4, testimony before UK Iraq Inquiry (June 23, 2010), 7.
29. George W. Bush, "Graduation Speech at West Point," June 1, 2002.
30. OSD Policy, "Sovereignty and Anticipatory Self-Defense," Aug. 24, 2002, http://papers.rumsfeld.com.
31. On the doctrine's revolutionary implications, see Roberts 2003: 46–48.

highly optimistic assumptions about what would follow the war. Specifically, these assumptions, which came to inform U.S. policy, were: (1) advanced U.S. technology would obviate the need for a large invasion force; (2) American troops would be welcomed as liberators by the Iraqi people; (3) Iraq's administrative and security apparatus would remain largely intact; and (4) the limited postwar reconstruction that might be necessary could be financed largely through sales of Iraqi oil (Bensahel 2006: 456–58; Gordon and Trainor 2006: 158–87; Ricks 2006: 76–79). The belief that a large-scale protracted stabilization mission would be unnecessary in Iraq further reduced any incentive to secure UN approval as a means of legitimating the war and facilitating sustained international burden sharing. Kori Schake, a senior NSC staffer who subsequently became responsible for international coalition management on Iraq, candidly recalls that the administration's war advocates "didn't have an extended stabilization period in mind, so they didn't make the argument, we need UN approval because that's the only way to durably hold the allies."[32]

No Need for a Large Invasion Force

Rumsfeld and his collaborators in the Office of the Secretary of Defense were adamant that significantly fewer troops would be needed to invade Iraq and topple Saddam's regime than the existing war plans foresaw. The off-the-shelf war plan, OPLAN 1003-98 developed by General Zinni in the late 1990s, envisioned a lengthy seven-month buildup of nearly four hundred thousand U.S. troops in the Middle East before the launch of offensive operations (Gordon and Trainor 2006: 26). But from late 2001 onward, Rumsfeld pushed General Tommy Franks, the new commander at Central Command, to repeatedly slash the troop numbers. By mid-2002, CENTCOM's "running start" plan foresaw a launch of offensive operations against Iraq without a lengthy buildup, using only one heavy division, or less than twenty thousand ground troops with air support (ibid., 50, 54; Ricks 2006: 34; see also Franks 2004: 373). As Walter Slocombe, a former senior defense official in the Clinton administration who subsequently advised the Bush administration on Iraq reconstruction, explains, "Rumsfeld had this fantasy of invading Iraq with twenty thousand troops—and it might have been enough for the initial combat phase of the war, given that Saddam had probably decided, sensibly, that he was not going to fight the American army this time."[33]

32. Author interview with Kori Schake (Jan. 21, 2011). See also Kreps 2011: 130–33.
33. Slocombe, author interview.

But Rumsfeld also had a broader agenda. The secretary of defense believed that the U.S. military had stagnated over the previous decade. His goal was to substitute speed, surprise, and advanced technology for the military's traditional emphasis on sheer mass.[34] Rumsfeld thus saw the Iraq War as an opportunity to prove that the Powell Doctrine, with its requirement of "overwhelming force" that hawkish U.S. conservatives had long perceived as an impediment to action, was outdated—and the secretary of defense and his collaborators were willing to assume significant risks to that end. Marc Grossman, then a senior State Department official, explains with only slight exaggeration that the Pentagon's civilians were "more interested in proving the Powell doctrine wrong than in getting rid of Saddam Hussein."[35]

Welcoming Iraqis

It was on the war's aftermath that the administration's hawks, notably senior civilians at OSD who also provided guidance to the military planners, were willing to take the greatest risks. Serious planning for "phase 4," the transition that would follow the end of major combat operations in Iraq, did not begin until November 2002—almost one year after the administration had begun developing its updated plans for a U.S. invasion. Franklin Miller, a senior NSC staffer working on defense policy in the Bush administration, recalls that the Pentagon "had concentrated very heavily on phases 1, 2, and 3 of the war [i.e., the force generation, deployment, and major combat phases] from August until November 2002, because there were things that had to be done under a presumed time pressure."[36] The postwar planning that was subsequently carried out before the launch of offensive operations focused primarily on short-term humanitarian issues. There was only limited, last-minute planning for administering postwar Iraq, and the possibility that American troops might have to assume primary responsibility for maintaining—let alone restoring—political order was hardly considered at all (O'Hanlon 2004: 33–34; Bensahel 2006: 454–62; Gordon and Trainor 2006: 138–63).

The leading war advocates at OSD—Rumsfeld, Wolfowitz, and Feith—anticipated that it might be possible to do without a transitional

---

34. Author interview with Col. Michael Trahan, Deputy Dir. for Operations (J-3), CENTCOM, 2001–3 (Jan. 26, 2011). See also E. Cohen 2003: 228–30.
35. Author interview with Marc Grossman, UnderSecState for Political Affairs, 2001–5 (Jan. 13, 2011). See also Gordon and Trainor 2006: 53–54; Haass 2009: 199.
36. Author interview with Franklin C. Miller, Senior Dir. for Defense Policy, NSC staff, 2001–5 (Feb. 23, 2011).

U.S. administration by almost immediately handing off responsibility to a new interim Iraqi government made up of former expatriates (Feith 2008: 369). American forces, those officials insisted, would be welcomed as liberators by a friendly Shia populace. Hence the Americans' task would be limited to enabling the Iraqis to help themselves—which reinforced the belief that a small number of U.S. forces would be sufficient (Bensahel 2006: 456–57; Ricks 2006: 98). Deputy Secretary Wolfowitz in particular did not make that argument only in public as a means of "selling" the war. In the intramural debates at the Pentagon and the NSC, as well, "he portrayed a very welcoming Iraqi populace made up of Shias who would throw palm fronds and flowers in front of the tanks as they rolled into Baghdad. And he had a wealth of Iraqi expatriates who supported that view."[37] The most influential among Iraq's expatriates was Ahmed Chalabi, who had built up a close relationship with Wolfowitz going back to the 1990s and now headed the Iraqi National Congress (INC), an umbrella Iraqi opposition group. The civilians at OSD "listened to Ahmed Chalabi very closely," explains a former senior administration official. "And Chalabi's siren tune was: Iraq will be a bastion of democracy in the Middle East."[38]

A Functioning Iraqi Security Apparatus

The leading hawks also insisted, and most other U.S. officials accepted, that once American troops had removed the top layer of Baath party officials who were tainted by their loyalty to Saddam, Iraq's administrative structure and security apparatus would continue to function. The country's army and police force, in particular, would remain largely intact and could be used to stabilize the country. As Stephen Hadley explains, "We assumed that we would have about 135,000 Iraqi army forces available to help us maintain postconflict order, and that we would use them to help us with postconflict reconstruction."[39] Those optimistic assumptions appeared to warrant the conclusion that U.S. forces would need to offer assistance for only a short period of time (Bensahel 2006: 457–58).

Wolfowitz and other OSD officials asserted in the final weeks leading up to the war that by August 2003—less than half a year after the invasion—the number of U.S. troops in Iraq could be scaled back from 150,000, which is the invasion force the administration ultimately

---

37. Author interview with Gen. Bantz Craddock, Senior Military Assist. to SecDef, 2002–4 (Feb. 16, 2011).
38. Author interview with Richard Armitage, DepSecState, 2001–5 (Jan. 31, 2011). See also Woodward 2004: 19–20; Ricks 2006: 56–57.
39. Hadley, author interview. See also Feith 2008: 366; Gordon and Trainor 2006: 157.

[203]

agreed on, to about 34,000 (Ricks 2006: 97, 106; Shelton 2010: 484). CENTCOM's war plan, developed under strict guidelines from OSD, foresaw that three years later, by mid-2006, only a small U.S. assistance force of 5,000 troops would remain in the country.[40] These best-case scenarios were rapidly shattered in the aftermath of the invasion, as Iraq's administrative structure and security apparatus collapsed and the country descended into chaos. The situation was made significantly worse by the decision of Paul Bremer, the U.S. civil administrator, to entirely disband the Iraqi army and implement a broad de-Baathification policy in late May 2003.[41]

Defraying Reconstruction Costs through Oil Sales

Finally, the administration's leading war advocates expected that the limited postinvasion reconstruction that might be necessary could largely be paid for out of Iraq's own oil reserves. Wolfowitz insisted that with the international sanctions lifted after Saddam's removal, Iraq would be able to rely on annual oil exports worth $15 billion to $20 billion. "To assume we're going to pay for this is just wrong," he asserted in congressional testimony (quoted in Schmitt, *NYT*, Feb. 28, 2003). In the internal policy meetings, too, "Wolfowitz was very compelling in his argument that the Iraqi oil was going to pay for this, and he said it over and over," explains a former senior Pentagon aide.[42] Wolfowitz even commissioned a small group of people to work through the oil issues and project Iraq's future oil production in barrels per day—assuming the absence of major internal instability. "He built a very convincing argument that the cost to [the United States] was going to be major combat operations and then it would be paid for."[43]

To some extent, those best-case assumptions may have reflected the administration's ideological opposition to nation building.[44] During the 2000 presidential election campaign, Condoleezza Rice famously

40. CENTCOM, "Notional Ground Force Composition, Phase IV," PowerPoint briefing slide, Aug. 5, 2002, http://www2.gwu.edu/~nsarchiv/NSAEBB/NSAEBB214/Tab%20K%20-%20page%2010.pdf.
41. As a former senior officer bitterly concludes, "We created the insurgency. There was no insurgency until we disbanded the Iraqi army." Author interview with Col. John Agoglia, Deputy Chief of Plans (J-5), CENTCOM, 2001–3 (Feb. 1, 2011). See also Ricks 2006: 162–63.
42. Craddock, author interview.
43. Ibid.
44. "It was an ideological bent of the administration," insists one of Rumsfeld's former military assistants. Bucci, author interview. See also Gordon and Trainor 2006: 5, 14.

declared, "We don't need to have the 82nd airborne escorting kids to the kindergarten" (quoted in Gordon and Erlanger, *NYT*, Jan. 18, 2001). But regardless of the intellectual origins of those assumptions—and it may have been sheer wishful thinking—the result was that most U.S. decision makers felt no need to coordinate policy with foreign partners, let alone secure UN approval, to maximize longer-term burden sharing. As a former Pentagon aide acknowledges with hindsight, "We probably misunderstood the length of the commitment that we were getting into and the difficulties that would occur, which would then have required that kind of long-term support and participation from our allies. We thought we could go in there, get rid of Saddam and his buddies, put nicer people in place, and have a functioning country."[45]

THE STATE DEPARTMENT'S PUSH FOR A UN-BASED APPROACH

Secretary of State Colin Powell and his senior-level collaborators were not fundamentally opposed to invading Iraq. However, they did not view the Iraqi regime as an imminent threat to U.S. national security and thus disputed that the invasion needed to happen soon. "My objection had to do with timing, not with the fact of the war," explains Richard Armitage, then the deputy secretary of state. "I wanted to get Afghanistan in a better place and thought we would be better served waiting until after President Bush was reelected in the fall of 2004."[46] Grossman, the third highest-ranking official at the State Department, held a similar view. "I wasn't for not fighting," he recalls, "I just wasn't for fighting him [Saddam Hussein] off the top of the list." Grossman's conviction was that if the United States went through multiple consultations with international partners and took the time to build up international support, then "in the fall of 2003 we could have gone to war with a UN-backed coalition that looked more or less like the one that we had used in 1991."[47]

Beginning in the spring of 2002, the State Department organized several policy workshops with regional experts, scholars, and Iraqi exiles as part of its "Future of Iraq" project, which made the senior diplomats aware of the likely difficulties and costs of postwar stabilization

---

45. Bucci, author interview.
46. Armitage, author interview. On Powell's views see Feith 2008: 245–46; DeYoung 2006: 376, 399.
47. Grossman, author interview. In 1991, international partners had contributed almost three hundred thousand troops to major combat operations. Weitsman 2014: 60.

(Herspring 2008: 106–7; Haass 2009: 226–28).[48] Grossman subsequently testified before Congress that even under the best of circumstances, a considerable contingent of outside military forces would have to remain deployed in Iraq for several years after a U.S. invasion to maintain stability and ensure the provision of basic public services (Dao, *NYT*, Feb. 12, 2003). Furthermore, Powell and his staff were skeptical of OSD's plans to quickly install an interim Iraqi government of former expatriates led by Chalabi. They doubted that such a narrowly based government would be viewed as legitimate by the local population, and hence they favored instead a period of international trusteeship aimed at laying the foundations for a more representative Iraqi government. "Our view was that the future of Iraq needed to be decided by all Iraqis and not just by Iraqi exiles," Grossman explains. "Therefore you needed to find a way, even if it took a little extra time, to enfranchise Iraqis living in Iraq to participate in this conversation as well."[49]

President Bush, lobbied by OSD, initially disregarded the State Department's proposal of an international trusteeship structure for postwar Iraq (Feith 2008: 279; Rice 2011: 193). It was not until *after* the 2003 invasion, when it became clear that Chalabi's "externals" were not nearly ready to form an effective government and Iraq's administrative structure began to implode, that Washington scrambled to establish a Coalition Provisional Authority (CPA) under Ambassador Bremer, which incorporated several elements of the State Department's trusteeship proposals (Bensahel 2006: 461–62; Haass 2009: 259–60). As one former OSD official candidly admits, "We thought those expatriates were going to ride in on white horses right behind our tanks, they would be welcomed with open arms, and they would take over. I think the State Department understood a little better that that was not necessarily a good assumption."[50]

In short, senior State Department officials viewed the Iraqi regime in 2002 as less threatening than did their hawkish colleagues at OSD and the office of the vice president, and they anticipated a significantly more complex and burdensome stabilization effort following a U.S. invasion. Outside powers, the senior diplomats believed, not only would need to maintain security for several years, but should also take over primary responsibility for Iraqi governance during a transitional period in order to facilitate the development of a more inclusive Iraqi political process. Given those less sanguine expectations about the postinvasion phase,

48. On the Future of Iraq project see also Woodward 2004: 282–83.
49. Grossman, author interview. For an OSD perspective on this debate see Feith 2008: 253–79.
50. Bucci, author interview.

Powell and his collaborators recommended that the president take the time to build up solid multilateral support at the United Nations and elsewhere before invading Iraq.

Powell: UN Approval Needed for Burden Sharing

Armitage says that he and his State Department colleagues "worried about what would happen after the war," and consequently they urged the president to seek a UN resolution of approval in order to "get friends and allies on board should [the United States] have to go to war—to help with the burden."[51] Secretary Powell himself made an impassioned plea to the president for seeking UN approval during a private conversation on August 5, 2002: "I told the president that when we break this we're going to own it, and when the government falls [in Iraq] we're going to be the government, and you may not want to be the government of this country—so let's try to get the UN resolution."[52] Involving the United Nations, Powell further elaborated, might provide an alternative to war in the (unlikely) event that Saddam decided to cooperate. But it would be crucial in case of a military confrontation, to maximize support from international allies and partners for both combat and postcombat stabilization.[53] According to Bush (2010: 238), during that conversation in August 2002, Powell "was more passionate than I had seen him at any NSC meeting. He told me . . . the military strike would be the easy part. Then America would 'own' Iraq . . . [and] a UN resolution was the only way to get any support from the rest of the world."

Powell and his staff thought that UN approval would be less relevant to ensure short-term domestic support for the war from Congress and the American public. "The United Nations is not a domestic political factor here," Grossman explains.[54] Given the persistent demonization of Saddam Hussein in the U.S. media over the previous decade, a policy of regime change inaugurated during the preceding Democratic administration, and the transformed public attitude towards the use of force after 9/11, it was clear that the domestic task would be relatively easy. Hadley, who chaired the deputies committee and participated in most NSC meetings where the issue of UN involvement was discussed, confirms that "we didn't seek support from the UN instrumentally in order to deal with the domestic problem, because domestic support really was not a

---

51. Armitage, author interview. See also Haass 2009: 225; DeYoung 2006: 399–402.
52. Author interview with Colin L. Powell (Feb. 2, 2011). See also Woodward 2004: 150–51.
53. Powell, author interview. See also DeYoung 2006: 401–2.
54. Grossman, author interview.

problem." The driving consideration, Hadley clarifies, was "whether further support from the UN would help us put together and keep together the international coalition. That's what we focused on."[55]

Ever since the president's axis of evil speech in January 2002, senior Bush administration officials had relentlessly insisted that Iraq constituted a serious threat to American security. That prompted Congress to adopt a joint resolution providing the president with wide-ranging authority to use military force against Iraq as early as October 2002—when the UN negotiations had just begun (Woodward 2004: 203–4; Ricks 2006: 61–63). Sustained burden sharing facilitated by UN approval could still be helpful for maintaining domestic support in case of an open-ended commitment, but few in the administration expected such a commitment, and in the short run Congress was effectively locked in. Zalmay Khalilzad, himself a neoconservative and at the time a senior presidential adviser on Middle East policy, laconically notes that "the domestic American politics had changed because of 9/11, and the congressional decision reflected the urgency that people felt."[56]

Finally, contrary to what some scholars have argued, those in the Bush administration who advocated a UN-based approach were not motivated by concerns that a unilateral invasion might result in "international political costs" in the form of negative issue linkage, or reduced international cooperation with the United States in other policy domains.[57] Powell, asked whether he was concerned about issue linkage, straightforwardly declares, "I didn't think through all of that, I did not expand the problem out to cooperation on counterterrorism and Afghanistan and things like that."[58] Grossman confirms that concerns about reduced international cooperation with Washington beyond the issue of Iraq were not a major factor in the State Department's thinking.[59] The hard-liners at OSD and in the office of the vice president certainly did not worry about international retaliation in the form of issue linkage, given their belief that decisive U.S. leadership would induce other countries to follow in America's "slipstream" (Woodward 2004: 377; Gordon and Trainor 2006: 162). Hadley is categorical: "I don't remember anybody

---

55. Hadley, author interview.
56. Author interview with Zalmay Khalilzad (Jan. 20, 2011).
57. Thompson (2009: 156) claims that in 2002–3 "the United States did not seek UN involvement primarily for burden sharing." Instead, "U.S. decision makers chose the UN path because they worried about the international political costs" (161). Those costs, he argues, might have included negative issue linkage (18–19).
58. Powell, author interview.
59. Grossman, author interview.

making the argument that we needed international sanction on Iraq to keep people cooperating with the U.S. in other areas."[60]

SILENCE FROM THE TOP-LEVEL GENERALS

Senior uniformed officers on the Joint Staff, in the services, and at U.S. combatant commands around the world shared (and may have partially influenced) the State Department's concerns and policy outlook before the Iraq War. However, the three top-ranking generals who enjoyed direct access to the president—JCS chairman Myers, vice chairman Pace, and CENTCOM commander Franks—were exceedingly deferential to OSD and never challenged the civilian war advocates' optimistic assumptions in front of either the president or the NSC. Rumsfeld's authoritarian management style, coupled with the climate of national insecurity after 9/11, made it very difficult for other uniformed officers to effectively challenge the war plans and highlight the war's likely costs.

Concerns of Senior Military Planners

In late July and early August 2002, the *Washington Post* carried several front-page stories noting that "much of the senior uniformed military, with the notable exception of some top Air Force and Marine generals, opposes going to war anytime soon" (Ricks, *WashPo*, Aug. 1, 2002; see also Ricks, *WashPo*, July 28, 2002). The senior officers doubted that Iraq, whose weapons capabilities had been crippled by a decade of international sanctions, constituted a serious threat to American security, and they believed that the country could continue to be contained (Gordon and Trainor 2006: 27; Shelton 2010: 485). Retired four-star generals such as Norman Schwartzkopf and Anthony Zinni, commanders of CENTCOM during the 1991 Gulf War and Operation Desert Fox, respectively, spoke out publicly in favor of continued containment and expressed serious reservations about the wisdom of a war for regime change (Keller, *NYT*, Aug. 24, 2002; Ricks 2006: 51, 81–82).

Among senior military officers on active duty, planners on the Joint Staff were particularly worried about the seemingly unstoppable march to war. According to General John Abizaid, director of the Joint Staff until late 2002 (he subsequently became deputy commander and then commander of CENTCOM), the predominant view on the Joint Staff was that "even if the Iraqis were moving towards weapons of mass destruction, it

---

60. Hadley, author interview.

would be a while before they would really constitute a big enough threat. So there seemed to be plenty of time."[61] The senior officers were especially concerned that a war against Iraq in 2002 or early 2003 would divert America's attention and resources away from the strategic threat of transnational terrorism. Lieutenant General Gregory Newbold, until late 2002 the director for operations on the Joint Staff, recalls that as the policy debate increasingly focused on Iraq, "the military's reaction—as you can imagine, I had extensive contacts with other senior American officers around the world, as well as in Washington—the reaction was confusion. Why Iraq? We all thought it was a sideshow, irrelevant to the key issue, and that was Al-Qaeda."[62]

In addition, the senior officers believed that the material costs of invading Iraq would be much higher than the civilian war advocates anticipated. The military viewed Secretary Rumsfeld's insistence on repeatedly cutting the troop numbers for both major combat operations and postcombat stabilization as a reckless gamble, which would dangerously expose the armed services if OSD's optimistic assumptions turned out to be incorrect.[63] Army leaders were especially worried about this, given that their service would bear the heaviest burden for Iraq's long-term stabilization. "It was clear to everybody that not only did we have the wrong capability on the front end, but certainly the wrong capability on the back end," remembers a former commander of U.S. Army troops in Iraq.[64]

By the fall of 2002, senior Joint Staff officers were becoming increasingly concerned about the lack of detailed planning for postwar stabilization. "None of us thought that the postwar planning assumptions coming out of OSD were very robust," explains General Abizaid.[65] Partially for that reason, Abizaid and his uniformed colleagues repeatedly emphasized to their civilian superiors at the Pentagon, as well as to Generals Myers and Pace, that the troop numbers for Iraq needed to be increased. Furthermore, the senior Joint Staff officers recommended that greater emphasis be put on postwar planning and that the

61. Abizaid, author interview. Senior military planners at CENTCOM and on the army staff agreed with this assessment. Author interviews with Col. Paul Hughes, Dir. of NatSec Policy on the army staff, 2000–2002 (Apr. 1, 2011), and Col. Michael Trahan, DepDir. for Operations at CENTCOM, 2001–3 (Jan. 26, 2011).
62. Author interview with LTG Gregory Newbold (Jan. 25, 2011). On the military's consternation about the Iraq focus, see Herspring 2008: 99–100.
63. Trahan and Miller, author interviews. See also Shelton 2010: 480–82.
64. Author interview with Maj. Gen. John Batiste, Commander, U.S. Army First Infantry Division, 2002–5 (Feb. 22, 2011).
65. Abizaid, author interview. See also Schmitt and Shanker, *NYT*, Sept. 26, 2002; Gordon and Trainor 2006: 140.

administration secure multilateral buy-in upfront so as to facilitate "burden sharing [and] get as big a force of allied units as possible assembled for postwar activities as we could."[66] According to Newbold, senior planners on the Joint Staff "shared a strong feeling that the UN had to be part of the decision-making process, endorsing what action [the United States] would take."[67]

Planners at CENTCOM, the regional combatant command that held primary responsibility for developing the Iraq war plan under guidance from General Franks, had similar concerns and formulated similar recommendations. "We believed that [after the invasion] the Iraqi army could potentially surrender en masse, or desert," remembers Col. John Agoglia, then CENTCOM's J-5 deputy head of strategic plans and policy. "The answer was, quite frankly, more forces."[68] The CENTCOM planners "got more into the UN discussion in the summer of 2002," he explains. By then, it was clear from the latest war plans that "we would have less U.S. forces there, so additional allies would be helpful."[69] Senior planners at CENTCOM therefore understood that advance UN approval would help facilitate postwar burden sharing. "We knew that the greater level of international support we had, the better it would be for the post-conflict side of the equation," Agoglia affirms. The CENTCOM planners expressed their views on the desirability of UN approval and more specific assurances of international burden sharing to senior civilian officials at OSD, as well as to General Franks—but it is unclear whether those views were relayed upward to Rumsfeld and the president.[70]

Yes-Men at the Top

Since adoption of the 1986 Defense Reorganization Act, the chairman and vice chairman of the JCS are supposed to speak for the military in U.S. policy debates, representing the military's interests and concerns vis-à-vis the president and the NSC. President Bush reportedly did not take a firm and final decision to invade Iraq until December 18, 2002, when he told the NSC that "war is inevitable" (quoted in Feith 2008: 342). Until then, JCS chairman Myers, his deputy, General Pace, and CENTCOM commander Franks could have disputed the wisdom of attacking

66. Abizaid, author interview, confirmed by LTG Michael Dunn, Vice Dir. of Strategic Plans and Policy, Joint Staff, 2001–3 (Jan. 31, 2011). On Abizaid's efforts to alert OSD to the invasion's long-term costs see also Woodward 2006: 143.
67. Newbold, author interview.
68. Agoglia, author interview.
69. Ibid.
70. Agoglia and Trahan, author interviews.

Iraq by questioning the civilian war advocates' optimistic assumptions in front of the commander-in-chief. Furthermore, though more controversially, the top-ranking generals could have spoken out during congressional hearings and encouraged press leaks by the military aimed at stimulating a more informed public debate on the risks and likely costs of invading Iraq (O'Hanlon 2004: 40–41; Wong and Lovelace 2008). Finally, as a last resort, they could have resigned in protest (Desch 2007: 108).

General Myers subsequently (2009: 223) acknowledged that "few military professionals were comfortable" with the civilian war advocates' prediction of a smooth and short stabilization phase after the end of major hostilities in Iraq. In the run-up to the invasion, however, Myers and Pace never forcefully challenged or contradicted Secretary Rumsfeld and his civilian collaborators on the war plans and related assumptions in front of either the president or the cabinet.[71] Hadley, who attended most senior-level policy meetings on Iraq, emphasizes that "notwithstanding reports that have come out since, nobody among the senior military mentioned any of those reservations to the president. Nobody dissented."[72] Several sources indicate that Rumsfeld, intent on quashing any dissent within the Pentagon, had selected Myers and Pace for the top military posts precisely because of their known malleability (Gordon and Trainor 2006: 4; Woodward 2006: 57–74; Herspring 2008: 67; Shelton 2010: 426).

Frank Miller, the director for defense policy on the NSC staff, was confidentially contacted by various senior military officers, who expressed significant concerns about force levels, the lack of adequate planning for phase 4, and the limited international support:

> I heard those concerns from two-stars, three-stars, and four-stars. And I reported those views to Dr. Rice, to Steve Hadley, to Andy Card [the White House chief of staff], to Scooter Libby. So, those views were known. But it's one thing for me to say, "These are the concerns I'm hearing," . . . and when the president asks the chairman and the vice chairman: "Anybody got any concerns?" nobody says anything—that expresses a very different message.[73]

In short, Generals Myers and Pace failed to speak up in the internal debates on Iraq, and by so doing, they de facto empowered the administration's most hawkish civilian officials because their silence could be interpreted as tacit consent. As a former senior uniformed officer who

71. Craddock, author interview. See also Ricks 2006: 89; Woodward 2006: 72.
72. Hadley, author interview.
73. Miller, author interview.

served at OSD in the run-up to the war acerbically remarks, "Secretary Rumsfeld wanted yes-men around him, and that's what he got."[74]

Besides Myers and Pace, the only other senior military officer who had regular access to the president in the months leading up to the war was General Franks, the CENTCOM commander. Yet Franks's deference to Rumsfeld reportedly bordered on sycophancy, and he followed OSD's guidance with little questioning (Woodward 2002: 251; Herspring 2008: 103). Rumsfeld, who was intent on maintaining full control over the planning process, also actively encouraged Franks to disregard criticism or advice from the Joint Staff. "This was going direct OSD to CENTCOM and it was bypassing the Joint Staff," recalls Abizaid.[75] With little or no support from Generals Myers, Pace, and Franks, and with the Pentagon's civilian leadership agitating for war, it was very difficult for other senior military officers to convey their concerns about the likely war burden to the president and the NSC.

Secretary of State Powell, himself a former JCS chairman, and Armitage, his deputy, maintained multiple channels of communication with the uniformed side of the Pentagon. "Powell and Armitage were always as well informed as anyone in the national security circle about military matters," explains a former senior State Department official.[76] Armitage acknowledges that senior military officers often called him on the telephone to express their concerns about troop numbers, the perceived rush to war, and the lack of solid international support. "You usually get through to the deputy," he explains. "That leaves less fingerprints."[77] Yet Powell could not openly admit to be speaking on behalf of the military in cabinet-level meetings—it would have been improper, and Rumsfeld was extremely sensitive about the State Department's known contacts with uniformed officers.[78] Directly questioned about it, Powell denies that he was speaking for the military in his August 5 meeting with the president, when he expressed concerns about a potentially open-ended commitment and made the case for involving the United Nations. "It was my concern," he insists, though it was influenced by his "own personal experience as a soldier of thirty-five years."[79]

74. Batiste, author interview.
75. Abizaid, author interview. See also Shelton 2010: 447, 478; Herspring 2008: 112.
76. Author interview with Lincoln P. Bloomfield, AssistSecState for Pol-Mil Affairs, 2001–5 (Apr. 7, 2011). See also Herspring 2008: 103.
77. Armitage, author interview.
78. Author interviews with senior administration members. The media first hinted that "Powell's stance ha[d] produced an unusual alliance between the State Department and the uniformed side of the Pentagon" in mid-2002. See Ricks, *WashPo*, Aug. 1, 2002.
79. Powell, author interview.

In principle, the chief of staff of the Army and the commandant of the Marine Corps—Generals Erik Shinseki and James Jones, both reportedly skeptical of the war plans—could have requested a personal meeting with the president to convey their views. However, that would have been a highly unusual measure for the service chiefs to take, since they have no statutory role in policy debates. General Shinseki did ultimately challenge the civilian war advocates' optimistic assumptions: pressed to provide his own estimate of the troop numbers needed to stabilize Iraq during an open congressional hearing on February 25, 2003, he pointed out that "several hundred thousand soldiers" would probably be required for that purpose.[80] But Shinseki's was a lonely voice, and with the launch of offensive operations less than a month away, it was arguably too late for his warning to have much impact.

Secretary Rumsfeld was convinced that the military had gained too much influence in previous years, and he took up his post in 2001 determined to reduce the authority of the Joint Chiefs (E. Cohen 2003: 230–32; Shelton 2010: 403). Miller is scathing in his assessment: "Rumsfeld was a tyrant. He suppressed any form of dissent in the building."[81] One important question then remains: How was the secretary of defense able to maintain such tight control? Intimidation appears to have played an important role. As Miller explains, "By personally interviewing any nominee for flag rank [as opposed to letting the services put forward their own candidates, as had long been the norm], Rumsfeld was politicizing the promotion system and making it very clear [to the senior officers] that if they crossed the line, their career was over."[82]

When the Bush administration took office in early 2001, initially there was significant pushback against Rumsfeld's reform agenda and his autocratic management style from within the armed services and the army staff in particular. Rumsfeld's first eight months as secretary of defense were far from successful. His plans to "transform" the U.S. military into a leaner fighting force relying more heavily on speed and advanced technology resulted in significant friction with the services. By the fall of 2001, speculations were rife that Rumsfeld might be the Bush administration's first cabinet-level casualty (Bacevich 2007: 252; Desch 2007: 103). Yet the terrorist attacks of September 11 and the initial success of the ensuing Afghanistan campaign boosted the secretary's authority and standing, allowing him to push ahead with his agenda.[83] Without

80. Statement by Eric Shinseki, *DOD Authorization for Appropriations for Fiscal Year 2004: Hearing Before the Senate ArmedServ Committee*, 108th Cong. (Feb. 25, 2003), 241.
81. Miller, author interview.
82. Ibid. See also Herspring 2008: 12–13; Woodward 2006: 73.
83. Trahan, author interview. See also E. Cohen 2003: 227–28; Bacevich 2007: 253.

9/11, it is doubtful whether President Bush would have been able to hold on for as long as he did to a defense secretary whose relationship with the uniformed side of the Pentagon was noticeably tense from the beginning.

The radically changed U.S. discourse on national security after 9/11 also explains why disgruntled military officers did not more systematically leak their concerns about the likely costs of war to the public, as they had previously done in the 1990s. As General Newbold explains, "Following 9/11, with the nation under attack, on the part of the military there was a great sense of mission and duty and a desire to frankly crush Al-Qaeda. Given this context, it is hard then to stand up and speak against actions that were framed as being part and parcel of the response to 9/11."[84] The civilian hard-liners' relentless insistence that the goal of regime change in Iraq was central to the administration's war on terror undoubtedly made it more difficult for those who had reservations, in the military and elsewhere, to speak out and articulate an alternative narrative without appearing disloyal, unpatriotic, or dangerously naive (see also Ricks 2006: 66; Herspring 2008: 112).

THE OUTCOME: A HALF-HEARTED ATTEMPT AT THE UNSC

Absent vigorous intramural opposition and/or publicly voiced reservations from the uniformed leaders, the bureaucratic political dynamics that had decisively steered U.S. policy toward a multilateral course of action leading up to previous interventions aimed at internal political change in Haiti and the Balkans were not activated in the run-up to the 2003 Iraq War. While civilian policymakers were probably aware of the military's concerns, there was no compelling need to reassure the top-ranking generals about burden sharing and exit strategies, since there was no risk that they would veto the intervention. President Bush, prodded by Secretary Powell, still decided to involve the United Nations in the summer of 2002—but the administration as a whole, dominated by hard-liners, had a low threshold of tolerance for the costs of multilateral engagement.

Toward Resolution 1441

Vice President Cheney and Secretary Rumsfeld strenuously objected to involving the United Nations. "They fought us every inch, by every

---

84. Newbold, author interview.

manner possible," Armitage recalls.[85] Nevertheless, on September 7, Bush informed his foreign policy team that he would seek a Security Council resolution to bring the UN weapons inspectors back into Iraq and get some support for an ultimatum threatening war (Bush 2010: 238–39; Rice 2011: 180). Over the preceding weeks, not only Powell, but also Prime Minister Blair had repeatedly urged the U.S. president to seek UN approval before invading Iraq (Blair 2010: 399, 404; Bush 2010: 232).

The president heeded Powell's advice to involve the United Nations, but he also seems to have agreed with Rumsfeld and Cheney that the UN process would be valuable only insofar as the SC could swiftly provide some support for military action at little cost to the United States (Thompson 2009: 139–40). According to John Negroponte, at the time the U.S. permanent representative to the SC, "the effort to get a UN resolution was half-hearted at best from the point of view of the president of the United States in the fall of 2002."[86] Negroponte's British counterpart, an experienced multilateral negotiator, cautioned in a secret cable in late September 2002 that Washington and London were "start[ing] from a point where the other 13 members of the Council will, at best, have serious doubts about the use of force"—which would make it difficult to garner "the necessary nine votes for an explicit pre-authorization of military action."[87] Nevertheless, the Bush administration decided to float a draft resolution on September 26 that presented Iraq with a set of stringent disarmament requirements and foresaw an automatic authorization of "all necessary means" in case of noncompliance (Blix 2004: 76–78; Gordon and Shapiro 2004: 109). Predictably, the draft had only limited support at the SC, with France and Russia completely opposed and only five out of the council's fifteen members backing the proposal (Kessler and Lynch, *WashPo*, Sept. 27, 2002).[88]

The administration's leading war advocates, irked by those difficulties, argued that Washington should force a vote on the September 26 draft. Wolfowitz in particular insisted during an NSC meeting on

---

85. Armitage, author interview. See also Woodward 2004: 157, 176, 180; Cheney 2011: 398; Rice 2011: 180.

86. Author interview with John D. Negroponte (Feb. 15, 2011).

87. Jeremy Greenstock, "Iraq: Handling the Security Council," secret and personal note to Sir Michael Jay, UK UnderSecState for Foreign Affairs, Sept. 3, 2002, http://www.iraqinquiry.org.uk/media/52504/greenstock-jay-security-council-2002-09-03.pdf.

88. France took the lead in opposing a pre-authorization of military action. The view in Paris was that if, after the adoption of a first resolution, the UN weapons inspectors reported that Iraq had blatantly failed to cooperate, a second resolution would have to be adopted to authorize the use of force. See Woodward 2004: 222–23; Chirac 2011: 269–70.

October 15 that "there are worse things than having our . . . draft defeated or vetoed by France" (quoted in Feith 2008: 315; see also Lynch and De-Young, *WashPo*, Oct. 16, 2002). The British, however, worried that a defeated UN resolution would be politically disastrous and eventually made it clear that they, too, deemed the initial U.S. draft unacceptable (Woodward 2004: 221; Straw 2012: 378). Hence after mid-October 2002, the United States moved away from its request of an automatic authorization of military action in case of noncompliance. Over the following weeks, Washington, London, and Paris negotiated a compromise text, and with all three of them finally pulling in the same direction, on November 8 the SC adopted Resolution 1441 by a unanimous vote of 15–0 (Gordon and Shapiro 2004: 110–12; Thompson 2009: 141–42).

Resolution 1441 offered Iraq a "final opportunity" to comply with its disarmament obligations, established a new UN weapons inspections regime, and threatened "serious consequences" in case of Iraqi noncooperation. However, it did not explicitly authorize military action. As Ambassador Negroponte declared at the time, "This resolution contains no 'hidden triggers' and no 'automaticity' with respect to the use of force."[89] Michael Wood, the UK foreign office's legal adviser, similarly concluded in a confidential memo that Resolution 1441 "does not itself authorize the use of force, or revive the authorization of force given in SCR 678" (the 1990 Persian Gulf War resolution).[90]

President Bush and his advisers nevertheless felt that they had obtained what they needed in terms of legitimacy for military action. "We didn't feel as though an additional resolution was necessary for a military operation," explains a senior State Department official who was directly involved in negotiating 1441.[91] U.S. policymakers expected that 1441 would help legitimate the war by signaling that military action was a last resort. Khalilzad, the former presidential adviser, explains that "you didn't want to create an impression of the inevitability of military action regardless of what Saddam does."[92]

The UN Inspections Regime—Pretext for War?

The UN weapons inspectors, headed by Swedish diplomat Hans Blix, reentered Iraq in late November 2002 (Blix 2004: 95–96; Woodward

---

89. UNSC, record of 4644th meeting, Nov. 8, 2002 (Doc. S/PV.4644), 3.
90. Michael Wood, "Iraq: Legal Basis for the Possible Use of Force," Nov. 6, 2002, http://www.iraqinquiry.org.uk/media/52579/wood-ps-legal-basis-2002-11-06.pdf.
91. Author interview with William B. Wood, Acting AssistSecState for IO Affairs, 1998–2002 (Jan. 25, 2011).
92. Khalilzad, author interview.

2004: 234). The inspections, backed by the threat of military force, were off to a reasonably good start: the United Nations Monitoring, Verification and Inspection Commission (UNMOVIC) conducted some three hundred inspections during its first two months of operation, many of them unannounced, including on suspicious sites pointed out by U.S. and allied intelligence. No illicit weapons material was discovered, but about seventy Iraqi Al-Samoud missiles, which exceeded the allowed range, were destroyed under UNMOVIC supervision (Blix 2004: 156, 190; Gordon and Shapiro 2004: 143).

However, the Bush administration's patience with the inspections was clearly limited. Beginning in the summer of 2002, with the president's approval, Secretary Rumsfeld had ordered a silent buildup of tens of thousands of American troops in the Persian Gulf under the guise of training exercises and increasing operational capacity for the Afghan theater.[93] In late November, acting on orders from OSD, General Franks then set in motion the deployment of a full invasion force of almost 130,000 American troops (Franks 2004: 409–10). It thus appears that the Pentagon's civilian hawks were able to set the United States on a default path toward military action. In the late fall of 2002, Rumsfeld could disingenuously advise the president that it would be politically unwise to "leave 150,000 troops sitting on Iraq's border forever" (quoted in Bush 2010: 251; see Gordon and Shapiro 2004: 165; Woodward 2004: 261). By the time the UN inspectors were fully operational at the end of 2002, Powell, the reluctant warrior, had been outmaneuvered in the bureaucratic game: as a former military commander, he understood only too well that given the large-scale troop buildup, there wasn't much time left for UN diplomacy (Gordon and Shapiro 2004: 124–25).

CENTCOM's timeline, about which the president had already been briefed in August 2002, foresaw a launch of U.S. ground operations against Iraq around March 10, 2003.[94] From the point of view of an administration determined to go to war, the UN inspections regime was thus never more than a sideshow, to be tolerated until the point when General Franks was ready to launch the invasion. The Bush administration was "never interested in the inspections, really," concludes Greenstock, Britain's UN ambassador at the time. "They were just looking for a degree of legitimacy that they could milk out of the system."[95] Negroponte, his former American counterpart at the UN, essentially agrees:

---

93. Craddock, author interview. See also DeYoung 2006: 394.
94. CENTCOM, "Operational Timeline/Force Flow," PowerPoint briefing slide, Aug. 5, 2002, http://www2.gwu.edu/~nsarchiv/NSAEBB/NSAEBB214/Tab% 20K.pdf.
95. Greenstock, author interview.

"The president wasn't really prepared to give the inspections regime much of a chance. If you set up a UN institution to carry out a regime of inspections and you are serious about it, it's a little bit silly to expect that you are going to produce results in two or three months."[96]

The Failed Effort to Obtain a Second Resolution

When the Americans made it clear to their allies around mid-January 2003 that an invasion of Iraq had become inevitable, David Manning, Blair's principal foreign policy adviser, informed Condoleezza Rice that for Britain to be able to participate in the war, a serious effort had to be made to obtain a second UN resolution authorizing the use of force.[97] On January 31, Blair personally traveled to the White House to repeat that same point. Bush ultimately gave in to Blair's request (Bush 2010: 244; Rice 2011: 201). But the United States was never committed to obtaining a second resolution. As Greenstock explains, "The prime minister persuaded the president that there should be at least American condonement of that attempt. We never got real American support in it."[98]

The immediate goal in Washington and London was to persuade at least nine out of the SC's fifteen members to vote in favor of a second resolution authorizing force. The expectation was that France, whose foreign minister, Dominique de Villepin, had indicated on January 20 that Paris might veto such a measure, would then abstain, allowing it to be adopted. As a senior U.S. official who was involved in the SC negotiations explains, "We thought the French did not have a strategic enough reason to veto. They might threaten to veto, but at the end of the day, none of us really believed they would go that far."[99] Out of the council's ten nonpermanent members, however, Washington and London could initially count on only Spain's and Bulgaria's support.[100] That put all the weight on the six nonpermanent members who remained uncommitted: Mexico, Chile, Pakistan, Angola, Cameroon, and Guinea. All those countries were skeptical of military action, yet they were also concerned about alienating the United States (Gordon and Shapiro 2004: 149–51; Thompson 2009: 151–52).

96. Negroponte, author interview.
97. David Manning, testimony before the UK Iraq Inquiry (June 24, 2010), 84–85.
98. Greenstock, testimony before the UK Iraq Inquiry (May 26, 2010), 28.
99. Author interview with senior State Department official involved in UN diplomacy, June 1, 2011, confirmed by Armitage, author interview. See also Bush 2010: 246.
100. Prime Minister José Maria Aznar of Spain was firmly aligned with the United States, and Bulgaria was waiting to have its NATO accession ratified at the time, which gave Washington significant leverage over its foreign policy.

The United States, Britain, and Spain introduced a draft second resolution at the SC on February 24, 2003 (Lynch, *WashPo*, Feb. 25, 2003; Blix 2004: 196). The draft stated that Iraq had "failed to take the final opportunity afforded it in Resolution 1441"[101]—apparently following specific advice from the UK's attorney general, who had earlier explained in a secret memo that such a phrase would be sufficient to authorize the use of force.[102] Jean-Marc de La Sablière, France's permanent representative to the SC at the time, confirms that the draft was interpreted by everyone on the council as an attempt to authorize the "serious consequences" that had merely been threatened in Resolution 1441.[103] However, the six nonpermanent members remained unpersuaded. Rice (2011: 202) remembers that the Latin Americans, in particular, "were proving more difficult than we had expected." Seeking to break the impasse, on March 7 the British foreign secretary, Jack Straw, floated an amended draft resolution with a final ten-day deadline by which Iraq would have to fully disarm. The amended draft foresaw an automatic authorization of the use of force after expiration of the deadline, unless the council concluded on or before that date that Iraq had "demonstrated full, unconditional, immediate and active cooperation" (Blix 2004: 112–13; Thompson 2009: 153).

Seeking to persuade the uncommitted six to support the use of force, between the end of February and early March 2003, Washington and London applied significant last-minute diplomatic pressure. Yet there was no sustained effort at persuasion or high-level offer of inducements. "Contrast the way that the Bush administration handled the second UN resolution in 2003 with [Secretary of State] Jim Baker's effort on the 1991 Gulf War," Negroponte suggests, and it becomes clear that in 2003 the president and his principal advisers "didn't really focus much on diplomacy with the other Security Council members leading up to the Iraq War."[104]

In 1990–91, the U.S. president had been deeply involved in a months-long diplomatic effort to secure UN approval, personally traveling to several foreign capitals, while Secretary Baker visited twelve countries on five continents, offering inducements amounting to hundreds of millions of dollars (Baker 1995: 305–25; Thompson 2009: 61). By contrast, in early 2003, President Bush merely called Vicente Fox and Ricardo Lagos,

---

101. See "U.S.-British Draft Resolution Stating Position on Iraq," *NYT*, Feb. 25, 2003.
102. Peter Goldsmith, "Iraq: Interpretation of Resolution 1441," secret legal advice to the British government, Feb. 12, 2003, http://www.iraqinquiry.org.uk/media/46490/Goldsmith-draft-advice-12February2003.pdf.
103. Author interview with Jean-Marc de La Sablière (May 18, 2011). See also Chirac 2011: 279.
104. Negroponte, author interview.

respectively his Mexican and Chilean counterparts, on the telephone, warning them that bilateral relations were at stake and reportedly threatening trade reprisals (Lynch, *WashPo*, Mar. 23, 2008; Lagos 2012: 219). President Fox sought concessions from Washington to help him "sell" a possible compromise to his own domestic audience, and he thus linked Mexico's cooperation on Iraq to progress on a new immigration agreement with the United States. Bush, however, rejected such a bargain (Weiner, *NYT*, Oct. 28, 2002). In his memoirs, Fox (2008: 382) candidly remembers that although Washington was wooing Mexico's vote, "the United States didn't have much to offer in the way of carrots to Mexico."[105]

Given how deeply unpopular the prospect of a war for regime change was around the world, securing explicit UNSC approval for the Iraq War would undoubtedly have been difficult.[106] French president Jacques Chirac's declaration on March 10, 2003, that he would veto the draft SC resolution then on the table "whatever the circumstances" (i.e., regardless of how many other council members supported it) probably doomed the prospect of adopting a second resolution with an explicit ultimatum.[107] The uncommitted six, with political cover from France, could now better resist the pressure from Washington and London. In that sense, Chirac's veto threat indeed "changed the game."[108] On March 17, Washington and London declared that the SC negotiations were over, publicly blaming France's "intention to veto any ultimatum no matter what the circumstance" (Younge et al., *Guardian*, Mar. 18, 2003; see also Woodward 2004: 357–59).

UN Approval within Reach

The available evidence indicates that even after Chirac's veto threat, the Bush administration would have stood a reasonable chance of securing UN approval for the use of force had it been willing to follow a different approach based on what came to be known as the "benchmarks proposal."[109] In the days between March 8 (thus starting before Chirac's March 10) and March 16 (when Bush informed Blair that the UN process should be abandoned), Greenstock, Britain's UN ambassador, launched

---

105. Newnham (2008) indeed indicates that the Bush administration offered more substantial economic inducements to recruit its informal coalition of the willing after the invasion than it did to secure UN approval beforehand.
106. On global opposition to the Iraq War see Sobel, Furia, and Barratt 2012.
107. On Chirac's veto threat see Gordon and Shapiro 2004: 152–53; Chirac 2011: 281.
108. Greenstock, testimony before UK Iraq Inquiry, 33–34.
109. I discuss this counterfactual in greater detail in Recchia 2015.

a final effort to find a compromise agreement with the council's uncommitted six. Together with Blix and Juan Gabriel Valdés, Chile's UN ambassador who informally represented the six, Greenstock worked out a list of five demanding benchmarks that Iraq would have to meet within a short time frame. The list, circulated to the entire SC on March 12, included: (1) allow thirty Iraqi scientists identified by UNMOVIC to travel abroad for interviews, along with their families; (2) hand over all anthrax and mustard gas stores still unaccounted for, or provide evidence of their destruction; (3) destroy all remaining Al Samoud ballistic missiles; (4) surrender all mobile production laboratories for biological and chemical weapons, and (5) account for all unmanned aerial vehicles and other remotely piloted vehicles (Blix 2004: 245; Gordon and Shapiro 2004: 151–54; Lagos 2012: 216).

The United States reluctantly allowed the British to move ahead with the proposal. However, President Bush made it clear that the benchmarks resolution had to be adopted within the next few days, and Iraq should be given no more than a single week to demonstrate its compliance (Bumiller and Barringer, *NYT*, Mar. 13, 2003; Blix 2004: 245). Blair (2010: 428) recalls that "it was indeed a hard sell to George [Bush]. His system was completely against it." The uncommitted six, for their part, were sympathetic to the benchmarks proposal but insisted on a longer time frame of thirty to forty-five days. "The biggest point of diversion was the timetable imposed upon Iraq for compliance," remembers Lagos (2012: 215). Furthermore, the six requested that the benchmarks resolution entail no ultimatum or "automaticity." Their view was that after expiration of the deadline, the SC should assess Iraq's implementation of the benchmarks, based on a report from the inspectors, and only in case of certified noncompliance it would then authorize military action (Blix 2004: 248; Lagos 2012: 217).

Blair says that he pleaded with President Bush to extend the deadline,[110] and Greenstock declared at the time that if he got "traction" on his benchmarks proposal, Britain might consider dropping the operative paragraph that foresaw an automatic authorization of force in case of Iraqi noncompliance (Blix 2004: 248). But Washington was unwilling to compromise on either automaticity or the one-week deadline. "What we weren't seeing," recalls a former senior British diplomat, "was serious American engagement in the negotiation in trying to find a formula that would work."[111]

---

110. Tony Blair, testimony before the UK Iraq Inquiry (Jan. 21, 2011), 91.
111. Stephen Pattison, head of UN affairs, UK Foreign Office, 2001–3, testimony before the UK Iraq Inquiry (Jan. 31, 2011), 60, confirmed by Greenstock, testimony before Iraq Inquiry, 35.

Had the Bush administration more wholeheartedly supported the benchmarks approach, compromising on automaticity and agreeing to postpone the start of military operations by up to six weeks, it could have moved the council's undecided members out of France's orbit, thereby isolating France and increasing the political cost to Chirac of continued opposition. A two-step process would have been necessary for the benchmarks approach to ultimately yield UN approval for the use of force. First, the SC would have had to adopt a second resolution containing the benchmarks and specifying a deadline for Iraq's compliance. Second, after the deadline expired and the weapons inspectors issued their final report, the SC would have had to adopt a further resolution acknowledging Iraq's failure to comply with the benchmarks and thereby authorizing the use of force. In the face of support by a nine-member majority for a resolution acknowledging Iraq's failure to comply, a French abstention would have been the most likely outcome.[112] Greenstock essentially told the UK Iraq Inquiry as much: "The benchmarks [could have offered some] sort of escape route from what Chirac had said, . . . [however] the Americans were closed to compromise."[113]

In hindsight, it would have been extremely difficult for Iraq to meet several of the benchmarks. Baghdad could hardly have accounted for its outstanding anthrax and mustard gas stores, given that the relevant documentation had probably been destroyed years earlier, and even after the invasion no usable WMD stocks were found inside Iraq. Furthermore, Iraqi scientists interviewed abroad could have provided indicting accounts of Saddam's attempts to deceive the international community about his WMD programs, which might have convinced the inspectors that Iraq was not cooperating as required. Blix declared in 2010, reflecting on the benchmarks, that "they didn't have the anthrax. . . . So I doubt very much they would have [been able to] fulfill that condition. . . . The other one was the mobile biology laboratories. They didn't exist. . . . They didn't have them, so how could they have complied with that?"[114]

It appears that the decision to go to war in March 2003 rather than waiting another forty-five days seeking to obtain a SC vote explicitly authorizing the use of force was based on a fairly straightforward cost-benefit analysis in Washington. With strong U.S. domestic support for military action and most senior administration officials expecting that

112. Paris had not vetoed a SC resolution in opposition to either Washington or London since the late 1970s. See *Global Policy Forum*, "Subjects of UN Security Council Vetoes," 2009, https://www.globalpolicy.org/component/content/article/196/40069.html.
113. Greenstock, testimony before Iraq Inquiry, 35.
114. Hans Blix, testimony before the UK Iraq Inquiry (July 27, 2010), 79.

toppling Saddam and stabilizing Iraq would be easy, President Bush saw little reason to engage in further taxing negotiations at the SC— especially since there could be no certainty about the final outcome. If he waited much longer, Bush also risked appearing indecisive vis-à-vis an opponent that he and his administration had increasingly portrayed as a vital, imminent threat to the United States. "We were so leaning forward," Armitage explains. "The momentum that had built in the administration didn't favor waiting at all."[115]

General Abizaid, who by early 2003 was deputy commander at CENTCOM, rejects the argument that American forces would have been incapable of fighting in the Iraqi summer heat and that U.S. military leaders pushed the president to go to war by March 2003. Even in the summer, Abizaid explains, U.S. forces could have avoided the heat by fighting at night, as they had already done during the 1991 Gulf War: "It would have been a problem, but it was not an insurmountable problem. I believe it was not a military decision, it was a political decision, and then some of the political leadership came up with this idea that it couldn't be done later. Of course it could be done. It could be done anytime. I didn't feel any great pressure from our military commanders on the ground."[116] Armitage, a former navy officer who served three combat tours in Vietnam, remembers telling President Bush not to feel pressured by the prospect of Iraq's summer heat: "I said, Mr. President, don't be rushed in your decision by rising daytime temperatures, because we own the night—and it's a lot cooler then."[117] British policymakers were hearing similar things from their chiefs of staff: coalition troops could stay deployed for several more months if needed, and fighting in the summer would be a manageable problem.[118]

A Limited Coalition and Heavy U.S. Burden

In the run-up to the Iraq War, the United States assembled a coalition of the willing made up of more than thirty countries that offered their political endorsement. This allowed President Bush to boast in late March 2003 that "we've got a huge coalition," which was larger on paper than the coalition assembled in 1991 by his father for the Persian Gulf War (quoted in Bumiller, *NYT*, Mar. 28, 2003). Yet most coalition members in 2003 were either small developing countries heavily dependent

115. Armitage, author interview.
116. Abizaid, author interview.
117. Armitage, author interview.
118. Jack Straw, testimony before UK Iraq Inquiry (Feb. 2, 2011), 75.

on U.S. economic aid (Panama, Honduras, El Salvador, the Dominican Republic, Micronesia, Palau, and the Marshall Islands), or Eastern European countries aspiring to NATO membership (Bulgaria, Romania, Slovakia, Georgia, Albania, and the three Baltic states).[119] As a former senior military officer who was involved in coalition management for the Iraq War explains, "If you are one of those tiny little countries, and the United States is going to give you armored personnel carriers, or if you are an Eastern European country and the U.S. is sponsoring NATO membership for you, then a UN mandate matters less to you."[120]

Apart from Britain's sizable contribution of 41,000 troops, only two other U.S. allies—Australia and Poland—contributed limited troop contingents to the initial invasion.[121] By contrast, in the 1991 Gulf War, U.S. partners had contributed almost 300,000 troops to initial combat operations (Weitsman 2014: 60). After the 2003 invasion, in the face of a rapidly deteriorating security situation and looming humanitarian disaster, the SC went back to cooperating on Iraq in a newfound spirit of pragmatism, beginning with the adoption of Resolution 1483 on May 22, 2003. As Negroponte explains, the French and the Russians supported SC involvement in the invasion's aftermath, because "it gave them a seat at the table—it gave them a voice in the governance of Iraq."[122] SCR 1483, while emphasizing the special responsibilities of the United States and the United Kingdom as occupying powers, also called on all member states "to help meet the humanitarian and other needs of the Iraqi people by providing food, medical supplies, and resources necessary for reconstruction and rehabilitation."[123]

SCR 1511, adopted unanimously on October 16, 2003, then authorized a "multinational force under unified command to take all necessary measures to contribute to the maintenance of security and stability," and "urge[d] Member States to contribute assistance, including military forces, to the multinational force."[124] Nevertheless, since the U.S.-led invasion of March 2003, launched without UN approval, continued to be viewed as illegitimate by large segments of the world's population, foreign leaders, even those aligned with Washington on other issues,

119. White House, "Coalition Members—Operation Iraqi Freedom," Mar. 27, 2003, http://georgewbush-whitehouse.archives.gov/news/releases/2003/03/20030327-10.html. See also Weitsman 2014: 134–35.
120. Trahan, author interview.
121. Australia and Poland contributed, respectively, two thousand and two hundred troops. See n. 1, above.
122. Negroponte, author interview.
123. SCR 1483 (2003), § 2.
124. SCR 1511 (2003), § 13, 14.

were reluctant to meaningfully share in the burden of postwar stabilization. Only after the United States agreed to partially offset the financial costs of those contributions was it able to recruit about 16,000 troops from other international partners besides Britain (Richter, *LA Times*, June 22, 2003).[125]

During the early stabilization phase in 2003–4, the principal international troop contributors besides the United States and Britain were Denmark (about 600 troops), Georgia (about 2,000), Italy (3,200), Japan (600), South Korea (3,600), Poland (2,500), Romania (about 800), Spain (1,300), and Ukraine (about 1,600).[126] Yet the improvised multinational coalition showed little staying power, and it soon began to fall apart as the operation became protracted and casualties mounted (Malone 2006: 229; Ricks 2006: 346–48). Some of the largest troop contributors, such as Italy, Spain, and South Korea, had signed on for a "peacekeeping" mission in 2003, but as the security situation in Iraq deteriorated, it became clear that there was little domestic support in those countries to take on an active combat role. According to one study (Ricks 2006: 347), by the fall of 2004, more than half of the remaining troop contributors were former Communist countries, many of them candidates for NATO accession, where support for U.S. policy remained comparatively strong.

By May 2007, at the height of the Iraqi civil war, when American troops in Iraq had "surged" to over 150,000, the non-U.S., non-UK component had shrunk to only about 7,000 troops that largely limited themselves to noncombat support missions.[127] The visible lack of burden sharing contributed to growing U.S. congressional pressure to withdraw all American troops (Zeleny and Hulse, *NYT*, 28 Mar. 2007). In the absence of significant, sustained contributions to stabilization and reconstruction from international partners, the overall cost of the Iraq War to American taxpayers between 2003 and 2011 exceeded $1 trillion by even the most conservative estimates.[128]

The lack of a vigorous civil-military debate in the run-up to the 2003 Iraq War yielded a flawed U.S. strategic assessment and inadequate war

125. See also Joseph A. Christoff, *Stabilizing and Rebuilding Iraq: Testimony Before the House Subcommittee on IOs, Human Rights, and Oversight*, 110th Cong. (May 9, 2007), 5-8.
126. Christopher M. Blanchard and Catherine Marie Dale, "Iraq: Foreign Contributions to Stabilization and Reconstruction," *CRS Report for Congress* (Dec. 26, 2007), 3–6, 11–18.
127. Blanchard and Dale, "Iraq: Foreign Contributions," 11–18.
128. Amy Belasco, "The Cost of Iraq, Afghanistan, and Other Global War on Terror Operations Since 9/11," *CRS Report for Congress* (Mar. 29, 2011). For a much higher estimate, see Stiglitz and Bilmes, *WashPo*, Sept. 5, 2010.

plan, notably with regard to phase 4 stability operations. It also allowed the Bush administration's civilian hawks—Rumsfeld, Cheney, and their respective subordinates—to set U.S. policy with their highly optimistic assumptions about the war and its aftermath practically unquestioned. Defense analyst Michael O'Hanlon (2004: 40–41) argues that "the uniformed military in fact shares some of the blame for the mistakes made in planning the Iraq stabilization mission [given that] no member of the armed forces of the United States went public with his objections." O'Hanlon's point is well taken—all the more so if one considers that, as this chapter has shown, the top-ranking generals (notably Myers and Pace) not only failed to express the military's concerns in public when it became clear that Rumsfeld was deaf to criticism but also neglected to candidly express those concerns during private meetings with the president and his cabinet.

Had the JCS chairman and vice chairman more clearly conveyed to President Bush (and to the Congress) the military's concerns about the likely high costs of stabilizing Iraq, it would probably have been more difficult for the civilian war advocates to build up intragovernmental support for quick military action. If nothing else, greater pushback from the military leaders could have persuaded the administration to make more significant efforts to coordinate U.S. policy with international partners and secure advance UN approval so as to maximize the prospect of sustained burden sharing on Iraq's stabilization and reconstruction. As the former U.S. intelligence officer Paul Pillar (2011: 78) notes, "Assume that the Bush administration and the American people anticipated the costly mess that would follow a toppling of Saddam . . . . Under those assumptions, it is highly unlikely that the administration would have proceeded with its plan for war and inconceivable that Congress and the American people would have gone along if it had." At the very least, one might add, Congress and the American people (and thus presumably the president) would have viewed UN approval and more specific assurances of operational support from major international partners as all but essential before embarking on such a high-stakes mission.

Conclusion

Political philosophers since John Stuart Mill (1837: 374) have argued that multilateral approval for military intervention is normatively desirable because it constrains powerful states and makes blatantly self-serving interventions less likely. Especially when the use of force is justified by reference to humanitarian objectives, a powerful state planning to intervene "can never be sure whether it is really distinguishing its own national interests from the universalizable interests that all the other nations could share" (Habermas 2006: 184). Therefore, from an ethical standpoint, prospective interveners should always test their own unilateral anticipation of what might be acceptable from the viewpoint of an "impartial spectator" by submitting their policy proposals to a formal process of multilateral vetting and authorization (see also Doyle 2015: 198–204).

This book has investigated the value of multilateral approval, not so much from the viewpoint of Mill's impartial spectator as from the perspective of very partial U.S. policymakers who are motivated by their own patriotism, values, personal experiences, and the organizational interests of the bureaucracies they serve. Multilateral bodies such as the United Nations and NATO play important roles in U.S. decision making on armed intervention—but, as the previous chapters show, they matter for reasons that partially differ from those highlighted in other studies. When U.S. policymakers seek advance approval from the UNSC or NATO's NAC, they are rarely motivated by feelings of moral obligation or by strategic concerns about negative issue linkage. Instead, policymakers typically seek IO approval when they anticipate an open-ended commitment, especially in the absence of imminent threats to American security, in order to facilitate sustained international burden sharing and thereby maintain congressional support.

Yet policymakers often differ in their threat perception, anticipated operational commitment, and thus ultimately their cost-benefit analysis vis-à-vis multilateralism. Particularly when multilateral approval appears difficult to secure because the intervention aims to change the internal politics of a foreign country (and other IO member states are thus reluctant to offer their approval), the most hawkish civilian leaders in Washington may initially be willing to bypass relevant IOs to maximize U.S. freedom of action. In those circumstances, America's top-ranking generals and admirals can play a central role in steering U.S. policy toward the UN or NATO by threatening to veto an intervention altogether. Even the most heavyweight hawks among the civilian leadership can then be expected to recognize the value of securing IO approval as part of a broader bureaucratic strategy aimed at reassuring the reluctant warriors and averting a military veto. The prospect of sustained burden sharing, facilitated by IO approval and the potential exit ramp that a handoff to NATO or the UN can provide are likely to alleviate the military's concerns about costly quagmires, reducing its opposition and paving the way to a presidential decision to intervene. The military has several instruments at its disposal to influence U.S. decision making on armed intervention, ranging from intramural persuasion to congressional testimony, press leaks, public statements, coalition building with organizations outside the executive branch, and threats of resignation as a last resort.

At the same time, the president and to a lesser degree the secretary of defense can seek to ensure the support of the JCS chairman and other high-ranking military officers by appointing loyalists known to share the administration's political orientation. When that happens, the Joint Chiefs are unlikely to forcefully express the military establishment's concerns, as demonstrated by the experiences of the Vietnam War and the 2003 Iraq War. As H. R. McMaster has shown in his painstakingly researched account of U.S. civil-military relations during the Vietnam War, "loyalty was the criterion [President Lyndon] Johnson and [Secretary of Defense Robert] McNamara thought essential for their appointees" (McMaster 1998: 110). Having appointed pliable loyalists such as Generals Earle Wheeler and William Westmoreland to the top military posts, the president and his secretary of defense never had to submit their policy of "graduated pressure" to a rigorous feasibility check, and consequently they embarked on a very costly and drawn-out military adventure, "taking actions disconnected from military realities and without full appreciation of their consequences" (ibid., 108, and 324–26 more generally). Similarly, prior to the 2003 Iraq War, President Bush and Secretary of Defense Rumsfeld appointed malleable individuals—Generals Myers, Pace, and Franks—to the top military posts. Partially as a consequence, in the "run-up to the assault on Iraq, . . . the military acted [in many ways] like Wheeler and Westmoreland" (Betts 2012: 221; see also Herspring 2008: 65–125).

Such instances of extreme deference on the part of America's military leaders, however, resulting from a politicization of the appointments process, are relatively rare and likely to be short-lived. The services will be embittered by such perceived corruption of their professional independence; Congress will become suspicious if the top-ranking generals simply parrot the administration's official stance in formal hearings; and most fundamentally, as Samuel Huntington (1957: 84–85) noted, such "subjective" (i.e., politicized) civilian control can be expected to yield flawed use-of-force policies with strategically suboptimal outcomes that might undermine U.S. national security. Together, these factors will sooner rather than later cause the pendulum to swing back in the direction of greater military independence and assertiveness.

Johnson's perceived failure in Vietnam not only resulted in a devastating blow to his presidency but also stimulated greater professional independence on the part of the military in subsequent decades (Bacevich 2007: 238–41). Likewise, the enormous difficulties the United States encountered in Iraq after the 2003 invasion resulted in greater professional independence and assertiveness on the part of the military leaders. During President George W. Bush's second term in office, senior U.S. military officers pushed back against civilian plans to use force in pursuit of regime change in Iran (Smith and Baxter, *Sunday Times*, Feb. 25, 2007; Porter, *Asia Times*, June 9, 2008). Similarly during the Barack Obama administration in 2012 and 2013, the Joint Chiefs publicly highlighted the risks and likely operational costs of a humanitarian intervention aimed at toppling Syria's political regime (Youssef, *Miami Herald*, Mar. 7, 2012; Londono, *WashPo*, Aug. 30, 2013). In 2014, the U.S. military leaders moved to support limited air strikes against Islamist insurgents in both Syria and Iraq—yet so far, those strikes have helped defend rather than overthrow established political authorities as well as the broader regional status quo.

FURTHER RECENT EVIDENCE OF THE MILITARY'S INFLUENCE

The main case studies in this book (Haiti, Bosnia, Kosovo) that illustrate the military's ability to steer U.S. intervention policy toward the UN and NATO are all from the 1990s. As explained in the introduction, there are good reasons for this selection: in each case, it was clear from the outset that securing multilateral approval would be difficult and time-consuming, and consequently the most interventionist policymakers were initially willing to bypass relevant IOs. That said, Bill Clinton, under whose presidency those interventions occurred, is known to have had a somewhat rocky relationship with the military, especially during this first term in office (see, e.g., Kohn 2002; Feaver 2003: chap. 6). Therefore, my case selection might be viewed as biased. I believe that such concerns are unwarranted. Arguments that civil-military relations were in "crisis" during the early 1990s rely heavily on Colin Powell's unusually assertive stance as JCS chairman. But Powell retired from the military in October 1993 and exercised only limited influence on U.S. decision making in the three aforementioned cases.

There is evidence that for a much longer period of time—since the early Cold War, across Democratic and Republican administrations—America's top-ranking generals and admirals have exerted significant influence over military intervention decision making (Betts 1991; Bacevich 2007). Even during the George W. Bush administration, which, as the Iraq case study shows, was marked by a high degree of civilian dominance over the military, the top-ranking generals exerted considerable influence over intervention decisions when the civilian leadership was divided. Probably the clearest example of this is the decision-making process in the run-up to the 2003 Liberia intervention, discussed below; but there is also evidence that the military effectively vetoed a U.S. humanitarian intervention in Darfur in 2005–6.[1] If anything, in light of protracted commitments in Afghanistan and Iraq, present-day military leaders appear more reluctant than ever to deploy American ground troops in peacekeeping and stabilization missions overseas, especially when the overarching goal is human-rights-related.

Liberia, 2003

In 1999, civil war broke out in Liberia when a rebel group backed by neighboring Guinea, the Liberians United for Reconciliation and Democracy (LURD), began to launch systematic attacks on Liberian government forces in the country's north. In 2003 a second rebel group, the Movement for Democracy in Liberia, emerged in the south. By the early summer of that year, the two rebel groups were converging on the Liberian capital, Monrovia. The national government led by Charles Taylor was under siege, and the humanitarian situation was rapidly deteriorating, with hundreds of thousands of civilians fleeing to neighboring countries (Kuperman 2008: 156–57).

1. On Darfur, see Hamilton 2011: 77–79.

In late June, UN secretary-general Kofi Annan and several West African leaders began to call for a humanitarian military intervention. The United States, they argued, should play a lead role, given its unique capabilities and strong historical ties to Liberia, founded in 1847 by freed American slaves.[2] Senior civilian officials in the Bush administration, notably Assistant Secretary of State for African Affairs Walter Kansteiner and NSC Director for African Affairs Jendayi Frazer, supported the idea of a U.S.-led intervention. National Security Adviser Condoleezza Rice was reportedly sympathetic and especially receptive to arguments about the United States' unique responsibility vis-à-vis Liberia.[3] However, America's military leaders and the Pentagon more generally were initially opposed. They expressed doubts about a potentially open-ended commitment that might end in a Somalia-like quagmire. JCS chairman Richard Myers publicly sought to disabuse civilian interventionists of the notion that the situation in Liberia could "give way to any instant fix" (quoted in Marquis and Shanker, *NYT*, July 25, 2003; see also Ross 2005: 60).

With the civilian leadership divided (Secretary Rumsfeld and Vice President Cheney remained very reluctant), policy officials who supported U.S. intervention needed to reassure the generals by addressing their principal concerns in order to keep the possibility of a U.S. troop deployment on the agenda. "We wanted an answer for every argument that DOD was going to spring at us," Kansteiner remembers. "We wanted to show that [American forces] weren't going to get trapped—so this wasn't going to be unilateral."[4] Before the Pentagon leaders reluctantly gave their go-ahead, they requested concrete assurances that longer-term peacekeeping would be handed off to a follow-on multilateral force made up of non-U.S. troops. General Bantz Craddock, then the senior military assistant to the secretary of defense, recalls that the uniformed leaders "did not want to go in without a commitment that there would be a UN force generated that we could hand it off to. Our plan was to go in for a very limited amount of time, and there was a lot of pressure on the State Department to keep that moving."[5] Furthermore, the Pentagon was opposed to deploying U.S. troops before a cease-fire agreement was reached between Liberian government forces and rebels out of concerns about becoming embroiled in an African civil war.[6]

2. "UN Lobbies for Liberia Force," BBC News, June 29, 2003.
3. Author interviews with Walter Kansteiner (Jan. 18, 2011) and Jendayi Frazer (Jan. 27, 2011). See also Stevenson, *NYT*, July 2, 2003.
4. Kansteiner, author interview.
5. Author interview with Gen. Bantz Craddock (Feb. 16, 2003).
6. Frazer, author interview. See also Weisman and Shanker, *NYT*, Aug. 9, 2003.

Securing multilateral approval was not particularly difficult on this occasion. Since the UN secretary-general and several regional heads of state had persistently called on Washington to take the lead in a humanitarian operation, signaling widespread international support, nobody at the UNSC fundamentally objected to the deployment of a robust stabilization force to Liberia (Stevenson and Marquis, *NYT*, July 23, 2003; Barringer, *NYT*, Aug. 2, 2003). But the Joint Chiefs, by opposing any U.S. intervention in the absence of concrete assurances that other countries would take over the longer-term burden, were able to exert considerable influence on related Security Council negotiations. John Negroponte, then the U.S. permanent representative to the SC, confirms that the Bush administration came to view a multilateral mandate foreseeing a rapid handoff to a follow-on UN mission as essential. "The U.S. military didn't like the idea of intervening in Africa," he explains, "they'd rather let somebody else do it. So we were going to do the emergency part of it and then back out of it, by having this other force take over."[7]

The military's principal concerns were effectively addressed before President Bush decided to intervene. First, the Economic Community of West African States (ECOWAS) endorsed the intervention and pledged to raise three thousand troops that would soon be deployed as peacekeepers to Liberia.[8] Second, the UNSC adopted a resolution on August 1 that authorized military action and committed the council "to establish . . . a follow-on United Nations stabilization force" under regional leadership within a maximum of two months.[9] Finally, under strong pressure from the United States, Taylor resigned from the Liberian presidency on August 7, opening the way to a cease-fire between government forces and rebels (Sengupta, *NYT*, Aug. 8, 2003). After some further hesitations, President Bush finally ordered the deployment of several hundred marines to Liberia on August 14 (Ross 2005: 64; Kuperman 2008: 159). A U.S. quick-reaction force took control of Monrovia's international airport, facilitating the subsequent deployment of a larger contingent of Nigerian and other West African peacekeepers. Another small U.S. contingent landed at Monrovia's seaport, rehabilitated it, and created a safe passage to the city so that emergency food aid and fuel could reach its starving inhabitants (Collins, *Army Magazine*, Feb. 2004).

The limited nature of the U.S. deployment clearly reflected a compromise between the Bush administration's civilian interventionists and the reluctant military leaders. As a State Department official explained at the

7. Author interview with John D. Negroponte (Feb. 15, 2011).
8. Kwasi Kpodo, "West African Nations Pledge 3,000 Troops for Liberian Intervention Force, Call for U.S. Lead," Associated Press, July 4, 2003.
9. SCR 1497 (2003), § 2.

time, "The Pentagon [was] dead set against" sending in any larger American force (quoted in Weisman and Shanker, *NYT*, Aug. 9, 2003). Frazer confirms that "DOD was doing options that were more and more limited, or showing how, if you did this option, it would take fifty thousand troops—so they were basically saying, it's not feasible."[10] Reflecting the military's desire, this was a short in-and-out mission. The quick-reaction force was withdrawn on August 24 after barely ten days, and the last marines left Liberia by the end of September. The United States handed off all longer-term peacekeeping and stabilization tasks to a follow-on UN mission (UNMIL) made up of about fifteen thousand non-American troops (Ross 2005: 65–67; Kuperman 2008: 159).

Libya, 2011

In February 2011, after "Arab spring" uprisings in Tunisia and Egypt, large numbers of Libyan citizens took to the streets protesting against Muammar Qaddafi's corrupt and authoritarian rule. The Libyan protests turned violent after Qaddafi's security forces killed more than a dozen protesters on February 17, quickly resulting in widespread gun battles between government forces and rebels. Within days, the rebels gained control of important cities along the coastline to the east of the Libyan capital, Tripoli. However, by early March the rebels' advance was stopped by the superior firepower of Qaddafi's forces. On March 6, Libyan government troops supported by airpower launched a brutal counterattack, driving the rebels into retreat and retaking several rebel-held cities (Hendrix, Faiola, and Sockol, *WashPo*, Mar. 7, 2011).[11]

Until then, the UNSC had limited itself to imposing an arms embargo on Libya, freezing the assets of Qaddafi family members, and referring the Libyan case to the International Criminal Court.[12] French president Nicolas Sarkozy was at the forefront in advocating a tougher international response. Beginning in late February, he had begun to call for Qaddafi to leave, while urging the imposition of a no-fly zone over Libya to "prevent the use of that country's warplanes against [its] population" (quoted in Watt and Wintour, *Guardian*, Feb. 23, 2011). Sarkozy was soon joined by British prime minister David Cameron, who supported the idea of a no-fly zone and offered to contribute UK "military assets" to a multilateral operation aimed at averting a humanitarian catastrophe (MacDonald, *Wall Street Journal*, Mar. 1, 2011). With the pressure mounting on U.S.

10. Frazer, author interview.
11. See also Christopher M. Blanchard, "Libya: Unrest and U.S. Policy," *CRS Report for Congress* (Apr. 25, 2011).
12. SCR 1970, adopted on Feb. 26, 2011.

leaders to take a firm stance on the humanitarian crisis in Libya, on March 3 President Obama demanded that Qaddafi "step down from power and leave" immediately, although Obama initially avoided references to a possible military intervention (Landler, *NYT*, Mar. 3, 2011).

The U.S. national security team met to discuss military options on March 9 (Clinton 2014: 366). Confronted with a humanitarian crisis that did not clearly threaten important American interests, the administration was divided over how to proceed. Senior civilian policymakers of liberal Wilsonian persuasion—notably NSC staffers Samantha Power and Benjamin Rhodes, as well as ambassador to the UN Susan Rice—supported military intervention. Secretary of State Hillary Clinton was initially "sympathetic [to arguments in favor of intervention], but not convinced" (Clinton 2014: 364). Meanwhile, the uniformed leaders and Secretary of Defense Robert Gates had deep reservations (Stolberg, *NTY*, Mar. 29, 2011; Clinton 2014: 370; Gates 2014: 511). In previous days General James Mattis, head of Central Command, had publicly cautioned that even imposing a no-fly zone would be "challenging" and carry significant risks, since it would require the United States to destroy Libya's air defenses (Bumiller, *NYT*, Mar. 1, 2011; see also DeYoung and Whitlock, *WashPo*, Mar. 2, 2011).

Secretary Gates and JCS chairman Michael Mullen initially pushed back against demands for U.S. military action. Gates, as the Pentagon's civilian leader, took the lead in publicly highlighting attendant risks and potential longer-term costs (Sanger and Shanker, *NYT*, Mar. 2 and 7, 2011). The secretary of defense, like most military officers a political realist in foreign affairs, believed that the humanitarian crisis in Libya "was not a vital national interest of the United States," and thus he "adamantly opposed" military intervention in the pursuit of regime change (Gates 2014: 511–12; see also Clinton 2014: 366). As the momentum toward intervention increased, Gates publicly expressed doubts that "other allies [would be] prepared to work with [the United States]" to share related burdens and risks, pointing to the absence of UN approval and noting that there was "no unanimity within NATO for the use of armed force" (quoted in Bumiller, *NYT*, Mar. 1, 2011). Gates therefore signaled that IO approval, combined with concrete assurances of international burden sharing, was essential for the Pentagon to come on board. Over the next several days, lest there be any doubt of where the Pentagon stood, Gates further insisted in private meetings that he viewed "a UN Security Council resolution and explicit regional participation" as necessary conditions for U.S. intervention in Libya (Gates 2014: 515).

Moreover, as Gates subsequently recalled, in the intramural debates during the run-up to the intervention, he and Admiral Mullen emphasized that before the president deployed U.S. military assets in Libya, several other criteria ought to be fulfilled: the mission's objectives needed to be clearly achievable, there had to be a viable exit strategy, and preferably there should be evidence of solid domestic support—in line with the Weinberger-Powell Doctrine for using force.[13] Therefore, although the Pentagon leaders recognized that regime change in Libya was the administration's ultimate *political* objective, they were adamant that the *military* mission be limited to imposing the no-fly zone and protecting civilians from large-scale attacks by government forces. Gates strongly "oppose[d] the idea of making regime change a military objective" because in his view such an objective would be virtually impossible to achieve "without people on the ground."[14] As the secretary of defense emphatically declared before the Senate Armed Services Committee, "the last thing this country needs is another enterprise in nation-building."[15]

Meanwhile, beginning in the second week of March, the situation on the ground rapidly deteriorated, with Libyan government forces retaking most rebel-held cities. By March 14, Qaddafi's loyalists seemed poised to crush the rebellion's last stronghold in the eastern city of Benghazi. Qaddafi's promise to "cleanse Libya house by house" and his threat to show the inhabitants of Benghazi "no mercy" were seized upon by advocates of humanitarian intervention in the United States and elsewhere as evidence of the regime's intent to commit mass atrocities (Kirkpatrick and Fahim, *NYT*, Mar. 17, 2011).[16] Around this time, Secretary of State Clinton, who had until then remained noncommittal, joined Power, Rhodes, and Rice in backing U.S. military intervention. Clinton hints in her memoir that she was convinced on the occasion of a March 14 meeting with Mahmood Jibril, the chairman of Libya's rebel-led Transitional National Council, arranged in Paris by President Sarkozy (Clinton 2014: 365, 369–70; see also Gates 2014: 511; Michaels 2014: 21).

It is unclear whether any of the Obama administration's civilian interventionists initially argued that the United States and its closest allies should intervene without UN or NATO approval in case neither could be secured. In any event, the point became moot when President Obama made it clear that he saw eye to eye with the Pentagon on this matter and insisted that he was "not going to act alone or without international sanction" (quoted in Gates 2014: 515). Ultimately, securing multilateral approval proved to be fairly straightforward, and no

---

13. Robert Gates, *Operation Odyssey Dawn and the Situation in Libya: Hearing Before the Senate ArmedServ Committee,* 112th Cong. (Mar. 31, 2011), 17.
14. Ibid.
15. Ibid., 22.
16. Kuperman (2013: 110–13) claims that Western advocates of military intervention significantly exaggerated the threat of mass atrocities.

protracted negotiations were necessary. Earlier in March, two regional IOs, the Gulf Cooperation Council and the Arab League, had endorsed the imposition of a no-fly zone over Libya, and several Arab countries, including Qatar and the United Arab Emirates, pledged concrete operational support (Bronner and Sanger, *NYT*, Mar. 12, 2011).[17] Such evidence of strong regional backing made senior State Department officials confident that Russia and China could be persuaded to abstain on an "all necessary means" resolution at the UNSC (Clinton 2014: 367, 370). The Arab League resolution, in particular, reportedly "strengthened the hand of the interventionists . . . inside the Barack Obama administration" (Williams and Bellamy 2012: 278).

Russian authorities agreed to abstain at the SC, after it became clear that most nonpermanent members supported a no-fly zone and Washington assured Moscow that the operation would be limited, with no military occupation (Clinton 2014: 371). Consequently, Ambassador Rice, with crucial British and French support, was able to secure the adoption of SCR 1973 on March 17. The resolution authorized the United States and its allies "to take all necessary measures . . . acting nationally or through regional organizations . . . to protect civilians and civilian populated areas under threat of attack . . . [and] to enforce compliance with . . . a ban on all flights" in Libya.[18] Earlier on March 17, President Obama had decided in a meeting with his principal foreign policy advisers, assuming the SC would offer its approval, that the United States was going to intervene (Gates 2014: 518; see also Wilson and Warrick, *WashPo*, Mar. 19, 2011).

Military operations began on March 19 with U.S.-led strikes against Libya's air force and air defense system, as well as against Libyan government forces en route toward the last rebel stronghold, Benghazi (Michaels 2014: 22). Besides the United States, ten other allies participated in the initial Libyan air campaign (Weitsman 2014: 165). The Obama administration would have liked the campaign to be implemented as a NATO mission from the outset. However, France was reluctant to involve the alliance, and Turkey was opposed to NATO's enforcing anything but a limited no-fly zone. Consequently, the initial phase of the campaign, called Operation Odyssey Dawn by the United States, was implemented by a U.S.-led coalition outside the NATO framework (Clinton 2014: 374–76; Michaels 2014: 20–24). Only on March 24 did NATO's NAC agree to enforce the no-fly zone. This opened the way for the Atlantic alliance to take over command and control of the mission, renamed

17. See also Wissam Keyrouz, "Gulf States Back Libya No-Fly Zone," AFP Newswire, Mar. 7, 2011.
18. SCR 1973 (2011), §§ 4, 8.

Operation Unified Protector, on March 31 (Michaels 2014: 24–25; Weitsman 2014: 167).

Yet by the time President Obama committed the United States to military intervention on March 17, the Pentagon's most serious concerns had been effectively addressed. First, the military mission was going to be limited to imposing a no-fly zone and protecting civilians from large-scale attacks by Libyan government forces. Promoting regime change was not part of the military mission.[19] That clearly reflected Secretary Gates's and the uniformed leaders' "preoccup[ation] with avoiding mission creep and avoiding an open-ended . . . commitment."[20] President Obama, who was personally sympathetic to the concerns of his generals, also made it clear in his public statement announcing the intervention that U.S. involvement would last "days, not weeks" (quoted in Cooper and Myers, *NYT*, Mar. 18, 2011).

Second, there was evidence of significant U.S. domestic support for a limited military operation. On March 1, the Senate had unanimously adopted a nonbinding resolution sponsored by Robert Menendez (D-NJ), calling for Qaddafi's resignation and urging the UNSC to impose a no-fly zone over Libyan territory.[21] In subsequent days, leading senators, including John Kerry (D-MA), chair of the Foreign Relations Committee; Mitch McConnell (R-KY), the Senate minority leader; and John McCain (R-AZ), ranking member of the Armed Services Committee, went further, calling for more decisive U.S. military action beyond imposing a no-fly zone (Berger, *NYT*, Mar. 6, 2011).

Third, the operation enjoyed solid multilateral backing from the UNSC and various regional bodies, most notably the Arab League. Paragraph 4 of SCR 1973 also explicitly "exclude[ed] a foreign occupation force of any form on any part of Libyan territory." The United States and its partners had thus committed themselves to a limited aerial operation, which precluded an invasion and subsequent occupation of the country. Secretary Gates, asked in late March about the likelihood that U.S. ground troops might be drawn against their will into a stabilization force for Libya, could point to that passage in the UN resolution to buttress his own opposition, claiming that this was "virtually impossible."[22]

Finally, several European allies led by Britain and France had pledged that they would carry most of the operation's burden after the initial degradation of Libyan air defenses. When NATO took over command

---

19. Gates, *Operation Odyssey Dawn*, 5.
20. Ibid., 27.
21. *A Resolution Strongly Condemning the Gross and Systematic Violations of Human Rights in Libya*, S. Res. 85, 112th Cong. (Mar. 1, 2011).
22. Gates, *Operation Odyssey Dawn*, 20.

and control of the mission on March 31, Secretary Gates declared before Congress that "this transition was part of the package and part of the plan with our allies, from day one."[23] More specifically, Gates explained, the Pentagon was assured before launching the air campaign that "the United States would come in heavy and hard at the beginning" to neutralize Qaddafi's air defense and airpower capabilities, "but, the idea all along was—and it was the agreement that was made with our allies— that . . . there would be a transition and we would recede to a support role as soon as we had reached the point where those air defenses had been suppressed."[24]

Accordingly, by the end of March, the United States handed off most of the longer-term burden to its European and international partners. After April 4, U.S. aircraft ceased to participate in strike sorties on a day-to day basis, although the United States maintained a stand-by strike capability and continued to provide crucial capabilities for electronic warfare, aerial refueling, and intelligence (Castle and Cowell, *NYT*, Apr. 4, 2011).[25] U.S. aircraft flew only 16 percent of all strike sorties in Operation Unified Protector, with France, Great Britain, Canada, Italy, Denmark, Belgium, and Norway shouldering most of the combat burden over several months. The NATO mission was concluded on October 31, ten days after Qaddafi was captured and killed by rebel fighters (Michaels 2014: 32; Weitsman 2014: 172-74). In the operation's later stages, U.S. fighter aircraft and drones had to reenter the fray, and there were some tensions when European stocks of laser-guided munitions began to wane earlier than anticipated (Gates 2014: 522; Michaels 2014: 27). Nevertheless, in line with the Pentagon's wishes, the United States was able to minimize its commitment. As Vice President Joseph Biden declared in October, "The NATO alliance worked like it was designed to do, burden sharing . . . . We carried the burden a lot of other places . . . and this was really burden sharing" (quoted in Rettig, *US News & World Report*, Oct. 31, 2011).

IMPLICATIONS FOR THEORY AND POLICY

The theory and findings presented in this book about the military as a driver of multilateral engagement suggest new avenues for research and have implications for both theory and policy. First, while my findings

---

23. Ibid., 12.
24. Ibid.
25. See also Adm. Michael Mullen, *Operation Odyssey Dawn and the Situation in Libya: Hearing Before Senate ArmedServ Committee*, 112th Cong. (Mar. 31, 2011), 30.

support Huntington's arguments about the importance of an independent military, they challenge his somewhat rigid distinction between
military affairs and policy and his related insistence that the uniformed
leaders should stay out of policy debates on the use of force. Second, the
argument developed in this book suggests that previous scholarship
may have underestimated the potential for the bureaucratic politics paradigm to generate explanatory theories in political science. Finally, my
argument yields specific recommendations for policymakers intent on
advancing American interests abroad while minimizing the costs of foreign intervention.

Objective Control Revisited

To what extent may, or should, the uniformed leaders participate in
policy debates on the international use of force? According to Huntington, debates about whether to use force, when to do so, and for what
objectives, are inherently political; political activity by generals and
admirals weakens their professionalism; and a non-professional military
risks undermining the nation's security. The solution he advocated was
"objective civilian control," a division of authority whereby the uniformed leaders concentrate on military operations, or the art and science
of "managing violence," while abstaining from participation in policy
debates about the use of force (Huntington 1957: 80–85).

Yet as several critics have pointed out, Huntington problematically
assumed there could be a clear distinction between military affairs and
policy. In reality, "there can be no clear distinction between the ends and
means of war, [because] what ends are possible to think about depends to a
large extent on the means by which they are to be pursued" (Burk 2002: 13;
see also Gibson 2008: 71–73). The available military means must be taken
into account in the formulation of policy and strategy—and since uniformed
leaders are best able to assess those available means (along with the cost of
their employment), they have an important role to play in debates about
both policy and strategy. "Effective civil-military relations in practice rely
on a dialogue," maintains Hew Strachan (2006: 67). A candid dialogue
among leaders at the civil-military nexus appears more desirable than ever
when it comes to devising so-called nontraditional military missions, with
ambitious objectives that may include anything from peacekeeping to
counterinsurgency to the democratization of war-torn societies.

Most contemporary scholars of civil-military relations recognize the
value of this dialogue between civilian policymakers and top-ranking
generals. Hence those scholars insist, or at least acknowledge, that the
uniformed leaders should challenge the civilian leadership in intramural
debates about armed intervention. By laying out the military's own

perspective and explaining the likely costs of any prospective force deployment in terms of financial assets, lives lost, and impact on the armed services' readiness, the military leadership contributes to the development of successful intervention policy. "No useful purpose is served," as one scholar explains, "if military professionals adhere to the 'can do' syndrome (regardless of the threat, mission, or contingency), without clearly indicating the likely costs involved" (Sarkesian 1998: 111; see also Cook 2002; Desch 2007). However, scholars and analysts remain divided over how uniformed leaders ought to respond if civilian authorities plainly disregard their advice, embracing optimistic assumptions and cost-benefit assessments that the military regards as unwarranted.

Traditionalists emphasize that once the military leaders have expressed their professional judgment and concerns, they ought to play no further role in policymaking. The historian Richard Kohn, in an article coauthored with former JCS chairman Richard Myers, offers a stark formulation of the traditionalist viewpoint: "Once military advice has been offered, automatic consent by the military in strategic and political matters is necessary—regardless of whether or not the military advice is heard, listened to, and considered" (Myers and Kohn 2007: 148; see also Feaver 2003; Nielsen 2005). Public resignation of senior military officers over policy disagreements, Kohn (2009) insists, is morally and politically wrong, although quiet retirement may be acceptable under exceptional circumstances.

Revisionists, on the other hand, contend that when civilian authorities disregard the generals' advice or, worse, deliberately seek to mislead the American people about the likely costs and risks of armed intervention, the uniformed leaders may legitimately voice their concerns to the public. The generals may leak their concerns to the media, express them in open congressional hearings and press conferences, or resign as a last resort before more vigorously challenging the administration, so as to foster "a sophisticated and informed discussion on the uses of military force" (Strachan 2006: 79; see also Sarkesian 1998; Gibson 2008: 122–23). These latter arguments have gained more prominence in the aftermath of the 2003 Iraq War, as it became clear that the lack of adequate planning for the occupation was due to a significant degree to Secretary Rumsfeld's disregard of professional military advice and the failure of the JCS to convey the military's concerns to the president, Congress, and the public (O'Hanlon 2004: 33–45; Wong and Lovelace 2008; Milburn 2010).

It is axiomatic that in a democracy, the dialogue between civilian authorities and the military has to be "unequal," as Eliot Cohen (2003: 209) points out, since "the final authority of the civilian leader [ought to be] unambiguous and unquestioned." Nevertheless, one counterintuitive implication of the argument developed in this book is that those who believe that the United States ought to display greater deliberation in military intervention decision making and work harder to secure multilateral support should probably welcome the generals' reluctance to use force for internal political change and their bureaucratic leverage. Conversely, those who believe that the United States should intervene more often, at an earlier stage in foreign crises, and that the costs of multilateralism to the United States tend to exceed its benefits may be inclined to call for stricter civilian control of the military. Put differently, without questioning the principle of ultimate civilian control, our views on the appropriate civil-military balance might have to reflect to some degree our broader normative attitude toward armed intervention and multilateralism as instruments for advancing America's interests abroad.

A Theory of Bureaucratic Politics

In its emphasis on civil-military bargaining, this work also advances our understanding of the role of bureaucratic politics in foreign-policy decision making. The central tenets of the bureaucratic politics paradigm, as developed by scholars such as Graham Allison and Morton Halperin, are: first, policy decisions are usually the outcome of bargaining and coalition building among officials from various agencies and departments; and second, how those officials view the interests at stake in a given situation is substantially affected by their specific organizational membership, which is often summed up in the aphorism "where you stand depends on where you sit" (Allison and Zelikow 1999: 255; see also Allison and Halperin 1972). Critics have emphasized that the bureaucratic politics approach may be able to explain particular decisions after the fact, but it cannot yield general explanatory theories, given that where officials stand on any issue is never completely determined by their organizational membership—and even if it were, it would be difficult to predict the outcome of bureaucratic bargaining (Krasner 1972; Welch 1992: 121–22). Therefore, in recent years the bureaucratic politics paradigm has somewhat fallen out of fashion among political scientists, although policy analysts and historians, who are more interested in understanding particular decisions than in developing general theories, have continued to show significant interest in this approach.

The argument and the evidence from the preceding chapters, however, suggest that fruitful insights may be gained by joining the bureaucratic politics paradigm with insights from research on civil-military relations. For the bureaucratic politics paradigm to yield general explanatory theories, two conditions need to be fulfilled. First, the representatives of specific governmental organizations (e.g., uniformed leaders representing the military establishment) usually have to stand at roughly the same place in interagency debates on a particular matter, for roughly the same reasons. Second, they need to have the ability to actually steer the policy process in their preferred direction, and their influence should follow a regular pattern in order to be predictable.[26]

America's top-level generals and admirals, unlike most civilian appointees to senior policy positions, rise to their position through the ranks of their organization. Hence they are significantly more parochial than civilian appointees, meaning that their policy outlook tends to reflect the armed services' preferences and concerns (Betts 2001: 126–32; Szayna et al. 2007: 68). When it comes to debating military intervention, the uniformed leaders consistently display fairly distinctive attitudes: they are concerned about limiting the armed services' liability, and when they anticipate open-ended commitments that they feel are unwarranted by the limited U.S. interests at stake, they usually counsel against intervention, emphasizing attendant risks and likely operational costs. Furthermore, in the United States, the senior generals and admirals can exert an extraordinary amount of influence on related decision making, given their professional expertise and the high public confidence that the military enjoys.

The bureaucratic politics approach as such is undoubtedly a "research orientation that serves to sensitize the analyst" rather than a full-fledged theory in the same way that realism and liberalism are broad paradigms in international relations rather than specific explanatory theories (Halperin and Clapp 2006: 344). However, this book suggests that just as realism and liberalism can yield more specific explanatory theories connecting hypothesized causal variables to outcomes (e.g., realist theories about the effect of international anarchy on war, or liberal theories about the democratic peace), so it is possible to derive specific theories from the bureaucratic politics paradigm that help us explain empirical regularities in foreign policy. Since the policy outlook of senior military officers usually reflects their organizational background, and given the military's unique influence, a greater focus on civil-military relations may allow researchers to account for some apparently puzzling regularities in U.S. national security policy. That said, the extraordinary nature of the military's impact on policymaking in the United States is likely to limit the extent to which those findings apply to other countries.

Looking beyond the United States

In the United States, the uniformed leaders' ability to mobilize Congress and public opinion in opposition to use-of-force policies they view

---

26. For a useful discussion see Welch 1998.

as exceedingly costly provides the military with extraordinary leverage. But there are few, if any, other democracies where the uniformed leaders enjoy a similar ability to mobilize public opinion and thus comparable influence over policymaking. Meanwhile, in nondemocratic regimes, the generals may well dominate the policy process—but where the military can simply impose its will on the polity, we are unlikely to witness the patterns of intense civil-military bargaining that characterize policymaking on armed intervention in the United States. In short, the nature of civil-military relations in the United States is unique, and thus any theory that draws heavily on evidence from U.S. civil-military relations will be limited in its geographic scope.

What are the implications of this for understanding the multilateral use of force by other countries? It is likely that alternative theories, which explain policymakers' efforts to secure multilateral approval as the result of norm internalization, fears of soft balancing, or concerns about short-term public support have more explanatory power when it comes to accounting for the behavior of prospective interveners besides the United States. One might plausibly hypothesize that different types of states seek multilateral approval for different reasons, depending on factors such as their national history, domestic regime type, and relative power position in the international system. This suggests that further research may be needed into the scope conditions of particular theories and hypotheses.

For instance, in states with strong parliamentary control over national security affairs, as in most of continental Europe, the specific configuration of parliamentary coalitions and the impact of public opinion on related coalition dynamics might have a decisive impact on decisions to intervene unilaterally or multilaterally. In the absence of a common threat perception, junior coalition partners, who frequently hold more extreme, radical pacifist or isolationist stances, might preclude military intervention altogether *except* as part of a multilateral mission.[27] Furthermore, in countries with a history of unsuccessful unilateral military missions (most notably Germany, Italy, and Japan, where aggressive expansionism during World War II resulted in complete military defeat), the modern populace and principal political parties may have internalized the requirement of multilateral approval, making straightforwardly unilateral intervention all but unthinkable.[28]

27. On the impact of coalition government on foreign policy see Auerswald 1999; Kaarbo and Beasley 2008.
28. For a similar argument see Krause 2004.

In contrast, for presidential democracies with a high degree of executive branch independence in national security affairs or for straightforwardly authoritarian regimes, the preferences of parliament and public opinion can be expected to have little impact on the government's decision to intervene and whether to seek multilateral support. Nevertheless, small- and medium-power states might still be driven to seek multilateral approval before intervening, out of international systemic considerations. Policymakers in France or Nigeria, for instance—two regional powers with only limited parliamentary control over national security affairs—may be motivated by concerns about negative issue linkage in their efforts to secure multilateral approval.[29] Ultimately, when investigating why countries other than the United States seek multilateral approval for their armed interventions, we might do well to think more about equifinality--i.e., the possibility that there may be different causal pathways to the same outcome.

Policy Implications

Finally, the argument developed in this book has important implications for policymaking, especially in the United States. Theories are most likely to be relevant for policy when they not only explain phenomena of interest but are also prescriptively rich in the sense of yielding useful recommendations (George and Bennett 2004: 279). More specifically, as Stephen Walt (2005a: 33) notes, good "theoretical work (combined with careful empirical testing) can identify the conditions that determine when particular policy instruments are likely to work."

I theorized in chapter 1 that advance approval from the UNSC or NATO's NAC functions as a catalyst for sustained burden sharing with international partners and, furthermore, may offer an exit ramp for U.S. troops as it facilitates the establishment of follow-on multinational missions. By clarifying the value of advance IO approval to the United States, my research sheds light on the conditions under which such approval is likely to be particularly helpful. For limited air strikes and commando operations that have a low chance of resulting in open-ended commitments, the costs of securing multilateral approval in terms of protracted diplomacy, side payments, and loss of secrecy probably outweigh any attendant burden-sharing benefits. Conversely, for more ambitious military operations that aim at changing the internal politics of foreign countries, the long-term payoffs of a multilateral course of action are likely to outweigh the initial costs of securing IO approval.

29. On French and Nigerian intervention policy see, respectively, Treacher 2003; Coleman 2007: chap. 3.

The argument presented in chapter 2 and the evidence from subsequent chapters further suggest that interventionist civilian leaders tend to underestimate the long-term material costs of military operations aimed at internal political change. Such false optimism often makes the benefits of multilateral support seem negligable, and the result might be a flawed policy with a heavy material burden on the United States. Therefore, interventionist policymakers should pay greater heed to military leaders and other skeptics who tend to emphasize the long-term costs of interventions aimed at internal political change. That is likely to yield more rigorous U.S. strategic assessments and adequate efforts to secure international support.

Perhaps most important, U.S. policymakers should bear in mind that unless the United States intervenes with IO approval, the leaders of foreign partner states may find it difficult to subsequently contribute troops and other resources for postcombat stabilization. Washington might be able to belatedly secure a UN mandate after the end of major combat, reflecting a desire by other members of the SC to gain some leverage over U.S. policies on the ground. But as demonstrated by the Iraq experience between 2003 and 2011, that is unlikely to be sufficient to retroactively legitimate the intervention and function as a catalyst for meaningful postcombat burden sharing. Policymakers should not delude themselves by unrealistically expecting that, as some recent scholarship implies, the United States may be able to pursue an approach to military intervention "that is largely *unilateral* . . . in early phases and then *multilateral* for postcombat phases of operations" (Kreps 2011: 166, emphasis added).

The only exception to this rule was the 2001 Afghanistan intervention, in which the United States initially intervened unilaterally and was subsequently able to secure explicit UN and NATO approval, as well as significant international participation, for longer-term stabilization efforts.[30] The reason for this appears to have been that although the United States made only very limited efforts to coordinate its policy with foreign partners before the start of offensive operations, the intervention itself, launched in the immediate aftermath of 9/11/2001, was credibly justified on grounds of self-defense and enjoyed broad international support. In most other cases of intervention, where U.S. assertions of self-defense are likely to leave international audiences unpersuaded, American leaders will find it difficult to secure sustained burden sharing on stabilization and reconstruction *unless* they have secured explicit IO approval before the intervention.

30. Nevertheless, as Weitsman (2014: 117–18) notes, the United States consistently carried most of the burden in Afghanistan, in contrast with other cases discussed in this book.

WHAT THE FUTURE MIGHT HOLD

Prediction in the social sciences is notoriously problematic. Human agents are reflective—they can adapt to and change their social and material environments. Phenomena such as strategic interaction and adaptive change make most social scientific generalizations necessarily contingent and time-bound. Nevertheless, social scientists may be able to diagnose current trends on the basis of their theories and investigations, and that may warrant the development of plausible scenarios for the short- and medium-term future (George and Bennett 2004: 129–31).

What, then, might the future hold in terms of U.S. military intervention policy and the role of multilateral organizations? First, civil-military relations are seemingly back to normal after an interlude of extraordinary deference to civilian authorities on the part of the top-ranking generals under Secretary of Defense Rumsfeld. The uniformed leaders have reasserted their professional independence, and for the near future, they can be expected to offer their frank and vigorous contribution to U.S. policy debates about armed intervention. Furthermore, because the costs of the unilateral Iraq invasion turned out to be much higher than civilian policymakers anticipated, U.S. civilian leaders now appear more willing to listen to and follow the generals' advice. As a result, in recent years either U.S. ground troops have been kept entirely out of foreign political conflicts, or their role has been limited to providing essential training and support, often in the context of multilateral missions. As President Obama told the *New York Times* in August 2014, "A lesson that I now apply every time I ask the question, 'Should we intervene, militarily?' [is] 'Do we have an answer [for] the day after?' "[31]

For the foreseeable future, therefore, the United States is unlikely to intervene unilaterally to promote domestic political change abroad absent a national consensus that the security of American citizens or key allies is imminently threatened. At the same time, it may become increasingly difficult for the United States to obtain the explicit approval of relevant IOs, and notably the UNSC, for future military interventions. The shift away from unipolarity is likely to increase the cost to the United States of persuading other SC members—such as China, Russia, India, and Brazil—to vote in favor of resolutions authorizing U.S. intervention or to at least abstain. Furthermore, as U.S. partner states democratize, their leaders must take into account the preferences of their people to a greater degree, and U.S. interventions are often highly unpopular among domestic audiences in Latin America, Asia, and the Middle East. John

31. Barack Obama, interview with Thomas L. Friedman, *NYT*, Aug. 8, 2014.

Ruggie (2006: 43) reminds us that "in the run-up to the 2003 Iraq War the United States had the most trouble not with authoritarian states or kleptocracies but with other democracies—and not only in 'old Europe' France and Germany, but also in Canada, Chile, Mexico, and Turkey."

Because UNSC approval is likely to be increasingly difficult to obtain, some scholars and pundits argue that the United States can be expected to rely more on improvised coalitions of the willing or seek the endorsement of regional IOs (see, e.g., Kagan, *Financial Times*, May 13, 2008; Kreps 2011: 165–66). Ad hoc coalitions of the willing may be helpful for the purpose of increasing short-term U.S. domestic support. However, such improvised coalitions tend to be made up largely of small states with modest financial resources and military capabilities. Even when more powerful states participate, coalitions of the willing have limited staying power, and consequently they are clearly suboptimal for the purpose of burden sharing on stabilization and reconstruction.

In principle, to lock in multilateral support, the United States could rely on the endorsement of regional IOs, first and foremost NATO, as a substitute for UNSC approval. However, the 1999 Kosovo experience, in which NATO approved a U.S.-led intervention without UN cover after months of pushing and prodding by Washington, will probably remain the exception. Major European countries such as Germany, Italy, and France had important national interests at stake in the Balkans, which facilitated a NATO consensus on the use of force that may be difficult to achieve elsewhere. If one adds to this the growing "intervention fatigue" among European publics after a protracted engagement in Afghanistan, it is hard to imagine that, absent a direct external attack on a NATO member state, the Atlantic alliance could endorse any future "out of area" interventions in Central Asia, Africa, or the Middle East without prior authorization from the UNSC. Other regional IOs, such as the OAS, the African Union, and the Arab League, are even less likely to endorse U.S.-led interventions targeting one of their own members in the absence of UN approval, given persistent sensitivities in most of the developing world to Western interference. Endorsements from regional IOs might usefully complement UN approval, providing additional legitimacy and facilitating burden sharing, but they are unlikely to become a viable substitute for the UNSC.

In short, advance approval from the UNSC is likely to remain of paramount importance as a catalyst for sustained international burden sharing. Since U.S. policymakers will probably find it more difficult to secure UN approval in the future, we may see more vote trading and side payments at the SC as Washington seeks to persuade skeptical member states to support U.S.-led military interventions. In the face of a rising China and resurgent Russia, the SC can thus be expected to function even more than has hitherto been the case like a classic great-power concert or security regime, relying on reciprocity, logrolling, and mutual accommodation among its principal members. At the same time, given the growing costs to the United States of securing UN approval and the military's reluctance to intervene in the absence of clear threats to American security, hawkish civilian policymakers in Washington may find it altogether more difficult to persuade the president to authorize interventions involving the risk of open-ended commitments.

Finally, the global power shift away from the United States and its principal allies has implications for arguments that emphasize concerns about negative issue linkage as a determinant of U.S. multilateralism. Twenty or thirty years from now, in the aftermath of a hypothetical U.S. unilateral intervention widely perceived as illegitimate around the globe, rising powers such as China, India, and Brazil would presumably have greater leeway to reduce their cooperation with the United States across different issue areas. In other words, negative issue linkage, while not a major concern at present, might further constrain U.S. policymaking in the future. Some scholars argue that U.S. unipolarity and the incentive for most other countries to accommodate the United States are unlikely to disappear anytime soon (Norrlof 2010; Beckley 2011). Nevertheless, the exceptional freedom of maneuver that the United States has enjoyed since the end of the Cold War may be coming to an end. Growing concerns about issue linkage might thus reinforce the aforementioned trends toward greater U.S. restraint, with the consequence that even in the absence of norm internalization, U.S. unilateral interventions (at least major interventions with significant numbers of "boots on the ground") could become exceedingly rare.

Summing up, for the foreseeable future, the United States is likely to become more cautious and multilateralist in its approach to military intervention. Given a military leadership that vigorously conveys its concerns about the risks and operational costs of intervention, a foreign policy elite that appears to have internalized the lessons of a difficult experience in Iraq, and perhaps growing concerns about negative issue linkage, multilateralism may well be overdetermined—especially when the goal of U.S. intervention is to change the internal politics of foreign countries. If one adds to that the growing costs to the United States of actually securing IO approval, the conclusion would be that U.S. humanitarian and other ambitious interventions aimed at internal political change may simply become less frequent. To the extent that the United States continues to intervene directly, as opposed to relying on local partners, it is likely to limit itself to narrowly targeted missions, relying on commando raids and unmanned aerial vehicles, to minimize the risk of open-ended commitments. Of course, exogenous shocks and other unforeseeable circumstances could significantly affect one or several of the aforementioned variables, leading U.S. foreign policy into altogether different directions. However, the ingrained preferences and concerns of America's uniformed leaders with regard to armed intervention are here to stay, and they will continue to shape U.S. foreign policy in consequential and sometimes counterintuitive ways.

Appendix

LIST OF OFFICIALS INTERVIEWED

(With relevant positions held and date of interview)

Abizaid, Gen. John P. (USA, ret.), Director, Joint Staff, Oct. 2001–Nov. 2002; Deputy Commander, Nov. 2002–July 2003, and Commander, July 2003–Mar. 2007, CENTCOM — January 20, 2011

Agoglia, Col. John F. (USA, ret.), Deputy Chief of Planning (J-5), CENTCOM, 2001–May 2003 — February 1, 2011

Armitage, Richard L., Deputy SecState, Mar. 2001–Feb. 2005 — January 31, 2011

Asmus, Ronald D., Deputy AssistSecState for European Affairs, 1997–2000 — April 5 and 21, 2010

Babbitt, Harriet, U.S. PermRep to the OAS, 1993–97 — July 10, 2009

Batiste, Maj. Gen. John (USA, ret.), Senior Military Assistant to the Deputy SecDef, 2001–Aug. 2002; Commander, First Infantry Division, U.S. Army, 2002–5 — February 22, 2011

Bennett, Douglas J., AssistSecState for IO Affairs, 1993–95 — March 30, 2011

Bennett, Virginia, Political Counselor, U.S. Mission to the UN, New York, 2000–2003 — June 1 and 3, 2011

Bloomfield, Lincoln P., AssistSecState for Pol-Mil Affairs, 2001–5 — April 7, 2011

Bowman, Adm. Frank L. (USN, ret.), Deputy Director of Operations (J-3), Joint Staff, Dec. 1991–June 1992; Director for Pol-Mil Affairs (J-5), Joint Staff, June 1992–July 1994 — April 27, 2011

Bucci, Col. Steven P. (USA, ret.), Military Assistant to the SecDef, 2001–5 — January 19, 2011

Burleigh, Peter, Deputy U.S. PermRep, Aug. 1997–Dec. 1999, and Acting PermRep, Sept.1998–Aug. 1999, UN, New York — April 3, 2010

[251]

Christiansen, John, OSD Desk Officer for the Caribbean, 1990–93; Director, OSD Haiti Task Group, 1993–97 — July 15, 2009

Craddock, Gen. Bantz J. (USA, ret.), Senior Military Assistant to the SecDef, Aug. 2002–4; SACEUR, 2006–9 — February 16, 2011

De La Sablière, Jean-Marc, PermRep of France to the UN, New York, 2002–7. — May 18, 2011

Dobbins, James, U.S. PermRep to the EU, 1991–93; Special Haiti Coordinator, DOS, 1994–95; Special Envoy for Kosovo, 1998–99, and Afghanistan, 2001 — July 10, 2009

Dobriansky, Paula, UnderSecState for Global Affairs, 2001–5 — February 1, 2011

Duffy, Thomas, Adviser for Political Affairs, U.S. Mission to the UN, New York, 1999–2003 — June 12, 2011

Dunn, LTG Michael M. (USAF, ret.), Vice Director of Strategic Plans and Policy (J-5), Joint Staff, June 2001–June 2003 — January 31, 2011

Errera, Philippe, Counselor in Charge of Pol-Mil Affairs, French Embassy in Washington, DC, 1999–2003 — January 22, 2011

Feinberg, Richard, Senior Director for Inter-American Affairs, NSC staff, 1993–96 — June 22, 2009

Fisher, Louis, Specialist in Constitutional Law, U.S. Library of Congress — July 8, 2009

Flavin, Col. William J. (USA, ret.), Deputy Director of Special Operations for the SACEUR, 1995–99; Director of Doctrine, Concepts, and Training, U.S. Army Peacekeeping and Stability Operations Institute, U.S. Army War College,1999–2013 — January 18, 2011

Frazer, Jendayi, Director for African Affairs, NSC staff, 2001–4. — January 27, 2011

Fuerth, Leon S., National Security Adviser to the VP, 1993–2001 — March 9, 2010

Gallucci, Robert, AssistSecState for Pol-Mil Affairs, 1992–94 — April 20, 2011

Gelbard, Robert, U.S. Special Balkans Envoy, 1996–99 — March 22, 2010

Greenstock, Jeremy, UK PermRep to the UN, New York, 1998–July 2003 — March 30, 2011

Grossman, Marc, AssistSecState for European Affairs, 1997–2000; UnderSecState for Political Affairs, 2001–5 — January 13, 2011

Hadley, Stephen J., Deputy Assistant, 2001–5, and Assistant to the President for National Security Affairs, 2005–9 — January 18 and 24, 2011

Hakim, Peter, President, Inter-American Dialogue, Policy Think Tank, Washington, DC, 1993–2010 — June 22, 2009

Halperin, Morton H., Consultant to the SecDef, 1993; Senior Director for Democracy, NSC staff, 1994–96; Director of Policy Planning, DOS, 1998–2001 — March 10, 2010

Hamre, John J., Deputy SecDef, 1997–2000 — February 17, 2010

Hughes, Col. Paul (USA, ret.), Director of National Security   April 1, 2011
Policy, U.S. Army staff, 2000–2002; Senior Staff Officer, Office of
Reconstruction and Humanitarian Assistance (OHRA) and
Coalition Provisional Authority (CPA) in Iraq, Jan.–Aug. 2003

Hunter, Robert, U.S. PermRep to NATO, 1993–97   March 11, 2010

Jeremiah, Adm. David (USN, ret.), Vice Chairman, Joint Chiefs   January 28, 2011
of Staff, 1990–94

Johnstone, Ian, Legal Adviser, 1994–95, and Senior Political   April 2, 2010
Officer, 1997–2000, Office of the UN Secretary-General

Joseph, Robert G., Senior Director for Proliferation Strategy,   February 2, 2011
Counter-Proliferation and Homeland Defense, NSC staff, 2001–5

Kansteiner, Walter H., Director for African Affairs, NSC staff,   January 18, 2011
1991–92; AssistSecState for African Affairs, 2001–3

Kaufmann, Col. Gregory (USA, ret.), Chief of Staff, 1997–98, and   March 10, 2010
Director, 1999–2000, OSD Balkans Task Force

Kerrick, LTG Donald L. (USA, ret.), Director of European   March 22, 2010
Affairs, NSC staff, 1994–95; Deputy Assistant to the President for
National Security Affairs, Jan. 1997–Aug. 1999; Assistant to the
JCS Chairman, Aug. 1999–July 2000

Khalilzad, Zalmay, Senior Director for Near East and North   January 20, 2011
African Affairs, NSC staff, May 2001–Dec. 2002; U.S. Special
Envoy for Afghanistan, Dec. 2001–Nov. 2003; Ambassador-at-
Large for Free Iraqis, Dec. 2002–Nov. 2003

Kojm, Christopher, Staff Member, House Foreign Affairs   August 9, 2009
Committee, under Lee H. Hamilton (D-IN), 1984–98

Kozak, Michael, Acting AssistSecState for Western Hemisphere   June 23, 2009
Affairs, 1989; Deputy Special Haiti Adviser, DOS, 1993–94; Head
of Haiti Working Group, DOS, 1994–96

Kross, Gen. Walter (USAF, ret.), Director, Joint Staff, 1994–96.   February 11, 2011

Lake, Anthony, Assistant to the President for National Security   June 26, 2009
Affairs, 1993–97

Larkin, Barbara, Staff Member, Senate Foreign Relations   April 2, 2010
Committee, 1986–95; AssistSecState for Legislative Affairs,
1996–99

Malone, David, Deputy PermRep of Canada to the UN, New   December 8, 2009
York, 1993–94

Matheson, Michael, Principal Deputy Legal Adviser, DOS,   July 30, 2009
1989–96

Miller, Franklin C., Senior Director for Defense Policy and Arms   February 23, 2011
Control, NSC staff, 2001–5

Negroponte, John D., U.S. PermRep to the UN, New York,   February 15, 2011
2001–4; Deputy SecState, 2007–9

[253]

Newbold, LTG Gregory S. (USMC, ret.), Director for Operations (J-3), Joint Staff, Oct. 2000–Oct. 2002 — January 25, 2011

Norris, John, Director of Communications for the Deputy SecState, 1999–2001 — April 26, 2010

O'Brien, James C., Adviser to the U.S. PermRep to the UN, 1994–97; Principal Deputy Director of Policy Planning and Special Balkans Envoy, DOS, 1997–2001 — March 9, 2010

Owens, Major, Member, House of Representatives, 1983–2007; Chair, Congressional Black Caucus Haiti Task Force, 1993–94 — July 12, 2009

Owens, Adm. William (USN, ret.), Vice Chairman, Joint Chiefs of Staff, March 1994–Feb. 1996 — January 27, 2011

Pastor, Robert, Senior Political Adviser to the Carter-Powell-Nunn diplomatic mission to Haiti, Sept. 1994 — June 23, 2009

Pezzullo, Lawrence, Special Haiti Adviser, DOS, 1993–94 — June 24, 2009

Pickering, Thomas, U.S. PermRep to the UN, New York, 1989–92; UnderSecState for Political Affairs, 1997–2000 — January 14, 2011

Powell, Gen. Colin L. (USA, ret.), Chairman, Joint Chiefs of Staff, 1989–93; SecState, 2001–5 — February 2, 2011

Ralston, Gen. Joseph W. (USA, ret.), Vice Chairman, Joint Chiefs of Staff, 1996–2000; SACEUR, 2000–3 — March 17, 2009

Riedel, Bruce, Director for Gulf and South Asia Affairs, NSC staff, 1991–93; Senior Director for Near East and North African Affairs, NSC staff, 1997–2002 — December 15, 2010

Rossin, Lawrence, Haiti Policy Director, Office of Inter-American Affairs, NSC staff, 1993–94 — July 25, 2009

Rubin, James P., Senior Adviser to the U.S. PermRep to the UN, 1993–96; AssistSecState for Public Affairs, 1997–2000 — April 9, 2010

Schake, Kori, Director for Defense Strategy and Requirements, NSC staff, 2001–5 — January 21, 2011

Schulte, Gregory L., Director, NATO Bosnia Task Force, 1992–98; Balkans Policy Director, NSC staff, 1998–99; Executive Secretary of the NSC, 2003–5 — March 9, 2010

Scowcroft, Brent L., Assistant to the President for National Security Affairs, 1989–93 — March 22, 2011

Sestanovich, Stephen, Ambassador-at-Large and Special Adviser to the SecState for the New Independent States of the Former Soviet Union, 1997–2001 — March 4, 2010

Slocombe, Walter B., Deputy UnderSecDef, 1993–94, and Under SecDef for Policy, 1994–2001; Senior Adviser, CPA in Iraq, 2003 — March 11, 2010, and June 9, 2011

Soderberg, Nancy, Deputy Assistant to the President for National Security Affairs, 1994–96; Alternate U.S. Representative to the UN, New York, 1997–2001 — July 29 and 30, 2009

Solana, Javier, NATO Secretary-General, 1995–99; EU High Representative for Common Foreign and Security Policy, 1999 –2009 — March 24, 2011

Talbott, Strobe, Deputy SecState, 1994–2001 — July 9, 2009

Trahan, Col. Michael W. (USA, ret.), Senior Military Assistant to the UnderSecDef for Policy, June 2000–Sept. 2001; Deputy Director for Operations (J-3), CENTCOM, Sept. 2001–June 2003 — January 26, 2011

Vendrell, Francesc, Senior Political Adviser to the UN Envoy for Haiti, 1992–93; Head, UN Mission to Afghanistan, 2000–2001; EU Special Representative for Afghanistan, 2002–9 — June 27, 2009

Veroneau, John, AssistSecDef for Legislative Affairs, 1999–2001 — April 7, 2010

Vershbow, Alexander R., Director for European Affairs, NSC staff, 1994–97; U.S. PermRep to NATO, 1997–2001 — April 2, 2010

Wald, Gen. Charles F. (USAF, ret.), Vice Director for Strategic Plans and Policy (J-5), Joint Staff, Oct. 1998–Jan. 2000; Commander, CENTCOM Air Forces, Jan. 2000–Nov. 2001; Deputy Commander, EUCOM, Dec. 2002–July 2006 — March 8, 2010

Ward, George F., Principal Deputy AssistSecState for IO Affairs, 1992–96 — April 4, 2011

Warner, Edward L., AssistSecDef for Strategy and Requirements, 1993–97 — April 12, 2011

Watson, Alexander Fletcher, AssistSecState for Inter-American Affairs, 1993–96 — June 23, 2009

Weisman, LTG David S. (USA, ret.), Vice Director for Strategic Plans and Policy (J-5), Joint Staff, 1995–98; U.S. Military Representative, NATO Military Committee, Oct. 1998–June 2001 — February 16, 2011

Wisner, Frank, UnderSecDef for Policy, 1993–94 — July 16, 2009

Wolff, Alejandro, Executive Assistant to Secretary of State Madeleine Albright, 1998–2000 — March 31, 2010

Wood, William B., Political Counselor, U.S. Mission to the UN, New York, 1993–98; Acting AssistSecState for IOAffairs, 1998–Dec. 2002; U.S. Ambassador to Afghanistan, 2007–9 — January 25, 2011

References

Abbott, Kenneth W., and Duncan Snidal. 1998. "Why States Act through Formal International Organizations." *Journal of Conflict Resolution* 42 (1): 3–32.

Albright, Madeleine. 2003. *Madam Secretary*. New York: Miramax.

Allison, Graham, and Morton Halperin. 1972. "Bureaucratic Politics: A Paradigm and Some Policy Implications." *World Politics* 24 (S1): 40–79.

Allison, Graham, and Philip Zelikow. 1999. *Essence of Decision: Explaining the Cuban Missile Crisis*. 2nd ed. New York: Longman.

Annan, Kofi A., with Nader Mousavizadeh. 2012. *Interventions: A Life in War and Peace*. London: Allen Lane.

Auerswald, David P. 1999. "Inward Bound: Domestic Institutions and Military Conflicts." *International Organization* 53 (3): 469–504.

Auerswald, David P., and Peter F. Cowhey. 1997. "Ballotbox Diplomacy: The War Powers Resolution and the Use of Force." *International Studies Quarterly* 41 (3): 505–28.

Avant, Deborah D. 1996. "Are the Reluctant Warriors out of Control? Why the U.S. Military Is Averse to Responding to Post–Cold War Low-Level Threats." *Security Studies* 2 (2): 51–90.

Bacevich, Andrew J. 2007. "Elusive Bargain: The Pattern of U.S. Civil-Military Relations since World War II." In *The Long War*, edited by Andrew Bacevich. New York: Columbia University Press.

Baker, James A. III. 1995. *The Politics of Diplomacy*. New York: Putnam.

Baker, William D. and John R. Oneal. 2001. "Patriotism or Opinion Leadership? The Nature and Origins of the 'Rally 'Round the Flag' Effect." *Journal of Conflict Resolution* 45 (5): 661–87.

Ballard, John R. 1998. *Upholding Democracy: The United States Military Campaign in Haiti, 1994–1997*. Westport, CT: Praeger.

Baum, Matthew A., and Tim J. Groeling. 2009. *War Stories: The Causes and Consequences of Public Views of War*. Princeton, NJ: Princeton University Press.

Beckley, Michael C. 2011. "China's Century? Why America's Edge Will Endure." *International Security* 36 (3): 41–78.

Bellamy, Alex J. 2002. *Kosovo and International Society*. London: Palgrave.

Bennett, Andrew. 2001. "Who Rules the Roost? Congressional-Executive Relations on Foreign Policy after the Cold War." In *Eagle Rules? Foreign Policy and American Primacy in the Twenty-First Century,* edited by Robert J. Lieber. Upper Saddle River, NJ: Prentice Hall.

Bensahel, Nora. 2002. "Humanitarian Relief and Nation Building in Somalia." In *The United States and Coercive Diplomacy,* edited by Robert J. Art and Patrick M. Cronin. Washington, DC: USIP.

——. 2006. "Mission Not Accomplished: What Went Wrong with Iraqi Reconstruction." *Journal of Strategic Studies* 29 (3): 453–73.

Betts, Richard K. 1991. *Soldiers, Statesmen, and Cold War Crises.* 2nd ed. New York: Columbia University Press.

——. 2001. "Compromised Command: Inside NATO's First War." *Foreign Affairs* 80 (4): 126–32.

——. 2012. *American Force: Dangers, Delusions, and Dilemmas in National Security.* New York: Columbia University Press.

Biersteker, Thomas J., and Cynthia Weber. 1996. "The Social Construction of State Sovereignty." In *State Sovereignty as a Social Construct,* edited by Thomas J. Biersteker and Cynthia Weber. New York: Cambridge University Press.

Blair, Tony. 2010. *A Journey: My Political Life.* New York: Knopf.

Blechman, Barry, and Tamara Cofman Wittes. 1999. "Defining Moment: The Threat and Use of Force in American Foreign Policy." In *The New American Interventionism,* edited by Demetrios P. Caralay. New York: Columbia University Press.

Blix, Hans. 2004. *Disarming Iraq.* New York: Pantheon Books.

Boutros-Ghali, Boutros. 1996. *Les Nations Unies et Haïti 1990–1996.* UN Blue Book Series, vol. 11. New York: UN Department of Public Information.

——. 1999. *Unvanquished: A U.S.-UN Saga.* New York: Random House.

Branch, Taylor. 2009. *The Clinton Tapes: Wrestling History with the President.* New York: Simon & Schuster.

Brody, Richard A. 1991. *Assessing the President: The Media, Elite Opinion, and Public Support.* Stanford, CA: Stanford University Press.

Brooks, Risa. 2009. "Militaries and Political Activity in Democracies." In *American Civil-Military Relations,* edited by Suzanne C. Nielsen and Don M. Snider. Baltimore: Johns Hopkins University Press.

Brooks, Stephen. 2012. "Review of Sarah Kreps, *Coalitions of Convenience.*" *H-Diplo/ ISSF Roundtable* 4 (7): 7–13.

Brooks, Stephen G., and William C. Wohlforth. 2008. *World Out of Balance.* Princeton, NJ: Princeton University Press.

Brown, Chris. 2010. "Rules and Norms in a Post-Western World." In *On Rules, Politics and Knowledge,* edited by Oliver Kessler, Rodney Bruce Hall, Cecelia Lynch, and Nicholas Onuf. London: Palgrave Macmillan.

Burg, Steven L. 2003. "Coercive Diplomacy in the Balkans: The U.S. Use of Force in Bosnia and Kosovo." In *The United States and Coercive Diplomacy,* edited by Robert J. Art and Patrick M. Cronin. Washington, DC: USIP.

Burg, Steven L., and Paul L. Shoup. 1999. *The War in Bosnia-Herzegovina: Ethnic Conflict and International Intervention.* London: M.E. Sharpe.

Burk, James. 2002. "Theories of Democratic Civil-Military Relations." *Armed Forces & Society* 29 (1): 7–29.

Busby, Joshua W., and Jonathan Monten. 2008. "Without Heirs? Assessing the Decline of Establishment Internationalism in U.S. Foreign Policy." *Perspectives on Politics* 6 (3): 451–72.

Busby, Joshua W., Jonathan Monten, Jordan Tama, and William Inboden. 2013. "Congress Is Already Post-Partisan." *Foreign Affairs* (online), January 28.

References

Bush, George W. 2010. *Decision Points*. New York: Crown.

Carter, Ashton, and William Perry. 1999. *Preventive Defense: A New Security Strategy for America*. Washington, DC: Brookings Institution.

CCGA (Chicago Council on Global Affairs). 2012. "Foreign Policy in the New Millennium." Results of a 2012 survey of American public opinion. http://www.thechicagocouncil.org/sites/default/files/2012_CCS_Report.pdf.

Cecchine, Gary et al. 2013. *The U.S. Military Response to the 2010 Haiti Earthquake*. Santa Monica, CA: RAND.

Chapman, Terrence L. 2011. *Securing Approval: Domestic Politics and Multilateral Authorization for War*. Chicago: University of Chicago Press.

Chapman, Terrence L., and Dan Reiter. 2004. "The United Nations Security Council and the Rally 'Round the Flag Effect." *Journal of Conflict Resolution* 48 (6): 886–909.

Cheney, Dick, with Liz Cheney. 2011. *In My Time: A Personal and Political Memoir*. New York: Threshold.

Chirac, Jacques. 2011. *My Life in Politics*. New York: Palgrave Macmillan.

Chollet, Derek. 2005. *The Road to the Dayton Accords: A Study of American Statecraft*. New York: Palgrave Macmillan.

Chomsky, Noam. 1993. "The Pentagon System." *Z Magazine*, February.

Christopher, Warren. 1998. *In the Stream of History: Shaping Foreign Policy for a New Era*. Stanford, CA: Stanford University Press.

Cimbala, Stephen J., and Peter K. Forster. 2010. *Multinational Military Intervention: NATO Policy, Strategy and Burden Sharing*. Burlington, VT: Ashgate.

Clark, Wesley K. 2001. *Waging Modern War*. New York: Public Affairs.

Claude, Inis. 1966. "Collective Legitimization as a Political Function of the United Nations." *International Organization* 20 (3): 367–79.

Clinton, Bill. 2004. *My Life*. New York: Knopf.

Clinton, Hillary Rodham. 2014. *Hard Choices*. New York: Simon & Schuster.

Cohen, Eliot. 2003. *Supreme Command: Soldiers, Statesmen, and Leadership in Wartime*. New York: Anchor.

Cohen, Herman J. 2000. *Intervening in Africa: Superpower Peacemaking in a Troubled Continent*. New York: St. Martin's.

Coleman, Katharina P. 2007. *International Organizations and Peace Enforcement*. New York: Cambridge University Press.

Cook, Martin L. 2002. "The Proper Role of Professional Military Advice in Contemporary Uses of Force." *Parameters* 32 (4): 21–33.

Cordesman, Anthony H. 2001. *The Lessons and Non-Lessons of the Air and Missile Campaign in Kosovo*. Westport, CT: Praeger.

Cortell, Andrew P., and James W. Davis. 1996. "How Do International Institutions Matter? The Domestic Impact of International Norms and Rules." *International Studies Quarterly* 40 (4): 451–87.

——. 2000. "Understanding the Domestic Impact of International Norms: A Research Agenda." *International Studies Review* 2 (1): 65–87.

Daalder, Ivo H. 2000. *Getting to Dayton: The Making of America's Bosnia Policy*. Washington, DC: Brookings Institution.

Daalder, Ivo H., and Michael E. O'Hanlon. 2000. *Winning Ugly: NATO's War to Save Kosovo*. Washington, DC: Brookings Institution.

Davidson, Jason W. 2011. *America's Allies and War: Kosovo, Afghanistan, and Iraq*. New York: Palgrave Macmillan.

Desch, Michael C. 1999. *Civilian Control of the Military*. Baltimore: Johns Hopkins University Press.

——. 2007. "Bush and the Generals." *Foreign Affairs* 86 (3): 97–108.

——. 2009a. "Hartz, Huntington, and the Liberal Tradition in America: The Clash with Military Realism." In *American Civil-Military Relations*, edited by Suzanne C. Nielsen and Don M. Snider. Baltimore: Johns Hopkins University Press.

——. 2009b. "Liberalism and the New Definition of 'Existential' Threat." In *Existential Threats and Civil-Security Relations*, edited by Oren Barak and Gabriel Sheffer. Lanham, MD: Lexington Books.

DeYoung, Karen. 2006. *Soldier: The Life of Colin Powell*. New York: Vintage.

Dobbins, James et al. 2003. *America's Role in Nation-Building: From Germany to Iraq*. Santa Monica, CA: RAND.

Doyle, Michael W. 1983. "Kant, Liberal Legacies, and Foreign Affairs," pt. 2. *Philosophy and Public Affairs* 12 (4): 323–53.

——. 2015. *The Question of Intervention: John Stuart Mill and the Responsibility to Protect*. New Haven, CT: Yale University Press.

Drew, Elizabeth. 1995. *On the Edge: The Clinton Presidency*. New York: Touchstone.

Dueck, Colin. 2006. *Reluctant Crusaders: Power, Culture, and Change in American Grand Strategy*. Princeton, NJ: Princeton University Press.

Eichenberg, Richard C. 2005. "Victory Has Many Friends: U.S. Public Opinion and the Use of Military Force, 1981–2005." *International Security* 30 (1): 140–77.

ElBaradei, Mohamed. 2011. *The Age of Deception: Nuclear Diplomacy in Treacherous Times*. London: Picador.

Falk, Richard. 1995. "The Haiti Intervention: A Dangerous World Order Precedent for the United Nations." *Harvard International Law Journal* 36 (2): 341–58.

Fang, Songying. 2008. "The Informational Role of International Institutions and Domestic Politics." *American Journal of Political Science* 52 (2): 304–21.

Feaver, Peter D. 2003. *Armed Servants: Agency, Oversight, and Civil-Military Relations*. Cambridge, MA: Harvard University Press.

Feaver, Peter D., and Christopher Gelpi. 2004. *Choosing Your Battles: American Civil-Military Relations and the Use of Force*. Princeton, NJ: Princeton University Press.

Feinstein, Lee, and Anne-Marie Slaughter. 2004. "A Duty to Prevent." *Foreign Affairs* 83 (1): 136–50.

Feith, Douglas J. 2008. *War and Decision: Inside the Pentagon at the Dawn of the War on Terrorism*. New York: Harper.

Finnemore, Martha. 2003. *The Purpose of Intervention: Changing Beliefs about the Use of Force*. Ithaca, NY: Cornell University Press.

Fisher, Louis. 1997. "Sidestepping Congress: Presidents Acting Under the UN and NATO." *Case Western Reserve Law Review* 47: 1237–79.

——. 2013. *Presidential War Power*. 3rd rev. ed. Lawrence: University Press of Kansas.

Fox, Vicente, with Rob Allyn. 2008. *La Revolución de la Esperanza: La vida, los anhelos, y los sueños de un presidente*. Mexico City: Aguilar.

Franks, Tommy. 2004. *American Soldier*. New York: Regan Books.

Gates, Robert M. 2014. *Duty: Memoirs of a Secretary at War*. New York: Knopf.

Gellman, Barton. 2008. *Angler: The Cheney Vice Presidency*. New York: Penguin.

George, Alexander L., and Andrew Bennett. 2004. *Case Studies and Theory Development in the Social Sciences*. Cambridge, MA: MIT Press.

Gibbs, David N. 2009. *First Do No Harm: Humanitarian Intervention and the Destruction of Yugoslavia*. Nashville: Vanderbilt University Press.

Gibson, Christopher P. 2008. *Securing the State: Reforming the National Security Decisionmaking Process at the Civil-Military Nexus*. Burlington, VT: Ashgate.

Girard, Philippe R. 2004. *Clinton in Haiti: The 1994 U.S. Invasion of Haiti*. London: Palgrave.

References

Golby, Jim, Kyle Dropp, and Peter Feaver. 2013. "Listening to the Generals: How Military Advice Affects Public Support for the Use of Force." Washington, DC: Center for a New American Security. http://www.cnas.org/publications.

Goldgeier, James M. 1999. *Not Whether but When: The U.S. Decision to Enlarge NATO.* Washington, DC: Brookings Institution.

Gordon, Michael R., and Bernard E. Trainor. 2006. *Cobra II: The Inside Story of the Invasion and Occupation of Iraq.* New York: Pantheon.

Gordon, Philip H., and Jeremy Shapiro. 2004. *Allies at War: America, Europe, and the Crisis over Iraq.* New York: McGraw-Hill.

Grieco, Joseph, Christopher Gelpi, Jason Reifler, and Peter D. Feaver. 2011. "Let's Get a Second Opinion: International Institutions and American Public Support for War." *International Studies Quarterly* 55 (2): 563–83.

Grimmett, Richard. 2007. "Congressional Use of Funding Cutoffs since 1970 Involving U.S. Military Forces and Overseas Deployments," *CRS Report for Congress,* January 16.

Haass, Richard N. 2009. *War of Necessity, War of Choice: A Memoir of Two Iraq Wars.* New York: Simon & Schuster.

Habermas, Jürgen. 2006. *The Divided West.* London: Polity.

Halberstam, David. 2001. *War in a Time of Peace: Bush, Clinton, and the Generals.* New York: Touchstone.

Halper, Stefan, and Jonathan Clarke. 2004. *America Alone: The Neo-Conservatives and the Global Order.* New York: Cambridge University Press.

Halperin, Morton H., and Priscilla Clapp, with Arnold Kanter. 2006. *Bureaucratic Politics and Foreign Policy.* 2nd ed. Washington, DC: Brookings Institution.

Hamilton, Rebecca. 2011. *Fighting for Darfur: Public Action and the Struggle to Stop Genocide.* New York: Palgrave Macmillan.

Hartz, Louis. 1955. *The Liberal Tradition in America.* New York: Harvest Books.

Helis, James E. 2012. "Multilateralism and Unilateralism." In *The U.S. Army War College Guide to National Security Issues,* edited by J. Boone Bartholomees, Jr. 5th ed. Vol. 2. Carlisle, PA: U.S. Army War College.

Hendrickson, Ryan C. 2002. *The Clinton Wars: The Constitution, Congress, and War Powers.* Nashville: Vanderbilt University Press.

Herspring, Dale R. 2008. *Rumsfeld's Wars: The Arrogance of Power.* Lawrence: University Press of Kansas.

Hildebrandt, Timothy, Courtney Hillebrecht, Peter M. Holm, and Jon Pevehouse. 2013. "The Domestic Politics of Humanitarian Intervention: Public Opinion, Partisanship, and Ideology." *Foreign Policy Analysis* 9 (3): 243–66.

Hoffmann, Stanley. 2005. "American Exceptionalism: The New Version." In *American Exceptionalism and Human Rights,* edited by Michael Ignatieff. Princeton, NJ: Princeton University Press.

Holbrooke, Richard. 1998. *To End a War.* New York: Modern Library.

Holsti, Ole R. 2001. "Of Chasms and Convergences: Attitudes and Beliefs of Civilians and Military Elites at the Start of the New Millennium." In *Soldiers and Civilians: The Civil-Military Gap in American National Security,* edited by Peter D. Feaver and Richard H. Kohn. Cambridge, MA: MIT Press.

Horowitz, Michael C., and Allan C. Stam. 2014. "How Prior Military Experience Influences the Future Militarized Behavior of Leaders." *International Organization* 68 (3): 527–59.

Howell, William, and Jon Pevehouse. 2007. *While Dangers Gather: Congressional Checks on Presidential War Powers.* Princeton, NJ: Princeton University Press.

Huntington, Samuel P. 1957. *The Soldier and the State.* Cambridge, MA: Belknap Press.

Hurd, Ian. 1999. "Legitimacy and Authority in International Politics." *International Organization* 53 (2): 379–408.

——. 2007. *After Anarchy: Legitimacy and Power in the United Nations Security Council.* Princeton, NJ: Princeton University Press.

IICK (Independent International Commission on Kosovo). 2000. *The Kosovo Report.* New York: Oxford University Press.

Ikenberry, G. John. 2001. *After Victory: Institutions, Strategic Restraint, and the Rebuilding of Order after Major Wars.* Princeton, NJ: Princeton University Press.

Jervis, Robert. 2005. *American Foreign Policy in a New Era.* New York: Routledge.

Kaarbo, Juliet, and Ryan K. Beasley. 2008. "Taking It to the Extreme: The Effect of Coalition Cabinets on Foreign Policy." *Foreign Policy Analysis* 4 (1): 67–81.

Keohane, Robert O. 1990. "Multilateralism: An Agenda for Research," *International Journal* 45 (4): 731–64.

Keohane, Robert, and Joseph Nye. 1985. "Two Cheers for Multilateralism." *Foreign Policy* 60 (Autumn): 148–67.

King, Gary, Robert O. Keohane, and Sidney Verba. 1994. *Designing Social Inquiry.* Princeton, NJ: Princeton University Press.

Kohn, Richard H. 2002. "The Erosion of Civilian Control of the Military." *Naval War College Review* 55 (3): 8–59.

——. 2009. "Always Salute, Never Resign." *Foreign Affairs* (online), November 10.

Krasner, Stephen D. 1972. "Are Bureaucracies Important? (Or Allison Wonderland)." *Foreign Policy* 7 (Summer): 159–79.

Krause, Joachim. 2004. "Multilateralism: Behind European Views." *Washington Quarterly* 27 (2): 43–59.

Kreps, Sarah. 2007. "The 1994 Haiti Intervention: A Unilateral Intervention in Multilateral Clothes." *Journal of Strategic Studies* 30 (3): 449–74.

——. 2010. "Elite Consensus as a Determinant of Alliance Cohesion: Why Public Opinion Hardly Matters for NATO-Led Operations in Afghanistan." *Foreign Policy Analysis* 6 (3): 191–215.

——. 2011. *Coalitions of Convenience: United States Military Interventions after the Cold War.* New York: Oxford University Press.

——. 2012. "Author's Response." *H-Diplo/ISSF Roundtable* 4 (7): 28–35.

Kretchik, Walter E., Robert F. Baumann, and John T. Fishel, 1998. *Invasion, Intervention, "Intervasion": A Concise History of the U.S. Army in Operation Uphold Democracy.* Fort Leavenworth, KS: U.S. Army Command and General Staff College Press.

Kull, Steven. 2002. "Public Attitudes toward Multilateralism." In *Multilateralism and U.S. Foreign Policy,* edited by Stewart Patrick and Shepard Forman. Boulder, CO: Lynne Rienner.

Kull, Steven, and I. M. Destler. 1999. *Misreading the Public: The Myth of a New Isolationism.* Washington, DC: Brookings Institution.

Kupchan, Charles. 1992. "Getting In: The Initial Stage of Military Intervention." In *Foreign Military Intervention: The Dynamics of Protracted Conflict,* edited by Ariel E. Levite, Bruce W. Jentleson, and Larry Berman. New York: Columbia University Press.

——. 2011. "The False Promise of Unipolarity: Constraints on the Exercise of American Power." *Cambridge Review of International Affairs* 24 (2): 165–73.

Kuperman, Alan J. 2008. "A Small Intervention: Lessons from Liberia 2003." In *Naval Peacekeeping and Humanitarian Operations,* edited by James J. Wirtz and Jeffrey A. Larsen. New York: Routledge.

——. 2013. "A Model Humanitarian Intervention? Reassessing NATO's Libya Campaign." *International Security* 38 (1): 105–36.

References

LaFeber, Walter. 2009. "The Rise and Fall of Colin Powell and the Powell Doctrine." *Political Science Quarterly* 124 (10): 71–93.

Lagos, Ricardo. 2012. *The Southern Tiger: Chile's Fight for a Democratic and Prosperous Future.* New York: Palgrave.

Lake, Anthony. 2000. *Six Nightmares: Real Threats in a Dangerous World and How America Can Meet Them.* New York: Little, Brown.

Lake, David A. 1999. *Entangling Relations: American Foreign Policy in Its Century.* Princeton, NJ: Princeton University Press.

Larson, Eric V., and Bogdan Savych. 2005. *American Public Support for Military Operations from Mogadishu to Baghdad.* Santa Monica, CA: RAND.

Leurdijk, Dick A. 1994. *The United Nations and NATO in Former Yugoslavia: Partners in International Cooperation.* The Hague: Netherlands Atlantic Commission.

Lindsay, James. 1995. "Congress and the Use of Force in the Post-Cold War Era." In *The United States and the Use of Force in the Post-Cold War World.* Queenstown, MD: Aspen Institute.

Malone, David M. 1998. *Decision-Making in the UN Security Council: The Case of Haiti, 1990–1997.* Oxford: Clarendon Press.

——. 2006. *The International Struggle over Iraq: Politics in the UN Security Council, 1980–2005.* New York: Oxford University Press.

Malval, Robert. 1996. *L'Année de toutes les duperies.* Port-au-Prince: Editions Regain.

Manchester, William. 2008. *American Caesar: Douglas MacArthur 1880–1964.* New York: Back Bay Books.

March, James G., and Johan P. Olsen. 2009. "The Logic of Appropriateness." In *The Oxford Handbook of Public Policy,* edited by Michael Moran, Martin Rein, and Robert E. Goodin. New York: Oxford University Press.

Mastanduno, Michael. 1997. "Preserving the Unipolar Moment: Realist Theories and U.S. Grand Strategy after the Cold War." *International Security* 21 (4): 49–88.

McDougall, Walter A. 1997. *Promised Land, Crusader State: The American Encounter with the World since 1776.* Boston: Houghton Mifflin.

McMaster, H. R. 1998. *Dereliction of Duty: Johnson, McNamara, the Joint Chiefs of Staff, and the Lies That Led to Vietnam.* New York: Harper Perennial.

Michaels, Jeffrey H. 2014. "Able but Not Willing: A Critical Assessment of NATO's Libya Intervention." In *The NATO Intervention in Libya,* edited by Kjell Engelbrekt, Marcus Mohlin, and Charlotte Wagnsson. New York: Routledge.

Milburn, Andrew R. 2010. "Breaking Ranks: Dissent and the Military Professional." *Joint Forces Quarterly* 59 (4): 101–7.

Mill, John Stuart. (1837) 1989. "The Spanish Question." In The *Collected Works of John Stuart Mill,* edited by John Robson. Vol. 31. Toronto: University of Toronto Press.

Miller, Russell A. 2010. "Germany's Basic Law and the Use of Force." *Indiana Journal of Global Legal Studies* 17 (2): 197–206.

Morgenthau, Hans J. 2005. *Politics among Nations: The Struggle for Power and Peace.* Revised by Kenneth Thompson. New York: McGraw-Hill.

Morris, Justin. 1995. "Force and Democracy: UN/US Intervention in Haiti." *International Peacekeeping* 2 (3): 391–412.

Moskovitz, Eric, and Jeffrey S. Lantis. 2004. "Conflict in the Balkans." In *Fateful Decisions: Inside the National Security Council,* edited by Karl F. Inderfurth and Loch K. Johnson. New York: Oxford University Press.

Müller, Harald. 1993. "The Internalization of Principles, Norms, and Rules by Governments: The Case of Security Regimes." In *Regime Theory and International Relations,* edited by Volker Rittberger and Peter Mayer. Oxford: Clarendon Press.

Myers, Richard B. 2009. *Eyes on the Horizon: Serving on the Front Lines of National Security*. New York: Threshold.

Myers, Richard B., and Richard H. Kohn. 2007. "The Military's Place." *Foreign Affairs* 86 (5): 147–49.

Nazirny, Kevin. 2007. *The Political Economy of Grand Strategy*. Ithaca, NY: Cornell University Press.

Newnham, Randall. 2008. "'Coalition of the Bribed and Bullied?' U.S. Economic Linkage and the Iraq War Coalition." *International Studies Perspectives* 9 (2): 183–200.

Nielsen, Suzanne C. 2005. "Rules of the Game? The Weinberger Doctrine and the American Use of Force." In *The Future of the Army Profession*, edited by Don M. Snider and Lloyd J. Matthews. Revised 2nd ed. New York: McGraw-Hill.

Norris, John. 2005. *Collision Course: NATO, Russia, and Kosovo*. Westport, CT: Praeger.

Norrlof, Carla. 2010. *America's Global Advantage: U.S. Hegemony and International Co-operation*. New York: Cambridge University Press.

Nouzille, Vincent. 2010. *Dans le secret des presidents*. Paris: Fayard.

Nye, Joseph. 2002. *The Paradox of American Power: Why the World's Only Superpower Can't Go It Alone*. New York: Oxford University Press.

O'Hanlon, Michael. 2004. "Iraq without a Plan." *Policy Review* 138 (December): 33–45.

Pape, Robert. 2005. "Soft Balancing against the United States." *International Security* 30 (1): 7–45.

Pastor, Robert. 2003. "The Delicate Balance between Coercion and Diplomacy: The Case of Haiti, 1994," In *The United States and Coercive Diplomacy*, edited by Robert J. Art and Patrick M. Cronin. Washington, DC: USIP.

Petraeus, David H. 1989. "Military Influence and the Post-Vietnam Use of Force." *Armed Forces & Society* 15 (4): 489–505.

Petritsch, Wolfgang, and Robert Pichler. 2004. *Kosovo-Kosova: Der Lange Weg zum Frieden*. Klagenfurt: Wieser.

Pew Research Center. 2011. "War and Sacrifice in the Post-9/11 Era: The Military-Civilian Gap." October 11. http://www.pewsocialtrends.org/files/2011/10/veterans-report.pdf.

Pezzullo, Ralph. 2006. *Plunging into Haiti*. Jackson: University Press of Mississippi.

Phillips, David L. 2012. *Liberating Kosovo: Coercive Diplomacy and U.S. Intervention*. Cambridge, MA: MIT Press.

Pillar, Paul. 2011. *Intelligence and U.S. Foreign Policy: Iraq, 9/11, and Misguided Reform*. New York: Columbia University Press.

Powell, Colin L., with Joseph E. Persico. 1995. *My American Journey*. New York: Random House.

Power, Samantha. 2003. *A Problem from Hell: America and the Age of Genocide*. New York: Harper Perennial.

Priest, Dana. 2003. *The Mission: Waging War and Keeping Peace with America's Military*. New York: Norton.

Rabasa, Angel et al. 2011. *From Insurgency to Stability: Key Capabilities and Practices*. Santa Monica, CA: RAND.

Rapport, Aaaron. 2012. "The Long and Short of It: Cognitive Constraints on Leaders' Assessments of 'Postwar' Iraq." *International Security* 37 (3): 133–71.

Rawski, Frederick, and Nathan Miller. 2004. "The United States in the Security Council: A Faustian Bargain?" In *The United Nations Security Council: From the Cold War to the Twenty-First Century*, edited by David M. Malone. Boulder, CO: Lynne Rienner.

References

Recchia, Stefano. 2007. "Beyond International Trusteeship: EU Peacebuilding in Bosnia and Herzegovina." Occasional Paper No. 66. Paris: EU Institute for Security Studies. http://www.iss.europa.eu/uploads/media/occ66.pdf.
——. 2013. "The Origins of Liberal Wilsonianism." In *Just and Unjust Military Intervention: European Thinkers from Vitoria to Mill*, edited by Stefano Recchia and Jennifer Welsh. New York: Cambridge University Press.
——. 2015. "Chirac Said 'Non'—Or Did He? Revisiting U.S.-UN Diplomacy on the 2003 Iraq War." *Political Science Quarterly*, forthcoming.
Reus-Smit, Christian. 2005. "Liberal Hierarchy and the License to Use Force." *Review of International Studies* 31 (S1): 71–91.
Rice, Condoleezza. 2011. *No Higher Honor: A Memoir of My Years in Washington*. New York: Random House.
Ricks, Thomas E. 2006. *Fiasco: The American Military Adventure in Iraq*. New York: Penguin.
Rieff, David. 1999. "A New Age of Liberal Imperialism?" *World Policy Journal* 16 (2): 1–10.
Risse-Kappen, Thomas. 1997. "Between a New World Order and None: Explaining the Reemergence of the United Nations in World Politics." In *Critical Security Studies*, edited by Keith Krause and Michael C. Williams. Minneapolis: Minnesota University Press.
Roberts, Adam. 1999. "NATO's 'Humanitarian War' over Kosovo." *Survival* 41 (3): 102–23.
——. 2003. "Law and the Use of Force after Iraq." *Survival* 45 (2): 3–56.
Rosenau, James N. 1969. "Intervention as a Scientific Concept." *Journal of Conflict Resolution* 13 (2): 149–71.
Ross, Blair A. Jr. 2005. "The U.S. Joint Task Force Experience in Liberia." *Military Review* 85 (3): 60–67.
Ruggie, John G. 1992. "Multilateralism: The Anatomy of an Institution." *International Organization* 46 (3): 561–98.
——. 2006. "Doctrinal Unilateralism and Its Limits." In *American Foreign Policy in a Globalized World*, edited by David P. Forsythe, Patrice C. McMahon, and Andrew Wedeman. New York: Routledge.
Rumsfeld, Donald. 2011. *Known and Unknown: A Memoir*. New York: Sentinel.
Russett, Bruce. 1994. "The Gulf War as Empowering the United Nations." In *War and Its Consequences: Lessons from the Persian Gulf Conflict*, edited by John O'Loughlin, Tom Meyer, and Edward Greenberg. New York: Harper Collins.
Sablière, Jean-Marc de La. 2013. *Dans les coulisses du monde*. Paris: Robert Laffont.
Salazar Torreon, Barbara. 2015. "Instances of Use of United States Armed Forces Abroad, 1798–2015." *CRS Report for Congress*, January 15.
Sarkesian, Sam. 1998. "The U.S. Military Must Find Its Voice." *Orbis* 42 (Summer): 96–114.
Sarooshi, Dan. 2008. "The Security Council's Authorization of Regional Arrangements to Use Force: The Case of NATO." In *The UN Security Council and War*, edited by Vaughan Lowe, Adam Roberts, Jennifer Welsh, and Dominik Zaum. New York: Oxford University Press.
Schnabel, Albrecht, and Ramesh Thakur, eds. 2000. *Kosovo and the Challenge of Humanitarian Intervention*. Tokyo: United Nations University Press.
Schulte, Gregory L. 1997. "Former Yugoslavia and the New NATO." *Survival* 39 (1): 19–42.

Schultz, Kenneth. 2003. "Tying Hands and Washing Hands: The U.S. Congress and Multilateral Humanitarian Intervention." In *Locating the Proper Authorities: The Interaction of International and Domestic Institutions,* edited by Daniel Drezner. Ann Arbor: University of Michigan Press.

Scognamiglio, Carlo. 2002. *La Guerra del Kosovo.* Milan: Rizzoli.

Sestanovich, Stephen. 2002. "Dual Frustration: America, Russia, and the Persian Gulf." *National Interest* 70 (Winter): 153–62.

Sewall, Sarah B. 2002. "Multilateral Peace Operations." In *Multilateralism and U.S. Foreign Policy,* edited by Stewart Patrick and Shepard Forman. Boulder, CO: Lynne Rienner.

Shelton, Hugh, with Ronald Levinson and Malcolm McConnell. 2010. *Without Hesitation: The Odyssey of an American Warrior.* New York: St. Martin's.

Slaughter, Anne-Marie. 2008. "Wilsonianism in the Twenty-First Century." In *The Crisis of American Foreign Policy,* edited by G. John Ikenberry, Thomas J. Knock, Anne-Marie Slaughter, and Tony Smith. Princeton, NJ: Princeton University Press.

Smith, Tony. 2012. *America's Mission: The United States and the Worldwide Struggle for Democracy.* Expanded ed. Princeton, NJ: Princeton University Press.

Sobel, Richard. 2001. *The Impact of Public Opinion on U.S. Foreign Policy since Vietnam.* New York: Oxford University Press.

Sobel, Richard, Peter Furia, and Bethany Barratt, eds. 2012. *Public Opinion and International Intervention: Lessons from the Iraq War.* Washington, DC: Potomac Books.

Soderberg, Nancy. 2005. *The Superpower Myth: The Use and Misuse of American Might.* Hoboken, NJ: Wiley.

Solingen, Etel. 2007. *Nuclear Logics: Contrasting Paths in East Asia and the Middle East.* Princeton: Princeton University Press.

Steinberg, James. 1993. "International Involvement in the Yugoslavia Conflict." In *Enforcing Restraint: Collective Intervention in Internal Conflicts,* edited by Lori Fisler Damrosch. Washington, DC: Council on Foreign Relations.

Stephanopoulos, George. 1999. *All Too Human: A Political Education.* New York: Little, Brown.

Strachan, Hew. 2006. "Making Strategy: Civil-Military Relations after Iraq." *Survival* 48 (3): 59–82.

Straw, Jack. 2012. *Last Man Standing: Memoirs of a Political Survivor.* London: Macmillan.

Szayna, Thomas S., et al. 2007. *The Civil-Military Gap in the United States: Does It Exist, Why, and Does It Matter?* Santa Monica, CA: RAND.

Tago, Atsushi. 2005. "Determinants of Multilateralism in US Use of Force." *Journal of Peace Research* 42 (5): 585–604.

Talbott, Strobe. 2002. *The Russia Hand. A Memoir of Presidential Diplomacy.* New York: Random House.

——. 2008. *The Great Experiment.* New York: Simon & Schuster.

Thompson, Alexander. 2006. "Coercion through IOs: The Security Council and the Logic of Information Transmission." *International Organization* 60 (1): 1–34.

——. 2009. *Channels of Power: The UN Security Council and U.S. Statecraft in Iraq.* Ithaca, NY: Cornell University Press.

Tocqueville, Alexis De. (1835) 2000. *Democracy in America.* Translated and edited by Harvey C. Mansfield and Delba Winthrop. Chicago: University of Chicago Press.

Treacher, Adrian. 2003. *French Interventionism: Europe's Last Global Player?* Aldershot, UK: Ashgate.

References

Trope, Yaacov, and Nira Liberman. 2010. "Construal-Level Theory of Psychological Distance." *Psychological Review* 117 (2): 440–63.

Trubowitz, Peter. 1998. *Defining the National Interest: Conflict and Change in American Foreign Policy.* Chicago: University of Chicago Press.

UNGA (United Nations General Assembly). 1999. "The Fall of Srebrenica: Report of the Secretary-General Pursuant to General Assembly Resolution 53/35." UN Doc. A/54/549. November 15.

Vincent, John R. 1974. *Nonintervention and International Order.* Princeton, NJ: Princeton University Press.

Voeten, Erik. 2005. "The Political Origins of the UN Security Council's Ability to Legitimize the Use of Force." *International Organization* 59 (3): 527–57.

Von Hippel, Karin. 2000. *Democracy by Force: U.S. Military Intervention in the Post-Cold War World.* New York: Cambridge University Press.

Walt, Stephen M. 2005a. "The Relationship between Theory and Policy in International Relations." *Annual Review of Political Science* 8: 23–48.

———. 2005b. *Taming American Power.* New York: Norton.

Wedgwood, Ruth. 2002. "Unilateral Action in a Multilateral World." In *Multilateralism and U.S. Foreign Policy,* edited by Stewart Patrick and Shepard Forman. Boulder, CO: Lynne Rienner.

Weitsman, Patricia A. 2014. *Waging War: Alliances, Coalitions, and Institutions of Interstate Violence.* Stanford, CA: Stanford University Press.

Welch, David A. 1992. "The Organizational Process and Bureaucratic Politics Paradigms: Retrospect and Prospect." *International Security* 17 (2): 112–46.

———. 1998. "A Positive Science of Bureaucratic Politics?" *Mershon International Studies Review* 42 (2): 210–16.

Weller, Marc. 2009. *Contested Statehood: Kosovo's Struggle for Independence.* New York: Oxford University Press.

Welsh, Jennifer. 2004. "Authorizing Humanitarian Intervention." In *The United Nations and Global Security,* edited by Richard Price and Mark Zacher. London: Palgrave Macmillan.

Westra, Joel. 2007. *International Law and the Use of Armed Force.* New York: Routledge.

Wheeler, Nicholas. 2000. *Saving Strangers: Humanitarian Intervention in International Society.* New York: Oxford University Press.

Williams, Paul D., and Alex J. Bellamy. 2012. "Principles, Politics, and Prudence: Libya, the Responsibility to Protect, and the Use of Military Force." *Global Governance* 18 (3): 273–97.

Woehrel, Steven. 2009. "Future of the Balkans and U.S. Policy Concerns." *CRS Report for Congress,* May 13.

Wong, Leonard, and Douglas Lovelace. 2008. "Knowing When to Salute." *Orbis* 52 (2): 278–88.

Woodward, Bob. 1996. *The Choice: How Bill Clinton Won.* New York: Simon & Schuster.

———. 2000. *Shadow: Five Presidents and the Legacy of Watergate.* New York: Touchstone.

———. 2002. *Bush at War.* New York: Simon & Schuster.

———. 2004. *Plan of Attack.* New York: Simon & Schuster.

———. 2006. *State of Denial.* New York: Simon and Schuster.

Zaller, John, and Dennis Chiu. 2000. "Government's Little Helper: U.S. Press Coverage of Foreign Policy Crises, 1946–1999." In *Decisionmaking in a Glass House,* edited by Brigitte L. Nacos, Robert Y. Shapiro, and Pierangelo Isernia. Lanham, MD: Rowman & Littlefield.

Index

Abizaid, John, 46, 209–10, 213, 224
Afghanistan 2001, 14, 24n5, 38, 46–47, 61–62, 104, 189, 198, 208, 214, 231, 246, 248
African Union (AU), 11, 28, 248
Agoglia, John, 211
Albania, 48, 151, 157, 225
Albright, Madeleine: and American exceptionalism, 36; and Bosnia, 42, 107–8, 116–18, 120–26, 129, 131, 133, 139–40, 142, 146, 148–49; disregard of for domestic public opinion, 38; and Haiti, 76, 80, 86, 93, 131; and Iraq, 191, 193–94; and Kosovo, 38, 150, 153–154, 156, 158, 160–62, 169–70, 172, 174, 178–80, 182–83, 185
"all necessary means" authorization: Bosnia, 145; Haiti, 93; Iraq, 12, 195–96, 216, 237; Kosovo, 179; and Resolution 1373, 2n1; and UN Security Council, 29; and Yugoslavia, 150
Allison, Graham, 5, 242
American exceptionalism, 7, 36–37, 39, 41
American ideology, 35–37
Annan, Kofi, 154, 191, 193, 232
Arab League, 28, 30, 237–38, 248
Arab spring uprisings, 234
Argentina, 88, 103
Aristide, Jean-Bertrand: Clinton administration plans to restore to

office, 71–72, 74–75, 79–83, 87, 93, 98; election of, 67; international opposition to plans to restore to office, 74–75, 77–78, 81, 100; power-sharing proposal regarding, 68–70, 78; resigns presidency, 104–5; restored to office, 66, 89
Armed Services Committees, 136–37, 166, 168, 176, 236, 238
Armitage, Richard, 64, 205, 207, 213, 216, 224
Aronson, Bernard "Bernie," 68
Asmus, Ronald, 160
Aspin, Les, 74, 108, 116
automaticity, 217, 222–23

Baker, James, 67–68, 72, 220
balance-of-threat theory, 21
Balkans. *See* Bosnia 1992–1995; Kosovo 1998–1999 (Allied Force); Yugoslavia.
Balkans Contact Group, 150, 161
benchmarks proposal, 193, 196, 221–23
Berger, Samuel (Sandy): and Haiti, 79; and Kosovo, 161–63, 167–70, 175, 179
Biden, Joseph, 137, 239
Blair, Tony, 193, 199, 216, 219, 221–22
blame avoidance, 24, 94
Blix, Hans, 217, 222–23

Bosnia 1992–1995: air strikes against, 111–12, 157, 164; and breakup of Yugoslavia, 108–109; Bush administration and, 109–10; Clinton administration and, 72, 110, 114–18, 124, 130–31; Congress and, 115, 136–38, 168; and Dayton peace negotiations, 138, 146, 149, 161; and ethnic cleansing, 149, 152–53, 158; and ethnic war, 107, 109, 114, 119–21, 127, 130–31, 136n79, 149, 163–64; and international peace-keeping, 9, 29, 109, 112, 116, 121, 125–27, 129, 132, 165–66; and IO approval, 2, *3*, 13–14, 22, 55–57; Madeleine Albright and, 116–17, 120–21, 123, 129–31, 150, 160–61, 169, 183; NATO and, 107, 111–15, 118–19, 121, 124–25, 127–28, 132–39, 182; military leaders and, 108, 118–128, 132–33, 171; public opinion and, 92, 109; Sarajevo, 9, 109, 111, 120, 123, 125, 134, 143; Srebrenica, 108, 111, 113–15, 128–29, 141–143. *See also* Lake, Anthony; Implementation Force (IFOR); Milosevic, Slobodan; Serbs; stabilization force for Bosnia (SFOR); United Nations Protection Force (UNPROFOR).
Bosnia 1993 (Deny Flight), 2, *3*, 56
Bosnia 1995 (Deliberate Force), 2, *3*, 13, 113–14, 133–36, 144–45
Boutros-Ghali, Boutros, 79, 93, 112, 149n104
Brazil, 21, 23, 55, 73n16, 74–76, 99–100, 10, 105–6, 247, 249
Bremer, Paul, 204, 206
Britain: and Bosnia, 112, 134, 143, 204, 206; and Iraq War, 10, 30, 190, 193, 218–23, 225–26; and Kosovo, 150, 155, 159, 173; as a U.S. military ally, vii, 26
burden sharing: and Bosnia, 108, 119–122, 131, 133–37, 140–42, 146, 148; and civil-military bargaining, 7, 12, 15, 67, 79, 148, 173–77; and Congress, 29–32; and cost-benefit analysis, 31–33; and domestic support for interventions, 25–31; and Haiti, 66–67, 79, 83–84, 89, 97, 105;

hypotheses about, vii–ix, 12–13, 17, 28, 31, 53–55, *57*, 61, 64, 96–97, 228–29, 245–46, 248; and IO approval, 4, 12–13, 17, 22n4, 26–28, 31, 35, 38, 53–55, 59, 61, 64, 108, 207–8; and Iraq, 189–90, 201, 205, 207–8, 210–11, 213, 215, 226–28; and Kosovo, 167–68, 171–77; and Liberia, 233; and Libya, 235, 238–39; military leaders emphasize need for, vii–viii, 15, 35, 41–42, 45–48, *57*, 58, 66–67, 79, 83–84, 119–121, 132–34, 136–37, 140–41, 148, 167–68, 210–11; and Syria, vii–viii. *See also* follow-on UN peacekeeping forces.
bureaucratic politics approach, 5, 33, 240, 242–43
Bush, George H. W., 67–70, 109, 149
Bush, George W.: and Afghanistan, 38, 63–64; "axis of evil" speech, 198, 208; and Darfur, 59; and Haiti, 104; and Iran, 230; and Iraq, 42, 188, 193, 197, 231; and Liberia, 233
Butler, Richard, 193, 195
Byron, Michael J., 85

Cameron, David, 234
Caputo, Dante, 69, 93
Carter, Jimmy, 88
casualties: in Iraq, 30, 226; in Libya, 28; and military decision making, 44, 49, 165; in Somalia, 120
Cédras, Raoul, 67, 70–71, 74, 80, 87–88, 100
Central Command (CENTCOM), 15, 63, 195, 189, 201, 204, 209–11, 218, 224, 235
Chalabi, Ahmed, 203, 206
Cheney, Richard, 72, 188, 197–200, 215–16, 227, 232
Chernomyrdin, Victor, 177
China: and Haiti, 63, 74–75, 77; and Kosovo, 183–84; veto power of, 38, 55, 75–76, 178
Chirac, Jacques, 126, 128, 221, 223
Christiansen, John, 85
Christopher, Warren: and Bosnia, 108, 116–17, 123–29, 133; and Haiti, 7–80, 97; and Kosovo, 149

civil-military bargaining, and Bosnia, 139; and burden sharing, 7, 12, 15, 67, 79, 148, 173–77; and civilian policymakers, 53; and Haiti, 76, 78–91, 105–6; hypotheses about, 91, 242, 247; and interventionist hawks, 7, 33, 35, 53–54, *58*, 61–62, 79, 83, 105–6, 123–26, 164, 169, 175–76, 212, 218, 226–27, 229, 249; and IO approval, 14, 35, 58, 139, 172; and Iraq, 189, 196, 221, 226–27; and Joint Chiefs of Staff, 1, 5, 34, 40–41, 44, 49–50, 52, 63, 66, 89, 106, 135, 142, 162, 195, 211, 213, 229, 231, 233, 241; and Kosovo, 177, 187; mentioned, 1, 5, 14; and military leaders, 53, 231; and need for dialogue, 240; and Office of the Secretary of Defense, 85, 89; and open-ended commitments, 53, 61, 79, 83; and parochial interests, 33; and the Pentagon, 48–49, 3, 68, 87, 203; scholarship on, 8, 34, 240, 242–43; and the United Nations, viii, 33, 35, 85–90; and Vietnam, 229.

Claes, Willy, 134
Clark, Wesley: and Bosnia, 122; and Kosovo, 157–58, 65, 169–70; and Somalia, 83
Clinton, Hillary, 235–36
Clinton, William (Bill): approval ratings of, 93, 114; and PDD 25, 46; relationship with military, 231
Clinton administration: and Bosnia, 107–8, 110–11, 114–16, 123–26, 128–31, 134, 137, 140, 143–44; credibility of undermined, 70, 72, 111–12, 114–16, 146; and Haiti, 2, 68–74, 77–80, 83, 87–88, 91, 93–98, 100–1, 103; and Iraq, 191–96, 198, 201; and Kosovo, 149, 155, 157–59, 163, 168–70, 173, 176, 180–84, 186–87; and Latin America, 100–3; liberal Wilsonians, 139, 178; and Somalia, 90–91, 95, 98; and *Harlan County* incident, 69–70, 72, 80, 85, 98
Coalition Provisional Authority (CPA), 206
coalition building: and Bosnia, 127, 154–56, 159; and bypassing IO approval, 60, 123, 237; and

domestic politics, 30–31, 92–93; and Haiti, 92–93, 99, 108, 123; and hypotheses about intervention, 5, 21, 29, 60, 159, 242, 244, 248; and Iraq, 9, 30, 197, 201, 205, 208, 221n105, 224–27; and Kosovo, 172–73; and Kuwait, 9; and Libya, 237; limitations of, 25; and military leaders, 6, 108, 168, 229; and NATO, 154–56, 159, 172, 237; policymakers' views of, 30–31, 37; versus IO approval, 10–12
coercive leverage: and Bosnia, 111; and Haiti, 7–78, 94; and Kosovo, 155, 160, 163, 165–66, 168, 170, 172, 174–77
Cohen, William: and Iraq, 193, 195; and Kosovo, 155, 160, 163, 165–66, 168, 170, 172, 174–77
collective self-defense, 9, *10*, 140, 178
Community of Caribbean states (CARICOM), 93
Congress. *See* U.S. Congress.
Congressional Black Caucus, 71, 104
congressional hearings, 50–52, 64, 90, 97, 121, 212, 214, 241. *See also* U.S. Congress.
constitutional frameworks, 19
cost-benefit analysis: and Bosnia, 141; and civil-military relations, 241; vis-à-vis multilateralism, 4, 31–33, 54, 106, 229
counterterrorism, viii, 21, 144, 183, 208. *See also* September 11, 2001, attacks; terrorism; war on terror.
Covenant on Civil and Political Rights, 19
Craddock, Bantz, 232

Darfur (2005–2006), 59, 231
Dayton peace negotiations, 138, 146, 149, 161
de Hoop Scheffer, Japp, 28
discourse analysis, 20
Dobbins, James, 80, 99, 184
Dole, Robert, 114–15, 137
domestic support for intervention: and Afghanistan, 62; and Bosnia, 107, 110–11, 114, 119–20, 123, 146; and burden sharing, 30–32, 45; coalitions and, 11, 31; and

domestic support for intervention
(*continued*)
  Congress, 44; and Haiti, 70, 73,
    77–78, 80, 90–91, 98, 106; and
    hawkish policymakers, 38; and
    IO approval, 2, 4, 7–8, 12–13, 17,
    23, 26, 35, 97, 139, 248; and Iraq,
    194, 196, 207–208, 223, 226; and
    Kosovo, 163–65, 168, 179–80; and
    Libya, 236, 238; internationally,
    4, 7–8, 55, 93, 101, 144, 155, 185,
    221, 247–48; and military leaders,
    44–45; and norm compliance, 23;
    and open-ended commitments,
    41–42; and skepticism about
    humanitarian intervention, 5; and
    Somalia, 90, 98, 123, 164. *See also*
    Weinberger-Powell Doctrine.
dovish officials, 6–7, 32–33, 35, 39–40,
    48, 53–54, 124

Eagleburger, Lawrence, 149, 159
European Union (EU), 29, 132, 138, 146, 182
European Union peacekeeping force
    (EUFOR), 138
executive branch, 24, 36, 94, 229, 245.
    See also Bush, George H. W.; Bush,
    George W.; Clinton administration;
    foreign policy; Obama, Barack.
executive-legislative relations, 14, 24, 44
exit strategy; and Bosnia, 103, 122, 133,
    136–38; civilian policymakers and,
    7, 42, 53, 137; and Haiti, 84–91;
    international organizations and,
    47; and Kosovo, 164; and Libya,
    236; military leaders demand, 6, 41,
    46–47, 66, 79, 82, 136–38

Federation agreement, 130
Feinberg, Richard, 72, 75, 101
Feith, Douglas, 200, 202
follow-on UN peacekeeping forces: in
    Bosnia, 109, 112–13, 119, 125–26,
    142, 157; in Haiti, 29, 66, 73–74,
    77–78, 83–89, 104–5, 132; in
    Kosovo, 172; in Liberia, 232–34; in
    Rwanda, 60; in Somalia, 84; UN
    resolutions and, 26, 66, 85–88; and
    U.S. exit strategies, 27, 47
foreign policy: and civil-military bar-
    gaining, 33, 117, 243–43; Clinton

administration and, 70, 72, 113–14,
    129–30, 139–40, 160, 173, 178,
    180–81, 194; George H. W. Bush
    administration and, 109; George W.
    Bush administration and, 197, 216,
    219n100; military and, 121; mul-
    tilateralism and, 37, 139–41, 249;
    Obama administration and, 237;
    Reagan administration and, 98;
    Tony Blair and, 219; U.S. Congress
    and, 94; and U.S. political culture,
    36, 92, 193
forum shopping, 14, 30
France: and Bosnia, 112–13, 126, 128,
    134–35, 142; and concerns about
    negative issue linkage, 245; and
    Haiti, 100, 105; and Iraq, 191–92,
    195, 216–17, 219, 221–23, 225, 248;
    and Kosovo, 150, 153, 155, 160, 173,
    177, 182, 237–39, 248; and Libya,
    234, 237; and Mali, 27; as a poten-
    tial U.S. military partner, 26; and
    World War II, 9
Franks, Tommy, 15, 68, 189, 201, 209,
    211, 213, 218, 229
Frazer, Jendayi, 232, 234
freedom of action: and Afghanistan, 38;
    and Bosnia, 147–48; and Kosovo,
    182–83; military leaders' views
    of, 46; multilateralism, 2, 7, 11, 20,
    32, 35, 55, 66; and policymakers,
    1, 4, 7, 20, 55, 79, 106–7, 146, 229;
    presidential, 24
Fuerth, Leon, 116–18, 120, 122, 132, 144

Gates, Robert, 38, 235–36, 238–39
Gelbard, Robert (Bob), 161–62, 180
Georgia (Russian Federation), 2, 75–76,
    225–26
Gergen, David, 98
Germany, 134–35, 150, 160, 244, 248
Gorbachev, Mikhail, 12
Gore, Al, 116, 138
Governor's Island Agreement, 69, 84.
    See also Haiti.
Grachev, Pavel, 143, 145
Gray, William, 97, 102
Greenstock, Jeremy, 193, 195, 218–19,
    221–23
Grenada, 10, 98, 100
Grossman, Marc, 11, 182, 202, 205–8

Gulf Cooperation Council, 28, 237
Gulf War (1991): China and, 75; and
    containment of Iraq, 190; and new
    international norms, 12; reestab-
    lishes confidence of U.S. public in
    the military, 42; and SCR 678, 195,
    217; SCR 687, 190, 195; U.S. builds
    multilateral support for, 2, 16, 220,
    224–25

Hadley, Stephen: on Iraq, 203, 207–9,
    212; on 9/11, 61, 197
Haiti 1993–1994 (Uphold Democracy):
    and civil-military bargaining,
    78–91; Clinton administration
    decides to intervene in, 70–73;
    Congress and, 68, 71–72, 81, 87,
    89–90, 94–97, 102, 104, 106; and
    domestic support for interven-
    ing, 71, 77, 91–94; and follow-on
    peacekeeping, 26–27, 29, 47, 66,
    73, 83–89, 104–5, 132; and Gov-
    ernor's Island Agreement, 69, 84;
    and hawkish civilian policymak-
    ers, 66, 79–81, 83, 90, 106; and
    hypotheses about intervention,
    22, 57; and hypotheses about U.S.
    multilateralism, 91–103; and IO
    approval, 2, 3, 14, 55, 78–79, 91–92,
    96–99, 104, 106, 132, 189, 215, 230;
    and lack of consensus among
    policymakers, 32, 79–81; interim
    multinational force enters, 88–89;
    and international norms, 96–99;
    intervention in controversial, 22,
    55, 76–78; Madeleine Albright sees
    as a precedent for intervening in
    Bosnia, 131–32; migrants from, 68,
    71, 73, 77, 93, 104; and military
    leaders and, 66, 69, 81–87; and
    negative issue linkage, 99–103;
    origins of the crisis in, 67–69;
    strategies for securing international
    support for intervening in, 73–76
Haiti 2004 (Secure Tomorrow), 3, 14, 56,
    103–6
Haiti 2010 (Unified Response), 105
Halperin, Morton, 5, 56, 87, 171–72,
    185, 242
Harlan County incident, 69–72,
    80, 85, 98

Hill, Christopher, 161, 180
Holbrooke, Richard: and Bosnia, 107,
    117–18, 124–26, 133–34, 138–39,
    141–42, 146; and Kosovo, 152, 173;
    view of multilateralism, 141–42
Hunter, Robert, 112, 114, 123, 141
Huntington, Samuel, 40, 230, 240
Hussein, Saddam, 9, 188, 190–91, 194,
    196–205, 207, 217, 223–24, 227
hypotheses about seeking IO approval
    for interventions: 18, 21–22, 31, 33,
    51, 54, 55, *57*; and Bosnia, 139–46;
    and Haiti, 67, 91–103; and Iraq,
    227, 229–30; and Kosovo, 178–79

Ikenberry, Jon, 26
Implementation Force (IFOR),
    136–138, 145
Inter-American Commission on Human
    Rights, 70
internal political change. *See* regime
    change.
International Atomic Energy Agency
    (IAEA), 190
International Criminal Court, 234
International Monetary Fund (IMF), 186
international norms: and Bosnia,
    139–40, 142, 146, 148; and burden
    sharing, 13; complying with, 17–20;
    emergence of new norms, 12–13, 17,
    242; emerging powers' interpreta-
    tion of, 55n34; and Haiti, 96–99, 106;
    and humanitarian intervention, 7,
    54; hypotheses about, 20–23, 38, 67,
    91, 96–99, 108, 139–40, 244, 249; in-
    ternalization of, 12–13, 17, 249; and
    IO approval, 7, 20, 96–99, 139–40,
    139–40, 146, 148, 177–80, 228; and
    Kosovo, 177–80, 184, 187; versus
    parochial interests as justification
    for policy decisions, 57; willingness
    of interventionist hawks to bypass,
    6, 20, 38. *See also* United Nations;
    United Nations Charter.
interventionist hawks: and Bosnia,
    107–8, 117–18, 120–21, 123–26, 135,
    140, 142; civilians, 15, 35–39, 53–54,
    61, 81, 191; and civil-military
    bargaining, 7, 33, 35, 53–54, *58*,
    61–62, 79, 83, 105–6, 123–26, 164,
    169, 175–76, 212, 218, 226–27, 229,

interventionist hawks *(continued)*
249; and Haiti, 66, 79–81, 83; and
hypotheses about IO approval,
33, *58;* and Iraq, 15, 63, 189, 192,
199–206, 212, 218, 226–27; and
Kosovo, 148, 161, 164, 169, 175–76,
183; and multilateralism, 6–7,
37–38; overoptimistic expectations
of, 15, 38, 83, 200–6; as policymakers, 38–39, 55, 80–81, 107–8,
117–18, 120–21, 135, 140, 180, 183,
192, 199–200; and Somalia, 90; and
Weinberger-Powell doctrine, 42;
willingness of to bypass IO approval, 6–7, 32, 66, 106, 142, 229
IO approval. *See* Bosnia 1992–1995; burden sharing; civil-military bargaining; domestic support for intervention; Haiti 1993–1994; hypotheses
about seeking IO approval for intervention; interventionist hawks;
Iraq 2002–2003; Kosovo 1998–1999;
North Atlantic Treaty Organization
(NATO); reasons for securing IO
approval; regime change; Somalia
1992; U.S. Congress.
Iran, 130, 198, 200, 230
Iraq 1991 (Provide Comfort), 2, *3,* 191
Iraq 1998 (Operation Desert Fox),
190–92, 194–96, 198, 209
Iraq 2002–2003 (Operation Iraqi
Freedom; Operation Enduring
Freedom): controversy over, 16, 22,
199, 248; hawkish interventionists
and, 15, 38, 42, 188–89, 197–200,
227; and international support, 30;
and IO approval, 2, *3,* 22–23, 55,
104, 189–90, 246, 249; mentioned, 9,
10, 13–14; military leaders and, 15,
63, 189, 209–15, 224, 229–31, 241;
multilateralism and, 10; need for
burden sharing underestimated,
46, 200–5, 226, 247; Project for the
New American Century and, 192;
and policy of regime change, 192,
203; and push for UN involvement, 207–9, 209–17, 219–24;
and sanctions, 191; and Security
Council Resolution 687, 191; and
Security Council Resolution 1194,
192–93, 196; and Security Council

Resolution 1441, 189–90, 217, 220;
and Security Council Resolution
1511, 225–26; and training for
counterinsurgency, 46; weakness
of international coalition, 224–26;
weapons inspection and, 191–94,
196, 217–19. *See also* Central Command (CENTCOM); Powell, Colin;
Rumsfeld, Donald; United Nations
Special Commission (UNSCOM).
Iraq 2014, 230
Iraqi National Congress (INC), 203

Johnson, Lyndon, 229–30
Joint Chiefs of Staff (JCS): and Afghanistan, 62; and Bosnia, 108–10, 116,
118, 120–22, 125–27, 133, 135–38,
142, 155; and civil-military bargaining, 1, 5, 34, 40–41, 44, 49–50, 52,
63, 66, 89, 106, 135, 142, 162, 195,
211, 213, 229, 231, 233, 241; and
Darfur, 59; and Haiti, 63, 7, 79,
81–87, 89, 104, 132, 134–35; and
Iraq, 15, 189, 194, 197, 209, 227,
241; and Kosovo, 55–56, 148, 160,
162–65, 167–60, 170–73, 175–76;
and Libya, 235; and multilateralism, 16, 84, 134; and risk aversion,
40, 109–10, 118, 121, 136, 162–63,
169, 230; Rumsfeld determines
to reduce authority or, 214; and
Rwanda, 60; and Syria, vii, 60, 230.
See also military leaders; Pentagon.

Karadzic, Radovan, 113, 119
Kaufmann, Gregory, 155, 165
Kerrick, Donald, 5, 122, 11, 137, 162
KFOR (stabilization force for Kosovo),
176–77
Khalilzad, Zalmay, 208, 217
Kissinger, Henry, 72
Kosovar Albanians, 147, 149, 151–53,
156–58, 174
Kosovo 1998–1999 (Allied Force): and
burden sharing, 29; and definition of military intervention, 9,
10; discussions of U.S. unilateral
action in, 55, 155–56, 159–62, 168,
178; ethnic violence in, 148–49,
151–54, 157–58, 174; importance
of to Serbs, 148; indecisiveness of

NATO's campaign in, 156–59; and IO approval, 2, 3, 13–14, 22–23, 55, 57, 178–87, 248; and Madeleine Albright, 161–63, 169–70, 172–76, 178–80, 182–83, 185; military leaders and, 47–48, 55–56, 164–77; NATO airstrikes in, 29, 147–48, 153–55, 157, 162; NATO and United States plan military action in 1998, 151–153; NATO peace-keeping in, 166–67; NATO's role in reassuring U.S. military leaders, 169, 171–77; and willingness of hawkish interventionists to bypass IO approval, 38, 55, 148, 155–56, 159–62, 183. *See also* Dayton peace negotiations; Kosovo Liberation Army (KLA); Milosevic, Slobodan; Rambouillet agreement.

Kosovo Liberation Army (KLA), 149–53, 164

Kreps, Sarah, 31–32, 33n15, 91

Kross, Walter, 85, 90, 96, 122, 133, 135, 137

Kuwait, 9–10, 12, 190–91

La Sablière, Jean-Marc de, 105, 220

Lagos, Ricardo, 220, 222

Lake, Anthony: and Bosnia, 107–8, 113, 116–17, 124–27, 129–30, 133, 139–42; and civil-military bargaining, 49, 66, 140–41, 146; and Haiti, 79–80, 82, 87, 88n59, 92, 96–98, 102

Latin America, 68, 74, 75, 78, 92, 99–103, 106, 220, 247

Lavrov, Sergey, 179

Lebanon, 10, 25, 98

legitimation effect, 16, 26–28, 76

liberal Wilsonians: and American exceptionalism, 36; and Kosovo, 178; and Libya, 235; and multilateralism, 37–38, 139–40, 178; views on armed intervention, 20, 235

Liberia 2003 (Joint Task Force), 2, 3, 14–15, 24n5, 26–27, 47, 56, 92n68, 231–34

Libya 2011 (Odyssey Dawn/Unified Protector), 2, 3, 15, 28, 146, 200, 234–39

logrolling, 2, 11, 53, 73, 76, 249

Lugar, Richard, 175

MacArthur, Douglas, 8

Macedonia, 151, 157, 161

Major, John, 126

Manning, David, 219

Mastanduno, Michael, 21

McNamara, Robert, 229

media: condemns Clinton's Bosnia policy, 114; and congressional opinion, 25; coverage of Bosnia, 112; coverage of Kosovo, 174; coverage of Haiti, 81; and domestic opinion, 207; international partners' use of, 113; military's use of, 50, 91, 241; policymakers' use of, 125

Menendez, Robert, 238

Mexico, 102, 104–5, 222

military intervention defined, 8–9, *10*, 78, 100, 102, 219, 221, 248

military leaders' attitudes toward obtaining UN approval for intervention: and Bosnia, 108, 122, 146; and Haiti, 48, 55–57, *58*, 60, 63, 78, 84–90, 106; and Iraq, 189, 194–95, 207, 209–16; and Kosovo, 176; and Liberia, 232–33. *See also* Joint Chiefs of Staff (JCS); Pentagon.

Miller, Franklin, 202, 212, 214

Milosevic, Slobodan: NATO airstrikes and, 147, 154; NATO diplomacy and, 151–52, 154, 156, 159, 173, 177; and siege of Sarajevo, 109. *See also* Bosnia 1992–1995; Kosovo 1998–1999.

Mladic, Ratko, 119, 128

moral norms, 96–97, 139, 180

Mullen, Michael, 235

multilateralism: and burden sharing, 21, 31; and civil-military bargaining, 14, 35, 57, 78–91, 121–26; coalitions-based versus institutions-based, 10–12; and Congress, 32; cost-benefit analysis of, 4–5, 32–33, 54, 229; costs of, 2, 73–76, 242; and controversial interventions, 54; hypotheses about, 13, 33, 57, 78, 91–103, 139–46, 177–87, 249; methods of evaluating, 20; military leaders and, 8, 57, 121–26; willingness of hawkish interventionists to bypass, 37–39

multilateral legitimacy: and burden
sharing, 12–13, 17, 46, 248; dovish
policymakers and, 6–7, 35; and
forum shopping, 30; hawkish policymakers and, 81, 140, 180, 217–18;
and international norms, 16–18,
139; liberal Wilsonians and, 20; military leaders and, 46; reasons U.S.
seeks, 17, 25–26; value of, 16–33.
See also hypotheses about securing IO approval for intervention;
reasons for securing IO approval.
Multi-National Force (MNF, Haiti),
88–89
Myers, Richard: and Iraq, 15, 63, 189,
197, 209–13, 227, 229; and Liberia,
232; mentioned, 241

National Security Act (1947), 51
National Security Council (NSC): and
Bosnia, 116–17, 119, 121–22, 126,
129–31, 156; and Haiti, 70–72, 75,
79, 82–83, 85–87, 91, 96–99, 101,
106; and Iraq, 189, 194, 201–3, 207,
209, 211–13, 216; and Kosovo, 163,
170, 179; and liberal Wilsonians, 36;
and Liberia, 232; and Libya, 235;
and Rwanda, 60
negative issue linkage: and Bosnia, 139;
and Haiti, 99–103, 106; hypotheses
about, 20–23, 99–103, 139, 142–43,
146, 148, 177, 183, 208, 249; and
international partners, 245; and
Iraq, 208; and Kosovo, 183–87; U.S.
policymakers avoid, 13, 17, 208
Negroponte, John, 64, 216–18, 220,
225, 233
neoconservatives, 36–39, 42, 188, 191,
197, 208
Newbold, Gregory, 210–11, 215
Non-Aligned Movement (NAM),
184–85, 195
nonbinding resolutions, 94–95, 238
noninterference/nonintervention, 7, 18,
35, 49, 54, 58–60, 74, 100
Noriega, Manuel, 101
norm internalization: and Bosnia,
139–41, 146, 148; and Haiti, 96–99;
hypotheses about, 12–13, 18–20,
67, 249; and Kosovo, 178–80, 187;
proof of, 19

North Atlantic Council (NAC):
and burden sharing, 4; and
civil-military bargaining, 58;
hypotheses about seeking approval
from, 35, 228, 245; and increasing
domestic support for intervention,
25–26; and increasing international
support for intervention, 26, 28;
and IO approval, 2, 3, 11, 30; and
Kosovo, 157, 159, 171–73, 176, 187;
and legitimation of intervention,
16; and Libya, 237; and reluctance
of other countries to approve U.S.
intervention, 55; and U.S. freedom
of action, 58
North Atlantic Treaty Organization
(NATO): and Afghanistan, 14,
47, 246; and Bosnia, 107, 111–15,
118–19, 121, 124–25, 127–28, 132–39,
182; and Bulgaria, 219n99, 225–26;
and burden sharing, 28–29, 61;
and Darfur, 59; and follow-on
peacekeeping, 29, 47; and former
Communist countries, 225–26; and
Germany, 19n3; and IO approval,
3, 4, 11, 13–14, 17–18, 28, 30, 33, 35,
54–57, *58*, 59, 61, 228, 248; and Iraq,
63; and Kosovo, 29, 47, 147–48,
151–59, 161–62, 166–67, 169, 171–87,
189, 195; and Libya, 235–39; public
opinion and, 92n68; U.S. military
leaders and, 8, 35, 47–48, 55–56,
58, 229; and Washington Treaty,
14, 62; willingness of interventionist hawks to bypass, 6, 39. *See also*
North Atlantic Council (NAC).
North Korea, 72, 198
Northern Iraq 1991 (Provide Comfort), 3

Obama, Barack: and Libya, 235–38; and
risk aversion, 247; and Syria, viii,
60, 230
O'Brien, James, 179
Office of the Secretary of Defense
(OSD): and civil-military relations,
85, 89; and Haiti, 89; and Iraq, 189,
201–4, 206, 208–11, 213, 218; and
Kosovo, 165, 173
open-ended commitments: and
Afghanistan, 62; and Bosnia, 121,

Index

131, 166–7; and burden sharing, 30–33; and civil-military bargaining, 53, 61, 79, 83; and Congress, 17, 25, 43, 44, 53, 55; and Darfur, 59; and Haiti, 66, 79, 83, 86, 96, 104–6, 131; and Iraq, 189, 213; and Kosovo, 55, 162–4, 180, 187; and Liberia, 232; and Libya, 238; military leaders' concerns about, 6, 15, 41, 43, 44, 46, 53, 59–62, 66, 86, 104–6, 121, 162–4, 167, 187, 189, 213, 232, 243; and obtaining IO approval, 4, 13, 228, 245, 249; and Rwanda, 60; and Syria, 60

Organization of American States (OAS), 11, 14, 18, 67, 70, 74, 77, 98, 100, 248

Organization of the Islamic Conference (OIC), 56, 143

Owen, David, 114

Owens, William, 64, 83–84, 90, 121, 124n43, 128, 132–33, 135

Pace, Peter, 15, 63, 189, 209–13, 227, 229
Panama 1989, 88, 100–1, 225
peacekeeping. *See* follow-on UN peacekeeping force.
Pentagon: attacked on 9/11, 61; and Bosnia, 118–20, 123–29, 131–34, 136, 138, 141, 146, 148; and civil-military bargaining, 48–49, 53, 68, 87, 203; and Haiti, 68, 70, 73, 80–82, 85, 87–91, 104; and Iraq, 197–98, 202–5, 210, 212–13, 215; and Kosovo, 163–70, 172–77, 183, 187; and Liberia, 232, 234; and Libya, 235–36, 239; and need for clear objectives, 41, 164; and need for exit strategy, 82, 136; and risk aversion, 70, 73, 80–81, 118–20, 124, 146, 176; strategic guidance document of (2012), 47. *See also* Joint Chiefs of Staff (JCS); military leaders.
Perry, William: and Haiti, 79, 82, 87; and Bosnia, 108, 116, 120, 124–5, 127, 129, 131–32, 144–45
Petraeus, David, 41
Pezzullo, Lawrence, 69–70, 79–80
Power, Samantha, 139, 235
Powell, Colin: assertiveness as Joint Chiefs of Staff chair, 231; and

Bosnia, 109–10, 116, 119–22, ; and Gulf War, 42; and Haiti, 61, 64, 67, 79, 81, 88n59, 104; and importance of exit strategy, 47; and IO approval, 48; and Iraq, 189, 197–98, 202, 205–8, 213, 215–16, 218; and multilateralism, 16, 189, 207–9. *See also* Weinberger-Powell Doctrine.
Powell Doctrine. *See* Weinberger-Powell Doctrine.
Presidential Decision Directive 25 (PDD 25), 46
preventive war, 37, 200
Primakov, Yevgeny, 192
process tracing, 33, 44, 57, 63, 187
Project for the New American Century (PNAC), 192
psychological research, 43
public opinion polls, 91–92

Qaddafi, Muammar, 234–35
Quadrennial Defense Review (2014), 47

"rally-'round-the-flag" effect, 23–24, 93
Ralston, Joseph: and civil-military relations, 44, 176; and Iraq, 194; and Kosovo, 163–65, 176–77
Rambouillet agreement, 153–54, 177
Reagan, Ronald, 98
reasons for securing IO approval: burden sharing, 38, 53, 64; and Bush administration, 38–39; civilians and, 53–54, 57–58, 79, 104; and Clinton administration, 98, 106, 115, 125, 140, 145–46, 178, 180, 235; growing cost of, 249; international norms, 38–39, 96–97, 146; international support and, 56, 92, 98–99, 246; and Haiti, 78–79, 91–92, 96–99, 104, 106; military veto, 54–55, 108; and NATO, 181–87; seen as a political issue, 48; theories about, 139–48, 178, 180, 187, 235, 245.
regime change: and Afghanistan, 62; and Bosnia, 189, 215; and civil-military bargaining, 8, 13, 35, 55, 57, 58, 59; and controversy, 22, 54; cost of underestimated, 246; as a goal of intervention, 3, 10, 36; and Haiti, 189, 215; and hawkish policymakers' willingness to

regime change (*continued*)
bypass IO approval, 55, 57, 188–89, 229; and IO approval, 1–2, *3*, 4, 8, 13, 58–59, 249; and Iraq, *3*, 15–16, 188–92, 194, 196–97, 207, 209, 215, 221; and Iran, 230; and Kosovo, 163; and Libya, 235–36, 238; military leaders' opposition to, vii–viii, 1, 7, 35, 37, 39–41, 43, 45, *58*, 59, 163, 189, 209, 230, 235–36, 238, 246; and need for domestic support, 247; and negative issue linkage, 22; and Syria, vii–viii
regional organizations, 11, 16, 18, 27, 30–31, 74, 84, 100, 103, 111, 145, 237–38, 248
Rhodes, Benjamin, 235–36
Rice, Condoleezza, 59, 197, 199, 204, 212, 219–20, 232
Rice, Susan, vii, 235–37
Riedel, Bruce, 194, 198
Rossin, Lawrence, 69n3, 79–80, 82, 98
Rubin, James, 169, 173–74
Rumsfeld, Donald: autocratic management style of, 209, 214; deference to by military leaders, 212–14, 229, 247; disregard of military advice, 210, 241, 245; and Iraq, 38, 188, 197–98, 200–2, 211–16, 218, 227, 229; and Liberia, 232
Russia: and Bosnia, 143–46, 150; and costs of IO approval, 2, 106, 178, 186; and Iraq, 191–2, 195–96, 247; and Kosovo, 171, 178, 183–87; and Libya, 237; and UN politics, 21, 38, 55, 73–76, 99–100, 145–46, 150–51, 178, 192, 247–49
Rwanda (1994), 39, 60, 72, 73n16
Ryan, Michael E., 135

sanctions: and China, 69; and Haiti, 69, 75; and Iraq, 188–91, 194, 196–97, 204, 209; and Yugoslavia, 150, 179; UN Security Council and, 69
Sarkozy, Nicolas, 234, 236
Schake, Kori, 201
Schulte, Gregory, 111, 132n66, 156
Schwartzkopf, Norman, 209
Scowcroft, Brent, 64, 68
Senate Foreign Relations Committee, 166, 175, 238

September 11, 2001, attacks, 14, 61–62, 196–99, 207–209, 214–15, 246. See also counterterrorism; terrorism; war on terror.
Serbs: and ethnic cleansing, 149, 152–53, 158; and hostage taking of UN peacekeepers, 112, 116, 119, 124, 141; and Kosovo, *3*, 148–53, 157–58, 163, 173; Muslim-Croat ground war against, 109, 114, 119–21, 127, 130–31, 136n79, 163; NATO air strikes against, 111–12, 119–20, 125, 135, 143, 153–58, 173, 185; President Clinton and, 109, 111–12, 124, 134; and siege of Sarajevo, 109, 111, 125, 134; President George H. W. Bush and, 149; Russian Federation and, 143–45, 150; and Srebrenica, 108, 111, 113–15, 127–29, 141–143; U.S. civilian policymakers and, 107, 116, 125–27, 133, 140–42, 146, 158, 162; U.S. military leaders and, 119–20, 131, 133–35, 141–42. *See also* Bosnia; Kosovo; Milosevic, Slobodan.
Sestanovich, Stephen, 186, 196
Shalikashvili, John, and Bosnia, 116, 119, 121, 126–27, 129, 130n54; and Haiti, 79, 82, 86–87
Sheehan, John, 119
Shelton, Hugh: Iraq and, 195, 197–98; Kosovo and, 155, 160, 163, 170, 174, 176–77
Shinseki, Erik, 214
short-term payoffs: and civil-military bargaining, 52; and coalitions of the willing, 248; Haiti, 82, 93, 96; Iraq, 207; and military hawks, 38, 61
side payments: multilateralism and, 2, 11, 19, 54, 195, 245, 248; and Russia, 178, 195
Slaughter, Anne-Marie, 37
Slocombe, Walter: and Bosnia, 119, 134; and burden sharing, 45; and Haiti, 81; and Iraq, 201; and Kosovo, 147, 167
Soderberg, Nancy, 70, 79, 87, 89, 99
soft balancing, 12, 21, 244
Solana, Javier, 64, 153

Somalia 1992 (Restore Hope): and Congress, 25; failure in, 72, 83–84, 91–93, 95, 98, 118–19; and *Harlan County* incident, 70; impact on subsequent U.S. policymaking, 90–91, 119–20, 137, 232; and IO approval, 2, *3*, 14, 56; and need for domestic support, 137, 165; and U.S. casualties, 69, 84, 91, 119
sovereignty, 9, *10*, 18–19, 55, 184
stabilization force for Bosnia (SFOR), 138, 165
Stephanopoulos, George, 94
Syria: vii–viii, 60, 230

Talbott, Strobe: Bosnia and, 145; and civil-military bargaining, 2, 80; Haiti and, 71, 73–74, 80, 86–87, 89, 96, 103; and IO approval, 30–31, 73–74, 87, 89, 96, 151; Kosovo and, 151, 159, 172, 184; mentioned, 64
Tarnoff, Peter, 75
Taylor, Charles, 231, 233. *See also* Liberia.
Tenet, George, 197
terrorism: in Lebanon, 98; and theories about intervention, 8, 14; military leaders' views of responses to, 210; UN resolutions and, 61–62; and U.S. response to 9/11, 198–200. *See also* counterterrorism; September 11, 2001, attacks; war on terror.
Thaci, Hashim, 149
Thompson, Alexander, 21–22, 208n57
Tocqueville, Alexis de, 1
Transitional National Council, 236. *See also* Libya.
Triangle Institute for Security Studies (TISS), 40

UN mission (UNMIL), Liberia, 234
UN stabilization mission in Haiti (MINUSTAH), 105
unilateral intervention: and Afghanistan, 246; and Bosnia, 107–8, 110, 112, 115–16, 118, 121–25, 130, 139–43, 146, 148, 149n2; and Haiti, 77, 80–81, 91–92, 98–101, 103; hypotheses about, 13, 15, 18–19, 21, 23, 31, 37, 59, 61, 228, 244, 246; and Iraq, 93, 200, 208, 247, 249; and Kosovo, 55, 155–56, 159, 161–62,

180, 182–83; and Liberia, 232; and U.S. public, 91–92
unipolarity, 23, 23, 36, 247, 249
United Nations: and Afghanistan, 246; and arms embargos, 110; and Bosnia, 9, 108–12, 116, 119, 122, 125; and burden-sharing, 29, 46–47, 61, 171, 176, 207–9; and civil-military bargaining, viii, 33, 35, 85–90; and Congress, 90, 94–96, 106, 226; cost of securing approval of for intervention, 2, 11, 54, 73, 77, 115, 141, 249; and degree of international support for interventions, 28–30, 56, 76, 143–46, 150–51, 171, 219–226, 246, 248; and Georgia (Russian Federation), 75–76; and Haiti, 66–67, 69–70, 73–75, 79–81, 83–88, 105, 132; and international norms, 54–55, 62, 96–99, 140, 150, 179–80, 184; and Iraq, 2, 15–16, 189–96, 199–201, 207–9, 217–19; and Kosovo, 150–51, 154, 171, 176, 178–180, 248; and Liberia, 232–34; and Libya, 235–36; Madeleine Albright and, 116, 140, 160; Non-Aligned Movement and, 184; and Persian Gulf War, 16; policymakers object to obtaining approval from, 38, 80–81, 215–17; policymakers willing to bypass obtaining approval from, 6–7, 39, 63, 79–80, 85, 118, 140, 178–80, 193–96, 200–1, 205, 236, 238; reasons for seeking approval of for intervention, 4, 17, 33, 228; and sanctions, 85, 191; and Somalia, 83–84, 95; and Syria, vii–viii. *See also* follow-on peacekeeping forces; military leaders' attitudes toward obtaining UN approval for intervention; United Nations Charter; United Nations Mission in Haiti (UNMIH); United Nations Monitoring, Verification and Inspection Commission (UNMOVIC); United Nations Protection Force (UNPROFOR); United Nations Security Council (UNSC); United Nations Security Council resolutions; United Nations Special Commission (UNSCOM).

United Nations Charter: Article 2, 54; Article 51, 62, 140; Chapter VII, 38, 62, 150, 179; international compliance with, 55; norms of, 22, 97; principle of nonintervention, 7; risks of noncompliance with, 21; Security Council and intervention, 11, 27, 38; violations of, 184.
United Nations Mission in Haiti (UNMIH), 69, 85
United Nations Monitoring, Verification and Inspection Commission (UNMOVIC), 218, 222
United Nations Protection Force (UNPROFOR), 109, 112, 115, 122, 125–27, 129, 133, 143
United Nations Security Council (UNSC):, and authorization for intervention, 18, 27, 73, 97, 107, 150–51, 178, 192, 235; divisions within, 12, 37, 192; and follow-on peacekeeping, 76, 109; U.S. policymakers' views of, 178, 180, 190, 220
United Nations Security Council resolutions: and "all necessary means," 12, 28, 93, 145, 150, 179, 195–96, 213, 237; and burden sharing, 26, 28, 171, 207; failed efforts to obtain, 219–23, 150; and follow-on peacekeeping, 26–27, 66; Iraq and compliance with, 192; and legitimization of intervention, 30; and need for support from other countries, 75–76, 78, 102–3, 143, 192, 195–96, 207, 219, 221, 247; Resolution 678, 195, 217; Resolution 687, 190, 195; Resolution 688, 3; Resolution 770, 145–46; Resolution 794, 3; Resolution 816, 3; Resolution 836, 3, 56, 69, 111, 143, 145–46; Resolution 867, 69; Resolution 940, 3, 26, 66, 73–76, 78, 86–87, 102–3; Resolution 1154, 192; Resolution 1194, 192, 196; Resolution 1199, 152, 179; Resolution 1368, 62; Resolution 1441, 190, 192, 215–17, 220; Resolution 1483, 225; Resolution 1497, 3, 26, 233; Resolution 1511, 225; Resolution 1529, 3, 104–5; Resolution 1973, 3, 28, 237–38; Resolution 2085, 27; United States and intervention and, 18, 19n3, 38, 146, 171, 178–80, 193, 196, 235; U.S. military leaders influence, 233. *See also* nonbinding resolutions.
United Nations Special Commission (UNSCOM), 190–94, 196
U.S. Atlantic Command (USACOM), 83, 85–86, 89
U.S. Congress: and Bosnia, 108, 115, 120, 123, 136–38; and burden sharing, 25, 29–30, 32; and civil-military bargaining, 53; and funding of interventions, 24–25, 42; and Haiti, 68, 71–72, 81, 87, 89–90, 94–97, 102, 104, 106; and hypotheses about intervention, 4, 53, 55, 241; and hypotheses about seeking IO approval, 4, 17, 31–32, 91, 106; and Iraq, 191, 194, 204, 206–8, 212, 214, 226–30, 241; and Kosovo, 163, 165–69, 174–77, 180, 187; and Latin America, 102; and Libya, 239; military leaders' relationships with, 35, 43–45, 50–51, 52, 55, 90, 121, 243; policymakers attempt to overcome lack of support for intervention within, 38; public confidence in, 50n28; and Somalia, 90; and U.S. public support for intervention, 24, 42, 46, 51; and Vietnam, 42. *See also* congressional hearings.
U.S. Constitution, 19, 180
U.S. State Department: and Bosnia, 109, 117, 124–25, 136, 138; and Haiti, 74, 79–80, 85–86, 96, 98; and Iraq, 199n27, 205–9, 213n78, 217; and Kosovo, 156, 160–62, 164, 166–67, 169–72, 174–76, 179–80, 182–84, 186; lack of combat experience of officials in, 36–37; and Liberia, 232–34; Libya, 237; and multilateralism, 56, 74, 96, 99, 138, 171–72, 182, 186, 205–9; and Rwanda, 60; and unilateralism, 62, 98 106, 161–62, 179, 182–83, 217
Universal Declaration of Human Rights, 19

Valdés, Juan Gabriel, 222
Vance-Owen peace plan, 110
Venezuela, 100, 102

Vershbow, Alexander: and Bosnia,
    126–27, 130, 141; and Kosovo, 153,
    166, 174
Vietnam: funding cut for, 25, 42; lessons
    of, 42, 45, 80, 108, 118, 120, 137,
    163–65, 229–30; mentioned, 224;
    and multilateralism, 10. *See also*
    Weinberger-Powell Doctrine.
Vorontsov, Yuri, 76

Wald, Charles, 156–57
war on terror, 15, 63, 189, 197, 215. See
    also counterterrorism; September
    11, 2001, attacks.
War Powers Resolution (1973), 24
Washington Treaty, 14, 62
Watson, Alexander Fletcher, 101
weapons inspections, 190, 192–94, 199,
    216–19, 222–23
Weinberger-Powell Doctrine, 42, 46,
    136, 202, 236
Weisman, David, 164, 162, 170–71
Westmoreland, William, 229–30

Wheeler, Earle, 229–30
Wilsonians. *See* liberal Wilsonians.
Wisner, Frank, 84, 90
Wolfowitz, Paul, 191, 197–98, 200,
    202–4, 216
Wood, Michael, 217
Woolsey, James, 79, 116

Yeltsin, Boris, 144, 184, 186–87
Yugoslavia: breakup of, 32, 108–10;
    NATO bombing of, 147, 154, 173;
    and compliance with UNSCR 1199,
    152; and ethnic cleansing, 147; KLA
    and, 151–52; poor performance of
    UN peacekeepers in, 92; and Ram-
    bouillet agreement, 153; Russia
    and, 184–85; sanctions against, 110,
    150; U.S. policymakers and, 2, 55,
    117, 178. *See also* Bosnia 1992–1995;
    Kosovo 1998–1999.

Zhirinovsky, Vladimir, 144
Zinni, Anthony, 195, 201, 209